A Tibetan Principality

The Political System of Sa sKya

A Tibetan Principality

The Political System of Sa sKya

C. W. CASSINELLI and
ROBERT B. EKVALL

UNIVERSITY OF WASHINGTON

Cornell University Press

ITHACA, NEW YORK

First published 1969

Library of Congress Catalog Card Number: 69-12977

Printed in the United States of America
by Kingsport Press, Inc.

Preface

This study is based upon extensive interviews with two sons of the royal family of the Tibetan principality of Sa sKya (pronounced "sah jah"), the wife of the elder, and the wife's uncle, who became an official tutor to the royal family. These four people were among a number of Tibetans brought to the University of Washington in the fall of 1960 by the Inner Asia Project of the Far Eastern and Russian Institute with the help of the Rockefeller Foundation. Robert B. Ekvall soon organized the four Tibetans into a continually functioning discussion group in order to obtain information on cultural and social conditions and practices in Tibet. For several months the anthropologist James F. Downs participated in these discussions, and he and Ekvall jointly published some of the results. Ekvall also relied heavily upon information obtained from the group in his books on Tibetan religious observances and nomadism.

In 1963, C. W. Cassinelli joined the discussion group and with the assistance of three graduate students—Frederick A. Cervantes, James W. Cayton, and Philip T. Clark—spent about seven hundred and fifty hours with the Tibetans getting information on the Sa sKya political system. All the discussions were conducted by Ekvall in the Tibetan language. In this book, Ekvall has assumed primary responsibility for the accuracy of the information on Sa sKya, and Cassinelli for the adequacy of the description of the political society based on this information. Whenever the word "we" is used in the text, it refers to the two authors.

[v]

The first of our respondents was NGag dBang Kun dGaa bSod Nams, the elder son of NGag dBang mTHu THub dBang PHyug, ruler of Sa sKya from 1936 until his death in 1950. Born in 1929, NGag dBang Kun dGaa bSod Nams was educated to succeed his father as spiritual head of the Sa sKya sect of Tibetan Buddhism and as governmental head of the Sa sKya polity. There was, however, a dispute over the succession upon his father's death, and NGag dBang Kun dGaa bSod Nams served three years as *pro tem* ruler. He then went to Khams in eastern Tibet, where he inspected monasteries of the Sa sKya sect, collected religious offerings, and came in close contact with important sponsors of the sect, such as the King of Derge. In 1954, as third in rank among Tibetan leaders, he accompanied the Dalai Lama and the Panchen Lama to Peking, where they met Mao Tse-tung, received a conducted tour of the showplaces of Communist China, and listened to the proposals and arguments of the Communists. From 1957 until 1959, NGag dBang Kun dGaa bSod Nams and his brother lived in Lhasa; during this period the Chinese attempted to persuade them to collaborate. When the Tibetan revolt broke out in 1959, the brothers fled through Bhutan to India.

NGag dBang Kun dGaa PHrin Las, the younger brother, was born in Sa sKya in 1934. In order to avoid dividing the family line, at about age seventeen he became a celibate monk. He received a thorough education in Sa sKya religious beliefs and practices, and several years of study in Lhasa gave him a good understanding of the doctrine and ritual of the dominant Yellow sect of Tibetan Buddhism. He traveled widely throughout Tibet on pilgrimages, on official religious and governmental business, and on tours to collect religious donations. From 1953, when his brother left Sa sKya, to 1957, when he himself went to Lhasa, NGag dBang Kun dGaa PHrin Las shared, with the other branch of his family, the responsibility for conducting the principality's religious and governmental affairs.

The third respondent, bSod Nams TSHe aDZom, the wife of
NGag dBang Kun dGaa bSod Nams, was born in Khams in
eastern Tibet in 1934. She received a fairly good Tibetan education, spent a number of years living with nomads, and with her
mother made a pilgrimage on foot to the holy places of central
Tibet. While on the pilgrimage, she met her future husband;
they were married when she was sixteen. As wife of a head of
the royal family, she was responsible for the domestic establishment of his palace, and she shared with a treasurer the responsibility for the palace's finances and business interests. She accompanied her husband on his travels after 1953.

Her uncle, Kun dGaa Bla Brang, usually known as sDe
gZHung Rin Po CHe, was the fourth respondent. He was born
in Khams in 1906 and entered the monkhood at the age of five.
At seventeen he was discovered to be an "emanation body" (a
concept explained in Chapter 3, section III). He became a renowned scholar of Tibetan Buddhism and for five years was in
charge of a monastery of three hundred monks, a position that
gave him important governmental functions in the local community of nomads. He later traveled extensively in eastern and
central Tibet, lecturing on religious doctrine, closely observing
Tibetan life, and giving advice on all kinds of personal problems.
As a tutor to the Sa sKya royal family, he saw government and
politics at first hand, without being a participant.

Our method in conducting the discussions was to introduce
topics of interest to us and then let the conversations go where
they would. Occasionally, of course, specific questions had to be
asked, but this approach was used as infrequently as possible.
During the year in which these conversations were carried on,
each important topic was brought up many times, sometimes
months apart, and the earlier information was compared with the
later. As the discussions progressed, we came to know Sa sKya
fairly intimately; we could recognize inconsistencies in our respondents' statements and review the subject once again. All the

respondents participated in the discussions, and the information presented here is never the opinion of one of them but a consensus of all four, frequently arrived at by spirited exchanges among themselves. Having a number of respondents allowed us to separate opinions and speculation from descriptions of clearly remembered facts. Whenever the Tibetans stated a generality, we asked for examples with the names of the participants, the time and place of the event, the wealth involved, and so forth. When such specifics were not available, we have prefaced the generality in the text by words such as "it was said that" and "reportedly." All four Tibetans were clearly aware of these problems of accuracy.

Our respondents' memories of people, events, and practices in Sa sKya were quite fresh. A large part of our discussions, however, concerned their own attitudes toward the organization and operation of the Sa sKya government. Although they had been subject to Chinese Communist arguments and propaganda and to American interviewing, and although the Communist takeover of Tibet had prompted them to reconsider the beliefs and practices they had always accepted, at the time of our interviews it was possible to recognize these extraneous influences and to eliminate them. As time passes, this separation of the old from the new will become more and more difficult.

The sudden flight from Tibet prevented our respondents from bringing out more than a few of the important documents and records of the Sa sKya principality. We believe, however, that the missing material, if it ever became available, would only give more concrete detail to our analysis.

It is difficult to write about a way of life different from one's own. When the life is that of one's friends, who have diligently and good-naturedly given its most intimate details, the difficulty increases. We have looked at Sa sKya from the point of view of modern Western social science; we have tried to be accurate in fact and logical in analysis. Our respondents may disagree with some of our conclusions, and so may other Tibetans. Personal involvements, the desire to make a favorable impression on foreigners, hindsight after the loss of Tibet to the Communists, and the nature of refugee politics may well make the material we present here somewhat controversial. We believe, however, that we have described government in Sa sKya as it actually existed; if we have, neither the personal honor nor the political fortunes of the Tibetans have been harmed.

The royal family of Sa sKya was divided into two branches, which for many generations had maintained a rather spirited rivalry. Since all our respondents were associated with one of these branches, we had to make every attempt to eliminate from our study any bias resulting from this division. Our method was to encourage our respondents to speak frankly about their disagreements with their relatives and especially about the vigorous contest over the succession to the throne after 1950. We thus obtained a fairly clear understanding of what they believed to be the issues in dispute and their positions on these issues. We did not include any of this material in the present study, but it enabled us to recognize the types of matters that seemed to have no relation to the issues in dispute, and hence to be unaffected by the rivalry, and to discover the types of matters that might be subject to bias, and to check them very carefully when we wanted to include them. Although we cannot describe the specific disputes, the existence of these disputes is an important piece of evidence in our study of the political system.

Tibetan words have been transliterated according to a system that uses Roman capitals to indicate the letter under which they are listed in a Tibetan dictionary and which (with the exception of the Tibetan "l") is the phonetically effective initial consonant. Thus the word "brGyud" is listed under the Tibetan equivalent of "g" and is pronounced "jed." Certain Tibetan letters are transcribed by use of two or three Roman letters, and hence some words contain two or three capitalized letters. The plural of Tibetan nouns is the same as the singular. We have used the standard transliterations for well-known names, such as

"Lhasa" and "Dalai Lama," and for place names that have no special connection with Sa sKya, such as "Tsangpo River" and "Rinphung Dzong."

We have regularly used only two untranslated Tibetan terms in the text. "KHri CHen" (pronounced "tree chen" and meaning "great throne") is the title of the hereditary head of the Sa sKya sect and the Sa sKya polity; "ZHabs Pad" (pronounced "shah pet" and meaning "lotus foot," an honorific) is the title of the Sa sKya prime minister or grand vizier. Except in Chapter 1, few proper names appear in the text. The most common and most important are these: "aKHon" (pronounced "kun"), the bone name of Sa sKya's ruling family; "aPHags Pa" ("pah bah"), the name of the thirteenth-century aKHon who was the most important figure in Sa sKya's political history; "NGag dBang mTHu THub dBang PHyug" ("nuk wahng too tohb wahng chu"), the name of the KHri CHen whose reign (1936–1950) is the focus of our study; and the names of the palaces of the two branches of the aKHon family, "PHun TSHogs" ("poon tsohk") and "sGrol Ma" ("droll mah"). Whenever possible, English equivalents are used for Tibetan terms and titles. The most important original Tibetan expressions are in the Glossary, listed by the English used in the text.

This study was made possible by the generous support of the Rockefeller Foundation and the Far Eastern and Russian Institute of the University of Washington under the directorship of Professor George E. Taylor. We also wish to thank Mr. Hans J. Meihoefer, who assisted in the preparation of the maps, and Professor Glen E. Alps, who made the prints of the seals (Plate 4).

C. W. C.
R. B. E.

Contents

Illustrations

PLATES

MAPS

Introduction

In 1936 a man named NGag dBang mTHu THub dBang PHyug became KHri CHen, or monarch, of the Tibetan principality of Sa sKya, thus assuming a throne that had been continuously occupied by members of his family since the thirteenth century. During these seven hundred years, the power and prestige of Sa sKya had fluctuated, but by the middle of the eighteenth century they became stabilized at a level that persisted into the twentieth century.

The domain of the KHri CHen in 1936 consisted of a number of noncontiguous areas in west-central Tibet that were remnants of a larger political unit. His capital was located in an enclave of about 2,100 square miles surrounded by territory controlled by governments in the Tibetan cities of Lhasa and Shigatse. This small area, which we call "Sa sKya proper," was a self-contained political unit of about 16,000 people.

Sa sKya got its name from the "pale earth" of its capital, Sa sKya gDan Sa, a town of about seven thousand inhabitants containing the royal aKHon family, the governmental officialdom, and two monasteries that were the headquarters of the Sa sKya sect of Tibetan Buddhism. Although Sa sKya was a *de facto* independent principality based on a special religious sect, its people were thoroughly Tibetan and, like other Tibetans, had been affected only slightly by the technology and beliefs of the modern world. Indeed, Sa sKya had fewer contacts with modernity than the larger, more important, and more accessible governmental capitals of Lhasa and Shigatse. There is every reason to believe that the beliefs, attitudes, and behavior of the people of Sa sKya had not changed substantially for several centuries.

Sa sKya was, in short, a traditional polity that had persisted into the contemporary period.[1] There have been few such political anachronisms and, to our knowledge, even fewer as little influenced by the forces of modernity. Since Sa sKya was also unusually small, it makes an excellent subject for a comprehensive study that attempts to describe the combination of social, economic, communal, ideological, organizational, and governmental factors that made its political system what it was. In our opinion, no other traditional polity has offered such an opportunity for analysis.

The goal of our analysis is to present a picture of twentieth-century Sa sKya as a polity in operation. Our emphasis is on the period from 1936 until 1950, the reign of KHri CHen NGag dBang mTHu THub dBang PHyug, because we have more detailed information about this period than about earlier times and because after 1950 Sa sKya came under the influence of the Chinese Communists. We have attempted to describe the structure of the Sa sKya government and the policy it pursued and to show how these political phenomena were correlated with the environment within which they occurred. The belief system of the people of Sa sKya, the manner in which they economized, their geographical location and its topography, their historical memories and traditions, and the pattern of social deference among them—these elements of the environment have been examined in some detail in order to show that such an environment was a natural concomitant of the type of governing found in Sa

[1] We do not imply that there was no change in Sa sKya in recent centuries, only that change had occurred within a stable structure of beliefs, attitudes, and institutions. For theories of such change, see Chalmers Johnson, *Revolutionary Change* (Boston: Little, Brown, 1966), esp. ch. 3. Our judgment that Sa sKya had experienced only this kind of change is based on its similarity to other societies whose past histories are better known.

sKya and that such governing was a natural accompaniment of this kind of environment. In other words, we have tried to show how in Sa sKya each of the generally recognized essential elements of any political society was related to all the others.[2]

Although our principal concern is with an accurate account and an adequate explanation of government and politics in Sa sKya, wherever possible we make comparisons with other similar political societies. Occasionally a feature of Sa sKya (such as its belief system) appears to be characteristic of a large number of those societies generally recognized as "pre-modern"; sometimes a feature (such as its method of religious observance) seems limited to only a few. Although there is no adequate classification of pre-modern polities, undoubtedly Sa sKya was basically different from the pre-literate political societies examined by anthropologists [3] and from the situation, described by Fustel de Coulanges,[4] where the polity and the religious group are identical. Nor was Sa sKya an "empire" or "historical bureaucratic polity," as conceptualized by S. N. Eisenstadt.[5] The dynamism and governmental initiative of the imperial systems was quite different from the static and passive nature of government in Sa sKya.

Land and people in Sa sKya were divided among a number of semi-independent agencies that we have called

---

[2] Our approach is based upon so-called "systems theory," derived from sources such as Talcott Parsons, *The Social System* (New York: Free Press of Glencoe, 1964), and David Easton, *A Systems Analysis of Political Life* (New York: John Wiley, 1965). Since, however, this theory is relatively undeveloped, we follow no formal scheme and use no special terminology. Johnson, *Revolutionary Change*, chs. 2–4, makes a useful attempt to synthesize the theory of social systems.

[3] See, for example, Lucy Mair's summary in *Primitive Government* (Baltimore: Penguin Books, 1962). There are, however, some similarities between Sa sKya and these pre-literate political societies.

[4] *The Ancient City* (Garden City, N.Y.: Doubleday, 1956).

[5] *The Political Systems of Empires* (New York: Free Press of Glencoe, 1963).

"establishments." [6] The royal family and many of the hereditary nobility had land and people of their own, but Sa sKya in the twentieth century had little resemblance to European "feudalism." [7]

The Sa sKya political system was clearly "traditional," for it had not changed substantially for several centuries, its strength lay in its continuity with the past, and it was (in large part) justified, or at least accounted for, by reference to this continuity. It may well have been an example of the literate, nonprimitive "traditional systems" that Eisenstadt compares with the "empires" that grew out of them.[8] The extremely small size of Sa sKya, it must be kept in mind, was not a major determinant of its political system. Although the style of governing was affected by the polity's size, the structure of government and the beliefs and attitudes associated with it came from a time, described in Chapter 1, when the Sa sKya domain was much larger.

Although we were unable to utilize a clear concept of the type of political society found in Sa sKya, we could not have collected our information nor have given it any structure without an idea of relevance that depended upon a tentative theory of "tradition." This theory will become evident as the text proceeds, but our exercise is best seen as presenting evidence (admittedly structured) to be combined with evidence from other sources in the search for a comprehensive theory. To put this another way, as in any such investigation generalities and specifics could not be separated.

[6] There was no concept of "establishment" in Sa sKya, and the word does not translate a Tibetan term. Our concept of establishment is explained in Chapter 3, section XII, and Chapter 9, sections IV and VII.

[7] F. L. Ganshof, *Feudalism*, trans. Philip Grierson (London: Longmans, Green, 1952), and Rushton Coulborn (ed.), *Feudalism in History* (Princeton, N.J.: Princeton University Press, 1956), two clear and succinct accounts of feudalism, provide the ground for this comparison. The possession of land and subjects by the Sa sKya nobility may have originated in some kind of "feudal" arrangement in past centuries.

[8] *Political Systems of Empires*, p. 149. Sa sKya was a "subject political culture," according to the scheme of Gabriel A. Almond and Sidney Verba, *The Civic Culture* (Boston: Little, Brown, 1965), pp. 17–18.

Our information about the reign of KHri CHen NGag dBang mTHu THub dBang PHyug came from members of the Sa sKya royal family, and thus Sa sKya was presented to us through the eyes and minds of its highest social, political, and economic stratum. A broader sample of the people of Sa sKya would naturally have been desirable, but there are four good reasons why the restricted source of our data is not a serious disadvantage to our study. In the first place, our respondents were much more familiar with the common man's experiences and attitudes than one might expect. The small population of Sa sKya proper and the size of its capital, a town of only 7,000, overcame much of the social distance between the royal family and their subjects. Many of the subjects described in this study were personal friends of our respondents; little of note occurred in the capital that was not brought by gossip to the ears of the highest dignitaries; and the official responsibilities of the royal family often brought its members in direct contact with their subjects. Two of our respondents, moreover, had lived closely with the common people elsewhere in Tibet, and they were able to supplement our information and to provide a check upon hasty generalizations about the subjects of Sa sKya.

Secondly, much is known about the attitudes of common men living in other times and places but having the same kinds of technology, the same standards of living, and the same types of religious and metaphysical orientations that we know were possessed by the people of Sa sKya.[9] Our only inference about the ordinary Sa sKya subject concerns his attitude toward his government. Although direct evidence would have been preferable, the inference appears reasonably sound, particularly because the same conclusions are suggested by the other elements of the political society. We might add here that very little information

[9] See the references in Chapter 3. Cf. Robert Redfield, *Peasant Society and Culture* (Chicago: University of Chicago Press, 1956). Ekvall lived almost eight years among the Tibetans and had constant and close association with commoners under tribal, monastic, and "kingly" political systems.

on the attitudes of pre-modern ruling classes has heretofore been available.

In the third place, in Sa sKya, as in other similar societies, the common people had little to do with government and politics, and the government did not pay much attention to their needs and attitudes. Our statements about governmental organization, functions, and perspectives consequently do not depend upon our inferences regarding the subjects' attitudes. If these inferences appear weaker than we believe, they can be discounted without seriously affecting the strength of the rest of our story.

Finally, we present our study of Sa sKya based only on the information provided by our respondents because Sa sKya, and most of Tibet as well, has now forever lost its former identity. Field work in any part of Tibet is impossible, and the existent information on Tibetan life prior to the Communist conquest consists primarily of random observations by foreign travelers. The memories of Tibetan refugees will fade and become distorted by their new environments, wishful thinking, and hindsight. We believe, in short, that the story of Sa sKya can best be told at this time.

We have attached a number of rather long appendixes to the text. They contain information about Sa sKya political society that did not conveniently fit into the main exposition; data upon which some of the text's generalizations and conclusions are based and which, in addition, illustrate our methods of reasoning; and material not relevant to government and politics but presumably of interest to students of Tibet and to those interested in pre-modern societies.

We believe that the story of Sa sKya is interesting as it stands. We hope that our analysis of Sa sKya's political system will contribute to the theory of "traditional" government and politics. This picture of Sa sKya may even help to clarify the process of "political development" now underway among such a large proportion of mankind.

A Tibetan Principality

The Political System of Sa sKya

Chapter 1

The History of Sa sKya

The people of Sa sKya were Tibetans and their history cannot be separated from the history of all Tibet. It was, indeed, an event of Tibet-wide significance—the invasion of Tibet by the grandson of Ghenghis Khan in 1239—that established Sa sKya as a permanent political unit. We shall begin our story of Sa sKya with a brief outline of the Tibetan past.

A knowledge of the "glorious" history of Sa sKya is essential to an understanding of the small twentieth-century principality. Many of the beliefs and institutions to be described in subsequent chapters had their origins centuries ago. More important, the Sa sKya political system was unusually dependent upon the past. The continuity of Sa sKya and its ruling family, the aKHon, and the former degree and extent of its government's power were probably the most important reasons for the maintenance of Sa sKya's political independence. This reliance upon the past will be a central theme in our analysis.

I

There are myths and legends about Tibetan history as early as the beginning of the Christian era, but the first written records date from the reign of the Tibetan king Srong bTSan sGam Po (c.629–649).[1] This famous man is believed to have promoted the

---

[1] Our outline of the history of Tibet is drawn from the following sources: J. Bacot, *Introduction à l'histoire du Tibet* (Paris: Société Asiatique, 1962); J. Bacot, F. W. Thomas, and C. H. Toussaint, *Documents de Touen-Huang relatifs à l'histoire du Tibet* (Paris: Libraire

useful arts, codified the law, introduced a system of writing, and established Lhasa as the political capital of Tibet. From Lhasa he extended his control until he came in contact with the Chinese and the Nepalese; he dealt with China as an equal and received tribute from Nepal. In addition to his Tibetan wives, he married a Chinese princess and a Nepalese princess, both of whom were strong Buddhists and undoubtedly influenced the king to encourage the propagation of Buddhism in Tibet. Under his direction, a number of Buddhist works were hand-written in the new Tibetan writing, and Tibetans today consider him an emanation of Avalokitesvara, the patron Bodhisattva of Tibet.

During the reign of his descendant King KHri Srong lDe bTSan (c.754–c.797), the Tibetan empire reached its greatest extent, including Hunza, parts of western China, and most of Turkestan. The empire received tribute from Bengal and the kingdom of Nan Chao as well as from Nepal; it had outposts in the Pamirs; and it came in contact with the Arabs, Persians, Turks, and Uighurs. When the Chinese failed to pay a tribute to KHri Srong lDe bTSan, his army briefly occupied Ch'ang-an, the capital of the T'ang dynasty. The king was also a great patron of Buddhism, inviting Padma Sambhava and other religious teachers to Tibet, building the monastery of Sam dByas, and establishing an institute for translating religious works. He declared in favor of the Indian school of Buddhism over the Chinese Chan school.

King KHri gTSung lDe bTSan, known as Ral Pa Can, who reigned from about 816 to about 836, was an especially devout

---

Orientalists Paul Genthner, 1946); Sir Charles Bell, *Tibet Past and Present* (London: Oxford University Press, 1924); Dalai Lama, *My Land and My People* (New York: McGraw-Hill, 1962); Tieh-tseng Li, *Tibet Today and Yesterday* (New York: Bookman Associates, 1960); Paul Pelliot, *Histoire ancienne du Tibet* (Paris: Librairie d'Amerique et d'Orient—Adrien-Maisonneuve, 1961); Luciano Petech, *China and Tibet in the Early Eighteenth Century* (Leiden: E. J. Brill, 1950); H. E. Richardson, *A Short History of Tibet* (New York: E. P. Dutton, 1962); and R. A. Stein, *La civilisation tibétaine* (Paris: Dunod, 1962).

patron of Buddhism. His enthusiasm and the favored treatment he gave to Buddhist monks aroused strong opposition from certain Tibetan noblemen who were adherents of the pre-Buddhist Bon religion, and it is said that he met death by assassination. He was succeeded by his older brother, KHri Dar Ma U Dum bTSan, known as Glang Dar Ma, who did what he could to destroy Buddhism in Tibet. He was assassinated by a Buddhist monk about the year 841.

During this period, from about 629 until about 841, a constant secular struggle occurred between the kings, determined to increase their power, and the nobility, determined to contain it. After the death of Glang Dar Ma, the Tibetan empire fell apart, more from this internal dissension than from outside pressure. About sixty years of political chaos followed, but then Buddhist leaders began to establish monastic communities and centers of learning that gradually attracted adherents and gained influence. The nobility became associated with these communities, often as patrons, and the religious centers developed into political centers as well. By the end of the twelfth century, Buddhism was dominant once again, and monastic communities such as TSHal, Bri Gung, and Sa sKya were established sects with varying interpretations of Buddhism and adherents and influence throughout all of Tibet.

In 1206, Ghenghis Khan invaded Amdo in the Tibetan northeast. He was met by a delegation of religious and secular notables of TSHal, who offered their submission to the Mongol in order to prevent his further advance. At this time, Ghenghis Khan sent an invitation to Sa sKya Pandita, the head of the Sa sKya sect, to come and negotiate with him, but the meeting never occurred. In 1239, Godan, Ghenghis Khan's grandson, sent his armies to within one hundred miles of Lhasa as a response to the Tibetans' failure to pay the tribute they had promised Ghenghis Khan. The leaders of TSHal then asked Sa sKya Pandita to represent them, and he succeeded in pacifying Godan's general. Upon invitation from Godan, Sa sKya Pandita visited the Mongol's court and tendered the submission of all the Tibetans. In 1249 he was made viceroy of Tibet, and the period of Sa sKya ascendency, to be described in some detail below, began.

The Sa sKya leaders took the Mongolian political system as their model. With the aid of the Mongols, they maintained a tenuous control over all Tibet until about 1350, when they were defeated in battle by Byang CHub rGyal mTSHan, of the noble house of PHag Mo Dru. This battle made Byang CHub rGyal mTSHan the strongest man in Tibet, and the Mongols, presented with a *fait accompli*, made him viceroy. For almost three hundred years the PHag Mo Dru and two other noble families attempted in succession to restore the kingly tradition, discarded many of the Mongol laws and institutions, and fought constantly with various religious sects and their noble supporters. The period ended when Gushri Khan, of the Oirat Mongols, defeated and killed the last Tibetan king in 1642.

II

During this "second rule of kings," the Yellow sect (dGe Lugs Pa) of Tibetan Buddhism, to become the dominant sect under the Dalai Lama, made its appearance and gained many adherents. Its founder was TSong KHa Pa, who arrived in central Tibet (from Amdo in northwestern Tibet) toward the end of the fourteenth century. He synthesized and systematized various Buddhist doctrines, insisted on the reform and purification of teaching and religious observance, and established the three great monasteries of Lhasa. One of his disciples became the first Dalai Lama. The third Dalai Lama was a protégé of the Mongol ruler Altan Khan, and one of Altan Khan's great-grandsons became the fourth Dalai Lama.

In 1642 the fifth Dalai Lama, a man of remarkable energy, ability, and statesmanship, was designated by Gushri Khan as the ruler of all Tibet. With this grant of power, and by virtue of being the head of the dominant religious sect, the fifth Dalai Lama made his office predominant in Tibetan politics until the arrival of the Chinese Communists. During these three hundred years, there were constant serious internal divisions and periodic interventions by the Chinese, Dzungarian Mongols, Nepalese, Dogras, and British.[2] In addition, at the height of their temporal powers the Dalai Lamas, or those who claimed to represent them, never had effective control of most of eastern Tibet, and they always recognized the autonomy of the political regimes of the Panchen Lamas in Shigatse and the aKHon family in Sa sKya.

The Dalai Lamas are held to be the emanations of Avalokitesvara, the "patron saint" of Tibet and one of the five principal Dhyani Bodhisattvas that are projections of the Buddhahood into the material plane.[3] According to Tibetan belief, the Buddhahood is also projected, in the form of Dhyani Buddhas, into the spiritual plane of meditation. The fifth Dalai Lama made his revered teacher abbot of the great monastery of bKra SHis lHun Po in Shigatse and announced that he was the emanation of one of these Dhyani Buddhas, Od PHag Med, or the Buddha of Boundless Light. Thus was born the institution of the Panchen Lama. The second Panchen Lama was an able and renowned man; the Chinese are said to have offered him control of all of gTSang and western Tibet. He accepted only the three districts of lHa rTSe, PHun TSHogs Gling, and NGam Rings, but subsequent Panchen Lamas extended the area of their governmental control.

From a doctrinal point of view, the Panchen Lama is a more exalted figure than the Dalai Lama, since the spiritual plane is higher than the material, but because of this spiritual characteristic, Panchen Lamas found it more difficult to engage in worldly affairs. The Dalai Lamas thus became both the temporal and

---

[2] The justice of the Chinese claim to Tibet does not concern us here. The important thing is that, until the arrival of the Communists, no Chinese government exercised any continued control over central and western Tibet.

[3] On the phenomenon of the "emanation," see Chapter 3, section III.

spiritual leaders of Tibet, although all Tibetans always have had the highest reverence for the Panchen Lamas.

III

The Tibetan past shows a unity among "all those who speak the Tibetan language," but this unity was cultural and, especially, religious rather than political. At least since the time of King Srong bTSan sGam Po in the seventh century, the Tibetans have seen themselves as different from the Mongols, Chinese, Nepalese, and others, and they have shared a presumption that they would act in concert whenever threatened by these outsiders. Even as late as the 1950's, however, this clear sense of Tibetanness was not seen as implying political unity. The Tibetans had not yet reached a nationalistic stage of development, a fact that is clearly manifested in the political ideas that underlay the principality of Sa sKya.[4] These ideas, the behavior of the Sa sKya government, and the history of Sa sKya can be understood only by reference to this cultural unity combined with an acceptance of political fragmentation.

The documented history of Sa sKya begins during the reign of KHri Srong lDe bTSan, King of Tibet from about 754 until about 797, when a member of the aKHon family, the future rulers of Sa sKya, was a well-known minister of the King.[5] The

[4] See Chapter 3.

[5] The historical account of Sa sKya is drawn from the following sources, in addition to those cited in note 1 above: Chandra Das, "Contributions on Tibet," *Journal of the Asiatic Society of Bengal*, L (1881), 240–242, *Narrative of a Journey round Lake Yamdo and in Lokha, Yarlung and Sakya in 1882* (Calcutta: Bengal Secretariat Press, 1887), pp. 60, 61, and *Journey to Lhasa and Central Tibet*, ed. W. W. Rockhill (London: J. Murray, 1902), pp. 239–241; Ippolito Desideri, *An Account of Tibet, 1712–1727* (London: Routledge, 1937), p. 131; George N. Roerich, *The Blue Annals* (Calcutta: Royal Asiatic Society of Bengal, 1949–1953), pp. 210–217, 405, 582, 1052, 1057; E. Gene Smith, "The History of the 'Khon to the birth of Sa-Chen Kun-dga'-snying-po According to the *Rgya Bod Yig Tshang*" (mimeographed paper, University of Washington, 1961) and "The Era of 'Grom-gon 'Phags-pa and the Apogee of Sa-skya-pa Power" (mimeographed paper, Univer-

history of Sa sKya is in effect the history of the aKHon, and, as with the Tibetan people as a whole,[6] myths account for the origin of the aKHon and legends describe their early activities.

The myth of the aKHon begins with the descent to earth of three brothers of the Gods of Clear Light, their point of landing being given as either the border area between gTSang and upper mNGaa Ris or near the "spirit lake" of the aKHon family, possibly north of rTSe gDong (Map 1). They were importuned to remain in the abode of men to act as governors, and the youngest, called gYu Se, gYu bSe, or dBu Se, agreed to do so. He had four sons, who, with the help of their uncle gYu Ring, the second of the three god-brothers, made war upon and reduced to vassalage the eighteen clans of the lDong, one of the six mythological tribes of prehistoric Tibet. As his wife, gYu Ring took a girl of the rMu (or sMu), another of the six tribes (a marriage that may also have involved a political alliance), and by her he had seven sons, known as the "Ma Sangs brothers." He and the six oldest ascended to the land of the gods by means of a rope. The youngest son, Ma Sangs rJe, remained on earth.

With Ma Sangs rJe the story of the aKHon family comes down to earth and becomes legendary. He married and had a son named THog TSHa dPaa Bo sTag.[7] This son married a female

---

sity of Washington, 1962); G. Tucci, *Tibetan Painted Scrolls* (Rome: La Libreria dello Stato, 1949), pp. 6–57, 625–629, 679; sTag TSHang Pa sRi Bhu-ti Bha-dra, *rGya Bod Yig TSHang* (MS, University of Washington Library, 1434?), ff. 184–190; and NGag dBang Blo bZang rGya mTSHo (the fifth Dalai Lama), *sGang Can Yul Gyi Sa La sPyod Pai mTHo Ris Kyi rGyal Blon gTSo Bor brJod Pai Deb THer rDZogs lDan gZHon Nui dGaa sTon dPyid Kyi rGyal Moi Klu dByangs ZHes Bya Ba bZHugs So* [Chronicles of the Land of Snow] (1643; Peking: Min Tsu Ch'u Pan Ch'u, 1957), pp. 122–139. Unfortunately, authoritative Sa sKya histories, such as the best and most up-to-date by AH Myes ZHabs, were not available.

[6] See Chapter 3, section V.

[7] Although the wife of Ma Sangs rJe was called "THog TSam Ur Ma" (thunderstorm) and her father "THog lHa Od Chen" (thunder god), there is every indication that these were proper names of human beings.

Klu, or naga (a serpent spirit), and their son, called Klu TSHa rTa Po Od CHen, married a woman who from her name was probably a queen or princess of the Mon, the several tribes of southern Tibet who were pushed southward or absorbed by the Tibetans. From this marriage issued a son named gYaa sPang sKyes, who may have been born on some enforced journey, for he got his name from his birth (sKyes) between the slate out-croppings (gYaa) and the high meadows (sPang). He apparently lived up to the circumstances of his birth, because in his wanderings he became involved with bSil Ma of gYaa Grum, the wife of sKya Rengs KHra Med, a Srin, or cannibalistic demon. gYaa sPang Skyes took the woman, killed the demon, and had a son who was called aKHon Bar sKyes—because he was born (sKyes) during the period (Bar) of hostility (aKHon) between his father and the demon—and "aKHon" became the bone name of the family. aKHon Bar sKyes married a woman of the country of gTSang and had a son, dKon Pa rJe Gung sTag bTSan, with whom the recorded history of the aKHon family, and thus of Sa sKya, begins.

IV

dKon Pa rJe Gung sTag bTSan is credited with irresistible charm and good looks, wisdom, and magical powers. His father told him to find good land and take it,[8] and he complied by seizing the plain of gNYan rTSe in upper gTSang north of Shigatse. His success as a homesteader—and one who no doubt had serfs and retainers—came to the attention of KHri Srong lDe bTSan, the King of Tibet (c.754–c.797) when the Tibetan empire was at its greatest expanse and power. The king made dKon Pa rJe Gung sTag bTSan a kind of chief counselor, and his long service in this capacity was so renowned that he took the

---

[8] The best land had eight characteristics: soil for agriculture, soil for building houses, water for drinking, water for irrigation, forests (of both the trees that turn red in winter and those that do not) for building, forests for fuel, grass nearby, and grass at a distance.

name aKHon dPal Po CHe, the one who had brought glory to the aKHon. He married a sister of a famous translator of religious works at the Tibetan court—one of the "seven men on trial," the first monks of the Tibetan monastic system—and had at least two sons. The elder son, who became another of the "seven men on trial," was the most gifted of the younger translators and eventually became an acknowledged master of metaphysics and tantrics, the use of meditation to experience fulfillment. Much of this fame came from the special initiations in tantrics he received from Padma Sambhava, the famous tantrist and magician. (Two of these eight "old sect" tantric initiations, the "reality" and the "thunderbolt-dagger," are considered by the Sa sKya sect as its specialities.) One tradition credits this elder son with having persuaded the Tibetan king to found the great monastery of bSam Yas.

The younger of the two sons of aKHon dPal Po CHe is known only as the father of the next aKHon. The Tibetans had no rule of primogeniture, and this is one of the many cases in which a younger brother of the aKHon family carried on its genealogical line. This next aKHon was rDo rJe Rin CHen, who also received many initiations from Padma Sambhava and who began the early Tibetan tradition of the secret mantra observances. His career was similar to that of his uncle, from whom he received additional initiations, except that he took a wife—the daughter of aBro dGra aDul—and had seven sons.

The story is that these seven brothers attended a public celebration and were so successful in the horse races, athletic competitions, and (possibly) competitive trading that members of their mother's family began to plot against them. The youngest of the seven wanted to raise troops and fight, but his brothers were reluctant to take arms against their relatives. They said there was no sense in fighting when there was land for all, and they scattered to Mang Yul (probably near Nepal), Gung THang (possibly near Nepal), gNYaa Lo Ro (possibly in southern Tibet), NYang SHab (the SHab Valley, Map 3, and the valley of

Shigatse), Grom Pa gYaa Lung (gYaa Lung, Map 3), and Srad (Map 1). The youngest brother stayed and fought for his ancestral lands. He had three sons, but the aKHon line was continued by the older of the two sons of SHes Rab Yon Tan, the sixth of the seven brothers and the one who went to Grom Pa gYaa Lung. The younger son of SHes Rab Yon Tan went to La sTod in northwestern Tibet, where he had many descendants. The elder son, TSHul KHrims rGyal Po, had three sons, and the oldest of these, gTSug Tor SHes Rab, remained in gYaa Lung and had seven sons. The fifth of these sons, aKHon dGe sKyabs, went to the SHab Valley—the others remained in gYaa Lung —and carried on the line of the aKHon family. The younger of the two sons of aKHon dGe sKyabs apparently had many descendants, but the elder, aKHon dGe THong, carried on the line through his only son, aKHon sTon Bal Po, who was famous for his religious achievements, having attained tantric realization in a cave east of the site of the future capital (Sa sKya gDan Sa, Map 3). His son was SHa Kya Blo Gros, who moved around in the SHab Valley and Bya Ru (perhaps rMa Bya, Map 3) and late in life went to gYaa Lung, the home of his ancestors. The elder of his two sons, Rog SHes Rab TSHul KHrims, took the full vows of a monk at an early age and achieved great learning and magical powers. According to tradition, the younger son, dKon mCHog rGyal Po, was born in 1034 at a place called sPyi lHas, a few miles from the future capital.

V

With dKon mCHog rGyal Po a new phase in the history of the aKhon family began. In the second half of the eighth century, a member of the family had been an important counselor to the king of Tibet, and his son had been one of the famous first seven Tibetan monks. But then, with the persecution of Buddhism by Glang Dar Ma and the disintegration of the Tibetan empire, the family's promise of religious and political leadership was unrealized and its members became wanderers, seeking land and position by force or through matrimonial alliances, getting involved in feuds and other troubles, and becoming dispersed and fragmented. In the second half of the eleventh century, the family once again began its movement toward pre-eminence in politics and religion.

According to Sa sKya tradition, Atisha, the great Indian Buddhist missionary to Tibet, while traveling through Tibet in 1042 or 1043, stopped in view of the "pale earth" of the future capital. As his companions made camp, Atisha made many gestures of religious worship toward the area of pale earth, explaining that from there would be manifested many emanations of three Bodhisattvas, sPyan Ras gZigs, PHyag Na rDo rJe, and aJam dPal dByangs, who would spread religious doctrine and benefit all living creatures. In some complicated way, it was indicated that emanations of the first two Bodhisattvas would be rare, but those of aJam dPal dByangs would be plentiful. This purported prediction took place when dKon mCHog rGyal Po of the aKHon family was eight or nine years old.

Some years later, dKon mCHog rGyal Po went to a religious celebration among the people of aBro. This celebration apparently involved elements of pre-Buddhist rituals,[9] and when he described them to his older brother, the brother charged him to remain true to the correct tantric doctrine received from Padma Sambhava and transmitted as the distinctive heritage of the aKHon family. The brothers thus were precursors of Sa CHen, the aKHon who formally stated a distinctive Sa sKya religious doctrine.

His older brother also urged dKon mCHog rGyal Po to go to aBrog Mi, a famous religious teacher who was at Mang mKHar (Map 3), to continue his studies and become fully initiated, but aBrog Mi would not accept him as a student. Instead, dKon

[9] These rituals included incantations, the ritual display of weapons, and masked dancing, especially a drum dance by a man wearing the mask of the "long-haired one."

mCHog rGyal Po studied at gYaa Lung with another teacher, Bla Ma gNam KHa U, who later dreamed that if dKon mCHog rGyal Po would leave the monkhood and marry, he would fulfill the prophecy of Atisha, for from him would issue a son who would be an emanation and who would also found a new religious sect and tradition. After the death of Bla Ma gNam KHa U, aBrog Mi agreed to receive dKon mCHog rGyal Po, who finally was initiated.[10] In accordance with the dream of his former teacher, dKon mCHog rGyal Po at the age of forty renounced the vows of the monkhood and married, an act for which he had the highest religious sanction.

While dKon mCHog rGyal Po was a monk, he built a monument to his father and brother and established a small monastery, which came to be called the "Sa sKya ruin" (Gog Pa), at a place called Bra O Lung (perhaps KHra U, Map 3). One day he was on a picnic with his novices, and from a mountain he saw an area of white, oily earth beside a stream. He announced that a monastery should be built on that spot, and he forthwith began to make the necessary arrangements. He secured permission from a local lord, four communities of monks, seven villages, and the Gu Ra Ba clan of the ZHang ZHung, a non-Tibetan people who were eventually absorbed by the Tibetans. Although no one asked for payment, in order to avoid future trouble dKon mCHog rGyal Po insisted on giving them, among other things, a white mare, a woman's robe, a jeweled rosary, and a coat of mail. Construction of the monastery began in 1073; with this act, the capital, the gDan Sa, or seat of power, of the "glorious" Sa sKya, or pale land, was founded. According to the oral tradition of the aKHon family, in the eleventh century most of the land was covered with scrub forest, there were few fields and people, and the climate was colder.

The original piece of land was small, but it was gradually

---

[10] The story is that dKon mCHog rGyal Po offered aBrog Mi seventeen horses and their loads, gained in trade, and a jeweled rosary purchased by renting grazing land to nomads.

enlarged by purchase, colonization, occupation, marriage alliances, and the religious offering of land and people to the head of the sect, and also by union with nearby people who traced their origins to the aKHon family. When the Mongols took a census of nuclear Tibet in the twelfth century, Sa sKya, with 3,630 families, or 21,780 people, was one of its three most populous districts, although the geographical limits of this population are not known.

The wife whom dKon mCHog rGyal Po married when he was forty apparently had no sons, so he took a second wife, Jo Mo ZHang Mo (the daughter of Gu Ra, a non-Tibetan), who in 1092 bore him a son, Kun dGaa sNYing Po, later often called Sa CHen. Sa CHen was the emanation of two Bodhisattvas, sPyan Ras gZigs and aJam dPal dByangs, and thenceforth, according to the prophecy of Atisha and the dream of Bla Ma gNam KHa U, every male member of the aKHon family has been an emanation of one or more of the three Bodhisattvas. Sa CHen expounded and codified a distinctive Sa sKya religious doctrine, which provided the foundation for later Sa sKya political and ecclesiastical power. He had four sons. The oldest went to India seeking religious instruction and initiation and died there, and little is known about the next two, who presumably were religious teachers. The family line was carried through the youngest of the four, dPal CHen Od Pa (1150–1203).

VI

dPal CHen Od Pa had two sons, Sa sKya Kun dGaa rGyal mTSHan (1182–c.1251), known as Sa sKya Pandita, and Zangs TSHa bSod Nams rGyal mTSHan (1184–1239). The elder son was both a scholar and a statesman; the younger occupied himself with carrying on the family line.

Sa sKya Pandita was a man of impressive learning and practical ability. His many writings include a masterly and original exposition of what is in effect a Tibetan system of logic and a set of maxims that may well have been the source of a later code of rules (gTan TSHigs) of the Sa sKya polity. In 1239, when the Mongol emperor Godan sent an army to within a hundred miles of Lhasa, Sa sKya Pandita was asked to represent the Tibetans. He pacified the army's commander and was invited to visit Godan's court in Liang-chow. With two of his nephews, Bla Ma aGro mGon aPHags Pa and PHyag Na rDo rJe, he eventually met Godan, tendered submission on behalf of the Tibetans, and was charged with controlling Tibet for the Mongols. He then wrote a letter to "all who speak the Tibetan language," urging them to accept a condition of vassalage because the Mongols had great power, had conquered the Uighurs and the Chinese, and indeed were irresistible. He specified the kinds, amounts, and schedules of tribute that the Tibetans were to pay. He stressed the severity of Mongol law. He did not, moreover, omit reference to himself: "This king [of the Mongols] is a Bodhisattva who has the greatest faith in the Buddhist teachings generally, and in the three gems [the Rare Precious Three] in particular. He protects the universe by good laws, and especially he has a great attachment to me, far above all others. He said, 'Preach religion with a tranquil mind; I will give you what you wish.' Above all he has a great attachment to aPHags Pa and his brother. Knowing how to govern freely, he has the good intention of being good to all peoples." [11] Sa sKya Pandita was undoubtedly trying to forestall objections to the terms he had negotiated and to get the Tibetans to accept the leadership of his family. He died at the court of Godan in 1251 or 1252.

Zangs TSHa bSod Nams rGyal mTSHan, the younger brother of Sa sKya Pandita, had five wives and seven children. One of his five wives was from the aBro family of the SHab Valley, one was the daughter of a petty king, one was a Mongol lady, the fourth was a serving woman of one of the other wives, and the fifth was the mother of his most famous offspring, Bla Ma aGro mGon aPHags Pa (1235–1280), known as aPHags Pa,

[11] The full text of the letter is in Tucci, *Tibetan Painted Scrolls*, p. 10.

and PHyag Na rDo rJe (1239–1278). The family line of the aKHon, however, was carried through Ye SHes aBung gNas, the son of the servant.

After the death of Sa sKya Pandita, aPHags Pa and his brother went to the court of Kublai Khan. In 1252, at the age of seventeen, aPHags Pa became the chaplain of the emperor, who had finally been converted to Buddhism. As his chaplain, aPHags Pa was entitled to receive offerings from the emperor.[12] When Kublai Khan received his first religious initiation, he gave aPHags Pa the thirteen myriarchies—units of ten thousand into which the Mongols divided their populations—of central Tibet, after his second initiation he gave him the three regions of greater Tibet, and after his third some very holy relics. aPHags Pa was also given the title Ti Shih, teacher of the emperor.[13] During his stay at the court of Kublai Khan, aPHags Pa sent back much wealth to the capital of Sa sKya, and his dPon CHen, or regent, SHakya bZang Po, began to build the great South Monastery (Map 5 and Plate 5), levying supplies and labor from the thirteen myriarchies. It is said that Kublai Khan wanted to make the Sa sKya sect official and forbid activity by all other sects, but aPHags Pa persuaded him to allow doctrinal differences to continue, probably because he realized that this pro-

[12] The relationship between the emperor and his chaplain is called "Yon mCHod" (fee offering), a contraction of "Yon bDag" (fee master), the one who makes an offering, such as wealth, land, people, or power, and "mCHod gNas" (offering rest), his spiritual superior who receives the offering. When the gift has been received, it is under the control of the receiver, but unless specified otherwise he cannot transmit this control to anyone else. This need to renew an offering to each mCHod gNas created political difficulties.

[13] aPHags Pa invented an alphabet, based on Tibetan writing, for the Mongol language, which Kublai Khan made official in 1269. Since, however, it was derived from a writing used for the relatively isolating language of Tibetan, the alphabet proved too complicated for the relatively agglutinative language of Mongolian, and after a while it was replaced by another system of writing. Official imperial documents written in the script of aPHags Pa are extant.

scription would further weaken his tenuous hold over the other Tibetan sects and factions and make him even more unpopular as a tool of the Mongols. aPHags Pa returned to Sa sKya in 1265, but was back in China in 1269. In 1277 he returned again to Sa sKya, feasted (according to tradition) 100,000 people, and held a great council. He died there, perhaps by poison, in 1280. His brother, PHyag Na rDo rJe, had died two years earlier, and poison is also suspected.

VII

After the death of aPHags Pa, the Tibetan political situation was confused. The power of the leader of Sa sKya over Tibet depended upon Mongol support and upon his occupying the office of Ti Shih, teacher of the emperor. Although aPHags Pa was succeeded as Ti Shih by members of the aKHon family, the office was also occupied by other people during the period of Sa sKya's ascendancy.[14] After aPHags Pa's death, his half-brother, Rin CHen rGyal mTSHan became Ti Shih, but he died, again possibly by poison, after only two years in office. The next Ti Shih was the son of aPHags Pa's brother, PHyag Na rDo rJe, but he too died young. The son of aPHags Pa's half-brother (by the servant wife) was bDag NYid CHen Po bZang Po dPal (1262–1322). He had a claim to succession, but he was suspected of complicity in the death of the last Ti Shih, and the Chinese exiled him, probably to Hainan. During his exile, his chaplain, Grag Pa Od Zen, of the family of KHang gSar, was made Ti Shih and held the office for eighteen years.

This family of KHang gSar was one of the four—the others were SHar Pa, Nub Pa, and Gung Pa—upon whose support the aKHon had relied in their dealings with the Mongols and the other people of Tibet.[15] The four, however, were constantly

---

[14] Names and dates of this period have not been satisfactorily determined. The genealogical chart in Tucci, *Tibetan Painted Scrolls*, is usually followed, but it contains mistakes in both.

[15] These four may have been factions rather than families.

seeking power for themselves, thereby confusing the succession
of leadership in Sa sKya and no doubt contributing to the brevity of Sa sKya's dominance in Tibet.

After sixteen years in exile, bDag NYid CHen Po bZang Po
dPal was allowed to return to Sa sKya, but he was forbidden to
participate in any worldly affairs. Tradition has it that at the age
of forty he married six wives, all from prominent families and
one a Mongol princess, and had thirteen or fourteen sons and
two daughters. He then took the vows of a celibate monk. He
apparently never received the title Ti Shih, but he was called
Kuo Shih (kingdom teacher) and Wang (king).

Some of this impressive number of sons died young. Those
that are accounted for were organized, in the order of seniority,
into the following four branches (or palaces) of the aKHon
family: gZHi THog, lHa KHang or Lo sTod, Dus mCHod,
and Rin CHen sGang or dGe sDings. Each branch had lands and
property assigned to it. The first three branches each contained
two brothers of the same mother; one was unmarried and presumably a monk, the other married in order to carry on the line.
The fourth branch had two unmarried brothers and one who
married. Three of these sons of bDag NYid CHen Po bZang Po
dPal became Ti Shih, and two others went to China in religious
capacities and were honored with other titles. During this generation Sa sKya lost its position as the dominant power in Tibet,
and the proliferation of offspring in the absence of primogeniture or some other clear principle of succession undoubtedly
contributed to this eclipse.

The gZHi THog, lHa KHang, and Rin CHen sGang
branches lasted only from four to six generations, and when they
died out their holdings were sooner or later transferred to the
other branches. The Dus mCHod branch lasted twenty-three
generations, from its founding until the twentieth century.[16]

---

[16] The marrying brother of the first generation of this branch took as
his wife one of his father's widows, the Mongol princess. She was young
when her first husband died.

VIII

During the period of Sa sKya power throughout Tibet, the position of the leader of Sa sKya depended upon his status as chaplain, or Ti Shih, of the emperor. Each new claimant to the chaplainship had to be invested by the emperor, and this required rather long residence at the imperial court. Moreover, the Ti Shih was a religious personage, and it was not exactly proper for him to engage in political affairs. These conditions necessitated the appointment of a second official under the Mongol emperor, the dPon CHen or Blon CHen (great official or great minister), who remained in Sa sKya to conduct the business of government and who naturally came to have great power. Each dPon CHen was proposed by the Ti Shih and approved by the emperor. The four dominant families competed intensely for the position; the tenure of the dPon CHen averaged about three and one-half years, with most of the incumbents dying in office. These officials were apparently so preoccupied with the struggle for power that they carried out their governmental functions rather badly, another reason for the disintegration of Sa sKya's power. There were, however, some exceptions: the first dPon CHen began the construction of the South Monastery, two others either compiled or revised the Sa sKya code, and another had some military success.

For seventy or seventy-five years Sa sKya was the dominant power among all the groups of Tibet, having a formal title, at least, to rule them. The control that Sa sKya managed to exercise was always dependent upon the Mongol emperors, and when the power of the emperors decreased and when they favored other Tibetans, Sa sKya could no longer even claim to be the government for all Tibet. Sa sKya never had its own sources of power; it lacked great wealth, large populations, and military strength. Moreover, as stated above, its internal structure had serious basic weaknesses that made positive political action difficult. Despite the brevity and tenuousness of Sa sKya ascendancy, the fact that it was once recognized as "the government of all Tibet" had the most important effects on its later self-image and on the attitude of other Tibetan governments, especially that at Lhasa, toward it. Because of its position in the fourteenth century, it was recognized by other Tibetans in the twentieth century as a "gZHung," a genuine government, a virtually autonomous political entity. Unquestionably this fact contributed to the maintenance of the miniature principality in a context dominated by much more powerful potential rivals.

IX

After Sa sKya was militarily defeated by the noble house of PHag Mo Dru in about 1350, the various branches of the aKHon family continued to engage in Tibetan politics. In the fifteenth century, one branch even attempted a rebellion against the PHag Mo Dru regime, but it was crushed. During the rebellion, other branches of the family allied themselves with the regime. In the same period, the rivalry of the branches of the aKHon developed into bloody warfare, and the PHag Mo Dru government intervened, pacified them, and set up a garrison in Sa sKya.

This intervention seems to have made its point. Sa sKya was on good terms with the last king of Tibet, sDe Srid gTSang Pa, but it managed to avoid involvement in his quarrel with Gushri Khan, who defeated and killed him in 1642, and it also was not touched by the invasion of Tibet by the Dzungarian Mongols in 1717. Sa sKya maintained friendly relations with the fifth Dalai Lama (1617–1682), who was anxious to consolidate his own power throughout Tibet. There were bitter feuds and actual warfare between the Yellow sect of the Dalai Lama and some of the older sects of Tibetan Buddhism, but Sa sKya did not become involved. The rulers of Sa sKya adopted a policy of neutrality in internal and external affairs, a policy well suited to their physical weakness and their prestige as a genuine gZHung. In the early eighteenth century, Sa sKya carefully dissociated itself from the Tibetan revolt against Chinese domination. In the first half of the eighteenth century, the principality mediated a dispute between the Lhasa government and Bhutan, and it mediated another between Lhasa and the Nepalese who invaded Tibet in 1788. When rivalry developed between the Dalai Lama in Lhasa and the Panchen Lama in Shigatse, Sa sKya sided with one or the other as events warranted in order to guard its independence and enhance its prestige.

In the eighteenth century, the religious and political power of Sa sKya was about the same as it was in the 1940's. Marriages had linked the aKHon family with outside notables, and sometimes territory and people—Mus (Map 1) is an example—were thus added to the Sa sKya domain. Sa sKya made religious converts in Amdo in eastern Tibet and the king of Derge became a staunch patron of the sect, but a reverse occurred when the NGor sect broke with the Sa sKya sect and established its own monastery of E Wam CHos lDan near Gyangtse in 1429.

X

After the aKHon family lost the title Ti Shih, the man who was head of the Sa sKya sect and polity had a variety of titles, including Gong Ma, or superior one. By the time of Gong Ma Kun dGaa Blo Gros (c.1728–c.1790), the title KHri CHen, or great throne, had been adopted.

When Gong Ma Kun dGaa Blo Gros became KHri CHen, only one branch of the aKHon family remained, but during the reign of his son, KHri CHen mTHu CHen dBang sDud sNYing Po (c.1763–c.1806), a new division of the family occurred. mTHu CHen dBang sDud sNYing Po had three wives and five sons, one of whom died young. Two of the remaining sons became monks, but neither the first son, Padma bDud aDul dBang PHyug, nor the second son, Yab CHen Kun dGaa Rin CHen, wanted to take the vows of celibacy, so a polyandrous marriage was arranged in order to prevent the family line from splitting. This marriage produced one son, sNGags aCHang aJam mGon rDo rJe Rin CHen, but it soon broke up. Although the brothers had the same mother and were close in age, Padma bDud aDul dBang PHyug was homely, having a remarkable lantern jaw, and Yab CHen Kun dGaa Rin CHen was exceptionally handsome.[17] Their wife, it is said, rather strongly preferred her good-looking husband, who was no doubt the father of her son. In addition to this domestic disagreement, it appears that at this time—the end of the eighteenth century—the office of KHri CHen was becoming more desirable, perhaps because it commanded a substantial income. In any event, when the brothers separated, Padma bDud aDul dBang PHyug set up the sGrol Ma palace and Yab CHen Kun dGaa Rin CHen established the PHun TSHogs palace.[18] The family line was split, and the brothers began to maneuver for the succession in anticipation of their father's death.

KHri CHen mTHu CHen dBang sDud sNYing Po was distressed by his sons' behavior and the split in the family. He retired to a monastery in Mus, where he died about 1806, but he somehow arranged to have his grandson, sNGags aCHang aJam mGon rDo rJe Rin CHen, become KHri CHen upon his death. The new KHri CHen was to occupy the palace of his grandfather, the gZHi THog palace, and revenue from the various sections of the Sa sKya domain was to be divided among the three palaces. When her son became KHri CHen, the former wife of his fathers, who had been living with him separate from both of them, moved into the PHun TSHogs palace with the handsome brother, bringing considerable wealth with her, although he had in the meantime taken another wife.

sNGags aCHang aJam mGon rDo rJe Rin CHen reigned as KHri CHen for a brief but undetermined period. While he was

[17] Likenesses of all members of the aKHon family were carefully preserved.

[18] The word translated as "palace" is "PHo Brang"—"male (honorable) abode"—a title that suggests political power. See Appendix A, section I, for the genealogies of the two palaces.

still quite young, he tired of the burdens of office and retired to a life of scholarship and contemplation, leaving no offspring. His grandfather's attempt to provide a smooth succession had come to nought, for now his fathers renewed their contest. From the vigor of this struggle it appears that the income assigned to the KHri CHen was now indeed a principal consideration. Because the time when branches of the aKHon family waged war on one another had passed, the dispute over the succession had to be mediated. No one in Sa sKya had sufficient prestige to mediate between members of the royal family, so the brothers agreed to accept as mediator their mother's brother, of the Lhasa noble house of Rang Byon Pa. An agreement was reached that whenever a KHri CHen died or resigned he was to be succeeded by the oldest male member of the aKHon family, irrespective of his branch of the family. This principle of seniority was adopted rather than the principle of alternation of the family's branches because alternation would not have solved the immediate problem. The agreement was signed by the two brothers and their uncle as mediator, and to increase its authority it was sealed by the Dalai Lama.[19]

XI

By the terms of the settlement, Padma bDud aDul dBang PHyug of the sGrol Ma palace became KHri CHen. He resigned after reigning for a relatively short time, but in the meantime his younger brother had died. Each of the brothers had a son by second wives, and the son of Padma bDud aDul dBang PHyug was older than the son of Yab CHen Kun dGaa Rin

---

[19] This document of mediation—a "Don CHod Yi Ge," or "affair settled letter"—is unfortunately not available. According to our respondents, the seal is supposed to be that of the eleventh Dalai Lama (1838–1856), but since sNGags aCHang aJam mGon rDo rJe Rin CHen became KHri CHen about 1806, it is more likely the seal of the tenth Dalai Lama (1816–1837).

CHen. The older cousin, bKra SHis Rin CHen of the sGrol Ma palace, became KHri CHen, but the younger cousin, NGag dBang Kun dGaa bSod Nams of the PHun TSHogs palace, challenged this succession on the basis of the principle that the palaces should alternate in providing the KHri CHen. This challenge was not taken seriously, however, because the original agreement was still fresh and the mediator was still alive.

KHri CHen bKra SHis Rin CHen died in office about 1865. According to the principle of seniority, NGag dBang Kun dGaa bSod Nams was now the rightful successor, but his right was challenged by a Jigs Med dBang rGyal rDo rJe of the sGrol Ma palace, the son of the deceased KHri CHen. This time mediation was necessary. Again the mediator had to come from outside Sa sKya, and this time the Dalai Lama himself served in this capacity. On the twelfth day of the first moon in the year 1866 a letter, sealed by the twelfth Dalai Lama, was sent to Sa sKya. This letter pointed out that an agreement on the principle of seniority had been made and ought to be kept. NGag dBang Kun dGaa bSod Nams of the PHun TSHogs palace then acceded to the office of KHri CHen. He was the first of his palace to become KHri CHen, following two successive KHri CHen from the sGrol Ma palace.

During his reign, mGon Po Nams rGyal, the chief of the NYa Rong tribe, who had been defeated in eastern Tibet by the army of the Lhasa government, fled westward across southern Tibet. He was given the right to pass through Sa sKya proper and the right of refuge if he wished to stay there. Some of his companions, who had their families with them, did settle in Sa sKya, but the chief went on to western Tibet, where Lhasa troops caught and killed him. It was said that he would have been safe had he remained in Sa sKya. The government at Lhasa was not pleased by Sa sKya's behavior and sent a protest, but it was not heeded. In another exercise of independence, NGag dBang Kun dGaa bSod Nams gave the vows of religious initiation to the fifth

Panchen Lama, who was reportedly in disfavor in Lhasa for not having come to the Dalai Lama to take his vows.[20]

KHri CHen NGag dBang Kun dGaa bSod Nams had a younger brother, who died at the age of twenty-five, one wife, of the noble Lhasa house of sNYing Ri Ba, and two sons, one of whom died young. The KHri CHen is said to have survived an attempt to poison him, but no details were available about the affair, the only mention of poison in the recent history of the aKHon family. NGag dBang Kun dGaa bSod Nams died in office about 1882.

According to the principle of seniority, it was now the turn of aJigs Med dBang rGyal rDo rJe of the sGrol Ma palace to become KHri CHen, but aDZam Gling CHe dGu dBang sDud of the PHun TSHogs palace, the surviving son of the deceased KHri CHen, challenged the succession. Once again the matter was referred to Lhasa for an opinion, and a letter, dated on the twenty-first day of the eighth moon in 1887, signed "Hu THog THu" by the regent for the thirteenth Dalai Lama, was received in Sa sKya. This letter made reference to the original agreement and its later reaffirmation by Lhasa and expressed the opinion that the principle of seniority ought to be adhered to. In the letter repeated reference was made to Sa sKya's status as a gZHung, a clear indication of Lhasa's recognition of Sa sKya's political autonomy. The receipt of this letter apparently ended the five-year contest for succession.

KHri CHen aJigs Med dBang rGyal rDo rJe had a younger brother, with whom he shared a single wife. The brother died young—in his twenties or thirties—and the marriage produced four sons. One of these, Drag SHul PHrin Las Rin CHen (1871–1935), married to carry on the sGrol Ma branch of the aKHon family, and the other three sons became monks. One of the three monks, aJam dByangs THub bSTan bZang Po, had a reputation for great piety. After his father's death, he and his

---

[20] Das, *Journey to Lhasa and Central Tibet*, p. 210.

mother left the sGrol Ma palace but remained in Sa sKya proper, reportedly because the widow did not get along well with the wife of her son Drag SHul PHrin Las Rin CHen. When his mother died, aJam dByangs THub bsTan bZang Po presented all the wealth of her establishment to the thirteenth Dalai Lama. The second of the three sons who became monks renounced his vows and married a daughter of a king of Sikkim. They had two sons, but the whole family died when the sons were young. The third monk remained obscure.

XII

KHri CHen aJigs Med dBang rGyal rDo rJe died in office in 1894. The oldest male member of the aKHon family then living was aDZam Gling CHe dGu dBang sDud of the PHun TSHogs palace, and he was invested as KHri CHen in about 1895 without any overt challenge to his succession. aDZam Gling CHe dGu dBang sDud had a single wife, of the family Sa dBang THon Pa, and two sons, NGag dBang mTHu THub dBang PHyug (1900–1950) and THub bsTan mKHas Grub rGya mTSHo (c.1906–c.1933). In 1922 the two brothers took a single wife, of the family Bya Rig Pa, but for some reason the younger brother withdrew fairly soon from this marriage. He later took a wife of his own, and made plans for setting up a new palace. He had the full right and power to take this action that would have split the aKHon line once again, but he died childless in his twenties. His widow returned to her home outside Sa sKya territory and later became a nun.

aDZam Gling CHe dGu dBang sDud reigned for twenty years. He was very interested in matters of government, his most notable accomplishment being the construction of a storage-pool system of irrigation in the capital. This was a very unusual system for Tibet, accomplished apparently against considerable domestic opposition, and it will be discussed several times in subsequent chapters. In 1915, at the age of sixty, he retired as KHri CHen, and he died in 1919.

Drag SHul PHrin Las Rin CHen of the sGrol Ma palace was in line for the succession according to the principle of seniority, and he became KHri CHen without delay and without a challenge. His wife was from the family of SHab rDo Zur, and they had two sons and four daughters. The sons, NGag dBang Kun dGaa Rin CHen (1902–1950) and NGag dBang Kun dGaa rGyal mTSHan (c.1903–c.1940), both married two daughters of the family of gZims Bon SHod.

KHri CHen Drag SHul PHrin Las Rin CHen was described as a retiring and meditative man, more concerned with his religious responsibilities than with worldly affairs. Governmental matters were left exclusively in the hands of his ZHabs Pad and other senior officials. According to our respondents, his wife was very interested in government and exercised considerable influence, behavior that was probably not atypical of the wives of the aKHon men, especially when these men were politically indifferent or deceased. In the dispute over the succession in 1950—to be described below—the principal challenge had to come from women because there were no males older than five years in the palace that challenged. Most of the wives of the aKHon were from noble families of the Lhasa and Shigatse regimes, and many of them no doubt tried to use their outside connections to influence affairs in Sa sKya.

XIII

KHri CHen Drag SHul PHrin Las Rin CHen of the sGrol Ma palace died in office in 1935. The oldest surviving male of the aKHon family was then NGag dBang mTHu THub dBang PHyug of the PHun TSHogs palace, two years the senior of the deceased KHri CHen's elder son, and a new kind of challenge was made to his succession. This new challenge was not to his right to succeed; it was an attempt to delay his accession.

NGag dBang mTHu THub dBang PHyug, like his father, aDZam Gling CHe dGu dBang sDud, had definite ideas about governmental policy, and during the reign of Drag SHul PHrin

Las Rin CHen he was not reticent about expounding them. Perhaps this behavior irritated or worried the sGrol Ma palace, or perhaps they sought a delay in the hope that something might turn up to prevent his becoming KHri CHen. In any event, the story (as told by our respondents) is that on the death of KHri CHen Drag SHul PHrin Las Rin CHen, his younger son, NGag dBang Kun dGaa rGyal mTSHan, went to Lhasa to get the approval of the regent, Rwa bsGreng, known as Reting—the thirteenth Dalai Lama had died in 1933—to this proposition: that NGag dBang Kun dGaa Rin CHen, the elder son of Drag SHul PHrin Las Rin CHen, serve as "interim KHri CHen" [21] until certain repairs on public buildings, already under way, were completed; once the repairs were finished, NGag dBang mTHu THub dBang PHyug was to become KHri CHen according to the principle of seniority. The regent apparently was not very interested in the affair, and he expressed the opinion that the proposition seemed all right.

The prestige of the Lhasa government was great enough to make even this unsubstantiated opinion of the regent a serious threat to the accession of NGag dBang mTHu THub dBang PHyug, who responded by sending a member of his grandmother's family—sNYing Ri Sa sNGags La, a nobleman under the Lhasa government—to the city of Lhasa as his representative. This representative took with him the original document that established the principle of seniority and the letters from the twelfth Dalai Lama and the regent of the thirteenth Dalai Lama that confirmed the principle. Upon seeing these documents and hearing the case of the PHun TSHogs palace, the regent Reting sent a letter—dated on the twenty-first day of the seventh moon in the year 1935 and addressed to the ZHabs Pad of Sa sKya— saying that there ought to be no delay because the rightful heir,

[21] The title was "KHri mJug" ("throne interim"), normally applied to the son of a deceased KHri CHen who occupies the throne until a KHri Ba is announced at a Great Assembly Meeting (see Chapter 7, section III).

NGag dBang mTHu THub dBang PHyug, had not agreed to a delay. Again there were several references to Sa sKya as a gZHung, and the regent mildly reprimanded the palaces for their disputes regarding the succession. Armed with this letter, NGag dBang mTHu THub dBang PHyug was able to become invested as KHri CHen within a year of his predecessor's death. His reign, from 1936 to 1950, is the period upon which our study of the principality of Sa sKya concentrates.

XIV

During the eighteenth, nineteenth, and twentieth centuries, Sa sKya occupied a relatively unchanging position in Tibet. The Sa sKya sect was established as an honorable if somewhat old-fashioned branch of Tibetan Buddhism, with a stable group of adherents and patrons and a sizable number of prospering monasteries. The Sa sKya government was recognized as an independent, although secondary, political entity, with jurisdiction over several noncontiguous areas in central and western Tibet. There is no reason to believe that during this period there were any significant developments in the domestic policy of the Sa sKya government, other than the construction of the irrigation storage pools in the capital and an occasional revision of the Sa sKya code. The problem of succession to the office of KHri CHen appears to have been by far the most important issue. (This importance will be shown to be quite natural, as the basic ideas and institutions of Sa sKya are later described and correlated.)

The disputes over the succession are obvious results of the absence of any of the devices used outside Tibet to establish inheritance and family continuity. Although women were made ineligible to become KHri CHen, the principle of primogeniture among males was foreign to Tibetan custom, there was no presumption of the right of a man to name his own heir, and no devices existed by which a decision of other-worldly forces could be ascertained. When informal agreements to guarantee that only one set of offspring would be produced by the aKHon family broke down, there was no way to effect a succession except by reference to an outside mediator with prestige equal to or greater than that of the aKHon family itself. In this way, the Lhasa government became involved in the domestic affairs of Sa sKya, an involvement that it seems to have considered embarrassing and inconvenient.

When the ruling house of Sa sKya split into the sGrol Ma and PHun TSHogs palaces, three principles of succession were available and none of them was ever accepted to the exclusion of the others. The original agreement on seniority, whatever the motives that led to its adoption, generally prevailed because it was supported by Lhasa. It was also a reasonable principle, because it worked to prevent the accession of a minor and the resulting difficulties of regencies and because it allowed for an approximately equal division of KHri CHen-ships between the two palaces. (In the beginning, the principle gave the sGrol Ma palace two KHri CHen in succession, but this would have been equalized for the PHun TSHogs palace in the 1950's.) The principle of seniority, however, was always subject to challenges based on two other principles, that the palaces should take turns in providing the KHri CHen and that a son should succeed his father. These challenges were always unsuccessful, but they were nevertheless made, thus creating the greatest problems (and no doubt the most excitement) of the miniature polity. According to our evidence, since the time when human feelings disrupted the carefully planned polyandrous marriage of the eighteenth century, only two successions, in 1895 and 1915, were achieved without some dispute.

Chapter 2

The Sa sKya Domain

In 1936 the government headed by the KHri CHen and located in the town of Sa sKya gDan Sa, the "capital," exercised its
power in the eleven separate areas throughout Tibet indicated on
Map 1. These areas undoubtedly were the remnants of the much
larger territories controlled by Sa sKya in previous centuries.

I

Two of the eleven small Sa sKya enclaves were in eastern
Tibet, well over six hundred miles and at least two months by
caravan from the capital, and hence they had only the most
tenuous connections with Sa sKya proper.[1] Other than a
hundred or so monks in the North and South Monasteries of the
capital, no people from these eastern areas were of any importance in the governmental and religious affairs of Sa sKya proper.
The great distance also made it impossible for legal cases and
revenue from these areas to reach the capital.

The capital had closer connections with the eight outlying
areas in western Tibet. Serious crimes, such as homicide, were
referred to the Law Officials in the capital; revenue in kind was
frequently brought to the capital upon special order of the
ZHabs Pad; all but one of the areas were visited by the so-called

[1] See Appendix B for the available information on these ten areas
outside Sa sKya proper. There was probably some other territory
belonging to Sa sKya, but it no doubt comprised very small areas and
included very few people.

[30]

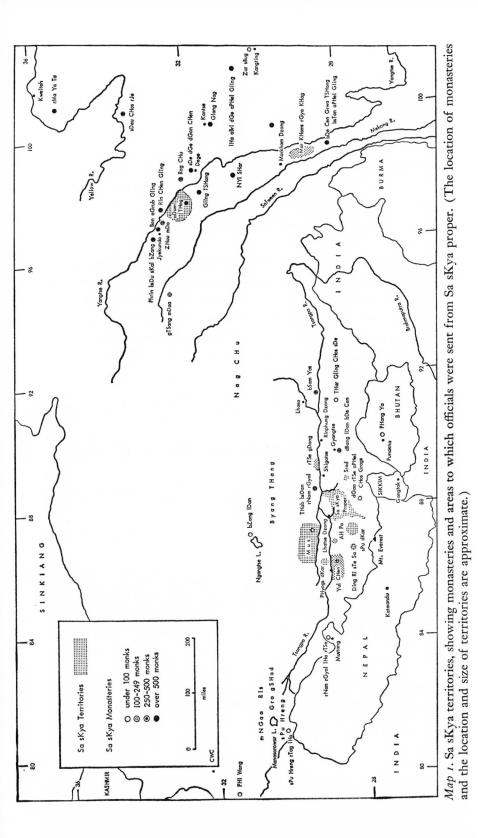

Map 1. Sa sKya territories, showing monasteries and areas to which officials were sent from Sa sKya proper. (The location of monasteries and the location and size of territories are approximate.)

"revenue collectors"; [2] the capital had better control over the officials (District Officers) in these areas; and people from them frequently occupied positions in Sa sKya proper, although not more than a half-dozen were in office during the 1940's.

All eleven areas were populated principally by members of the Sa sKya sect of Tibetan Buddhism, and apparently they constituted the only significant concentrations of such believers in all Tibet. The governmental power of the capital was undoubtedly connected with the existence of members of the Sa sKya sect; but regarding the western areas other than Sa sKya proper, it is impossible to say whether the retention of governmental control allowed the persistence of Sa sKya religious affiliation or whether the strength of this affiliation prompted rival governments to refrain from challenging Sa sKya political control.[3] In any event, by the twentieth century the political situation in western-central Tibet had been stabilized to the point where there were no serious rivalries among the governments of the area regarding control of settled populations. Occasional disputes occurred over boundaries and over very small territories and holy spots such as springs or hilltops, but all were settled by peaceful negotiations.[4]

The two easternmost Sa sKya territories operated under an arrangement in which the priority of other governments—the Lhasa government in Mar KHams rGya KHag and the Chinese in aDam THog—was recognized by their right to levy work from the inhabitants.[5] This situation clearly indicates that, at least in the past, the Sa sKya government was weaker in the east than it was in any of the areas in western Tibet, but the retention

[2] On these "collectors," see Chapter 12, section V.

[3] On the theoretical relation between religious and political affiliation, see Chapter 3, section VII.

[4] Two examples are the area TSHa Zur within the city of Lhasa, claimed by Sa sKya (see section V), and the Sa sKya monastery aJigs sKyob (Map 3), claimed in 1950 by Shigatse.

[5] The significance of the work levy is discussed in Chapter 9, section VII.

by Sa sKya of a large measure of independence in Mar KHams rGya KHag and aDam THog can be explained no more readily than its power in the west.

II

According to Sa sKya belief, Sa sKya political power expanded from the area of the capital until it encompassed all Tibet; it then contracted to the area we are principally concerned with, the area occupied by Sa sKya proper in the twentieth century. There is virtually no evidence that suggests reasons why Sa sKya proper retained its degree of political independence during the period of our study. Undoubtedly the physical presence of the aKHon family and the Sa sKya monasteries aided the retention of governmental control over the area, but the specific borders of Sa sKya proper were no doubt established by a large number of unrelated and fortuitous events of which there are no records. The religious homogeneity of the people and their nonpolitical relationships could as easily have been the results of a reasonably unified political system as the causes of it.

An examination of the geography of Sa sKya proper also gives few clues to the reasons for its size and shape. Its geographical and demographic characteristics are, however, some help in explaining its cohesiveness and persistence.

As shown in Map 2, Sa sKya proper occupied about 2,100 square miles of land, about the extent of the state of Delaware, and almost the entire territory was at least 12,000 feet in elevation. About 94 per cent of the principality's approximately 16,000 people lived below 15,000 feet in the valleys within five miles of the rivers (Map 4). The capital, with about 7,000 people,[6] or 44 per cent of the total population, was located in a

---

[6] This figure was given by the Chinese Communists after their conquest of Tibet; although our respondents considered it reasonably accurate, it may be modest because of the Communists' usual insistence on the sparseness of Tibetan population.

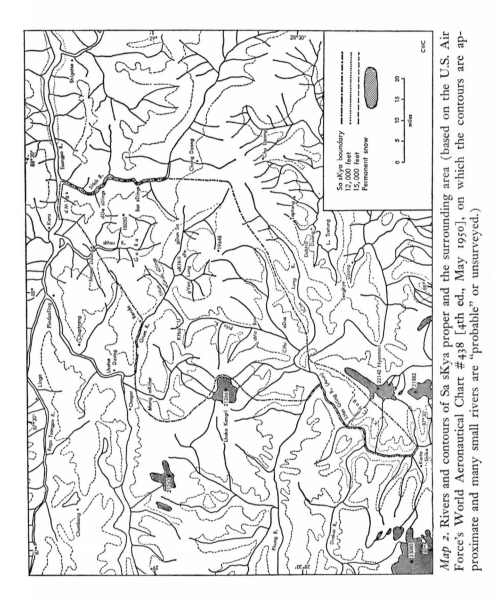

Map 2. Rivers and contours of Sa sKya proper and the surrounding area (based on the U.S. Air Force's World Aeronautical Chart #438 [4th ed., May 1950], on which the contours are approximate and many small rivers are "probable" or unsurveyed.)

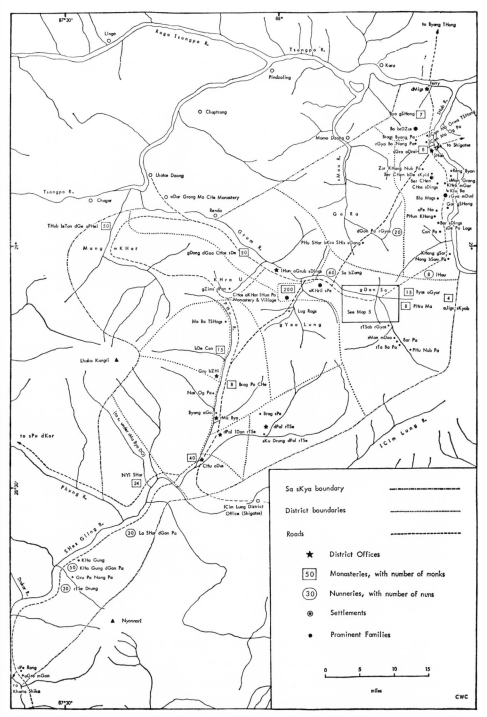

Map 3. Sa sKya proper (based on the U.S. Air Force's World Aeronautical Chart #438 [4th ed., May 1950], and on interviews).

relatively inaccessible place, about twelve miles from the nearest boundary. Its unifying force in the polity came from its importance as a religious and governmental center, rather than from any geographical or economic predominance. No doubt part of its relatively large population was attracted to and remained in the area for the excitements of metropolitan life.

Sa sKya's northernmost boundary ran about eight miles along the Tsangpo River to its confluence with the SHab River and then south up the SHab for about thirty-five miles until the river turns sharply to the east (Map 3). This was a tolerably "natural" boundary because both rivers were large enough to impede military movement across them and because, of course, they were easily identifiable. The SHab boundary was only about thirty miles due west of the more important and more powerful religious and political center of Shigatse, which controlled the area east of the SHab River. It took about a day and a half to ride from the SHab District Office at dGe sDings to the pass that leads to the fertile valley in which Shigatse is located. This proximity was offset by climatic conditions that sharply differentiate the east and west banks of the SHab. The east bank, controlled by Shigatse, was a desert unsuited even for grazing, and there were no more than a dozen families living in the whole area, with no signs of a previous larger population. The west bank, on the contrary, was quite fertile for this part of the world —it was the most fertile section of Sa sKya proper—and it had a population of over 2,500 people. The SHab Valley was also the home of at least six and perhaps nine or more of the Sa sKya noble families dating from the time of aPHags Pa in the thirteenth century. This suggests that Sa sKya power was well entrenched along this eastern border.

The eight miles of northern boundary along the Tsangpo River, which could here be crossed only by boat, gave Sa sKya a kind of corridor, but it is not clear to what. Apparently few goods were moved along the Tsangpo from Sa sKya east toward Shigatse, and in any event material could be moved in leather coracles down the SHab River during high water. Trade with

and religious donations from Byang THang to the north (Map
1) were important for Sa sKya, but access to the Tsangpo was
not necessary for this intercourse. Sa sKya collected a tariff on
wool and salt coming in from the north, and the eight miles of
the southern river bank were tolerably well supervised to prevent smuggling; but there is no way to tell whether this tariff
had any connection with the establishment of this part of Sa
sKya's boundary. The dMigs District (Maps 3 and 4) contained
about 630 people, and north of the Tsangpo across from Sa sKya
the land was farmed by a relatively sparse population under the
jurisdiction of Shigatse.

The western border of Sa sKya moved south from the
Tsangpo River about eight miles west of the SHab River and ran
southwest through low country close to Momo Dzong, an administrative unit of the Lhasa government. This area was very
lightly populated on both sides of the border. More day-to-day
contacts seem to have occurred across this border than anywhere
else on the Sa sKya periphery, and occasionally a farmer on one
side leased land to a farmer on the other, much to the annoyance
of both governments. This section of the boundary did not correspond to any natural impediments to movement or to any demographic patterns. There was a trade route from the SHab District Office to Momo Dzong, but it served only to connect
Momo Dzong with points to the east of Sa sKya. No trade of
any importance was conducted between Sa sKya and Momo
Dzong and other places to Sa sKya's immediate northwest.

From the sMau River near Momo Dzong, the Sa sKya border
ran about twenty-three miles through high uninhabited country
to the Grum River just east of Renda. Renda was a small settlement named after a prominent family, Re mDaa, whose ancestor
was a monk in the North Monastery in the Sa sKya capital and a
teacher of TSong KHa Pa, the fifteenth-century founder of the
Yellow sect of Tibetan Buddhism, the sect of the Dalai Lama.[7]

---

[7] See Helmut Hoffmann, *The Religions of Tibet* (London: George
Allen & Unwin, 1961), p. 161.

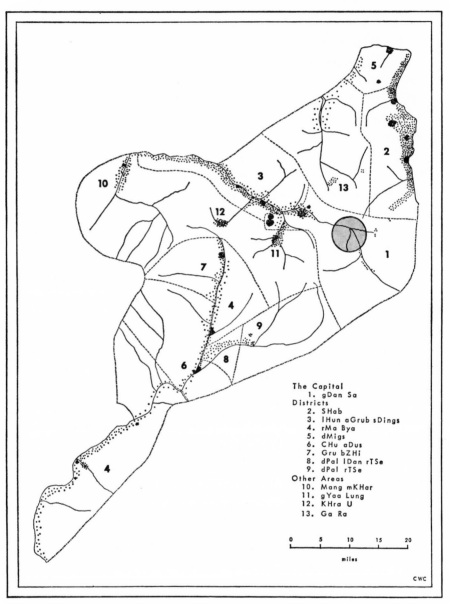

The Capital
　　1. gDan Sa
Districts
　　2. SHab
　　3. lHun aGrub sDings
　　4. rMa Bya
　　5. dMigs
　　6. CHu aDus
　　7. Gru bZHi
　　8. dPal lDan rTSe
　　9. dPal rTSe
Other Areas
　　10. Mang mKHar
　　11. gYaa Lung
　　12. KHra U
　　13. Ga Ra

0　　5　　10　　15　　20

miles

CWC

Map 4. Distribution of the nonherding population of Sa sKya proper. Each dot represents five people; the shaded area at the capital represents seven thousand people.

There is no explanation why Renda was just on the other side of the Sa sKya border.

The Grum River served as the Sa sKya border from Renda to about thirteen miles west of Renda, where the river turns north to join the Tsangpo. Somewhere along this line the Grum goes underground for some distance, thus preventing its use as a waterway. A moderate amount of traffic, however, moved on land from Sa sKya down the Grum Valley to the Lhasa administrative unit of Lhatse Dzong, a town of about 6,500 people. This was the principal avenue of Sa sKya trade with the west, but the western trade was much less important than that with the south, east, and north. The north bank of the Grum River, here controlled by the Shigatse government, was much more lightly populated than the Sa sKya south bank. Further up the Grum, within Sa sKya, the north bank was also more sparsely populated than the south (Map 4), because the north side of the Grum Valley is very narrow. Nothing along this section of the Grum River sharply separated the people of Sa sKya from the people under Shigatse control across the border, but neither was there anything that might have been expected to draw them together.

Whatever the reasons for the original location of this section of the Sa sKya border from where it left the Tsangpo River to where it left the Grum River, maintenance of this boundary no doubt was aided by the political division of the neighboring territory between the governments of Lhasa and Shigatse.

After the Sa sKya border left the Grum River, it circled to the west and south to encompass the area of Mang mKHar (Map 3), where there were about three hundred people engaged in agriculture, an undetermined number of herding families, and a Sa sKya monastery of about fifty monks. The location of this monastery, THub bsTan dGe aPHel, probably accounted for the inclusion of this outlying and relatively insignificant area within Sa sKya, because the monastery had been important in Sa sKya's religious and political history.

From Mang mKHar the border wandered about forty miles

due south through very high and uninhabited country to the confluence of the Phung and Arun (SHes Gling) Rivers (Map 2). This border was really an extended limit of the PHu Valley of Sa sKya. The valley, with its relatively large population of about 1,100 and with at least one noble family (Byang aGo) dating from the time of aPHags Pa, was one of the three principal geographical units of Sa sKya proper, and hence this section of the border was quite "natural."

The appendage called Ko CHag (Map 2), with about 730 people, was about thirty miles long, with its eastern border traversing very high country and the SHes Gling River forming its western boundary. The valley of the SHes Gling is narrow and the river was not fordable; the west bank, under the Shigatse government, had very few people. There was a route south from Sa sKya following the SHes Gling, but it was difficult and infrequently traveled. The people of Ko CHag carried on a small trade with Karta Shika, a Shigatse town. At the southernmost tip of Ko CHag lived the aGro mGon family of hereditary emanation bodies of the rNYing Ma Pa sect, a sect older than the Sa sKya sect. A daughter from this family is known to have married KHri CHen NGag dBang bSod Nams Rin CHen of Sa sKya in the latter part of the seventeenth century. Perhaps this family, which had an unbroken line since about A.D. 800, had had earlier connections with Sa sKya that might help to account for the inclusion of Ko CHag within Sa sKya.

North of Ko CHag the southeastern Sa sKya border passed across two river valleys that were at most sparsely populated and then reached high ground again a few miles north of the lCim Lung River. Through the southernmost part of this high country ran a trade route from CHu aDus to the lCim Lung District Office of the Shigatse government, a village of about 120 people about three miles from the Sa sKya border (Map 3). This was part of a caravan route, maintained the year round by the government, that traversed Sa sKya proper: it began at the SHab District Office, after coming from Shigatse, and passed through

Ga Ra, aKHril sPe, gYaa Lung, and rMa Bya to CHu aDus. From the lCim Lung District Office the route went to Dobtra Dzong, an administrative unit of the Lhasa government, and thence south to Sikkim, Nepal, and India.

From its intersection with the main caravan route, the Sa sKya border went northeast and north for about fifty-three miles through high and uninhabited country until once again it reached the SHab River. There were passes across this border leading from the capital to the east and to the southwest down the lCim Lung River, but they were rarely used.

III

Sa sKya proper consisted basically of the three valleys of the Grum, SHab, and PHu Rivers, with the SHes Gling Valley as an appendage (Map 2). The sMau Valley and the country upstream from Mang mKHar were areas well suited for raising animals, and thus they no doubt served as pasture complements of the farming areas along the main valleys. Viewed in this way, Sa sKya appears to have been reasonably compact.

According to the map, the SHab District Office was about thirty-five miles from the capital; the dMigs District Office, along the same main caravan route, about forty-four miles; the lHun aGrub sDings District Office, about eighteen miles; the monastery in Mang mKHar, about sixty-five miles; the rMa Bya District Office, about thirty-eight miles; the CHu aDus District Office, about forty-five miles; and the south tip of Ko CHag about ninety miles. A caravan could travel about fifteen miles a day, and a rider about thirty. Therefore, even if another half is added to the map distances to allow for the actual distances on the ground, the important districts were within about three days' riding time of the capital, and the farthest boundary to the south within about five days. This physical proximity no doubt contributed to the cohesiveness of Sa sKya proper, even though all communication was by land with only animal-power and without wheeled vehicles.

Another physical characteristic that aided the capital's maintenance of control over Sa sKya proper was the unsuitability of the high country along its borders for nomadic pastoralists. Tibetan nomads were not amenable to governmental control and often had to ignore political boundaries in their search for pastures, but in and around Sa sKya there were probably not more than a dozen or so nomad families. This part of Tibet, moreover, had relatively few sedentary herders, about two hundred families, or 6 per cent of the total population, in contrast to about 15 per cent in eastern Tibet.[8] Most of the Sa sKya herding families, moreover, were located well within the borders. Although Sa sKya herders and herders under other governments engaged in frequent minor disputes over grazing lands, the interactions between the two were probably minimal and provided little reason for serious quarrels or political aggrandizement.

Although it cannot be known how Sa sKya proper came to comprise the areas described above, the several reasons suggested for the maintenance of the individual sections of the boundary may also have had some bearing upon the original stabilization of the principality after the Tibet-wide political power of Sa sKya began to wane. In any event, the external environment seems to have been favorable to the persistence of Sa sKya's political independence. In the first place, the surrounding area was divided piecemeal between the governments of Lhasa and Shigatse, and as a consequence Sa sKya, despite its size, was not especially weak in its own context. In the second place, Lhasa and Shigatse resembled Sa sKya in their static and definitely nonagressive character—in recent times only rudimentary military forces existed in western Tibet—and these similar systems had no internal reasons for aggrandizement at one another's expense.[9] Third and most important, although the three govern-

[8] Sa sKya proper got a large proportion of its animal products from the Sa sKya territory of Mus and from the nomads of Byang THang (Map 1).

[9] Cf. A. E. Moodie, *Geography behind Politics* (London: Hutchinson's, 1947), p. 83.

Plate 1. Sa sKya gDan Sa, the capital, showing the north bank of the Grum River. The largest building at right center is the Government Building and North Monastery. (See Map 5.)

ments had sectarian differences, these were negligible compared to their shared devotion to the Tibetan variety of Buddhism. Once Sa sKya had established its right to exist by simply existing, it was no doubt accepted by its more powerful neighbors in the same way that it accepted them.[10] As we will later argue, the Sa sKya ruling class justified its political power almost exclusively by reference to its success in maintaining this power.

Another reason for the persistence of Sa sKya was that political fragmentation had no adverse effects upon what the Tibetans considered most important in life. Movement of people and goods was completely free, and travel along the main routes was reasonably safe. Religious observance, the outward manifestation of religion so vital to Tibetans, was in no way impeded by the political divisions. The western Tibetan's low level of technology and isolation from foreign pressures gave him no reason for setting up large-scale political organizations. The simple tasks expected of government could be performed in small political units.

IV

We have spoken throughout of Sa sKya's political independence from the larger, more powerful, and better-known governments at Lhasa and Shigatse. This independence is important to our study only to the extent that we are attempting to relate the structure exhibited and policy pursued by the Sa sKya government to the cultural, social, and economic environment of Sa sKya proper. As shown below, the Dalai Lama and his government were attributed a theoretical political superiority that was rather inconsistent with Lhasa's own recognition of Sa sKya as a gZHung and that had, moreover, little practical effect. Sa sKya was part of a political system that included Lhasa and Shigatse, but this system was largely formal and had virtually nothing to

[10] Our respondents liked to contrast the orderly political life of western Tibet—represented by the governments of Lhasa, Sa sKya, and Shigatse—with the chaotic conditions in eastern Tibet. Perhaps the people of Lhasa and Shigatse had similar feelings.

do with the day-to-day business of governing the area of Sa
sKya proper. In performing the essential governmental functions
of collecting and allocating revenue, maintaining judicial processes, and selecting official personnel, the government of Sa sKya
was answerable to no one.[11] It was not linked with Lhasa as part
of a federation or confederation, for there was no policy that
applied to both Lhasa and Sa sKya; it was not part of an empire
ruled by Lhasa, for the minor demands effectively made by
Lhasa were too weak and infrequent to constitute an imperial
relationship. The unity of western Tibet was cultural and religious; no one perceived a need for anything more than the most
superficial political coordination.

At least regarding Sa sKya proper, the independent political
power of the government at the capital was exercised on a
territorial basis; that is, the KHri CHen and his officials autonomously and exclusively performed governmental functions
within the boundary previously described and they had no such
ability on the other side of this boundary. If a subject of the
Lhasa or Shigatse governments fled to Sa sKya to escape punishment, his government had to request his extradition from the
government of Sa sKya, although a kind of "hot pursuit" arrangement was accepted; and the Sa sKya government had to
proceed similarly regarding its own fugitives. It is quite accurate
to call Sa sKya proper a miniature state.

All states need clearly defined borders, and those of Sa sKya
were defined in terms of specific villages, landmarks such as
streams and mountain ridges, and Tibetan measures of distances
such as paces, earshot (about 2,500 feet), and days' ride. There

---

[11] At the beginning of the eighteenth century, Ippolito Desideri said
that Sa sKya paid no taxes and owed no services to anyone (*An
Account of Tibet, 1712–1727* [London: Routledge, 1937], p. 131); and
G. Tucci characterized Sa sKya as "independent principality" ("Un
principato indipendente nel cuore del Tibet: Sachia," *Asiatica*, VI
[1940], 353–360). It is not meaningful to speak of "sovereignty" in the
case of Sa sKya. "Sovereignty" either is a concept of international law,
which did not apply to these Tibetan governments, or suggests an
absolute independence that no government possesses.

were no maps, but written descriptions of the boundaries were kept by the governments of Sa sKya and Shigatse and in each of the Dzong (administrative units) of the Lhasa government. When a dispute arose over the location of the boundary, the interested governments compared their records and negotiated. To settle one dispute over grazing land to the west of rMa Bya, officials from the Sa sKya and Lhasa governments took their respective records to the area and marked the border on the ground.[12]

The movement of people in either direction at any point on the border of Sa sKya proper was not supervised; and the movement of goods in and out of Sa sKya was also free, except for an inspection of material coming south across the Tsangpo River in order to collect a tariff of 1 per cent on salt and wool. This freedom of movement is another indication of the pacific relations among the governments of the area, and also of the limited scope of governmental action in this part of the world, for although the Sa sKya government was well aware of the importance of external trade, it made no attempt to regulate it or to derive revenue from it.[13]

V

The official relationships of the Sa sKya government with the government at Lhasa were clearly understood, although unofficial intrigues were not unknown. The people and the government of Sa sKya recognized the Dalai Lama as the religious and political leader of all Tibet and as the symbol of Tibetanness. He was the "lord" or "owner" of Tibet, and his government was the "central government." [14] This was, in effect, a recognition that the Dalai Lama had a claim to political control of Tibet. The

[12] No cases of such disputes in agricultural areas were remembered by our respondents. This reinforces our conclusions regarding the physical composition of Sa sKya.

[13] Sa sKya trade will be discussed further several times in following chapters, especially Chapter 10.

[14] "Owner" was "bDags Po" and "central government" was "sDe Pa gZHung."

ruling family of Sa sKya, nevertheless, would have considered it most improper if the Dalai Lama had attempted to give orders to the Sa sKya government or religious leaders or to influence the people of Sa sKya politically or religiously without reference to their officials. When asked about the possible results of such an attempt, our respondents answered that the question was not realistic, for "the Dalai Lama would have had no reason for making a pronouncement in Sa sKya." This statement may well be a rather neat summary of the attitude of Tibet's most powerful government, a very reasonable attitude considering the limited degree of its own power.

The pre-eminence of the Lhasa government was manifested in its relations with Sa sKya in both practical and symbolic ways. Sa sKya had an obligation to maintain a contingent of five hundred men in the Tibetan army controlled by Lhasa. These men were conscripted if no volunteers presented themselves; but, since the five hundred were drawn from all the Sa sKya territories in western Tibet and since Tibetan soldiers customarily remained in military service until retirement at age sixty or even later, only two or three men were sent each year from Sa sKya proper. The Sa sKya government was also responsible for equipping, rationing, and paying one hundred troops of the Lhasa army, again from all its western territories.[15] The job of providing these men and supplies for the Lhasa army was performed by an official of the Sa sKya government who in the 1940's had enough spare time to occupy another full-time position.

The Lhasa government also had the right to call for a levy in mass of all Tibetan men from ages fifteen to sixty for the defense of Tibet against outsiders. A request of this nature would always

---

[15] The amount of supplies requested by Lhasa varied from year to year, from twenty to forty donkey-loads of material, which the people of Sa sKya took to Shigatse where the Lhasa government picked it up. These military obligations had little effect upon the people of Sa sKya proper.

have been complied with because the Sa sKya government accepted Lhasa's authority in recognizing a genuine threat to Tibet. In 1950 the Lhasa government informed the Sa sKya government that a call for mass mobilization might soon be made. The Sa sKya government made plans for assembling its men and for receiving arms from Lhasa—it had only percussion-cap muskets in any quantity—but in 1951 the Dalai Lama approved the 17-point program with the Chinese Communists and the word to mobilize never came. Even in such an emergency, however, the Lhasa government would have accepted without question whatever troops were supplied by the Sa sKya government: "It would have been unthinkable for the Dalai Lama to make a direct appeal to the people of Sa sKya."

The responsibilities of the Sa sKya government for moving material and officials of the Lhasa government through Sa sKya territory was the second practical expression of Lhasa's superiority in western Tibet. When Lhasa was moving revenue in kind over a route that went through Sa sKya, the Sa sKya government was responsible for providing the means of transporting the material within its own boundaries, with only a token payment for its troubles. Such movement of goods was, however, very infrequent.

When officials of the Lhasa government were traveling through Sa sKya on any kind of official business, their means of transport were supplied by the Sa sKya government through its own transport levy, and they paid about 15 per cent of the going price for this service. These trips occurred between two and five times a year and were a measurable burden.[16] The government of Lhasa was obligated to provide the same services for Sa sKya officials traveling through Lhasa territory, but it did so with more reluctance and less grace. This relationship clearly implied that Lhasa was somewhat more than equal.

The principal symbolic expression of the superiority of the

[16] See Appendix D, section I.

Lhasa government and the Dalai Lama was the custom whereby each newly enthroned KHri CHen of Sa sKya traveled to Lhasa to pay his respects, to receive congratulations, and no doubt also to recommit the Lhasa government to its recognition of Sa sKya. Although every KHri CHen made this trip of deference, it was not considered especially pressing: NGag dBang mTHu THub dBang PHyug was invested as KHri CHen in 1936 but did not manage to get to Lhasa until 1947.

Three times a year—at the Tibetan New Year and once each in the summer and in the winter—there was a formal exchange of greetings and gifts between Sa sKya and Lhasa that symbolized the superiority of Lhasa, but that also symbolized Lhasa's acceptance of Sa sKya. On each of these three occasions, a rather important Sa sKya official was sent to Lhasa with letters of greetings and congratulations to the Dalai Lama, the Lhasa cabinet, and the Lhasa secretariat; he returned with three similar letters to the Sa sKya Government and the two palaces. In the New Year's letter to the Dalai Lama was three-tenths of an ounce of gold, and in each of the other two letters five ounces of silver. The gifts from Lhasa were more modest: seven ounces of silver to the Sa sKya Government and five ounces of copper to each palace. All the letters were accompanied by the traditional Tibetan scarves of greeting (KHa bDags); these were very large, as long as eighteen feet, and of equal size. The trips to Lhasa by the KHri CHen and his officials were too superficial to indicate a tributary status; at most, they may have symbolized such a status.

The pre-eminence of Lhasa was also illustrated by the use of the Lhasa government or the Dalai Lama himself as the mediator in the disputes between the two branches of the Sa sKya royal family over the succession to the throne. Reference to a mediator was a natural and common way for Tibetans to attempt to resolve disagreements, and in the case of the Sa sKya palaces no one in Sa sKya had enough prestige to serve as a mediator. Whenever a dispute was referred to Lhasa for mediation,

Lhasa's prestige virtually obliged the Sa sKya palaces to accept the proffered solution.

It must not be thought that Sa sKya was merely tolerated by the more powerful government and religious establishment at Lhasa. As said above, these unequal polities accepted one another's independence and propriety. The status of Sa sKya is nicely illustrated by an affair during the reign of KHri CHen NGag dBang mTHu THub dBang PHyug. In examining various governmental records shortly after his accession, the KHri CHen discovered that a small area containing a handful of families in the heart of the city of Lhasa itself was Sa sKya territory according to some ancient right. The area had been controlled by the Lhasa government for some generations, so the KHri CHen sent his records to Lhasa and, although there was initial resistance, the area was eventually returned to Sa sKya control in the 1940's. In 1954 the Sa sKya government sold part of this land to the Chinese Communists.[17]

The Lhasa government also recognized the right of its own subjects to leave its jurisdiction and become subjects of Sa sKya.[18] Once two young subjects of Lhasa became monks in a monastery at the Sa sKya capital. To be near them, their father, a subject of a Lhasa nobleman, moved his remaining family—his wife, another son, and the son's wife and child—to Sa sKya where they were given land in gYaa Lung by the PHun TSHogs palace. The palace thenceforth paid Lhasa an annual token sum (one Srang per person), and it was recognized that the people had become subjects of Sa sKya. Changes of allegiance were possible in any direction among the three governments of western Tibet, and they were sometimes effected by trading individual for individual or family for family.

[17] The district was called TSHa Zur; it was located somewhere in the area bounded by the Potala, the Sera Monastery, the Mint, and the "Cathedral" (Jo KHang).

[18] The concepts of "subject" and "allegiance" are explained in Chapter 3, section XII.

VI

The relations between the governments of Sa sKya and Shigatse were not so smooth. In their only symbolic relationship they were equal: at every New Year the two governments exchanged scarves, letters of greeting, and five copper coins; one year a Sa sKya official would go to Shigatse and the next a Shigatse official to Sa sKya. In practical relations with the larger and more powerful Shigatse government, Sa sKya was at a disadvantage. This discrepancy in power, however, was at least partially offset by a differential in prestige in Sa sKya's favor. This differential and, incidentally, the position of the Lhasa government with respect to the other two, are illustrated by the following story. In western Tibet the officials of both the Lhasa and the Sa sKya governments wore their hair in topknots as an insignia of office. Tibetan custom did not accord this right to Shigatse officials, and once the Panchen Lama complained to Lhasa that since Sa sKya officials could wear the topknot his officials also should be allowed this mark of distinction. The reply from Lhasa was that Sa sKya had this privilege because it was once the government of all Tibet (and thus the only unit other than Lhasa itself entitled to the status of gZHung); since the Shigatse government had no such past, the request was denied. The Panchen Lama could only acquiesce in this authoritative pronouncement.

Sa sKya was naturally quite aware of this distinction and had a tendency to suggest that Shigatse was not after all a "real government." This attitude no doubt added to the minor frictions that were bound to occur between the two smaller governments of western Tibet, whose capitals were only a few days apart. Despite all this, the Sa sKya rulers recognized that the Shigatse government was as effective as their own and hence also helped create the political stability differentiating western from eastern Tibet. Sa sKya, for example, would not have accepted an immigrant from Shigatse territory without obtaining the Shigatse government's consent, and it would have returned him had Shigatse so requested. Sa sKya treated immigrants from Lhasa territory in the same way, and both Lhasa and Shigatse were supposed to reciprocate. If an immigrant came to Sa sKya from eastern Tibet, no questions were asked and no inquiries made. The important thing in such situations was, according to our respondents, that every commoner had a definite political allegiance—in other words, that the cohesiveness of the western Tibetan polities was maintained.

VII

Sa sKya was accorded a strict formal equality in the generally accepted arrangements for settling disputes among the subjects of the three governments of western Tibet, although it was perhaps somewhat at a disadvantage in dealing with its more powerful neighbors. For example, homicide, the most serious grounds of dispute, was handled in the following way. On the insistence of the family of the slain man, a Sa sKya subject who had killed a subject of Lhasa or Shigatse in Sa sKya was tried by the Lhasa or Shigatse government, and a subject of Lhasa or Shigatse who had killed a subject of Sa sKya in Lhasa or Shigatse territory was tried by the Sa sKya government. When a subject of Lhasa or Shigatse killed a subject of Sa sKya in Sa sKya, the Sa sKya government had the right to try him, and when a subject of Sa sKya killed a subject of Lhasa or Shigatse in the latter's territory, the government of Lhasa or Shigatse had the right to try him.

Because Sa sKya was so small and isolated, it had very few contacts with non-Tibetan governments and thus had little use for the paraphernalia of diplomacy and international law. When, for example, a Sa sKya subject arrived at the Indian border on a trading venture, he had no documents from any government; the Indian officials heard his story and gave him a visa of limited duration. The same procedure was followed with subjects of Lhasa. Whenever a dispute arose between subjects of Sa sKya and subjects of Nepal, Sikkim, or Bhutan, it was dealt with directly by the officials of the respective governments on a basis of formal equality.[19]

VIII

The territory of Sa sKya proper was compact and its borders were clearly delineated; its localities were held together principally by the influence of the government and the monastic establishment located at the capital. We will show throughout our study that Sa sKya maintained itself primarily by its government's power and its subjects' acquiescence. Although Sa sKya's physical make-up contributed to its cohesiveness, nothing about its territory and its distribution of population suggested its government's degree of independence.

Sa sKya proper was, nevertheless, a relatively self-contained political society based on the territorial principle and recognized as such by all the other governments with which it had any significant contacts. Its independence was defined and maintained with a degree of sophistication and level of technology reasonably well adjusted to the functions and responsibilities of government in west-central Tibet before the arrival of the Chinese Communists.

[19] When our respondents fled Tibet through Bhutan in 1959, they were recognized by the government of Bhutan as "descendants of Sa CHen" (the great Sa sKya ruler) rather than as adjuncts of the Lhasa government. In 1951 the Chinese Communists insisted that Sa sKya maintain two representatives, one from its Government and one from its Religious Establishment, in both Lhasa and Shigatse. These four officials had documents that said they were accredited to Lhasa and Shigatse.

Chapter 3

Beliefs and Attitudes

Human beings always try to order their lives by developing systems of ideas or beliefs. Philosophy, science, religion, cosmology, ethics, ideology, and creeds and superstitions are all responses to the uncertainties, vagaries, and mysteries of life. They can explain experiences, predict or justify them, logically relate them to one another, or make them analogues of less problematic experiences. These responses always have some correspondence to the practical problems of daily life, even though they may proceed from the premise that the physical world and man's presence in it are basically chimerical. Although no one's beliefs are perfectly consistent, there seems always to be an urge to eliminate contradictions, and although no two people have identical beliefs, stable interactions among a number of people tend to be accompanied by the sharing of similar types of beliefs. It is thus possible to speak of "belief systems" or "ideologies."

Every system of beliefs includes accounts of man's relation to natural forces such as the weather, disease, and death and of his relations with his fellow man. The human relationships that constitute the polity or that are directly relevant to its existence are the subjects of specific beliefs that must be understood in order that the polity itself can be understood. Explanations of government's existence, justifications of individual governments, and attitudes of the government toward the governed, of the governed toward the government, and of the governed toward one another are intimately related to every political system. A complete account of any polity must show how these are integral parts of a larger belief system and how they are consistent with the organization and operation of the polity's government. In this realm of life, ideas about what is done and what ought to be done may well be more important than the things that people actually do.

I

Like many other "traditional" people, the Tibetans believed that they had little control over their physical environment, and as a result they viewed it as hostile. The immense Tibetan landscape and its violent weather made man seem unusually puny and hence reinforced the predisposition to seek supernatural defenses against an unfriendly nature. The magic and other superstitions that pre-dated the introduction of Buddhism to Tibet were incorporated into Tantric Buddhism.[1] Divination, for example, was commonly practiced and had a quasi-religious status supported by the methods of discovering important religious reincarnations such as the Dalai Lama himself. Although the Tibetan was often sharply skeptical of diviners, he retained his belief in the possibility of true forecasts, and important decisions, both private and governmental, were usually preceded by favorable divinations. Fetishes were also commonly used to protect against natural disasters and to assure that actions would have favorable results.

According to the Tibetan, the surface of the earth was owned by supernatural beings called "soil-owners" (Sa bDag). Their ownership was similar to human ownership of property; they divided the land among themselves and were as committed to the principle of private property as any mortal. These beings naturally resented the farmers who disturbed their land, and hence

[1] Although the Tibetans were perhaps more concerned with their religion than most traditional people, we are concerned here only with the religious beliefs that were directly relevant to the operation of the polity of Sa sKya. For a more detailed discussion of Tibetan religious concepts and the Tibetan world view, see Robert B. Ekvall, *Religious Observances in Tibet* (Chicago: University of Chicago Press, 1964).

they had to be placated by prayers, offerings, and the requisite worship. Although the Tibetan farmer's religion taught him some precautions, soil-owners often enough refused to be mollified and brought misfortune and sickness on interlopers. Mining was a doubly heinous offense because the earth was robbed as well as disturbed, and the soil-owners were notoriously miserly. No placation made mining even tolerably safe. The Tibetan farmer lived under the constant, jealous, irritated scrutiny of these supernatural beings, and his resulting insecurity and guilt no doubt contributed to his admiration of the nomad, who leaves the earth quite intact.

The more philosophical tenets of Tibetan Buddhism present an interpretation of existence and a prescription for salvation. The existence of human beings in a physical world is not considered real; it is the result of desire that in turn results from ignorance. Physical existence is valueless, and each man must liberate himself by the reduction of his desires and the accumulation of merit gained by concrete religious observances. Health, happiness, and success in this world are of relatively slight consequence; the proper preoccupation is with liberation (THar Ba) or Bodhisattvaship. There are, moreover, many worlds, each with its own gods and heaven.

Earthly history makes sense only within the frame of reference established by cycles of religion, each cycle beginning with the appearance of a new Buddha or Teacher and then moving through periods of culmination and decay. Tibet itself has been in decline since the "golden age" of the eighth century, when it was politically independent and powerful and when Buddhism was proclaimed the faith of the king and the religion of the state.

The thesis of the world's fundamental unreality is correlated with a conception of worldly events as more a series of adventitious changes than a succession of results each dependent on the one preceding. There is no single truth, for truth is not a matter of accurate description or inference, but a relationship between concepts of a system, and different systems are useful for different things. The Tibetan is consequently able to accept modern technology and the theoretical base of modern science while retaining his own metaphysical system.

II

The belief that events in this world are largely beyond human control is understandably associated with the characterization of the world as basically unreal and with the desire to escape from its capriciousness. These beliefs and attitudes are in turn associated with a relatively high degree of individualism, because other human beings are seen as part of the basically hostile environment and thus are not to be depended upon.[2] The important thing for the Tibetan Buddhist is the individual's progression toward liberation. The responsibility for this progression is his alone, and he meets it by the accumulation of virtue through acts of religious observance—saying prayers and hearing them said, making offerings, paying respect and adoration to holy things and holy people, and circumambulating religious objects or persons—and by the proper feeling of compassion toward all living things. Even this ideal of compassion is highly individualistic; one aids his neighbors or gives to beggars, for example, not to relieve their distress but to perform a virtue-producing duty that also manifests the compassion of the giver. Tibetan Buddhism has little in the nature of an abstract code of right and wrong in human relationships, other than the absolute prohibition against taking life.

The individualism of religious observance was supplemented by the doctrinal emphasis upon withdrawal from the world of affairs as a step toward liberation. The family was recognized as a biological unit, but it had no special sanctity. Procreation was only tolerated, surnames were uncommon, and fatherhood commanded no special status. The doctrine of reincarnation was

[2] Cf. Fustel de Coulanges, *The Ancient City* (Garden City, N.Y.: Doubleday, 1956), pp. 161, 167–168. See below, section IV, and Chapter 10.

inconsistent with reverence for ancestors and with stressing the continuity of family lines. Nothing special was expected of one's descendants, and so there was no strong incentive to guarantee a succession. According to strict doctrine, the bodies of the deceased should be fed to the vultures and other consumers of carrion, so that even death will contribute to life; hence there were few records of burial and symbols of the dead.

As an economic unit, the family was appreciated and even stressed, but again the doctrines of withdrawal from the world and the necessity of religious observance had a centrifugal effect. The individual might choose to withdraw from mundane affairs, to make substantial gifts to monasteries, or to leave home for an extended pilgrimage. Even daughters could absent themselves from home for a year to be spent in accumulating their own private religious merit. These individualistic religious principles may well have contributed to the weakness of the Tibetan political structure. Any man could, for example, enter a monastery at will, and monks could change monasteries, go on pilgrimages, or become hermits, all again at their own pleasure.

III

Tibetan Buddhism is unique in its doctrine that the Buddhahood, continuously manifested in the Bodhisattvas, is revealed in a succession of rebirths. These rebirths constitute the "emanation bodies" (sPrul sKu)—men who, in writings on Tibet, are often called "incarnation lamas" or "living Buddhas." These emanation bodies partake of the attributes of deity and receive worship; they are the foci of much of Tibetan religious observance. They have escaped from the forced round of birth and rebirth and have attained liberation, but because of compassion for all sentient beings they devote themselves to aiding those beings in the long progress toward the same liberation, and so they return in successive rebirths. They have the power of the liberated, which reflects in degrees the might of the divine, and they have transcendental or clairvoyant perception (mNGon SHes). The Ti-

betans revere and worship the emanation bodies for their compassion, power, and supreme wisdom, and seek from them aid
toward liberation, guidance in all the affairs of daily living, and
assurance concerning the great future of the hereafter. The
emanation bodies bestow benediction, and they bring to mundane affairs a touch of the divine (in so far as that term can be
used with reference to Buddhism).

The best known emanation bodies are the Dalai and Panchen
Lamas, but there were many others who were part of the whole
system but had in their persons and positions independence and
separate identity. Each was a savior in himself by reason of his
birth, and together they were the foundation of the impressive
Tibetan ecclesiastical organization. These emanation bodies also
often had political and government functions. Each of the three
governments of western Tibet—Lhasa, Shigatse, and Sa sKya—
was organized around a pre-eminent emanation, who was in
theory the final source of governmental power and who also
often actually exercised this power.

The Tibetan believes completely in his emanation bodies, the
continuously renewed saviors of his religion, so he also must give
credence to all their sayings and pronouncements. He was, however, often ready to mock these pontifications and compare them
to the vagaries of justice at the hands of a capricious officialdom,
thus apparently separating a human element from the divine.

As described in Chapter 1, all the male members of Sa sKya's
ruling family, the aKHon, were emanation bodies by birth. The
political effects of this status are discussed later in the present
chapter and elsewhere throughout the book.

IV

The system of fundamental beliefs sketched above is essentially
similar to those of many other societies that have been called
"traditional." The basic unreality of the physical world and
human existence within it, the lack of order in mundane events
and the power of magic, the relative absence of curiosity about

natural phenomena and of a desire to master them, and the individualistic ethics of accumulating virtue and ultimate withdrawal—all have been noted on many occasions in many contexts.[3] This system of beliefs corresponds rather well to these societies' experience of nature, both animate and inanimate, their levels of technology, and their methods of economizing. It is only reasonable to suppose that this type of religion, metaphysics, and ethics would be accompanied by a congruent set of beliefs about government that also corresponded to the relevant experiences of government, and the literature on these societies contains strong suggestions along these lines.

According to these suggestions, the average man sees government as part of the mysterious, unpredictable, and uncontrollable forces of nature. Governors, like the supernatural powers that control disease and the weather, may be mollified by the proper behavior, but nothing can really guarantee success in this approach. The feeling of helplessness toward natural events is also manifested toward government, which, like the powers behind nature, is credited with almost unlimited abilities. Any attempt to influence government in a concrete pragmatic way is, of course, unthinkable. The only feasible response is to be cun-

[3] See, among others, Lucian W. Pye, *Politics, Personality, and Nation Building* (New Haven: Yale University Press, 1962), chs. 4–5; Daniel Lerner, *The Passing of Traditional Society* (Glencoe, Ill.: Free Press, 1958), chs. 4, 5, 9; Richard H. Pfaff, "Disengagement from Traditionalism in Turkey and Iran," *Western Political Quarterly*, XVI (1963), 79–98; Oscar Lewis, *Pedro Martínez: A Mexican Peasant and His Family* (New York: Random House, 1964), pp. 492–497; Herbert A. Phillips, *Thai Peasant Personality* (Berkeley: University of California Press, 1965); Ronald Segal, *The Crisis of India* (Harmsworth, G. B.: Penguin Books, 1963), p. 156; Manfred Halpern, *Politics and Social Change in the Middle East and North Africa* (Princeton, N.J.: Princeton University Press, 1963), p. 11; and, particularly W. I. Thomas and F. Znaniecki, *The Polish Peasant* (Boston: Richard G. Badger, 1918), Vol. I, esp. p. 274 on the influence of the Roman Catholic "magical religious system." Robert E. Lane has succinctly summarized this type of thought in *Political Ideology* (New York: Free Press of Glencoe, 1962), pp. 432–434.

ning: to appear resigned to all that happens while maintaining a universal mistrust, and to derive the maximum benefit from any thing or person that happens to come under one's control.[4] The governors, for their part, have a tendency to fear the masses as intractable and unpredictable. These ideas and attitudes are correlated with the social distance between governors and governed and with the government's high-handed behavior.

As we said in the Introduction, in the absence of direct evidence of attitudes of the Sa sKya common people, we are obliged to rely on inferences from their physical and social environment and from evidence regarding the attitudes of other people, including other Tibetans, living in similar environments. These inferences suggest that the perception of government as mysterious and uncontrollable was consistent with the Sa sKya common people's otherworldly, magical orientation, with the high social status accorded their governors, and with the beliefs about and theories of governing possessed by the Sa sKya rulers (described below in the present chapter). This perception of government was not, however, consistent with the size of Tibetan polities and the mobility of the Tibetan people.

To be as mysterious as nature, government must be unfamiliar, aloof, and capable of arbitrariness. To give this appearance and to act in this way, it must be able to create and maintain a significant physical and social distance between itself and the common folk. Although the common people themselves help create this distance by their limited perspectives and their predisposition to believe that anything can happen, this passivity is not enough. The governor must be insulated by a large official hierarchy, and he must have a large amorphous population to provide scope for his capriciousness. The Lhasa government, however, the largest and strongest in Tibet, ruled about 160,000 people, divided into 53 districts averaging about 500 families each.[5] This is a small polity by any standards; and in Sa sKya

[4] Thomas and Znaniecki, *Polish Peasant*, I, 274-275.

[5] Pedro Carrasco, *Land and Polity in Tibet* (Seattle: University of Washington Press, 1959), p. 92.

proper, with a total population of 16,000, it was very difficult for the governors to stay aloof from the governed and to maintain an unrestricted scope of action.

The high mobility of the average Tibetan also worked against popular apathy and governmental arrogance. No Tibetan government could exist without people, and its prestige was roughly proportionate to the number of its subjects. Tibetan political units consequently tended to compete for people, at least in the sense that they had to avoid provoking their own subjects to the point of emigration. Few Tibetans were unaware of the possibility of leaving their homes in search of more favorable political conditions. Their experience with long-distance trading missions and extensive pilgrimages, both highly approved in the culture, suggested something other than dull resignation to their political superiors. And in the back of everyone's mind was the figure of the highly admired and envied nomad, the man who lived well and could make large religious donations, who did not commit the impiety of disturbing the earth, and, most importantly, who acknowledged no man as his master. No doubt many a peasant, oppressed by his burdens, dreamed of running away to join the nomads. Although all these dreams naturally could not be realized, the change was not impossible. The nomad communities also needed men, and former peasants would be welcomed for their skill at making hay and their willingness to perform menial tasks. A number of families left Sa sKya when they failed to make a decent living, and at least one family left when it disliked a political development.

Our inference about this part of the Sa sKya common man's attitude toward government must thus be a compromise. We infer that he was not in great awe of his government nor did he consider it incomprehensible, but he did believe that government was none of his business and that the governors had their own motives, which were not those of the average person. If this inference is incorrect, our error should have no effect upon our account of the interrelationships among the rest of the elements of the political society of Sa sKya.

V

One of the most important questions about people related by a political system is whether they consider themselves a unique group apart from this political relationship. The modern nation is the best example of this kind of mutual identification, but in 1950 Sa sKya, as indeed all Tibet, was still "pre-nationalistic." A sense of nationality, or anything similar to it, did not exist, because Sa sKya's social and economic arrangements did not have the degree of complexity that prompts a diversified population to seek a sense of belonging to a special in-group and an assurance that its political system is legitimate. Sa sKya, with its homogeneity and its acceptance of the facts of political power, got by with less elaborate foundations.

All the people of Sa sKya, from the butcher and the share-cropper to the royal family, considered themselves Tibetans and identified with other Tibetans who, they assumed, also identified with them. Tibetans recognized one another and defined themselves by reference to their religion, language, folkways, and geographical location.[6] Religion was the most important aspect of the Tibetan's life, and he naturally identified with those who shared his special variety of Buddhism. There were, however, a rather large number of people in Tibet who retained the beliefs and practices of the pre-Buddhist Bon religion, a shamanistic and animistic system that strongly influenced Tibetan Buddhism. These people were nonetheless considered to be genuine Tibetans, although not with the best credentials. Tibetans who were converted to Islam lost part but not all of their Tibetanness.

The Tibetans are linguistically remarkably homogeneous. Their frequent and lengthy trading ventures and religious pilgrimages helped minimize linguistic differences, and the close connection of their language with their religion helped prevent

[6] See Robert B. Ekvall, "The Tibetan Self-Image," *Pacific Affairs*, XXXIII (1960), 375–382, an essay based on interviews with people from all parts of Tibet.

borrowing from other languages. Tibetans also believed that their general patterns of behavior distinguished them from other people; the types of food eaten without hesitation and those avoided were considered especially important. It was believed, finally, that the Tibetans were those who inhabited a certain territory, although this was the least important index of identification.

The combination of these characteristics did not, however, suffice to define a Tibetan. Tibetans believed themselves to be somehow physically unique, to constitute (we might say) a special race.[7] Our respondents readily acknowledged that Tibetans vary greatly in their facial features, pigmentation, and bone structure, and that they had intermarried with all their neighbors from the Persians to the Chinese. This rejection of physical criteria prompted us to ask about a "Tibetan soul," but we were assured that all men are the same "on the inside." The thing that distinguished Tibetans from all other people was their descent from common ancestors indigenous to Tibet.

According to the myth, the Tibetans originated when a great monkey of the land of the snows mated with a female demon of the cliffs. From this union came six offspring, who belonged neither with the monkeys of the forest nor with the meat-eating demons of the cliffs. They were destitute and miserable until their father—by a Buddhist gloss called an emanation of Avalokitesvara, the patron Bodhisattva of Tibet—took pity on them and gave them barley, wheat, sesame, rice, and peas. With the practice of agriculture, they became the "black-haired people," the Tibetans. From their father they inherited their black hair and red faces, and faith, zeal, wisdom, and goodness; from their mother, a taste for meat, courage, physical strength, and the impulse to kill. After an indefinite period of time, the black-haired people appealed to heaven for a king to unite them and protect them against their powerful neighbors. This appeal was

[7] The Tibetan term for this concept is "Mi Rigs gCig"—"man lineage one."

granted, and the six lineage groupings received the first of a line of forty kings, the first seven of whom were mythical and the rest principally legendary.

The Tibetans' mobility and their uniform written language allowed them to recognize their basic linguistic and religious similarities and their differences from their Moslem, Hindu, and Chinese neighbors. This recognition led to the invention of a myth of origin, a not uncommon way to account for cultural similarities. Once this concept of a common ancestry was accepted, certain people who spoke the Tibetan language and who had lived for a long time among other Tibetans could not be denied the status of Tibetans even though they did not possess the characteristic considered most typical of the true Tibetan, the special religious beliefs and practices of Tantric Buddhism.

This sense of Tibetanness was very strong, but it was not the same kind of thing as a sense of nationality. The myth of the origin of the Tibetan people includes an early political unity; from the seventh to the ninth century, Tibet was under a single government; and recently there was at least a strong presumption throughout Tibet that all Tibetans should cooperate against foreign encroachments. Nevertheless, the social and economic conditions of the Tibetan people gave rise (as will be seen) to attitudes that must be considered pre-national and that overcame the influence toward political unity exerted by the homogeneous Tibetan culture.

VI

All the people of Sa sKya considered themselves Tibetans, but this identification had only one important political effect: no one but a Tibetan could become a member of the Sa sKya polity. If some non-Tibetan had wished to settle in Sa sKya, the government might have permitted him to sharecrop or to perform some useful non-agricultural function, but he could have had none of the privileges and responsibilities of the true member of the polity, except that he came under the jurisdiction of the criminal law. If this foreigner married a woman of Sa sKya, their daughters were considered Tibetans with Sa sKya allegiance and their sons would have been granted Sa sKya allegiance upon their requesting it. A Tibetan from anywhere outside Sa sKya was, of course, always eligible to become a subject of Sa sKya.

In the capital there were about fifteen men, descended from male Nepalese immigrants and married to Tibetan women, who had chosen not to take on Sa sKya allegiance and who were considered to have allegiance to Nepal, even though they were born and had lived all their lives in Sa sKya. By "remaining Nepalese," they did not have to take land and hence could devote themselves to commercial pursuits such as operating taverns. The Sa sKya government accepted this situation because it was not opposed to having these commercial functions performed, but it believed that agriculture was the only fitting occupation for its own people.

This insistence on Tibetan "blood" as a condition for membership in the polity expressed the Sa sKya government's recognition that its success depended in great part upon the homogeneity of its people. Again this homogeneity was conceived of in terms of ancestry. No matter how fervently he embraced the religion, how fully he mastered the language, and how thoroughly he adopted the customs, a Chinese, European, or Indian would never have been granted full standing in the Sa sKya political society.

Being a Tibetan was a necessary condition for membership in the Sa sKya polity, but there was naturally no conception of Tibetanness as a sufficient condition for any polity. Sa sKya, indeed, as a small encircled principality, had to insist on the reasonableness of political divisions among the homogeneous Tibetan people.

VII

The overwhelming proportion of the people of Sa sKya proper were members of the Sa sKya sect of Tibetan Buddhism, and it seems that most of the areas of Tibet that contained large concentrations of the Sa sKya sect were either fully or partially under Sa sKya political control.[8] This sectarian homogeneity was a result of past political developments, especially the contraction of Sa sKya political power within Tibet; there was no presumption that Sa sKya believers ought to have had their own government. The polity of Sa sKya, in other words, was not justified in terms of the unique religious composition of its population.

We asked our respondents about the reaction of the Sa sKya government to a hypothetical situation in which a group of people living under the Lhasa government, say a village of twenty families, changed their affiliation from the Yellow sect to the Sa sKya sect. The answer was that the Sa sKya government would definitely have considered the possibility of gaining political control over such a group, but it would have been interested only because the change in sects offered an opportunity to increase its lands and people. There was no suggestion of a right to bring these fellow sectarians within the polity. Indeed, it was explicitly recognized that changing from the Yellow sect to the Sa sKya sect, or from the Sa sKya sect to the Yellow sect, had no effect upon a man's allegiance to the Lhasa government or to the Sa sKya government. The Lhasa government felt no obligation to surrender control of any of its subjects who belonged to the Sa sKya sect, and the Sa sKya government's opportunity to increase its power in the hypothetical example would have been rather slight. This situation regarding religious affiliation makes an interesting contrast with the actual transfer to Sa sKya of the small area within the city of Lhasa described in Chapter 2: Sa sKya's effective claim to the area was based solely upon its ability to show it had fairly recently controlled the area; most of the area's inhabitants were members of the Yellow sect.[9]

Within Sa sKya proper there were a number of adherents of

[8] A member of the sect was called a "Sa sKya CHos Lugs Pa." The areas under Sa sKya control are described in Appendix B.

[9] See Chapter 2, section V.

an older Buddhist sect, the rNYing Ma Pa, or Old sect. Several Old sect families were prominent in Sa sKya's political, social, and religious affairs. Probably the most important was the hereditary noble family of SHar ZHabs Pad of the SHab Valley, which no doubt got its name from a family member who had been ZHabs Pad (prime minister) early in Sa sKya's history and which had subsequently supplied many high governmental officials, including a ZHabs Pad in the twentieth century. The family of aGro mGon of Ko CHag were lineage emanation bodies of the Old sect who maintained a temple. They were also hereditary nobles, and because of their religious status they were considered to have more prestige than other noble families. No members of the Yellow sect, however, seemed to have gained any official prominence within Sa sKya proper.

The sects of Tibetan Buddhism were not sharply distinguished from one another. Members of the Yellow sect and the Sa sKya sect visited one another's holy places and received blessings from one another's holy men, and monks of either sect preached in the other's monasteries. No religious formalities were required for a man to change sects, and no government objected to such a change; our respondents insisted that the government of Sa sKya had no right to control the religious affiliations of its subjects. Any non-Tibetan was, of course, eligible for conversion to all sects, and indeed welcomed.[10]

In summary, membership in the Sa sKya sect, the only characteristic other than their membership in the polity that distinguished the people of Sa sKya, was not seen as a justification for the Sa sKya government's control over them. As will be described below, the polity was viewed by its rulers as at least very useful in promoting the sect and at most indispensable in keeping

---

[10] There were few reasons why the average Tibetan would want to leave one sect to join another that was so similar. Such a change might have occurred when a man entered a monastery; by putting himself under the monastery's code of discipline, he came close to changing his political allegiance.

the sect alive, but this attitude is quite different from the concept of the polity's promoting the interests of the nation. The religious homogeneity of the people of Sa sKya proper undoubtedly was a major factor in the polity's viability, but it did not create anything resembling the modern political community.[11]

VIII

Throughout the discussions, our respondents insisted that the government of Sa sKya could not be understood without reference to religion. This insistence expressed their belief that religion is the most important aspect of human life and that all other aspects, including the political, derive their significance from their contribution to religion; and it was based on the recognition that both religious belief and political relationships were integral parts of the tradition by which the people of Sa sKya lived. A number of specific features of the polity were directly connected with religion, but generally the spheres of religion and government were kept quite separate. The strong individualism and otherworldliness of Tibetan religion naturally led to this separation, and the highly pragmatic character of the polity—its amorality and emphasis on power described below—can indeed be understood only by reference to such a religion.

Three important features of the polity of Sa sKya directly connected with religious belief were the government's maintenance of a large monastic establishment, the power of the KHri CHen, and the definition of the most serious transgressions to be

---

[11] One manifestation of this homogeneity appeared in our respondents' statement that, although a man could have the proper attitude toward the Sa sKya government without being a member of the Sa sKya sect, if there were two men equally qualified to perform an important governmental task, one of whom belonged to the sect and one of whom did not, the government would unhesitatingly have selected the member of the sect. For a work that discusses the several varieties of political community, from the local to the international, see Philip E. Jacob and James V. Toscano (eds.), *The Integration of Political Communities* (Philadelphia: J. B. Lippincott, 1964).

handled by the criminal law. Other than its basic function of maintaining "law and order," the most important occupation of the Sa sKya government was its promotion of religious observance by supporting the monasteries of the capital and the emanation bodies of the aKHon family. As shown below, however, this policy cannot be interpreted as the government's response to a political obligation.

Although the religious and governmental positions of the KHri CHen were in theory independent of one another, in practice his religious status was an element of his political power. For example, the personal intervention of the KHri CHen would have immediately overcome any resistance, by officials or subjects, to any governmental policy. Although in such a case the KHri CHen would have been acting in his governmental rather than his religious capacity, the people involved would naturally have responded to his religious status. The KHri CHen of Sa sKya, however, did not often come in direct governmental contact with their subjects.

The most serious transgressions to be dealt with by the criminal law were defined according to religious beliefs. In the order of decreasing seriousness, they were: killing an emanation body, a high monk, or a "realized one," an act that involved both taking life and profanation; killing one's parents, who as one's origins resemble the "realized ones"; desecrating religious objects, which are manifestations of the Buddha; and taking other human life, the most serious breach of the Buddhist rule against destroying any kind of life. The wickedness of these acts was directly implied by religious tenets.

Except for homicide and desecration, there was little correspondence between religious standards and political propriety. A small but significant example is the separation of a man's religious worthiness from his political activities. High governmental office was readily given to monks who had broken their vows of celibacy or against taking life—the rigors of monastic life were recognized as incompatible with certain personalities—and in the

Sa sKya government a number of men had as monks reached high positions and then broken their vows without any apparent ill effect on their official careers. One man broke his vow of chastity with a nun, who was of course also sworn to chastity. He apologized to his monastery by paying for a "big tea" (a feast for all the monks), and later he was promoted to a higher governmental position. In another case, a monk, while in one of the highest positions in the government, took up with a lady friend and lived with her and their children for many years. He did not acknowledge his new status and continued to dress as a monk, until some of his friends persuaded him of the unseemliness of his behavior, whereupon he changed his garb, made amends to his former monastery, and continued exercising his rather important governmental responsibilities.

This separation between religious worth and political activity is also illustrated in the case of a wealthy hereditary nobleman who, the story has it, was determined to increase his political power by any available means. One of the most effective was to eliminate his rivals or opponents, and he was credited with involvement in two attempts at assassination, one successful and one frustrated. In evaluating this man, however, it was said that he was scrupulous in his religious observance and that he supported the monastic establishment. He was acknowledged as a ruthless seeker of power, but this behavior was not considered relevant to his goodness or badness as a person. This attitude toward personal power seems to be connected with the attitudes toward government and the polity discussed below.

IX

One of the principal goals of our investigation of Sa sKya was to discover how the existence of government was accounted for and whether there were any theories that justified particular governments. The Tibetan word for government was "gZHung," meaning "center"; it connoted unity and centralization in the sense of coming together and organizing for common goals. The possession of government, it was said, is one feature that distinguishes men from animals.

Religion definitely had no connection with the existence or justification of government. There was no idea of divine or supernatural forces participating in the creation of government, supporting its continuation, or justifying its power. Although the Sa sKya government spent the larger part of its resources supporting the monasteries in the capital and the hereditary emanation bodies of the aKHon family, no one suggested that it was justified by its contribution to religious observance. No one said that the subjects of Sa sKya were obliged to obey their government because it contributed to their "salvation." There is every reason to believe that the Sa sKya subjects approved of this support of religion,[12] but there is no reason to suppose that they saw this activity as obligating them to comply with their government. It had definitely not occurred to the rulers that the subjects might be so obligated.

The KHri CHen was an emanation body whose position in the Sa sKya sect was comparable to that of the Dalai Lama in the Yellow sect. In addition to being the focus of the religious beliefs and observances of the people of Sa sKya, the KHri CHen (as will be shown in Chapter 7) was the autocratic head of the Sa sKya government, but in theory his religious and political positions were not connected. The subject of Sa sKya was supposed to have one attitude toward the KHri CHen as a religious figure and a different attitude toward him as a governmental figure. Toward the KHri CHen as a religious figure, and toward his monastic hierarchy, the proper attitude was reverence based on faith.[13] Toward the KHri CHen as a governmental figure, and

---

[12] See especially Chapter 11 on the levy of monks. On this kind of support for "traditional" government, cf. Pye, *Politics, Personality, and Nation Building*, p. 79.

[13] The word translated "reverence" is "Mos." The word translated "faith" is "Dad Pa": it denotes a specific religious concept, not just a general trust.

toward his civil hierarchy, the proper attitude was a respect for authority in the strict sense that, after a careful evaluation of the official's ability, the subject accepts the official as one qualified to take care of him. This attitude did not imply a commitment to any specific official or government; it was a recognition by the subject that he would profit by doing what his governor told him to do. The attitude was most significantly called "Yid CHes," literally "great intelligence." Religious faith had no connection with governmental affairs and situations.

X

Although we had little difficulty getting direct answers to questions about divine sanction for government and the government's responsibilities for religious observance, our respondents never quite understood questions about the right of the Sa sKya government to rule its people. To us, however, the implications of what they said about government were clear: government was seen as the only agency possessing enough power to guarantee social harmony.[14] When we asked them what right the government of Sa sKya had to use its power to resolve situations such as those created by homicide, and why the resolution was not left to the people most vitally concerned, as was done in other areas of Tibet, the answer was that where government is effective there are few homicides and that where there are laws and courts homicides cannot be private affairs. This answer did not deal with the problem of government's right to govern; instead it emphasized the power of government to provide harmony or, as is now said, "law and order." This view of government implies that government's power serves the interest of the governed and thus that on pragmatic grounds the governed are wise to support and comply with their government; it includes nothing resembling the modern concept of legitimacy, which implies that government is justified by some factor independent

[14] The word for harmony is "mTHun Po"; it refers specifically to relations among people. The word for power is "dBang."

of it and, by virtue of this justification, has a moral right to the compliance of the governed.[15] This absence of a moral justification will be seen more clearly when the problem of accounting for specific governments is examined below.

The belief of the rulers about the function of government is consistent with our information on the structure and operation of the Sa sKya government and on the context within which this government existed. Whether the subjects shared the belief is the second question in this study we must answer by inference. Evidence from societies with belief systems and social systems similar to those of Sa sKya suggests that both governors and governed see government as the concentration of power that alone can guarantee harmony.[16] It is, in the second place, reasonable to assume some correspondence between the beliefs of the governed and the beliefs of the governors regarding the general

[15] For this concept of legitimacy, see C. W. Cassinelli, *The Politics of Freedom: An Analysis of the Modern Democratic State* (Seattle: University of Washington Press, 1961), ch. 7, and *Free Activities and Interpersonal Relations* (The Hague: Martinus Nijhoff, 1966), ch. 5.

[16] According to the southern Italian villager, "The state exists to force men to be good. A regime is worthy of respect if it has plenty of power and uses it rigorously to enforce obedience and to maintain law and order" (Edward C. Banfield, *The Moral Basis of a Backward Society* [Glencoe, Ill.: Free Press, 1958], p. 142). The ancient Indian writers saw the absence of a king as anarchy, which they wished to avoid at all costs; without a king there would be no sacrifices, no marriage, and even no society. (John W. Spellman, *Political Theory of Ancient India* [Oxford: Clarendon Press, 1964], p. 5). Also, Halpern, *Politics and Social Change*, pp. 17-18, finds the fear of anarchy predominant in Islamic societies; cf. A. L. Basham, "Some Fundamental Political Ideas of Ancient India," in C. H. Philips (ed.), *Politics and Society in India* (London: George Allen & Unwin, 1963), p. 17; and Hugh Nibley, "Tenting, Toll, and Taxing," *Western Political Quarterly*, XIX (1966), 609. Justus M. van der Kroef, "Javanese Messianic Expectations," *Comparative Studies in Society and History*, I (1958-1959), 299-323, explains the concept of "peace and order in harmony" and, pp. 304-305, describes the ruler's role in maintaining it. Fustel de Coulanges suggests that the fear of anarchy was important in early Greece and Rome (*Ancient City*, p. 121), and Thomas and Znaniecki suggest the same for Poland (*Polish Peasant*, p. 283).

function of government and regarding the reasons for accepting particular governments, discussed in the next section. Third, the high degree of individualism of Tibetan Buddhism and the absence of political communities in Tibet suggest that the average Tibetan was uneasy in interpersonal relationships and hence appreciated any power that served to stabilize them. Finally, our respondents said that the subjects of Sa sKya wanted only a little law and order and that they would "turn away" from a government that did not provide it.

Social harmony is the goal, and government provides the power to realize it. The Tibetans had a clear concept of power: it was the ability to take or to seize. Political power was measured by the amount of land and number of people under a government's control. The concept thus emphasized physical power, an emphasis that seems to be connected with an inability to understand more complex social relationships.

The Tibetans had a keen appreciation of the importance of power, and they saw it as independent of and prior to any specific accomplishments; for example, "great wealth comes to the powerful, but little power to the wealthy." The power possessed by a governor, or by any other man, is a result of his karma. This means, in effect, that his fate is to have power, and consequently no rational explanation of his power can be given. Karma may be thought of as a mark of supernatural favor, but there is no suggestion that any divine forces deliberately give power to a man so that he can perform the desirable function of maintaining worldly harmony through the agency of government. A ruler's power comes from his karma, which may be a result of his past acts or those of his ancestors, but there is no way to predict that a ruler will keep his favorable karma, or that he will lose it, to be deposed by someone else.[17]

---

[17] Spellman, *Political Theory of Ancient India,* p. 12, says that the concept of karma implies that kingship is dependent on neither god nor man. Also see R. Heine-Geldern, "Conceptions of State and Kingship in Southeast Asia" (data paper #18, Southeast Asia Program, Cornell University, Ithaca, N.Y., 1956), on the relation of karma to kingship.

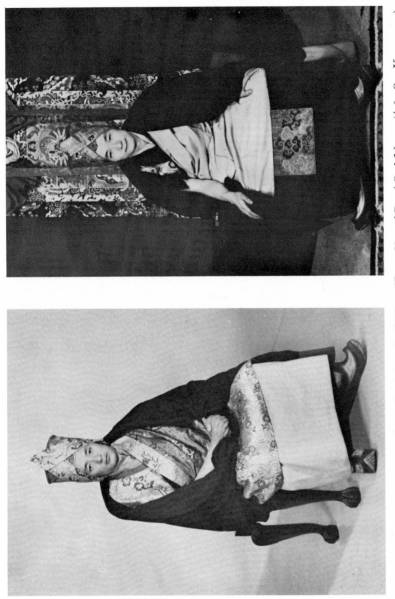

Plate 2. The principal respondents for the study, NGag dBang Kun dGaa bSod Nams (*left*, Sa sKya, 1949) and NGag dBang Kun dGaa PHrin Las (*right*, Sa sKya, 1952), the sons of the late hereditary ruler of Sa sKya. They fled Tibet after the Chinese invasion and now live in the United States.

Plate 3. NGag dBang mTHu THub dBang PHyug, the KHri CHen (hereditary ruler) of Sa sKya from 1936 until his death in 1950 (Sa sKya, 1946).

XI

After having established this theory of the existence of government, we asked our respondents to explain the right of the Sa sKya government to tell its subjects what to do and to maintain its independence of other governments. The answer was perfectly consistent: the Sa sKya government had the power to do these things, and it had had it for a very long time. The Mongol emperor's grant of Tibet-wide power to Sa sKya Pandita in the thirteenth century was seen as the key event in the history of the power of the aKHon family, although the century or two preceding the grant were not omitted from this "glorious history." Throughout the centuries the aKHon family had been the bearer of this power, and the reigning KHri CHen was the direct heir of the original grant, this recognition of Sa sKya as a gZHung. A constant comment on the dual function and position of the KHri CHen was that he could tell no one to have religious faith, but he could without question tell his subjects to obey, because and solely because he was their governor, that is to say, he had the power to govern.

When a government's "right to rule" is based on its power, the past takes precedence over the future. The longer the history of power of a regime or ruling family, the more powerful it currently appears. A prediction of future power cannot similarly serve to increase present power, especially among people with a limited ability to imagine things to come. The emphasis on power as the base of the polity seems to be one of the principal elements of "traditional" society's orientation toward the past.

Two additional points are relevant to this concept of government as power. First, the Tibetan equivalent of treason consisted in plotting to undermine the power of the government and especially the political power of the KHri CHen.[18] Second, one reason given for the right of government to intervene in situa-

---

[18] This equivalent was a violation of "allegiance," a concept explained below in section XII. The violation was called "Glo Ba Ring" (lungs far) or "NGo Logs" (face turned away).

tions created by acts such as homicide was that in these situations the interest of the subjects could not be separated from the interest of the government. This sounds very modern, but it did not mean that these interests were the same, because (as shown below) in Sa sKya a sharp distinction was made between the governors and the governed. What was meant was that the interests of the two converged: the governed were interested in maintaining social harmony, and the government was interested in maintaining its power. Our information contains no suggestion that the Sa sKya government felt itself obliged to guarantee harmony for its subjects, and information about similar societies appears to support a similar conclusion.[19]

When this conception of government as power is understood, the emphasis of the Sa sKya government on maintaining its own power becomes comprehensible. It is not surprising that the rulers paid more attention to their own power than to "making policy," and that they did not delegate their power in the "rational" way required by governments pursuing extensive regulative and promotive activities.[20] Polities such as Sa sKya can afford to have "overcentralized" governments because they have a very limited conception of what can be done by governmental action.[21]

[19] For two explicit statements on the absence of governmental obligation, see Spellman, *Political Theory of Ancient India*, p. 7, and Edgar L. Shor, "The Thai Bureaucracy," *Administrative Science Quarterly*, V (1960), 66–86.

[20] The concentration of power at the top of the Sa sKya governmental hierarchy is described in Chapters 5, 6, and 7. The same reluctance to "dilute" power is noted by Ernest W. Luther, *Ethiopia Today* (Stanford, Calif.: Stanford University Press, 1958), p. 39: delegation of authority is unseemly in the eyes of both the superior and the subordinate. See Chapter 12 on the policy of the Sa sKya government.

[21] Carrasco, *Land and Polity in Tibet*, p. 80, quotes from an official document of the Lhasa government: "Tibet is a country in which political and religious affairs are carried on simultaneously, with its chief aims the propagation of Buddhism and the seeking of happiness for all souls on earth." This statement is undoubtedly the result of outside influences.

In Sa sKya, as in other similar political societies, the principal governor was also a high religious figure. In some of the more "primitive" systems, these two positions may be conjoined because the overriding importance of the religious function is believed to require the support of governmental power.[22] In Sa sKya, however, such a requirement was not emphasized; indeed, our respondents expressly denied that the KHri CHen's religious functions depended in any way on his governmental power. This denial suggests that, when the conception of government as an agency of power necessary to establish social harmony is accepted, the religious functions, attributes, and powers of the chief governor serve principally to support his worldly power. The religious position of the KHri CHen, in other words, was a buttress to his worldly power, a buttress comparable to his high social status and to the pomp surrounding him. The religious positions of other monarchs may similarly support their governmental power.[23] This connection between governmental power and the supernatural must not be confused with the seventeenth-century European concept of the "divine right of kings," a concept designed to give a moral justification of governmental power.

XII

The idea that government is a force external to society required to maintain harmony within society naturally leads to a sharp distinction between the governors and the governed. Sa sKya had a more or less precise concept of the governed: they were the Mi Ser, a term that we translate "subject." To under-

[22] See Lucy Mair, *Primitive Government* (Baltimore: Penguin Books, 1962), and Fustel de Coulanges, *Ancient City*.

[23] The term "buttress" is used in this context by Pye, *Politics, Personality, and Nation Building*, p. 66. Heine-Geldern's accounts of both Hindu and Buddhist conceptions of kingship appear to support this thesis. See also P. Mercier, "The Fon of Dahomey," in Daryll Forde (ed.), *African Worlds* (London: Oxford University Press, 1954), p. 233.

stand this concept of subjecthood, two other concepts must be explained, "allegiance" and "establishment." [24]

A subject was a man who was obliged to make regular payments to the Government, the Religious Establishment, one of the two palaces, or a member of the hereditary nobility. We call the Government and the rest "establishments" to indicate that they all had (or could have had) subjects, and we use the term "Government"—as distinguished from "government," which means the totality of agencies that performed governmental functions—to refer to the most important of these establishments and the principal focus of our study. The payments to the establishments were in kind or in labor or in both, and they expressed part of the obligation the subjects owed for the benefits they received from the establishments. Revenue in kind was due when a subject farmed land that "belonged" to an establishment, and the payments in labor expressed his ultimate subordination to the Government.[25] When outside of Sa sKya, a subject identified himself as a "Sa sKya Mi Ser," and within Sa sKya as, for example, a "Religious Establishment Mi Ser" or a "Government Mi Ser."

A man usually became a subject of an establishment by being given responsibility for a portion of its land. People coming into Sa sKya from elsewhere in Tibet were normally required to take some land in order to become subjects and hence members of the Sa sKya polity. A number of people, however, had no responsibility for land, but they also were subjects of an establishment. If a man had someone, usually a brother, who took the responsibility for his father's establishment land, he could be without land and thus without an obligation to make payments in kind to an

---

[24] "Mi Ser" means "yellow people": it originally referred only to the clergy but was then extended to laymen in the sense described in the text. The term we translate "allegiance" is "Mi KHongs," literally "man midst." The concept of establishment is our own.

[25] The way in which land "belonged" to an establishment is described in Chapter 9, section IV. The obligation to provide labor as expressing ultimate power is discussed in Chapter 9, section VII.

establishment. He was, however, still a subject of his father's establishment, a relationship expressed by his obligation to pay it a yearly token "head tax." [26] A man who became the adopted heir of a family belonging to another establishment also owed this "head tax" to his former establishment. The palaces had a number of servants who farmed no land; they were subjects of a palace, but their responsibility to it was met by their labor and they owed it no other payments.

Every subject of the Religious Establishment and every subject of a nobleman also had allegiance to the Government, a relationship expressed by labor owed to the Government in addition to the payments in kind owed to the Religious Establishment or the noble. The subjects of the two palaces were exempt from working for the Government because the palaces were the "estates" of the two branches of the ruling aKHon family, and the royal family was naturally seen as independent of the Government, which after all consisted of its subordinates. Nevertheless, the Government's criminal-law procedures applied to palace subjects and its civil-law procedures were available to them.[27] Although palace subjects, unlike all other subjects, did not have allegiance to the Government, they had allegiance to Sa sKya, and this implied support of the Government.

"Allegiance" was the relationship of a subject to his establishment, but it also involved a proper attitude toward the establishment. A subject was responsible for complying with the rules and directives of his establishment. Allegiance also implied, for

[26] This tax was called "Mi KHral" (man tax), and it was only one or two Srang a year.

[27] The system of revenue is described in Chapter 9, and legal procedures in Chapter 6. Naturally, actual practice was not completely consistent with the theory of subjecthood. For example, there once was a subject of one of the palaces who occasionally refused to perform chores for it. He said that he was a subject of Sa sKya and had his principal allegiance to the Government, not to the palace. The palace did not believe it could force him to do the work, and its officials were rather embarrassed. This subject was also difficult in other ways.

subjects other than those of the Government, a responsibility not to embarrass one's establishment by running afoul of the Government. A nobleman was expected to apologize to the Government if one of his subjects broke its laws; the other establishments did not apologize for such transgressions, but they were nonetheless embarrassed.

Every subject in Sa sKya was expected to have the attitude of allegiance to the polity of Sa sKya as well as to his own establishment. Our respondents maintained that among Tibetans only the subjects of the three regimes of west-central Tibet—Lhasa, Shigatse, and Sa sKya—had a genuine allegiance; in other words, the other areas of Tibet had inferior political systems. The people of Sa sKya, as Tibetans, also had an allegiance to Tibet and to the Dalai Lama as the symbol and "owner" of Tibet.

The concept of allegiance to Sa sKya and to its several establishments is a specific example of the respect for authority described above (section IX) as the proper attitude of the governed toward their governors. Allegiance did not involve a moral obligation; it was part of the recognition that the benefits provided by government might be jeopardized if it did not have the full cooperation of its subjects.

XIII

The Mi Ser were the subjects or the governed. The men who held the higher positions in the institutions of government had an entirely different status; they were separated from the subjects by as rigid a social barrier as was possible in the small polity. The clearest expression of the difference between governors and governed occurred when a subject was appointed to a governmental position that carried "noble" status: [28] by virtue of this appointment, "he was taken out of the status of a subject." There was a strong suggestion that the governors were those men "naturally" qualified to control the subjects, and the concept of a common

[28] This "noble" status is strictly sKu Drag status, to be described and explained in Chapter 5, section I.

interest of the two groups, an interest identical to both, was no doubt hardly comprehensible to either.

Although we were unable to obtain any direct information on how the subjects of Sa sKya felt about their governors, we discovered the attitudes of the governors to the governed and the governors' opinions of the governed's attitudes toward them. According to our respondents, the subjects only wanted a little law and order. In providing law and order, the government had to be careful to follow tradition: the KHri CHen should always have asked himself if his actions were consistent with those of his predecessors. When tradition was violated, the subjects were disturbed and discussed the matter among themselves. The relationship of governor to the governed did not resemble that of a father toward his children; the governmental relationship was much more formal than the parental relationship and it involved much less personal commitment.

The subjects generally lived prudently and wanted to be left alone, but they were potentially very "fierce." They were difficult to accommodate, and could cause the government great inconvenience by expressing their displeasure with its actions in anonymous letters and gossip. The subjects certainly were not king, but they could not be pushed around without creating just too many headaches for the government. They all complained about paying their revenue in kind and labor; few refused to pay, but everyone stalled as much as he could. Outlying localities tended to resist interference, in what they considered their own affairs, by the government of the capital. They resented the arrest of one of their members, especially if the act prompting his arrest had occurred outside his home district, and they might well have secretly helped him to avoid it. Any overt resistance to a posse seeking a suspect would have been treated as rebellion, but no instances of such resistance were recalled.

XIV

Tibetan Buddhism was otherworldly in orientation, holding that a man should detach himself as much as possible from the chimerical relations and situations of this life; strictly followed, this precept would have made government impossible. Although worldly affairs can never be completely ignored, the attitudes expressed in the religion of Sa sKya no doubt were connected with the view that the Sa sKya government had only minimal functions. Yet even a small involvement in mundane matters is inconsistent with a religion of withdrawal; and the more positive role of government envisioned by KHri CHen NGag dBang mTHu THub dBang PHyug, described in Chapter 7, would obviously have contradicted the presuppositions of the society.[29]

When we posed this incompatibility, our respondents' first answer was that governmental activity was a manifestation of the religious concept of compassion; a man who has governmental power can renounce his own religious interests to take on the burden of his subjects' welfare. The concept of compassion is central to the phenomenon of the emanation body, whose compassion prompts him to remain involved in worldly affairs to help others to gain liberation, but the religion did not prescribe acts of compassion for the ordinary believer. Compassion, however, can explain only how an individual governor can justify his own actions in terms of his own progress toward liberation. Governing was here linked with compassion in a context that assumed the existence of government, the principal function of which was to provide social harmony. Compassion as the basic justification of the polity implies a relationship between governors and governed too intimate to be consistent with both the facts of governing in Sa sKya and the theory about it. It was explicitly denied that governors had any feeling toward their subjects comparable to that of parents toward their children, and government was apparently judged by and accepted for its ability to maintain harmony.

[29] This contradiction seems to resemble very closely the conflict between the "traditional" and the "rational" stressed by S. N. Eisenstadt in *The Political Systems of Empires* (New York: Free Press of Glencoe, 1963).

Despite their reference to compassion, our respondents recognized a continuing contradiction between religious tenets and political activity. There was a saying in Sa sKya that no progress could be made unless the gods were offended, and certain people were referred to as those who meet every problem by closing their eyes and praying. This contradiction was seen even more clearly when the government of Sa sKya began to consider some departures from its customary minimal role.

An interesting corollary of this increasing awareness of the contradiction between traditional religious values and the exigencies of governmental responsibility was our respondents' statement that the power of the subjects of Sa sKya had been increasing in modern times. Perhaps the subjects had in fact become less docile in their acceptance of their government, but in any event it was believed that they had and that this was a distortion of the proper relationship between government and governed that required the government to break with tradition and become much more active. The "rise of the masses" was seen as one manifestation of the Buddhist doctrine of universal degeneration,[30] but firm governmental action following the proper principles could no doubt successfully meet this new challenge. When the subjects have ideas regarding the correct course of governmental action, the government must make sure there is a consensus—the fragmentation of many opinions must be avoided —and then decide whether or not action ought to be taken. This combination of the right of the subjects to make suggestions and the power of government to accept or reject these suggestions may represent a first stage in the erosion of belief systems such as Sa sKya's.

[30] Other manifestations, occurring within the memory of our respondents, were a shorter life span—few people now live to be sixty, whereas formerly they lived to seventy, eighty, and even ninety—shorter grass and distances, a worsening of social relationships, and lower mountains. The Chinese Communist conquest was, of course, the greatest instance of universal degeneration.

XV

We have tried to show that a concept of the functions of government implying an account of the polity was an integral part of the general belief system of Sa sKya. There was no idea of a moral right possessed by the government to direct the activities of the governed, and thus no idea of a moral obligation between governors and governed. The relationship between the two was entirely pragmatic, based on converging rather than identical interests. This situation is not surprising, for one would not expect to find a concept of legitimacy in a belief system viewing social relationships as a necessary evil, to be minimized in order to preserve the integrity of the individual regarding both his worldly power and his progress toward liberation. Similarly, the absence of a political community, so closely associated with the concept of legitimacy, should cause no surprise.[31] In these respects Sa sKya may have been typical of societies that have passed the stage where religion and government are identical but that have not yet reached the stage where government is recognized as a useful instrument for innovation.

[31] Students of both legitimacy and the political community have recognized the modernity of these phenomena: see, for example, Seymour Martin Lipset, *Political Man* (Garden City, N.Y.: Doubleday, 1960), p. 78; Karl W. Deutsch, "The Growth of Nations," *World Politics*, V (1953), 184; and Hans Kohn, *The Idea of Nationalism* (New York: Macmillan, 1961), intro.

Chapter 4

Local Government

In Sa sKya proper there was an ideal division of governmental functions along territorial lines: a number of Headmen, each responsible for a group of contiguous families, were accountable to a District Officer, and the District Officers were accountable to the ZHabs Pad. (The capital had a special system.) Unsurprisingly, such symmetry was only an ideal. The actual arrangement was shaped by custom, accident, power, and lethargy, as well as by principles of organizational rationality. The details of the arrangements are interesting particularly because they show how these factors contributed to the problems of governing the small principality.

I

The governing of Sa sKya was complicated by the division of its population among the several establishments. The following account refers only to the people who had allegiance to the Government, with occasional specific mention of those with allegiance to the Religious Establishment. The arrangements for people with allegiance to a palace or to a nobleman are described elsewhere.[1]

[1] On these arrangements, see Appendix A, section II, and Chapter 8. See Chapter 3, section XII, on establishments and allegiance. Our estimates of the populations of the several areas was based upon our respondents' memories of their visits to the areas and of official statistics. These figures were then compared with data from similar environments elsewhere in the world. We believe our total figures are within 5 per cent of accuracy. The estimates of the divisions of people among

Of a total population of about 16,000 people, about 7,900, or over 49 per cent, were under the immediate jurisdiction of the several governmental agencies in the capital. Of the remaining 8,100 people, about 1,500 did not fit into the governmental scheme to be described. There were, first, about 340 monks and nuns who were principally under the discipline of their monasteries and nunneries. Next, there were seventeen noble families, with probably ten members each, who had a special political status described in Chapter 8. Finally, there were an estimated 200 families engaged in full-time animal-herding who were scattered throughout high country and consequently not closely integrated in the governmental arrangements for the farming population, although they had their own Headmen. Subtracting these three groups of people from the population outside the immediate jurisdiction of the capital leaves about 6,600 people, or about 1,300 families, governed after the pattern to be described.

About seven-eighths of these 1,300 families lived in eight formally defined districts; the remainder lived in four separate areas in central Sa sKya (Maps 3 and 4). The District Officers, who reported directly to the ZHabs Pad in the capital, had full charge over only those families with allegiance to the Government. They drafted and organized labor on a levy basis from the families with allegiance to the Religious Establishment and to noblemen, but they had no other official functions regarding these people. They had no jurisdiction at all over families with allegiance to the palaces. The District Officers thus were responsible for about 1,135 families with allegiance to the Government, or about 70 per cent of the people outside the immediate jurisdiction of the capital.

II

Only those families with allegiance to the Government or the Religious Establishment were organized under Headmen, the

---

the several establishments are rougher, but the total of our estimates for all the separate areas is very close to our respondents' memory of governmental statistics for all of Sa sKya proper.

lowest-level official in Sa sKya. Every Government and Religious Establishment family was supposed to have a Headman, but some who lived in isolated places or who were drifters sharecropping someone else's land did not. The number of these people could not be estimated.

Outside the area directly under the supervision of the capital, there were approximately thirty-nine Headmen for the nonherding population, perhaps seven of whom were affiliated with the Religious Establishment.[2] Each was responsible for from ten to thirty families. The two hundred herding families probably had about ten Headmen, all of whom were affiliated with the Government. When a Government Headman's families did not live in one of the eight districts, he reported directly to the capital, often consulting, however, with an important nobleman in the neighborhood. Some of the Headmen in charge of herding families—for example, in Mang mKHar and Ga Ra—reported directly to the capital even though their jurisdiction lay within a district, probably because the herders maintained many animals belonging to the Government. Religious Establishment Headmen always dealt directly with the head of the Religious Establishment, the Steward, in the capital. The SHab District, with almost 360 Government and Religious Establishment families, had only one Headman, a special situation described below.

The Headman was the official closest to those people of Sa sKya who lived outside the capital. In former times Headmen inherited their office (which was often of noble status) or were appointed by the capital.[3] In recent centuries Headmen were usually selected by the families within their jurisdiction, and it was said that they were less powerful than in the old days.

[2] The estimates of the number, location, jurisdiction, and affiliation of Headmen in this chapter are quite rough, based upon memories such as "There probably were two or three Headmen in that area."

[3] Headmen were formerly called sDe Pa Lags, meaning "district one honorable." The title was retained, without its implications of heredity and noble status, by some recent Sa sKya Headmen, and some noble families had the title in their names.

Although they were "popularly" selected, they were full members of the governmental hierarchy under the ZHabs Pad, a status recognized by their rank of Jo Lags, which entitled them to wear special insignia.[4]

The Headman was supposed to bring his people's needs and problems to the attention of his superiors and to protect his people from any injustices from above, as well as to direct and organize them according to regular and special orders. Headmen had to be literate in order to communicate with their superiors, but there were few scholars among them. Although they received no formally allocated income from their positions, at least part of their expenses in traveling on official business was met by government and they received gifts in kind and in labor from their people. Headmen were the only governmental officials in Sa sKya who could openly accept the gifts that came to all officials. All other such transactions, which were considered quite proper, always took place in private. Although the gifts and favors received from the subjects were of considerable value, most Headmen were independently rather prosperous and sought the position more for its significant local prestige than for economic gain.

III

The Headman, like all Sa sKya officials, had no fixed tenure of office. He served as long as he retained his mental and physical powers and avoided giving strong offense either to his people or to his superiors. Both Government and Religious Establishment Headmen were usually in office for a long time. When a vacancy occurred, every family of subjects sent at least one representative to an assembly for choosing the new Headman. The choice was supposed to represent a consensus, an example of the "harmony" that Tibetans and other similar people value so highly. When there was a single outstanding aspirant, the choice could be made by a shout of acclamation; in these circumstances cries of protest

---

[4] The status of "Jo Lags" and the grades within it are described in Appendix C, section I.

were not likely, but if a significant proportion of the people remained silent, the candidate was, at least for the moment, rejected. During the entire procedure of selecting a Headman, the initiative in calling the assembly, canvassing the people, calling for a vote, and so forth was completely unofficial. There were always some prominent or officious persons willing to be *ad hoc* leaders.[5]

Consensus was possible in groups that had as few as ten members and were never much larger than fifty. If a deceased or retired Headman had been a successful official, there was always a strong presumption for his son to succeed him, because the son would have wealth, prestige, and experience. The office, however, was not hereditary, and an unpopular son of a popular Headman could easily be rejected.[6] If for some reason there were two strong candidates for Headman, a compromise candidate would be sought. If a consensus appeared impossible, the decision might well be indefinitely deferred.

The process of succession is well illustrated by a situation in the settlement of aKHril sPe, near the capital. The Headman, a man in comfortable circumstances but not wealthy, died in the late 1940's. He was succeeded by the elder of two sons who lived with him, but the new Headman was in office only a few years before he too died. His sons were too young to replace him, and so his younger brother had a claim to the Headmanship. This younger brother, however, was not considered very responsible, and an excuse was found not to support him.[7] Several other

[5] Our respondents had observed the choice of a Group Official—see section XVI below.

[6] In Burma, only the headmen and the king were selected by heredity (Lucian W. Pye, *Politics, Personality, and Nation Building* [New Haven: Yale University Press, 1962], p. 70). For the use of the principle of heredity in the SHab District, see section X.

[7] The excuse was that since he was a sorcerer he was not suited for a lay position. This family was well known to our respondents; a brother of the father had been a religious collector in eastern Tibet, and a daughter was a nun and nursemaid in the PHun TSHogs palace.

aspirants for the position appeared, and a consensus could not be achieved. As a consequence, the Headmanship remained unfilled for several years.

When a new Headman was selected by this procedure, the ZHabs Pad or the Steward of the Religious Establishment was notified. Both officials could refuse to recognize the selection on grounds of the man's disloyalty or pronounced incompetence, and such a disagreement between the Steward and his subjects could be referred to the ZHabs Pad for resolution. When the subjects' selection was approved, the capital sent the new Headman a written authorization of office which said that he was entitled to wear the special Jo Lags insignia.

IV

The Headman, with his counterpart in the capital, the Group Official, was the only Sa sKya official whose selection required any approval or even consultation with those whom he governed. The ZHabs Pad had the final decision on an appointment, and if he believed the subjects were acting irresponsibly, he could ignore their choice and make his own appointment. In overriding the subjects' choice, the ZHabs Pad always risked (our respondents insisted) destroying the effectiveness of the office of Headman. Apparently the ordinary subject saw his Headman as a buffer against the unfamiliar, and no doubt somewhat suspect, higher officialdom. The ZHabs Pad, for his part, probably could expect better cooperation from the subjects when they had the Headman of their choice. They usually chose a man of substance, who had a real stake in the governmental and social system, so the ZHabs Pad's only problem was to make sure that there was a real consensus on the nominee. If a majority of the subjects had insisted on their man despite the opposition of a minority, his name could have been formally presented to the ZHabs Pad; but in this case the ZHabs Pad would no doubt have refused authorization and asked the subjects why they were so indecisive. The Headman was not important enough to get involved in factional disputes,[8] and hence the ZHabs Pad would probably not concern himself with the personal loyalties and policy orientations of the man selected by the subjects.

Once a Headman received his letter of appointment, he could be removed from office only by the ZHabs Pad. This action would be taken, after two warnings, when the man was not meeting his responsibilities to his superiors or when he had demonstrably lost the confidence of his subjects. A loss of confidence could be expressed in a written protest from the subjects to the capital, but the more usual method was to start a campaign of slander by word of mouth. When such a campaign could no longer be ignored, the capital sent someone to the Headman's area to investigate, and if the protest were judged genuine, the man was removed from office. No instances of removing Headmen were recalled by our respondents, but the following case illustrates the relationships among the subjects, the Headman, and the capital.

In the early 1950's there was an acting Headman in gYaa Lung (Map 3) who had been appointed by the capital because, for some reason, a consensus had not been reached among the subjects. This Headman was a man of letters, a great talker, an aggressive personality, and a sorcerer. He had the kind of personality that would never admit an error; he would go to great pains to prove the correctness of a small mistake or the truth of a trivial falsehood. Once he was called to the home of an old woman who was seriously ill. After performing divinations, he announced that she would recover. He had barely left the house when she died. This story was enjoyed by all who knew him, but not in the least because they disliked him.[9]

[8] On factions and policy, see Chapter 12.

[9] This Headman was imprisoned by the Chinese Communists. He and Brag sPe senior and junior (see Chapter 8, section II) refused to say that the Tibetan way of life was not the best way for Tibetans, and hence the other prisoners believed the three to be marked for liquidation. Two daughters of the late KHri CHen, NGag dBang mTHu THub dBang PHyug, were in the same prison, but later escaped.

Another man in the neighborhood aspired to the Headmanship and was consequently envious of the acting Headman. The Liaison Officers at the capital, whose function was to communicate messages to the ZHabs Pad (see Chapter 5, section IV), began to receive a number of complaints from the subjects of gYaa Lung about the way the acting Headman was conducting his office, and the ZHabs Pad eventually sent an investigator in the guise of a casual visitor to the area. This spy reported back that most of the people supported the acting Headman and that when he questioned those who had circulated the slander, they acknowledged that the envious rival had paid them to do so. The acting Headman was then brought to the capital and given a permanent appointment.[10]

V

The Headman in Sa sKya was supposed to take care of his people and to carry out orders from his superiors. He had no authority to make any final governmental decisions, although he could resolve some types of cases in conjunction with his superior, the District Officer. If a Headman were to be away from home for any length of time, he appointed a temporary substitute.

The Headman was a governor, but a governor who was concerned with almost every detail of his people's lives and who used his governmental power as sparingly as possible. In Sa sKya there was always a strong preference for resolving all problems without reference to formal governmental action; even the very important Law Officials at the capital welcomed the opportunity to refer to private mediation cases that they had already begun to investigate. The less frequently a Headman had to refer issues to his superiors, the more valuable he was considered; and, since he could make no final decisions on his own authority, he had to rely upon his persuasiveness, personal prestige, and status

[10] This appointment was made by NGag dBang Kun dGaa bSod Nams, who was at the time acting KHri CHen.

as a member of the governmental hierarchy. Once again the society emphasized harmony and consensus; and because Sa sKya was small and contained relatively few sources of discord, harmony was a real possibility. In all the situations described below, however, the Headman could, if it were necessary, call upon the full power of the government.

The Headman was supposed to resolve all disputes among his people, but he would intervene only when relatives or friends of the disputants had failed to mediate the quarrel. In a case of trespass by an animal, a common cause of quarrels, the procedure might have been something like this: the owner of the field apprehended the trepassing animal and took it to the Headman as proof that its owner was responsible for the damage to his crops; the Headman then contacted the owner and the three men went to inspect the damage; after this inspection, the Headman suggested a settlement. In a case of petty theft—one involving less than the value of four sheep—the Headman investigated, discovered the thief, and suggested a proper restitution. In a case of bodily assault, the Headman tried to get the attacker to pay an indemnity and the injured man to accept it. Disputes over debts, interest payments, business agreements, water rights, and even quarrels among children were similarly dealt with by the Headman.

One of the Group Officials at the capital, who like the Headmen were supposed to handle such disputes, was generally recognized as an excellent official. His ability as a mediator is illustrated by the following anecdote. He once came upon some weeping children huddling outside a house while from within issued the sounds of a violent quarrel. Entering the house amid flying furniture, the Group Official quietly inquired of the man and wife the nature of their disagreement. The three thereupon sat down and resolved the matter.

When the Headman was unsuccessful in resolving disputes among his people, he announced that he was going to refer the dispute to his District Officer. At this point the associates of the disputants would try once again to mediate their differences, making every effort to avoid involvement with the higher official and the consequent use of formal governmental procedures. If this last attempt at private settlement failed, the Headman brought the case to the District Officer, and after consultation the two of them arrived at a decision for which they were jointly responsible. In Sa sKya there was always an emphasis upon sharing responsibility for decisions among at least two governmental officials. (Perhaps the idea of shared responsibility was derived from a desire to maintain interpersonal harmony and stability by avoiding the appearance of undue individual initiative and innovation; outward conformity may well have been the complement of a high degree of religious and social individualism.) Despite the emphasis on shared responsibility, however, only the Headman and the District Officer, at the lowest level of governing, seem to have made any real joint decisions. Considerations of efficiency, as will be seen, apparently prevailed to create the final and unshared authority and power of the ZHabs Pad, although even he was supposed always to consult with the Chief Secretary.

The Headman and the District Officer together had the authority to use governmental techniques to resolve only those cases that are now described as "criminal." If the culprit in a case of theft or assault refused to accept the settlement proposed by the District Officer and the Headman, they could, again acting together, punish him, usually by administering a flogging, and the case would then be closed. The man who was wronged by theft or assault, incidentally, could receive a flogging himself if he insisted on restitution more generous than that proposed by the officials.

The other disagreements that the Headman was unable to settle and hence referred to the District Officer concerned matters such as trespass, debts, contracts, and water rights. When brought into these cases, the District Officer could only add his prestige and general influence to those of the Headman in attempting to get the disputants together. If a disputant refused to compromise, the case could only be referred to the capital. The reason for the inability of the District Officer and Headman to resolve these cases seems to be that the cases involved interpretations of written rules and regulations. Only the highest officials had the expertise necessary to make correct interpretations, and it would have been most improper to allow minor officials to have access to the venerated written codes.[11] In theft and assault, on the other hand, any sensible man with a knowledge of affairs could calculate a just retribution or an appropriate punishment.

VI

Another responsibility of the Headman was to help his people with their personal and especially their economic problems. If, for example, a poor man had no plow and no money to rent or buy one, he could approach his Headman, who would lend him a plow, or try to borrow one for him, or get him a loan. If the man were in real trouble, the Headman would try to negotiate an interest-free loan and other kinds of assistance from his neighbors. If the situation were too serious for local resources, the Headman would ask for assistance from the District Officer, who could, on his responsibility alone, draw upon the Government stores under his control. The Headman, however, again would have done everything possible to avoid involving his superior in the problems of his own people.

The Headmen of Sa sKya seem to have been well qualified to perform these paternal services for their people. They had, of course, the prestige of their governmental positions. Most of them also had personal wealth, although they were not always the richest subjects in their neighborhoods: the Headmen at aKHril sPe and gYaa Lung described above were comfortable but not wealthy. The many gifts and favors received by the

[11] See Chapter 6, section II, on the written code. The importance of the written word will also be seen in connection with government records (Chapter 9, section V).

Headman also helped him in aiding his people, a situation with some resemblance to the practice in less complex societies of presenting gifts to a chief and expecting largess from him as a method of tolerably equitable distribution. The resemblance was not too pronounced, however, for the people of Sa sKya were rather individualistic in their economic behavior.

One of the Government Headmen in the CHu aDus District (see Map 3) was Nas Og Pa, whose home appears on several maps of Tibet under the name of Nyope. Nas Og Pa was one of the richest men in Sa sKya, having gained his wealth from the largest herds of sheep in the principality. He had a large two-storied house, with good furnishings and lots of imported brass-ware, and he had a number of servants. Two married sons lived with him and supervised the farm and the flocks. It was presumed that one of them would succeed him as Headman. Nas Og Pa traveled to the capital periodically, and whenever there he visited the PHun TSHogs palace to pay his respects and receive blessings. These visits were quite unofficial, but they exemplify the close contacts between subject and royalty in the small polity.

Gru Pa Nang Pa and dPe Rang were Government Headmen in the Ko CHag area under the rMa Bya District Office (Map 3). Both had considerable wealth gained from flocks of sheep. dPe Rang had five sons: the eldest had been a religious collector; the second was a former monk who had once been a servant in the PHun TSHogs palace and after renouncing or breaking his vows went into trade with the areas south of Sa sKya; and the three youngest remained in their father's household. One of these last three would no doubt have succeeded his father as Headman.

VII

The Headman in his official capacity had certain functions that required him to notify his District Officer, or the capital if his jurisdiction was not in a district. In the event of a serious crime such as treason, homicide, major theft, arson, poisoning of water, and extensive desecration of religious objects, the Head-man notified the District Officer, who in turn notified the capital, which alone could deal with these grave issues. The Headman's responsibility was to be alert to such eventualities, and if any occurred among his people his reputation suffered. In case of marauders from the outside, the Headman and the District Officer together raised a militia. Whenever a communicable disease of human beings or animals occurred, the Headman notified the District Officer; the two of them imposed a quarantine and sent for practitioners of folk medicine, requesting more such specialists from the capital if the outbreak were serious. The Headman reported any damage to canals, roads, bridges, and public buildings to the District Officer, who dealt with the matter himself.

The Headman was responsible for moving his people's revenue in kind to storage at the District Office or the capital. He notified them of the amounts they owed, which were calculated in the capital. He kept the capital informed of births and deaths and the state of the crops, so that the revenue schedules could if necessary be adjusted. In cases of individual hardship, the Headman could ask that the family's payments be lessened or deferred. In the event that any governmental orders were unclear, the Headman went to the capital. In the fall he collected the seed grain and had it moved to storage, and in the spring he got it from storage and allocated it to his farmers. In performing these functions and the ones previously described, the Headman of the Religious Establishment directly contacted the Steward in the capital.[12]

Our respondents maintained that the Headman of Sa sKya considered themselves primarily the spokesmen for their people and secondarily officials of the government, and that the subjects

[12] Every subject family belonged to a bCu SHog, a "unit of ten," a classification left over from the Mongol census of the thirteenth century. These units, which had no fixed number of members, had no organization and were used by the Headmen, the Group Officials, and others only in the allocation of various chores and levies.

saw them in the same light. It must not be supposed that, because Headmen were elected spokesmen, they were viewed by their people as "representatives" in the modern democratic sense of "substitutes," the sense of men chosen by the people to govern because the people themselves are too numerous and too busy to be governors.[13] In choosing a Headman, the subjects of Sa sKya sought a man of prestige and character who could mediate their own differences and who would not be cowed by high governmental officials, noblemen, and other powerful people. They sought protection from someone who was superior but not too superior; the idea of "self-government" was completely foreign to their beliefs and experiences.

Our respondents also claimed that the office of headman was a very successful institution, both for the subjects and for the capital, and that to bring every family under a Headman and every Headman under a District Officer was one of the most needed reforms in the Sa sKya governmental structure. Given the presuppositions of the political system, these opinions seem to be correct, even though we were unable to discover what the ordinary subject thought of his Headman and District Officer.

The relatively few families who lived in isolated places and had no Headman were probably at a disadvantage in not having the paternal care described above. These families may have had to pay more in revenue to the government, because revenue-farmers were sent to collect grain and other material from subjects who had no Headman. Sometimes revenue-farmers were requested by the subjects themselves to help in the management of their land, an indication of inefficiency and disorganization.

VIII

There were eight districts in Sa sKya proper (see Maps 3 and 4). The District Officers had full jurisdiction over families with allegiance to the Government and they were responsible for

---

[13] See C. W. Cassinelli, *The Politics of Freedom: An Analysis of the Modern Democratic State* (Seattle: University of Washington Press, 1961), ch. 7.

organizing corvée labor from all families save those with allegiance to the palaces. In all other respects, there were great variations among the districts. The three northern districts of SHab, dMigs, and lHun aGrub sDings were reasonable administrative divisions of the Sa sKya government; at least four of the five districts in the valleys of the PHu and SHes Gling Rivers to the south were not. Each of at least three of the southern districts was dominated by a single noble family; there were no nobles in dMigs and lHun aGrub sDings and no single dominant family in SHab. The three northern districts contained almost two-thirds of all families outside the capital with allegiance to the Government and almost two-thirds of all families outside the capital who were responsible for corvée labor.[14] None of the eight districts was of recent origin, and information regarding the reasons for their establishment was not available.

The largest district was SHab, with slightly over 400 subject families. About 240 of these families had allegiance to the Government, 115 to the Religious Establishment, 35 to the nobility, and 20 to the palaces. Thus the SHab District Officer had about 1,200 people for whom he was completely responsible and about 1,950 people whose labor had to be coordinated periodically. SHab was a rational administrative unit because it included a concentration of population separated sharply enough from other concentrations, except on its northern boundary with the dMigs District. Even this boundary may have been more rational than it appears, for the SHab Valley was the area containing the majority of the hereditary nobility outside the capital, and the estate of the northernmost noble, lCam Mo Grwa TSHang, was just south of the SHab-dMigs border. The situation in this district led to a special governmental arrangement, described in section X.

The dMigs District comprised the northern panhandle of Sa

[14] A recent District Officer in the Sa sKya territory of Mus (Map 1), where there was no nobility, was the subject monk Gar CHung sGang, who resigned as Government Steward (Chapter 5, section II) to take the position. He also was a professional administrator.

sKya. It contained about 110 subject families, about two-thirds
with allegiance to the Government, one-third to the Religious
Establishment, and four to the sGrol Ma palace. The District
Officer of dMigs collected the only tariffs levied by the Sa sKya
government, and he maintained along the Tsangpo River the
only patrol of the Sa sKya border. Like SHab, the dMigs District
was a tolerably rational unit in terms of size and distribution of
population, and an official of some status was required for the
supervision of the border. The District Officer had perhaps four
Headmen under him, and there was probably one for the subjects of the Religious Establishment.[15] One of the recent District
Officers here was a monk who had come to the capital from the
Sa sKya territory of rTSe gDong (Map 1) to enter governmental service. Sometime prior to 1936 he resigned from his position
in the capital to become District Officer at dMigs. The fact that
he was a professional administrator, rather than a local notable as
in the case of other District Officers, further suggests the administrative rationality of his district.

The lHun aGrub sDings District extended along the Grum
River to the west of the capital. It contained about 280 subject
families, 20 with allegiance to the palaces and the remainder
divided between about three-quarters to the Government and
one-quarter to the Religious Establishment. This district was also
a rational unit, and it may have contained as many as ten Government Headmen, with perhaps three other Headmen attached
to the Religious Establishment. In the 1950's the District Officer
of lHun aGrub sDings was from a prosperous family of hereditary practitioners of medicine who had their clinic near the
District Office and who had hereditary Jo Lags rank. The position, however, was not hereditary, because the incumbent's
father had not been District Officer.

IX

The rMa Bya District included the east bank of the PHu
River and the noncontiguous area of Ko CHag, the southern

[15] See note 2 above.

appendage to Sa sKya. The northern part of the district contained about thirty-five Government families, about seven Religious Establishment families, four families with allegiance to a
nobleman, and perhaps two Government Headmen. Ko CHag
had about sixty Government families, thirty-five Religious Establishment families, thirty-five families with allegiance to the
palaces, and perhaps three Headmen, one of whom may have
been affiliated with the Religious Establishment. The District
Officer of rMa Bya was thus fully responsible for 95 families and
in charge of the corvée labor of about 140 families.

The District Officers of rMa Bya were apparently always
members of the noble family Byang aGo, whose nobility dated
from the time of aPHags Pa in the thirteenth century. However
the district may have originated, in recent times it was clearly the
domain of this rich and renowned family. It was not known why
Ko CHag was included in the rMa Bya District, but our respondents offered a reasonable and significant conjecture: Ko
CHag may once have been an independent district, a status that
it lost through the incompetence of some District Officer or the
capital's displeasure with some prominent local family; the capital then may have given it to rMa Bya as a mark of favor, or
someone in rMa Bya may have been aggressive enough to acquire it.

The Gru bZHi District was located on the west bank of the
PHu River; it contained about thirty Government families with
probably two Headmen, ten Religious Establishment families,
and ten with allegiance to the wealthy noble family of Ma Ba
TSHogs. This family apparently always supplied the District
Officers of Gru bZHi. The duration of the family's noble status
was not known, but whatever it was and whenever the district
was created, the nature of the district strongly suggests some
connection between the two.

The dPal rTSe District had only about ten Government families, with a single Headman, and about seven more attached to
the nobility of the area. This smallest district seems to have been
the preserve of the noble family sKu Drung dPal rTSe, whose

nobility dated from the last half of the eighteenth century.[16] One member of the family resigned a high position in the capital to replace his deceased brother as District Officer.

The dPal lDan rTSe District had about twenty Government families with two or three Headmen and twenty families with allegiance to the palaces. The district occupied the lower half of the valley whose upper half was the dPal rTSe District, and it was directly bordered by the District Offices of rMa Bya on the north and CHu aDus on the south. There were no prominent families in the district, and it was not recalled who had recently occupied the position of District Officer. We can only speculate that the district's existence and extent were somehow connected with the establishment, for reasons not connected with administrative rationality, of the districts surrounding it.

CHu aDus was another small district, with about fifty families divided four to one between the Government and the Religious Establishment, and with perhaps two Government Headmen. The District Office with its cluster of about twenty families was on the east bank of the PHu River, and the rest of the district's territory extended northward along the west bank. It had no nobility, its Officers were not remembered, and again we can only guess that its reason for being was connected with the creation of its neighboring districts.

The five smaller districts had only one-third of the total population outside the capital, and their average population was only about 22 per cent of the average population of the three northern districts. The presence of the three important noble families —Byang aGo, Ma Ba TSHogs, and sKu Drung dPal rTSe—was probably the key to this southern pattern of districts, even though three other such families—in Ga Ra, gYaa Lung, and KHra U—were not favored with District Offices. The only criticisms of the Sa sKya district as a device for allocating governmental authority on a territorial basis are that there were too

[16] The other noble family of the district, Brag sPe, gained this status only in 1948.

many small districts in the southern part of the country and that the rMa Bya District should not have included Ko CHag. The proliferation of districts, however, was not a serious matter; they had very low operating costs, and larger governmental units in this lightly populated area would have provided few advantages. The attachment of Ko CHag to the rMa Bya District, on the other hand, must have led to some inefficiency, but in the Sa sKya political system power and prestige were at least as important as administrative rationality.

X

The SHab District was exceptional because of its relatively large and rich population, its concentration of noble families, and its administrative arrangements. After the capital, the SHab Valley was the most populous locality in Sa sKya; and because of its favorable land and climate, it was the most prosperous of all. This economic advantage was most probably connected with the presence of ten noble families and perhaps a handful of formerly noble families, and it created at least ten quite wealthy subject families.[17] These prominent families created a problem for the Sa sKya government because they naturally had to be treated most circumspectly, particularly because of their influence upon the subjects in their immediate vicinities. In Sa sKya the residence of a wealthy noble or subject was usually the nucleus of a grouping of lesser families, who looked to their established neighbor for aid and protection.[18] The government had to compete, as it were, with the local notables for the attention of these subjects.

The SHab District Office was established well before the split in the royal aKHon family in the eighteenth century, and it was supposed to have replaced one of the branch palaces that the

[17] Only two of these prominent families—dPe rGyal sDe Pa Lags and SHar ZHabs Pad—could not be located on Map 3.

[18] This is in addition to any families that had allegiance to a nobleman. Compare the centripetal force of the Burmese man of *pon*, in Manning Nash, *The Golden Road to Modernity* (New York: John Wiley, 1965), pp. 85 ff.

royal family had occasionally set up. It appears that the SHab Valley was made a district and thus put under direct governmental control in order to counterbalance the power of its prominent families. This power was only partially checked, however, because in addition to the centripetal attraction described above, the administrative arrangement of the SHab District favored vested local interests over those of the central government.

The district had six rather irregular subdivisions.[19] There was a Government Headman in only one of them, but the other five had what might be called "unofficial headmen." A single family in each subdivision, three noble families and two subject families, always provided the man who functioned in this semi-official capacity.[20] These five men were expected to mediate disputes, to help the poor and unlucky, and to report any serious crimes to the SHab District Officer and cooperate with him in handling them. If their people requested it, they were supposed to help in the collection of revenue and to request adjustments of the revenue schedule. These five men were not chosen by the subjects nor appointed by the government, and hence they were not entitled to any insignia of office. It was said that if the subjects had wanted help in approaching the Government or Religious Establishment, they would have had to organize among themselves in order to approach their "unofficial headman." From what we learned about the Headmen of Sa sKya, these people of SHab were at a definite disadvantage.[21]

The only Headman in the SHab District was a member of the prominent subject family Bar sDings sDe Pa Lags. This family had formerly been hereditary Headmen with accompanying noble status. Although in recent times Headmen in Sa sKya were neither hereditary nor noble, it would have been very surprising

[19] They were called "TSHo."

[20] The five families were KHro mGar, CHos sDings, Klu Ba, Gar SHong, and Nang bSam Pa.

[21] In Ko CHag the families of KHa Gung and aGro mGon also provided "unofficial headmen."

if the Headman of this subdivision of SHab had come from some other family. This is another example of the retention of power by the local notables against the centralizing influence of the capital.[22]

The District Officer at SHab was said to have had an uncommonly difficult job that involved constant negotiations with the families of power and prestige. Since the SHab Valley was the richest area of Sa sKya, the District Officer there also had a greater opportunity for personal enrichment, as will be seen in section XII. From every point of view, who occupied this office was a matter of some importance.

Sometime before 1936 a member of a fairly well-established SHab subject family was appointed District Officer. In 1947 he was replaced by a former monk named Bar Ma THogs Med, who came from a rTSe gDong family with allegiance to a nobleman. As a monk in a rTSe gDong monastery, he gained a reputation as a scholar, a man of affairs, and an outspoken, politically minded independent. He eventually renounced his vows and took Government land in rTSe gDong, but the news that such an astute and learned man had left the monkhood soon reached the capital and he was sent for. The sequence of events then becomes unclear, but at one point Bar Ma was offered a high governmental position carrying noble status, which he refused in order to take or to continue in the position of District Officer at SHab. (It might be surmised that he refused noble rank because his background had tempered his admiration of the nobility.) In any event, as District Officer he gained a reputation of fearlessness in his dealings with the SHab nobility (over such official matters as the transport levy [23]) and with officials of noble rank from the capital who came through the SHab District requesting or demanding special treatment. He always main-

[22] Our respondents believed that the presence of so many local notables in SHab would have made it impossible to get Headmen for all the subjects of the district.

[23] See Chapter 9, section VIII, and Appendix D, section I.

tained that he was on the side of the subjects and this reportedly made him quite popular among them.[24] Bar Ma was a professional administrator in a position that called for one.

XI

In the Sa sKya governmental organization the District Officer occupied a low rank, just above the Headman and equal to that of the valet of the KHri CHen's wife; the valets of the male members of the ruling family had a greatly superior status.[25] This ranking indicates several aspects of a polity with a hereditary ruler; the physical persons of royalty have the greatest symbolic and practical importance; prestige is a function of nearness to the source of governmental power; and the officials directly responsible for the welfare and mundane obligations of the ordinary member of the polity are not held in very high esteem. This last attitude is not to be explained solely as an expression of indifference to the well-being of the mass of the governed. It is more a reflection of the limited perspective of this kind of government, which neither expects much from its subjects nor conceives of doing much for them.

The position of District Officer also carried only a rather small official remuneration in the form of a parcel of land to be farmed by the District Officer or his family or let out to sharecroppers. District Officers, however, also received the gifts that in Sa sKya were *de rigueur* but never openly acknowledged. These gifts no doubt provided some consolation for the District Officers, and

[24] Bar Ma's reputation led the Chinese Communists to contact him, but they had no success. They emphasized a concept—Mi dMangs (man populace)—that included everyone; he was defending the subjects (Mi Ser), a concept that implies a governing class.

[25] Under the Lhasa government "gZHis KHa"—which we have translated both "District" and "District Officer"—means "estate." The Lhasa title "gDZong dPon" is equivalent to the Sa sKya "gZHis KHa." The rank of the District Officer was "orange" Jo Lags (see Appendix C, section I).

Plate 4. The seal of the Sa sKya Government (*left*), used by the ZHabs Pad (prime minister), and the seal of the PHun TSHogs palace (*right*), used by the head of the palace.

Plate 5. The South Monastery (*center*), with the palaces of the royal family in the background. (See Map 5.)

Plate 6. Members of the KHri CHen's party during their trip to Lhasa in 1947 to obtain confirmation of the KHri CHen's accession to office: (*left to right*) dBon mDaa, secretary to the PHun TSHogs palace; Rang Byon, the KHri CHen's Valet; KHri CHen NGag dBang mTHu THub dBang PHyug; PHun KHang, the ZHabs Pad; and bDe CHen sGrol Ma, the rGyal Yum (wife of the KHri CHen).

the offices had enough local prestige and power to motivate certain noble families to retain control of a number of them.

The District Officers were appointed for indefinite tenure by the ZHabs Pad, and they were directly responsible to him. Some of the District Officer's functions have been described above in connection with the Headman. When a serious crime was committed, the District Officer investigated and, if the suspect had allegiance to the Government, turned him over to the capital. In unusually dry years, the District Officer had to preside with the Headmen over the allocation of water. He could utilize Government stores to relieve economic distress among the subjects under his jurisdiction, but no information was available on the frequency or generosity of such allocations. The Headmen of Sa sKya probably did what they could to help their people, and it is known that the capital provided very little economic aid. Although the District Officers were fairly close to the subjects, they probably did not give them any significant economic aid from Government supplies. There was a strong tendency in Sa sKya to accumulate—a tendency that will be examined later— and no District Officer would have lightly depleted the Government stores for which he alone was responsible.

In disputes involving debts, contracts, and so forth, that the District Officer and Headman could not resolve because one party to the dispute proved intransigent, the District Officer could make clear to both parties that if he had to refer the case to the capital, he would do what he could to insure that whoever frustrated his attempt at mediation, by refusing to compromise, would lose the case. The capital gave considerable weight to the opinions of the District Officers in these situations; and hence, although the District Officer was supposed to act only as a mediator in these disputes, he had some of the power of the arbitrator who makes a binding decision.

Other functions of the District Officer were to provide the animals and men to transport officials of the Lhasa government through Sa sKya, and to receive the revenue schedules from the capital, transmit them to the Headmen, and check and store the revenue material received from the Headmen. Regarding revenue and other demands made upon the subjects, the District Officer, like the Headman, was supposed to serve as a buffer between the capital and the village and farm. He also collected and stored the seed grain and distributed it in the spring. The District Officer was not responsible for the maintenance of dams and canals for irrigation—these were viewed as belonging to the people who used them—but he had the authority to initiate new irrigation projects, levying material and labor from the local people without reference to the capital. If his project was beyond the capacity of local resources, he could request material from the capital; but since the capital was always most reluctant to draw from its stores, such requests were probably rather infrequent.

The District Officer, finally, was responsible for keeping the principal roads (Map 3) in passable condition, the main caravan route in both summer and winter and the others in summer only.[26] If damage to a road was minor, the District Officer and the Headman called upon the inhabitants of the immediate vicinity for labor, giving them their meals and a token payment. If the job required more than ten days of labor for more than a few people, the District Officer had to get the approval of the ZHabs Pad, who provided the meals and token wages. If necessary, the District Officer could ask the capital for building materials such as stone and timber. The District Officers who had jurisdiction over the territory through which the main caravan route passed had the authority to draft one member from every family in their districts for maintenance of the road. Probably none of the

---

[26] On Map 3, the main caravan route—from the SHab District Office to the capital to the CHu aDus District Office—is represented by a heavier line. During the Tibetan winter, roads in flat areas were ignored in favor of traveling over the frozen fields.

roads in Sa sKya was very well maintained, and the people were reported as being rather unenthusiastic about this chore.

XII

The District Officer was appointed for an indefinite period and was responsible only to the capital. He was socially more distant from his people than the Headman was from his, and it was more difficult for the subjects to influence his actions and decisions. One of the District Officers at SHab was reportedly very high-handed and demanded frequent and generous gifts from the subjects. Bringing gifts to District Officers was a normal practice in Sa sKya, but this man was not satisfied with the usual gifts, and he got rich by exporting to Shigatse the meat, eggs, and oil bullied from his people. Eventually the people of SHab began to complain, the more resentful threatening to leave the valley or even Sa sKya itself. On the basis of this unrest, the KHri Chen and the ZHabs Pad investigated, and ultimately, despite his desire to remain in office, the District Officer "was allowed to resign." This story suggests that the District Officers appointed by the capital to supervise the administratively rational districts were vulnerable to persistent pressure from the subjects. Such pressure, however, was probably much less effective against the hereditary District Officers.

Every person with allegiance to the Government had the right to send a petition directly to the ZHabs Pad or the KHri CHen or both, provided that he had made at least two attempts to get his Headman and District Officer to act on his problem. Such petitions obviously indicated "disharmony," and it was said that the ZHabs Pad's natural action upon receiving one was to write to the Headman or District Officer inquiring about his ability to handle his job. Little evidence was disclosed regarding the frequency and effectiveness of these petitions, although occasions were remembered when the subjects of dMigs, SHab, and rTSe gDong bypassed their local officials and made direct contact with the capital. Since the distances in Sa sKya were short and everybody knew someone who could write a petition, this right to appeal over the heads of the local officials was probably not a completely ineffective check upon their doing things not approved by the capital.[27]

XIII

Four areas of Sa sKya outside the capital were not organized into districts. These were Ga Ra, Mang mKHar, gYaa Lung, and KHra U, containing about 13 per cent of the nonherding families outside the capital (Maps 2, 3, and 4). These four areas had small populations, but no smaller than the populations of half the districts. Mang mKHar and KHra U were isolated; Ga Ra and gYaa Lung were on the main caravan route.

Mang mKHar contained about twenty families owing allegiance to the Government, ten to the Religious Establishment, and twenty to the palaces. There were probably two Headmen in the area, but it had no nobles and no subject families of unusual wealth and prestige. The monastery of THub bsTan dGe aPHel was the most prominent feature of Mang mKHar, but the monastery officials had no dealings whatever with the Headmen or any other governmental personnel. (They were willing, however, to serve as mediators in private disputes.) South and east of the agricultural population were many herding families who probably had some Headmen of their own. All Headmen in the area reported directly to the capital.

The area of KHra U was also isolated. It contained about twenty-four Government families and twelve Religious Establishment families, with probably only one Headman among them. KHra U was the home of the formerly noble family gZims dPon, which, although it had lost certain special privi-

[27] In the nineteenth century, a District Officer of dPal lDan rTSe joined his people in opposition to the capital. Unfortunately, nothing was known about the incident.

leges, retained its dominance in its small locality. Indeed, this family—and the two noble families of Ga Ra and gYaa Lung—had a semi-official status comparable to that of the "unofficial headmen" of the SHab Valley described above. The Headmen in KHra U, Ga Ra, and gYaa Lung always notified the heads of these families of any unusual event, such as a serious crime or damage to government property, and they consulted with them when serious disputes or undue economic hardship occurred among the subjects. These "leading citizens" could use none of the techniques and none of the resources of the government. They could not, for example, in cooperation with a Headman punish anyone, nor could they draft labor or request material from the capital; they relied on their personal wealth and prestige to help stabilize their immediate neighborhoods.

The area of gYaa Lung contained about seventeen Government families, eight Religious Establishment families, nine palace families, and four families with allegiance to the noble family of the area, Lug Rags. The area of Ga Ra contained about thirty Government families, a few Religious Establishment families, and four families with allegiance to the noble family PHu SHar bKra SHis sGang. Each area had probably two Headmen, who worked with the nobility as did the Headmen of KHra U. Because the main caravan route went through these areas, these nobles had the additional responsibility of arranging for the transport of Sa sKya and Lhasa governmental officials.

South of gYaa Lung and north of Ga Ra were concentrations of herding families, with their own Headmen who reported directly to the capital. One of these Headmen from the sMau Valley used to visit the PHun TSHogs palace whenever he came to the capital. After presenting the KHri CHen with a small gift and receiving a blessing, the Headman would sit for some time with the KHri CHen and his family while they questioned him about conditions and events in sMau. Tibetans were always starved for news, and no social distance ever stood in the way of its communication.

XIV

As with most capitals, Sa sKya gDan Sa had its own system of
dealing with the governmental problems handled elsewhere by
Headmen and District Officers. This system applied to the area
shown in Map 5, but at aKHril sPe there was a Headman who
had charge of about forty Government families in his immediate
vicinity and about forty more in and near the CHos aKHor
lHun Po village (Map 3). In his territory there were also about
fourteen families with allegiance to the palaces and perhaps
twenty with allegiance to the Religious Establishment. The
aKHril sPe Headman reported directly to the ZHabs Pad and
cooperated closely with the capital concerning matters such as
the levy for transporting official dignitaries. He was much more
closely tied to the capital than were other Headmen.

The people of the capital were directly under the authority of
the ZHabs Pad in all those areas of governmental activity described above in connection with the Headmen and the District
Officers. The only officials between the subjects of the capital
and the ZHabs Pad in the governmental hierarchy were two
Group Officials, whose office had apparently evolved from the
office of Headman.[28] The Group Officials had less power than
Headmen; their principal authority concerned the distribution
of water for irrigation. The Group Officials had the same "Jo
Lags" rank as the Headmen, thus being fully authorized members of the governmental hierarchy, and like the Headmen they
received no formal pay, but only gifts and favors from their
people. The work of the two Group Officials was not divided
territorially or functionally; both dealt in the same capacities
with the same people.

Before 1945 disputes among the subjects of the capital had to
be referred first to the Group Officials, even though, unlike
Headmen, they had no authority to make final decisions in any
kind of case, and even though they could not, like the District

---

[28] One of the Group Officials had the title sDe Pa Lags (see note 3,
above).

Officers, threaten to work against a recalcitrant when his case was referred to higher authority. Our respondents estimated that a Group Official of average ability solved about 40 per cent of the disputes that came to his attention, and that a superior Group Official could settle about half of them.

In about 1945 the KHri CHen issued a special order allowing the subjects of the capital, if they were dissatisfied with the Group Officials' handling of their affairs, to go directly to one of the four Liaison Officers. The Liaison Officers (described in the next chapter) were high officials who had direct contact with both the ZHabs Pad and the KHri CHen. When we suggested to our respondents that the average subject might have had some difficulty approaching such august personages, the answer was that the Liaison Officers were very approachable men—"that was part of their job." This qualification for high office and the assumption that subjects in the capital had every right and every opportunity to speak directly to its occupants are good indications of the effect of the small size of the polity upon the relations between its governors and its governed.

Any dispute or other disturbance in the capital brought to the attention of the Liaison Officers, either directly or after the Group Officials had failed to settle it, was under the governmental authority of the ZHabs Pad. The Liaison Officers also were unable to make any final decisions. They served only as mediators of high prestige, but (like the District Officers) they could testify against recalcitrants should their efforts at unofficial settlement prove unsuccessful. The Group Officials, for their part, assumed a responsibility for keeping alert to any source of trouble and for unofficially intervening before matters became serious. The arrangement regarding all disputes, therefore, was that both the Group Officials and the Liaison Officers, although neither could make official decisions, did what they could to prevent problems being brought to the ZHabs Pad. The ZHabs Pad, of course, automatically took charge of serious crimes.

The 7,000 inhabitants of the capital were related in different ways to the Group Officials, the Liaison Officers, and the ZHabs

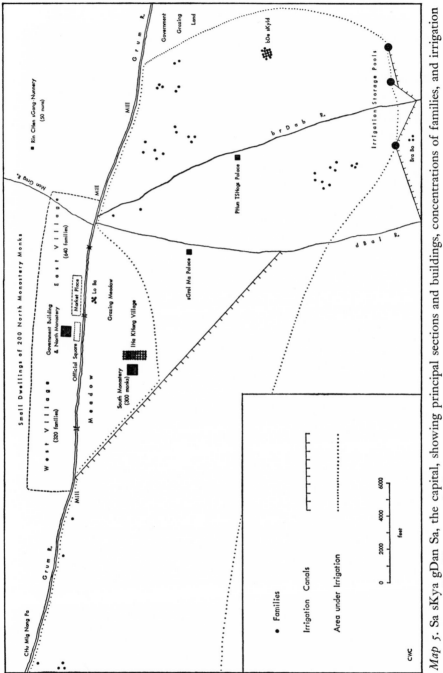

Map 5. Sa sKya gDan Sa, the capital, showing principal sections and buildings, concentrations of families, and irrigation arrangements. (See Plates 1 and 5.)

Chu Mig Nang Po

Grum R.

Small Dwellings of 200 North Monastery Monks

Rin Chen sGong Nunnery (50 nuns)

West Village (320 families)

Government Building & North Monastery

Official Square

Market Place

Meadow

Mon Grog R.

Mill

Mill

Lo Ba

Grazing Meadow

East Village (640 families)

South Monastery (300 monks)

lHa KHang Village

Grum R.

Government Grazing Land

bDa sKyid

brDab R.

Phun TSHogs Palace

sGrol Ma Palace

Irrigation Storage Pools

Bra Bo

dBal R.

Families

Irrigation Canals

Area under Irrigation

0   2000   4000   6000

feet

CWC

Pad. About 950 were monks, nuns, members of noble families, officials, and "foreigners," [29] none of whom were under the regular authority of the governing agencies. There were approximately 1,030 families of subjects engaged in agriculture who had the following allegiances: 13 to local noblemen, 106 to the palaces, 228 to the Religious Establishment, and 685 to the Government.[30] Revenue in kind was collected directly by each establishment from its subjects, from Government families by two officials appointed on a yearly basis by the ZHabs Pad. The Group Officials took no official part in the collection of revenue, but they did what they could to help the subjects meet their revenue responsibilities and to make sure that everyone kept enough seed grain for the next year, for the farmers of the capital, unlike those elsewhere, kept their own seed. The Group Officials also helped maintain the census of the capital population for revenue purposes.

The Group Officials offered their good offices and utilized their prestige to assist in solving disputes among the Government and Religious Establishment families; they had many fewer contacts, however, with the subjects of the palaces and the nobility, who reserved this function for themselves. The two Group Officials served as mediators for more than one thousand families.

The Group Officials, in cooperation with the aKHril sPe Headman and under the direction of the Transportation Official, organized the work levy to provide transport for traveling officials. In this capacity, they dealt again with about one thousand families, including those who lived to the south of the capital (Map 5). The same arrangements applied for labor levied

[29] The "foreigners" were the "Nepalese" (see Chapter 3, section VI).
[30] The 7,000 inhabitants of the capital consisted (approximately) of: royalty (2 families, of 10 each), 20 people; palace officials, all monks, 25; nobility (7 families, of 10 each), 70; monks and nuns, other than palace officials, 550; government officials and dependents, 65; minor officials and government menials, 20; servants of the palaces (15 families, of 5 each), 75; shopkeepers (36 "Nepalese" families, of 5 each), 180; artisans (167 families, of 5 each), 835; and farmers (1,030 families, of 5 each), 5,160.

to maintain government buildings, a task supervised by the Building Official.[31]

The Group Officials were also responsible for organizing the four troops of singers and dancers who performed for two days each in an annual summer ceremony designed to placate the gods that controlled hail.

XV

The principal responsibility of the two Group Officials was to supervise the use and maintenance of the pools and canals of the capital's irrigation system. As diagramed in Map 5, there were three of these storage pools.[32] The two to the east were used to irrigate the area bounded by the Grum River, the brDab River, and the dotted line to the east. The westernmost pool stored water for the area between the brDab River and the dBal River; this pool was normally supplied by water from the brDab, but when this river was low, water was taken from the dBal. Water from the dBal River was normally used to irrigate most of the area west of the long canal that joined the dBal with the Grum, and hence in unusually dry seasons it was necessary to divide water between the land to the east and the land to the west of the dBal. All three rivers, in addition, were directly tapped for irrigation.

The two Group Officials were jointly responsible for the entire system of irrigation. Each spring they personally inspected the pools and all the canals; and if any repair was needed, they levied labor from the more than one thousand families who worked land in the area. This levy of labor was the only one in Sa sKya that included families with allegiance to the palaces, no doubt because administrative divisions were impractical among a population so economically interdependent. Anyone who failed

[31] The Transportation and Building Officials are described in Chapter 5, section II; the transport levy in Chapter 9, section VIII, and Appendix D, section I.

[32] For another account of this system, see Robert B. Ekvall and James F. Downs, "Notes on Water Utilization and Rule in the Sakya Domain —Tibet," *Journal of Asian Studies*, XXII (1963), 293–303.

to do his share of work on the irrigation system had only to pay a small fine; the Group Officials used this income to buy refreshments for the more conscientious.

It was estimated that water from the storage pools was required in six or seven years out of ten, with a minimum of three and a maximum of six openings during each dry season. The Group Officials had full authority, with no need for approval from any higher official, to open the gates of the pools; anyone else caught taking water was fined or flogged. The usual procedure was for farmers in need of water to approach the Group Officials, who then jointly announced that the gates would be opened at dawn on a given date. They did not supervise the distribution of water to the farmers in need, who had to help themselves, but after surveying the area, they decided when the gates were to be closed.

The decision to divert water from the dBal River into the western storage pool was also made by the Group Officials. This diversion usually decreased the supply of water to the farmers to the west of the river, and hence it was a possible source of conflict between them and the farmers to the east of the river. Since the land in the capital was randomly divided among the several establishments, people of the same establishment could find themselves on opposing sides in such conflicts. The Group Officials' decisions regarding this diversion of water could be appealed to the Liaison Officers, and then to the ZHabs Pad. Appeals were rare, but one appeal to a Liaison Officer was recalled.

All these arrangements for supplying water provided many opportunities for disputes among the subjects. Sometimes private mediators could resolve them; when private mediation was not feasible or had failed, the Group Officials took over. If the Group Officials also failed, the dispute went to the Liaison Officers. If they in turn failed, it could be referred to the ZHabs Pad, but apparently the Liaison Officers' prestige (and their desire not to bother the ZHabs Pad) enabled them to settle virtually all disputes referred to them.

During the growing season in the capital a number of semi-official people kept watch over the growing crops. They were ordinary farmers serving on a rotation basis and loosely under the authority of the Group Officials. Their job was to check on anything that might injure the crops, such as stray animals, to try to settle any disputes among the farmers, and to report on problems such as human and animal sickness. They also were on the alert for illicit sexual relations in the fields and for illegitimate pregnancies, because these were invitations to supernatural retribution in the form of hail.[33]

XVI

The method of selecting the Group Officials resembled that of choosing Headmen, but consensus was not insisted upon. When a Group Official was to be chosen, the ZHabs Pad notified the people of the capital that an assembly was to be held to select candidates. Every family of subjects, except those with allegiance to the palaces, sent a representative or a formal proxy to the assembly; those who did not had to pay a fine. Once again the governing of the capital required the combination of people with different allegiances, although it was inconsistent to make the palace subjects responsible for working on the irrigation system and not to allow them a voice in the selection of the Group Officials.

These assemblies were held in summer in the meadow on the south bank of the Grum River and in winter in the official square on the north bank (Map 5).[34] About one thousand people attended, bringing refreshments, and they soon grouped themselves according to their preferences for the several candidates whose qualifications had usually been informally but thoroughly discussed prior to the assembly. Several unofficial and sponta-

[33] Illegitimate birth during the growing season was the offense. Expectant mothers without husbands were obliged to leave the area until the crop had been harvested, when they were free to return.

[34] Our respondents witnessed the selection of Group Official AH Ma in 1947.

neous leaders went from group to group, writing down the names of the candidates and the amounts of their support. They always attempted to narrow the number of candidates, but three to five men usually remained in contention. The large number of people involved in this process of selection prevented the consensus expected and usually achieved in the selection of Headmen.

When the number of candidates was fixed, their names were put on a "consensus paper," without any indication of their respective amounts of support, and the paper was sent to the ZHabs Pad. The ZHabs Pad, in consultation with the KHri CHen, selected one of the candidates as the new Group Official.

In the late 1940's the two Group Officials were Lo Ba Don sGrub and AH Ma Zla Ba Don sGrub. Both were from well established Government families that were prosperous but not wealthy. Our respondents considered AH Ma to have been a most able official, suited for much higher governmental positions. Before he became Group Official, he had gained a high reputation as a mediator, conciliator, and persuader. He was personally very popular and was a skillful singer, dancer, and musician.

XVII

Governmental power and authority in Sa sKya were allocated in a way that allowed lower officials to make very few final decisions. This arrangement was consistent with two basic beliefs about the nature of government: first, the emphasis upon "harmony," which led to the attempt to resolve minor disturbances through the process of mediation, without resort to the power of government; and, second, the belief that the power that defined government had to remain concentrated in order to persist, which led to the rather pronounced autocracy of the KHri CHen and the ZHabs Pad. The relative weakness of lower officials in Sa sKya may not, however, have been too inefficient in such a small polity, where personal contacts between subjects and officials were always possible.

Chapter 5

Central Government

The division of governmental functions among the several establishments in Sa sKya resulted in a rather confusing formal structure of government, but it did not seriously affect the autocratic power of the KHri CHen, the hereditary monarch, and the ZHabs Pad, his grand vizier. The Sa sKya hereditary nobility directly controlled about 3 per cent of the subjects, and the two palaces about 9 per cent.[1] Hence only 12 per cent of the people of Sa sKya were not governed by the officials of the Government and of the Religious Establishment described in this chapter. Ultimately, however, all the subjects were under the control of the royal family, and the ZHabs Pad was its principal agent in governmental matters.

About 20 per cent of the subjects in Sa sKya had their allegiance to the Religious Establishment. Its head, the Steward, was directly responsible to the KHri CHen and cooperated closely with the ZHabs Pad; the Religious Establishment was in effect a separately organized branch of the Government. The Government itself not only had direct control of 68 per cent of the people of Sa sKya and partial control of the remaining 32 per cent, but it also was the gZHung, the manifestation of the governmental function. Although the governing of Sa sKya was in detail rather diffuse, it was quite concentrated regarding important matters.

Although the KHri CHen was the only person who could

[1] The operations of the nobility as an establishment are described in Chapter 8, of the palaces in Appendix A, section 2.

innovate in governmental affairs, the day-to-day business of governing was conducted by the ZHabs Pad, who authorized almost all decisions and himself made a large proportion of them. These two most important offices will be examined in Chapter 7. In the present chapter, the other officials of the central government, who were in effect the assistants of the KHri CHen and the ZHabs Pad, will be described. Their functions and responsibilities, the manner of their appointment, their power and prestige, and their backgrounds are all both interesting and important.

I

The governmental apparatus of the capital consisted of about forty full-time employees, eleven officials of Jo Lags rank,[2] and thirty-nine officials of the highest rank. The employees were about twenty janitors and servants assigned to the government offices in the Government Building and the South Monastery (Map 5); two or three grooms for the Government's horses; five or six jailers; six men who were both policemen and floggers; and a steward, who had seven assistants, to wait on the Law Officials and to feed prisoners. Each year an additional sixteen men, drawn from the general population, were charged with keeping order at the capital during the New Year's celebrations.[3] Among the officials of Jo Lags rank were two men responsible for welcoming and housing important guests to the capital; seven heads of the artisans who worked for the Government; and the man in charge of the attendants in the government buildings. Other Jo Lags officials will be described throughout the present chapter.

The highest rank of officials had a status called "sKu Drag"; unlike the status of Jo Lags, it was intended to indicate a large social distance between the official and the subject. The word

[2] The rank of Headmen and District Officers (see Chapter 4 and Appendix C, section I).

[3] It is interesting that these men were called the "law ones" (KHrims Pa). See Chapter 6, section XIV.

"sKu" means "body" (an honorific), and "Drag" means "fierce" or "frightful"—an interesting way to describe governmental officials. sKu Drag status was probably hereditary at one time, but at least in the last several generations subjects as well as hereditary nobility gained the status by being appointed to high office.[4]

The status of sKu Drag contained gradations of rank, but all these ranks together formed a social stratum with a prestige surpassed only by the royal family and the highest officials of the monasteries. Although many sKu Drag officials were monks who shaved their heads, the most important symbol of sKu Drag status was the hair worn piled on the head in a topknot; the significance of the topknot is illustrated by the Panchen Lama's request that his officials be allowed to wear it. A Sa sKya sKu Drag official was once seized to prevent his committing an act of violence; before anyone of lower status could touch him, men of his own rank had to pull down his topknot.[5]

On formal occasions, sKu Drag who were laymen wore long satin robes and those who were monks wore the usual monk's costume.[6] The formal insignia identifying these high officials were special hats topped by buttons of different colors according to rank. Only the ZHabs Pad, for example, wore a coral-colored button. sKu Drag officials were addressed by a special honorific —"sKu NGo," literally "body-face"—and they received other formal signs of respect from the subjects.

[4] On the hereditary nobility and the status of sKu Drag, see Chapter 8, section II.

[5] The topknot is linked to the Tantric symbol of the thunderbolt. A less authoritative tradition is that it dates from one of the early kings of Tibet, who was a vigorous persecutor of the Buddhists and used this hair style to conceal his horns. On the incident regarding the Panchen Lama, see Chapter 2, section VI.

[6] A curious variation of official costume concerned sKu Drag who had formerly been monks. They could grow topknots and dress like lay sKu Drag, or they could continue to shave their heads and adopt, in place of monk's clothing, a special costume in the Mongolian style; they were thus called the Sog CHas, or "Mongolians." There were two such "Mongolians" in Sa sKya in the 1940's.

Service as a sKu Drag official did not affect the religious and organizational standing of a monk. Although an official position occupied all of a monk's time, he could without any formalities rejoin his monastery upon leaving governmental service. The principal purpose for using monks as Sa sKya governmental officials no doubt was to obtain men of ability.[7] The high individualism of Tibetan monastic orders allowed monks to accept the opportunity of serving in the Government and other establishments, a service that had a high priority in the culture.

In answer to persistent questioning, our respondents were emphatic that Sa sKya could not have been governed without officials of sKu Drag status. Without this differential in prestige between officials and subjects, how could the subjects be controlled? An aphorism was offered: "There is no religion without monks, and no government without [sKu Drag] officials." The social distance between governors and governed in Sa sKya seems to have been greater than in the politically disorganized areas of eastern Tibet and less than in the larger polity ruled from Lhasa.[8]

II

The status of sKu Drag was possessed by nine officials of the Religious Establishment, a dozen or more officials connected with the royal family, twenty-three officials of the Government, and from five to thirteen candidate officials.

The lowest level of sKu Drag officials of the Government consisted of the ten offices of what was called the Work Corps: [9] the Military Official, the Sedan Official, the Equerry, the Fuel Official, the Building Official, the Transportation Official, the

[7] Pedro Carrasco, in *Land and Polity in Tibet* (Seattle: University of Washington Press, 1959), p. 83, says that the Lhasa government divided responsibility of office between laymen and monks as a means of checking power. We discovered nothing similar in Sa sKya.

[8] Judgments based on our respondents' personal experiences.

[9] For the formal rankings of Sa sKya secular and monastic officials, see Appendix C, section II.

Government Steward, the Fodder Official, the Doorman for the ZHabs Pad, and the Liaison between the KHri CHen and the monasteries. These positions were formally of equal status; precedence in such matters as seating was determined by seniority in the corps.

Eight of these offices involved the supply of material, facilities, and labor, and two—the Doorman and the Liaison Official—handled personal contacts for the highest dignitaries. The functions of the Military Official were so slight that in the 1940's the job was performed by the man who was also the Equerry. None of the jobs specifically attached to the positions in the Work Corps fully occupied the incumbents; much of their time was spent fulfilling *ad hoc* assignments given them by the ZHabs Pad. All members of the Work Corps, except the Sedan Official, were appointed and dismissed by the ZHabs Pad without reference to the KHri Chen, but the KHri CHen, if he so desired, could make the final decisions.

Once each year the Military Official received from the ZHabs Pad the requests of the Lhasa government for military personnel and supplies. He then contacted the District Officer or Headman whose turn it was to supply the two or three yearly conscripts, or he selected the men himself if they were to come from the capital. He also arranged with all local officials to collect the small levy in money and kind for Sa sKya's share of the support of the Lhasa army. The Military Official kept 5 per cent of the goods and money he collected, and he was himself exempt from this levy.[10]

The Sedan Official was responsible for the transportation of the KHri CHen by sedan chair. He kept this chair in good repair; he selected, trained, and supervised the men and the mules that bore the KHri CHen when, perhaps twice a month, he left his palace; and he always rode by the chair and personally

[10] During the period of Sa sKya's Tibet-wide power, there was a dMag dPon (soldier official) who ranked higher than the Work Corps. The position of Military Official replaced this office.

directed the operation.[11] The KHri CHen always personally approved the appointment of this man who was responsible for his bodily safety. The Sedan Official had an assistant of Jo Lags rank; one of his duties was to precede the chair to inspect the road and arrange for a proper reception at settlements.

The Equerry was in charge of the horses and mules of the Government and the two palaces. He was responsible for their breeding, and he supervised their care in the stables in the east village in the winter and on the Government grazing land in the summer (Map 5). He also organized the annual horse races in which all officials, from the lowest Jo Lags to the ZHabs Pad, were supposed to have an entry. These races were very big and very competitive affairs. (One legend has it that the split in the ruling family originated from bad feeling over a horse race.) The organization of the races was a real responsibility. Our respondents insisted that the Equerry was a very important official because in controlling the horses he controlled the single most concentrated source of physical power in the principality. As we will show, however, there was little possibility that the Equerry (or anyone else) was capable of using physical power to challenge the regime.[12]

The Fuel Official was in charge of collecting, storing, and providing fuel for the Government Building, the South Monastery, and the two palaces. The fuel was principally cattle and sheep droppings, with some laurel-type brush used as kindling. It came principally in the form of revenue in kind from the herders, and the Fuel Official kept a small proportion for himself.

The Building Official was responsible for the structural main-

---

[11] There were eight human bearers, who worked in brief shifts of four and made their changes without losing a stride. They bore the KHri CHen when the road was rough or the distance short and when the proper style was required on approaching a settlement. At other times, the mules took over. The human bearers were by custom always from aKHril sPe, the home of the family sKye PHrang NGa, whose ancestor was a sedan-bearer for aPHags Pa. Sedan-bearing was a full-time job.   [12] See Chapter 12.

tenance of the Government Building, the South Monastery, the two palaces, and some of the monks' quarters and small shrines on the hillside behind the east and west villages (Map 5). He maintained a continuous inspection of these structures and supervised their annual whitewashing and painting. He had charge of stores of wood, stone, and adobe brick, but he needed the authorization of the ZHabs Pad to draw from them. The Building Official, again with the authorization of the ZHabs Pad, could call, through the Group Officials, for a work levy from the inhabitants of the capital and, if more labor was needed, he could notify the District Officers. He made some personal profit from the annual whitewashing and painting.

The Transportation Official arranged the levied transport facilities for personnel of the Government, the Religious Establishment, and the monasteries traveling on official business.[13] The traveler presented an authorization from the ZHabs Pad for the necessary men, animals, and equipment to the Transportation Official, who with the assistance of the Group Officials and the Headman of aKHril sPe levied them from the subjects of the area. If the traveler were as important as, say, the Chief Secretary, the Transportation Official contacted District Officers along the traveler's route, but lesser dignitaries arrived unannounced at outlying points.

The Government Steward had charge of the dishes, kitchen utensils, cutlery, and so forth in the Government Building and the South Monastery, some of which were very expensive. He had to be ready to produce the proper service at any time for unexpected but important guests.

The Fodder Official collected feed for the horses of the Government and the palaces, and was in charge of the Government's grazing land in the capital area.

The Doorman for the ZHabs Pad was posted outside the ZHabs Pad's office and announced all visitors. His job was little

[13] The transport levy is explained in some detail in Chapter 9, section VIII, and Appendix D, section I.

more than a formality, although he could occasionally impede or expedite appointments. The Doorman also handled the offerings to the "wrathful deities," which provided him with a little extra income.

The Liaison between the KHri CHen and the monasteries was a Government official appointed by the ZHabs Pad, although his job required him to report to the KHri CHen. His principal function was to inform the monasteries in Sa sKya that the KHri CHen was planning to visit them and to arrange for his proper reception. The Liaison usually retained for himself some of the material provided by the monasteries for religious offerings on these occasions.

III

The specific tasks of the Work Corps officials were not especially important, but at least in recent times they were not intended to be. The Work Corps, as its name suggests, was basically a pool of officials available for any job that the ZHabs Pad might need performed. They were sent with important messages; they investigated serious crimes, crop conditions, economic hardship, and other unusual circumstances anywhere in Sa sKya; they were sent to Lhasa and Shigatse for the periodic exchanges of courtesies; they greeted important visitors to the capital; they supervised the "great assembly distributions"; [14] and they handled the revenue in kind paid by the subjects of the capital. They had no permanent offices of their own; when not attending to their specific tasks and not on *ad hoc* assignments, they sat on call in a large room in the Government Building or the South Monastery. They remained available as long as the ZHabs Pad was in his office, even if this required missing a meal. As soon as the ZHabs Pad left for the day, the Work Corps immediately disappeared.

From the viewpoint of the Sa sKya royal family, the functions of the Work Corps officials were not very important and their

[14] Chapter 11, section X.

power within the governmental apparatus was rather slight. The ZHabs Pad appointed the Work Corps, without having to get the approval of the KHri CHen, and he dealt with it only indirectly through the Liaison Officers (described in section IV), thus maintaining a formal aloofness from it. According to Tibetan custom, very high officials had to refrain from rapid talk and expeditious action in order to maintain an aura of distance, dignity, deliberateness, and power.[15] The Work Corps was not considered high enough for such airs. The rewards for membership in the corps were the very desirable status of sKu Drag, an apparently modest income, association with government and hence the ability to tell people what to do, and the chance of promotion to a higher position. The normal line of advancement was through the Work Corps to higher offices, although as shown below there were many exceptions, especially during the reign of KHri CHen NGag dBang mTHu THub dBang PHyug.[16] Although membership in the Work Corps was desirable, it was not irresistible; in recent years several men resigned from the corps to take advantage of other opportunities.[17]

The Sa sKya system of government was quite autocratic, with the ZHabs Pad making most decisions, and hence someone had to

[15] As an example, our respondents said that for a Sa sKya official to accomplish a week's worth of business with the Lhasa government, he might have had to stay in that city for six months.

[16] A man who had been in the Work Corps, and who was considered an expert on governmental affairs, used to maintain that one should work his way slowly up the official hierarchy if he wished his power to be solidly based. Too rapid an advancement might only mean an equally rapid fall. This judgment seems sound enough, except in those cases where the official had the confidence of a KHri CHen interested in daily governmental affairs.

[17] A Transportation Official resigned to go into private business, and a Fuel Official to go to eastern Tibet with his stepson, who was a religious collector (see Chapter 11, section VIII); these resignations indicate a search for a better income. A Government Steward resigned to become the District Officer at Mus, and a District Officer at dMigs had resigned from the Corps of Candidates, also a sKu Drag position (see section VII, below).

be constantly available to carry out his orders. Since these execu-
tors were directly associated with the highest governmental
official, they had to be of high rank. The traditions associated
with government and the royal family, moreover, explain why
the rank of sKu Drag was given to men who maintained the
royal residences or the Government's tea service. Although the
members of the Work Corps had little power of initiative, their
enthusiasm and conscientiousness determined to a large extent
the short-term effectiveness of the governmental system. The
specific functions performed by each official were rather petty,
but they gave him some individual standing and security he
would not have had if the corps had been organized as no more
than a pool of factotums. Finally, the cost of the Work Corps
was not excessive, and it added to the dignity of the governmental apparatus.

IV

Between the Work Corps and the ZHabs Pad were thirteen
sKu Drag officials whose special functions constituted full-time
jobs. They were all appointed by the ZHabs Pad in consultation
with, or at least with the approval of, the KHri CHen.

The lowest in rank of these officials was the Archivist, who
had charge of the records kept in the Government Building. The
archives included population statistics, land records, revenue
schedules, records of all monastic and governmental personnel,
the reports of the Law Officials, and copies of all Religious
Establishment records. There were two indexes to the archives,
one kept by the Archivist and the other by the ZHabs Pad. No
records could be removed from the archives, and they could be
examined only on the authorization of the ZHabs Pad. The
Archivist also kept a written account of the daily activities of the
KHri CHen.

The position of the Archivist gave him little opportunity to
influence the course of governmental policy, although the
efficiency of the Government depended to some extent upon his

accuracy and thoroughness. His access to information was coun-
teracted by his isolation from other officials and from the subjects.[18]

At the next rank were four interesting and important officials,
the Liaison Officers. The principal function of these four officials,
who were formally equals, was to act as intermediaries for the
ZHabs Pad and to convey all communications to and from him.
The only people whom the ZHabs Pad met directly on a formal
basis were the Chief Secretary, the Steward of the Religious
Establishment, and the KHri CHen, although by special arrangement he would see any official informally. When the
ZHabs Pad was out of his office, he was always accompanied by
at least one Liaison Officer.

These four high-level intermediaries for the ZHabs Pad served
two purposes. They eliminated direct contacts between the man
who made the decisions and the men to whom the decisions
applied, an important function because Tibetans were very uneasy in face-to-face situations and whenever feasible used intermediaries. The Liaison Officers also kept the ZHabs Pad at the
proper social distance from lesser people in order to maintain an
aura of impersonal authority and power in the small polity and
to avoid improprieties such as a hesitation by the ZHabs Pad
or an expression of doubt by a subordinate or subject. The ZHabs
Pad needed some kind of insulation, and our respondents were no
doubt correct in their opinion that the device of the Liaison
Officer successfully provided it.

Although use of the Liaison Officers increased the chances of
accidental or intentional distortion in the chain of communication, they were not used for the most important communications. The highest officials dealt directly with one another, and
when a lower official or a private person had important informa-

[18] The Archivist replaced the Mi dPon (man official), a census-taker
and record-keeper of higher status during the period of Sa sKya's
Tibet-wide power.

tion, he bypassed the Liaison Officers and met informally with the ZHabs Pad.

As described in Chapter 4, the Liaison Officers were also responsible for maintaining harmony among the inhabitants of the capital, so they had to be approachable and skillful at mediation and pacification. In all their functions, they dealt directly with people, and principally with people who wanted something from the Government, if only the attention of the ZHabs Pad. Significantly, all of the seven men identified as having been Liaison Officers were laymen and from families of hereditary nobility. Perhaps monks were believed to lack insight into domestic affairs which Liaison Officers at any time might have been called upon to settle, and without doubt it was believed that noblemen had the poise, self-confidence, and dignity required of officials who dealt constantly with ordinary subjects. A former subject could perform satisfactorily in the Work Corps, where the jobs were not critical, or in the highest positions, where the prestige of the office sufficed to establish the dignity of its occupant. The Liaison Officers had themselves to supply at least part of their dignity.

Although nine officials formally outranked the Liaison Officers, only two—the Chief Secretary and the ZHabs Pad—had more power. As the normal channels of communication with the Government, the Liaison Officers naturally received many gifts. Since they were in constant contact with both officials and the subjects of the capital, they were very knowledgeable about affairs and personalities. And as the constant companions of the ZHabs Pad, they were in the public eye and associated with the personification of government. Their power was not great enough to shape the course of governmental policy, nor was it directed to this end. It was rather the power to influence rivalries and factions within the Government and especially to gain promotion to the highest offices of Chief Secretary and ZHabs Pad. Whenever a new Liaison Officer was to be appointed, the eligible lower officials were greatly excited. The appointment of a Liaison Officer was made only after personal consultation between the ZHabs Pad and the KHri CHen, with the Chief Secretary also usually in attendance.

V

At the next rank above the Liaison Officers were two formally equal Law Officials. Their judicial functions, in which they had a greater degree of independence from the ZHabs Pad than any other official of the Sa sKya Government, will be described in detail in Chapter 6. The Law Officials also were the only officials with a staff of their own, which they selected and discharged. The Law Officials received many gifts from people involved in cases before them, but our respondents said that they worked so hard they deserved this income.

There was no formal instruction in secular law in Sa sKya, so men who wanted to be Law Officials had to pick up the necessary knowledge of the Thirteen Pronouncements, the Sa sKya code, the customary law, and court procedure wherever they could. They were not allowed to attend sessions of the court, but they had access to the relevant documents, they could talk to the Law Officials and to the parties to cases, and they could participate in investigations in connection with cases. Unlike any other official, a Law Official upon retirement could recommend a replacement to the ZHabs Pad.

The staff of the Law Officials consisted of two court secretaries of Jo Lags rank, who recorded selected portions of the trials, made up the final reports of the trials, and drew up the terms of settlement; a steward to serve the Law Officials and handle the prisoners' rations; seven lackeys to help the steward and to maintain the courtroom; and six jailers and six policemen.

As specialists fully occupied in their specialty, the Law Officials had little opportunity to influence the course of governmental affairs. They had a great amount of influence upon the lives of the governed, but they had less power of innovation than judges in modern societies.

At the rank above the Law Officials were two formally equal Keepers of the Keys, who were in charge of the Government stores located under and beside the Government Building.[19] They carried the keys to these stores and also seals and wax used to seal the ropes that bound bales or bundles of various kinds of material. Only the ZHabs Pad, however, could authorize withdrawals from the stores; and when goods of some value were to be withdrawn, he accompanied the Keepers of the Keys to procure it. The ZHabs Pad also had the only complete inventory of these stores; it was kept by a Secretary and contained the sources of all additions to the stores and the reasons for all withdrawals. The Keepers of the Keys also had the keys to the Government Building, and each day they escorted the ZHabs Pad to his office.

The Keepers of the Keys were not especially important officials and they had little opportunity to influence the operation of government, although one of the most recent Keepers had established a reputation as an expert to be consulted on proper governmental procedure. Their high status was justified by reference to their possession of the symbols of government in the form of the keys and seals. In Sa sKya, moreover, there was a mild obsession with the accumulation of material goods, and this attitude may have contributed to the prestige of the men responsible for the stores.[20]

---

[19] These stores contained butter, tea, dried and frozen meat, dried fruit, salt, sugar, cotton and woolen cloth, satin, greeting scarves, tanned hides and leather, furs, brocade, silk, silver, gold, precious stones, and some rice, barley, and wheat. The Keepers of the Keys were not in charge of the great stores of revenue grain located near the South Monastery. On the sources of all this material, see Chapter 9.

[20] This tendency to accumulate is dealt with further in Chapter 12, section IV.

VI

Next in rank in the Sa sKya Government were the three formally equal Secretaries, who spent their entire time writing and copying governmental records and correspondence. They were occasionally assisted in routine copying by lower officials and Candidates, but to be official correspondence had to be written by the Secretaries themselves.

The high prestige of the Secretaries, who did no more than write what other people told them to write, came from their connection with the written word and especially from their close physical association with the ZHabs Pad, the personification of government. This prestige, combined with their access to all governmental records and correspondence, made the Secretaries natural candidates for higher office, especially if they had had some experience in more active positions such as Liaison Officer.[21] A Secretary had the great advantage of being well known to the ZHabs Pad and Chief Secretary, and perhaps even to the KHri CHen, but his position gave him little opportunity to prove himself an organizer and leader and to make a favorable impression among the lower officials and subjects. The Secretaries apparently had little influence on the conduct of government; at least they were not consulted on any important matters by the ZHabs Pad or the Chief Secretary. The position of Secretary, however, provided access to the system's most important decisions and to the men who made them.

The Chief Secretary was the highest Government official under the ZHabs Pad. His formal duties were to read all incoming correspondence, including letters addressed to the KHri CHen or the ZHabs Pad or both, and to check everything that the Secretaries wrote. He did no writing himself.

[21] SHar ZHabs Pad TSHe Ring dBang rGyal, the SHab nobleman who was the ZHabs Pad of Sa sKya from about 1916 until about 1937, was first a Liaison Officer and then a Secretary.

Although the Chief Secretary's formal duties had nothing to do with the actual business of governing and although the ZHabs Pad was in both theory and fact the head of the Government, every decision of the ZHabs Pad was supposed to represent the joint opinion of the two officials. This supposition was based on a reluctance, manifested in many areas of Sa sKya life, to give the appearance of taking individual initiative. At the two lower points in the governmental process where definitive decisions were made, the presumption in favor of consensus showed itself in the form of joint decisions: the Headman and the District Officer together punished recalcitrants in certain types of cases, and the two Law Officials together determined degrees of guilt and punishment.[22] Although the logic of governmental organization in the small polity led to the concentration of power in the hands of a single man, the ZHabs Pad, this logic could apparently be accepted only in conjunction with the fiction that the ZHabs Pad's decisions were really the decisions of two men.

The power of the Chief Secretary depended to a great extent upon his personal relationship with the ZHabs Pad, but, even if this were not too good, the prestige of the office and its access to information made the Chief Secretaryship the second most powerful Government office in Sa sKya. The man who was Chief Secretary from about 1915 until about 1937 worked closely with the ZHabs Pad of that period, and the two incumbents in the second half of the 1940's also cooperated closely. (There was no Chief Secretary from about 1936 to 1946.) The Chief Secretaryship and the Stewardship of the Religious Establishment were the offices from which a ZHabs Pad was most often selected.

Assuming mutual trust and confidence between the Chief Secretary and the ZHabs Pad, the Chief Secretaryship was probably a useful office. The ZHabs Pad had an experienced senior official

[22] On the Headman and District Officer, see Chapter 4, section V; on the Law Officials, see Chapter 6.

to consult with and to share his personal burden of final decision, but the authority and responsibility for these decisions were still his alone.

VII

Sa sKya officialdom also included a group of apprentice officials who were called the Corps of Candidates. There were usually at least five and not more than thirteen of these Candidates, who had no specific tasks to perform but who were given sKu Drag status.

Admission to the Corps of Candidates was granted by the KHri CHen on the recommendation of the ZHabs Pad to both nobles and subjects and both laymen and monks. Appointment as a Candidate meant that the appointee had committed himself to governmental service and to preparing himself for office while in candidacy, and that the Government had recognized him as a future official. Hence the Candidates were given sKu Drag status, even though they were not genuine officials. Entry into the corps was marked by a formal ceremony during which the initiate, if a layman, put on sKu Drag clothing and put up his hair in a topknot.[23] After the ceremony, his family gave a big party at which friends and relations offered him their formal congratulations.

Government officials usually began their careers in the Corps of Candidates and received their first regular appointments in the Work Corps, but there were many exceptions. Mature men who had experience in administering monasteries, or who had worked for other Tibetan governments, or who were outstanding economic successes, were occasionally brought directly into the Government or made officials after very brief terms as Candidates. (Appointments were also occasionally made from the staff of the Religious Establishment, but these officials had themselves usually been Candidates.) A young man could also spend the

[23] When a subject became a sKu Drag, he left the status of Mi Ser (see Chapter 3, section XIII).

normal minimum time of a year as a Candidate and then be appointed to a high office such as Secretary.

Acceptance to candidacy did not guarantee a governmental appointment, although there was a moderate turnover in the ranks of the Work Corps and Candidates could get appointments in the Religious Establishment and on the staffs of the palaces and of the KHri CHen. Candidates considered incompetent occasionally resigned their candidacies after several years of failing to get an appointment.

The Candidates were formally equal, with priority in matters such as seating determined by seniority in the corps. They had no superior or supervisor, but were expected to make themselves useful and to learn what they could. A Candidate with a special interest might have attached himself to some official or area of governmental concern; in the late 1940's, one of the secretaries of the Law Officials was a Candidate. The Candidates were also available, like the Work Corps, for special assignments from the ZHabs Pad, and when they were not occupied they were also supposed to be constantly on call outside the ZHabs Pad's office.

Young men became Candidates when they were about twenty years old, the normal age of marriage for laymen. Since Candidates received only token payment during candidacy, they were usually dependent on their families. This was a real burden if they came from outside the capital, and monks who could remain within the capital monasteries were at a definite advantage.

VIII

The Religious Establishment was an independent governmental hierarchy linked to the Government only at their highest levels. Its principal function was to provide the material means of support for the four to six hundred monks of the North and South Monasteries by collecting revenue in kind from the approximately 530 families who were its subjects. For some reason, probably because the right to collect revenue was seen as inseparable from civil and criminal jurisdiction, the Religious Establishment, through its Headmen and other officials, dealt with all the problems of its subjects until they reached the stage of reference to the Government's Law Officials.[24]

The Religious Establishment was headed by the Steward, an official of sKu Drag status whose prestige was only slightly lower than that of ZHabs Pad. A number of Headmen throughout Sa sKya reported to the Steward, and he had in the capital a full-time staff of eight sKu Drag officials and about twelve Jo Lags officials. He appointed, with the approval of the ZHabs Pad, all these officials. None of his sKu Drag officials were monks; perhaps it was believed that monks would have been more concerned with the standard of living in the monasteries than with the well-being of the subjects who helped support the monasteries. Two of the Religious Establishment's sKu Drag officials ranked with the Government's Liaison Officers, and the rest with the Work Corps. Neither the sKu Drag nor the Jo Lags officials had specific functions or titles; they all assisted the Steward as and when required. The sKu Drag came from both noble and subject families, and some were appointed from the Corps of Candidates. Younger men often acted as apprentices to the Jo Lags officials; frequently they were the sons or other younger relatives of these officials, another example of the principle of heredity at the lowest levels of officialdom.

The Steward of the Religious Establishment was always a monk in good standing in the North or South Monastery. When a Steward was to be appointed, the ZHabs Pad requested nominees from the two abbots who, after conferring with their subordinate officials, sent the names of not more than four men to the KHri CHen, who chose the Steward from this list. Two recent

[24]The origins of the Religious Establishment are most unclear. Its subjects could have been donated, as an act with religious merit, by the royal family, the Government, or the nobility. According to our respondents, the Religious Establishment in Sa sKya had less independence within the governmental structure than the religious establishment in Lhasa and more than the religious establishment in Shigatse.

appointments suggest that the KHri CHen could make sure that the name of his favorite was on the list; a ZHabs Pad could no doubt do the same.[25]

The functions of the Steward and his staff were similar to those of the officials of the Government, and they will be dealt with when appropriate in subsequent chapters. Since the Steward's job closely resembled that of the ZHabs Pad, it was excellent training for the highest office, and two of the most recent ZHabs Pad had previously been Stewards.[26]

The Steward usually maintained fairly close relations with the KHri CHen, with whom he consulted on religious affairs; and, at least in recent years, the Steward and the ZHabs Pad kept in close contact, discussing matters of mutual concern and especially anything unusually problematic for either of them. The two establishments drew on one another's treasuries so frequently that their finances were in effect a single operation.

IX

The KHri CHen had six personal assistants of very high sKu Drag rank who were always monks in good standing: a Butler, a Valet, a Religious Offerings Official, and a Treasurer, who ranked in that order just below the Secretaries; and a Body Servant and a Chef who ranked, respectively, just above and just below the Liaison Officers. These officials were recognized as

[25] The custom was that if the man picked for the Stewardship refused it, the KHri CHen used a chance method to select one of the nominees. No such cases were discovered, but the method resembles the chance selection of some monastery officials (see Chapter 11, section IV).

[26] Recent Stewards, with approximate dates of incumbency, were: lCam Mo Grwa TSHang (personal name unknown), from a noble SHab family, ?–1930; Bar sDings sDe Pa Lags PHrin Las mTHar PHyin, from a formerly noble family of SHab, 1930–1933; Nang bSam Pa (personal name unknown), from a noble SHab family, 1933–1938; PHun KHang bKra SHis bZang Po, a subject from SHab, 1938–1942; Nang bSam Pa, again, 1942–1958; rGya Bo Nang Pa CHos rNams rGyal, a subject from SHab, 1958–?. Nang bSam Pa and PHun KHang also served as ZHabs Pad.

part of the governmental organization by receiving their appointments from the ZHabs Pad and by having, with one exception, the right to attend the Great Assembly Meetings. The Butler, Valet, and Treasurer were also paid in the same way as the officials of the Government.[27]

The Butler handled household matters and served as the KHri CHen's contact with other people. He delivered messages from the ZHabs Pad, the Steward of the Religious Establishment, and monastery officials. He approved all interviews, both official and unofficial, and made all appointments. The Butler also accepted the gifts given to the KHri CHen at the various religious festivals.

The Valet was in charge of the clothing and other personal effects of the KHri CHen. The Offerings Official was in charge of all material used in religious offerings by the KHri CHen; as salary, he was allowed to keep about one-half of the material provided for these offerings. The Treasurer managed all the material goods, money, and valuables belonging to the office of the KHri CHen. He had a layman assistant of the highest Jo Lags rank.[28]

The Body Servant of the KHri CHen was a very high-ranking personal attendant, who was also a companion and often a confidant of the KHri CHen, but he was not recognized as a governmental official in full standing. He was given his food and lodgings and two new outfits of clothing each year, and he received many gifts from people seeking the attention of the KHri CHen.

The Chef of the KHri CHen, with two assistants whom he selected, prepared the food for the entire family of the KHri CHen and was the KHri CHen's official taster. Our respondents,

[27] The exception was the Body Servant. The Great Assembly Meeting is described in Chapter 7, section IV. The way in which officials were paid is discussed in Chapter 12, section V.
[28] The Treasurer also got a return from each religious collector, and each year he financed a three-day feast for the monks of the North and South Monasteries on the KHri CHen's birthday.

with their memories of the frequent assassinations by poisoning in Tibetan history, emphasized the care that had to be taken in making this appointment.[29]

The two palaces also had a number of officials of sKu Drag rank, but most of them had little to do with the business of governing. They were significant principally because their high rank clearly indicated the importance of a royal family in a hereditary monarchy. A man who, for example, was responsible for the safety of a male child of the royal family had a higher status than the Liaison Officers, who were among the most important and powerful members of the governmental organization.[30]

X

We were able to identify about 90 per cent of the men who held sKu Drag offices from the late 1920's until the middle 1950's. Almost all the Government and Religious Establishment officials above the ranks of the Work Corps were identified and the dates of their incumbencies calculated within a year or two. The missing 10 per cent were principally from the Work Corps and the staff of the KHri CHen, where there were greater turnovers. In addition, eight Candidates in the early 1950's were identified, and this may have been all there were.

Sa sKya officials usually stayed in office for a long time; there was definitely no policy of removing men from office after a brief period in order to prevent them from becoming too powerful.[31] Government and Religious Establishment officials above

[29] The KHri CHen also had two doormen, monks whose principal qualifications were large size and imposing appearance. The KHri CHen's wife had a nun as a butler and a layman as a valet.

[30] The structure and the officials of the palaces are described in Appendix A, section II. These officials are not included in the analysis that begins with section X below.

[31] Carrasco suggests that under the Lhasa government it was the practice to "change the guard" rather frequently so that power would not become too concentrated (*Land and Polity in Tibet*, p. 83).

the rank of the Work Corps remained in their positions until they retired or died; during the twenty-five years we are examining, only two officials resigned after a few years in office. Including the tenures of men who died prematurely in office, of the two men who were promoted to even higher positions, and of the three men who were discharged for an alleged direct act of disloyalty to the KHri CHen, the average incumbency was about sixteen years. The conquest of Tibet by the Chinese Communists cut short many careers and brought this average down.

The higher Government and Religious Establishment officials in Sa sKya usually attained their positions at the age of thirty or thirty-five and, except for those who benefited from the few opportunities for promotion, remained in these offices until they died or retired at sixty. This pattern of tenure was assisted by the Sa sKya custom of expecting officials to remain in office despite the accession of a new KHri CHen or the appointment of a new ZHabs Pad.

The twenty men who were identified as having served in the Work Corps and in the lower sKu Drag offices of the Religious Establishment were a smaller proportion of the men who actually held these offices, and they had briefer tenures of office than the men discussed above. Of the twenty, three resigned, two to go into trading and one to become a District Officer. Four were promoted to higher offices, and one was discharged for excessive exactions from the subjects and for helping himself too generously to Government supplies, for "eating wealth," as the Tibetans say.[32] The average tenure of office of these eight men was about six years. Only five of these twenty lower sKu Drag

[32] When either a noble or subject sKu Drag official was removed from office for incompetence or malfeasance, he received a letter describing his new status. He could have been put in the Candidate Corps, whether or not he had previously been a Candidate, thus retaining sKu Drag status. He could have been removed from sKu Drag status with no prejudice to his receiving a future sKu Drag appointment, or he could have been forbidden future sKu Drag status with no prejudice against his sons, or they too could have been disqualified.

officials seem to have made careers of their offices. However, the relatively high turnover in these positions was clearly not planned from above; it was principally the result of the incumbents' leaving for better opportunities.

The officials of the KHri CHen were not identified as thoroughly as those of the Government and Religious Establishment. During the reign of KHri CHen NGag dBang mTHu THub dBang PHyug, from 1936 to 1950, there seem to have been one Chef, one Valet, two Butlers, two Offerings Officials, two Body Servants, and four Treasurers. Only the turnover in the treasury was unusual: it is explained by one death and two resignations for personal reasons.

XI

Of the fifty officials identified, twenty-four were laymen, twenty were monks, two were former monks, and three began as monks and continued in office after breaking their vows. Eleven of the monks held positions—the Stewardship of the Religious Establishment and the staff of the KHri CHen—that could be occupied only by monks. Monks comprised about 30 per cent of those men occupying offices that could be held by either monks or laymen and about 46 per cent of all incumbents that were identified.

It is mildly incongruous that a society putting so much emphasis upon withdrawal from worldly affairs and devoting a large proportion of its resources to maintaining a monastic establishment should take so many men from their responsibilities of religious observance to participate in governmental affairs. Although the "compassion" of Tibetan emanation bodies required them to serve ordinary mortals, and although Tibetan monks were expected to aid in practical affairs by means such as divination, Tibetan Buddhism did not assign religious personnel to congregations of laymen, and hence Tibet had no explicit tradition of religious management of mundane matters. The use of monks as officials of the KHri CHen, and as attendants of the royal family, is explained in part by the status of the aKHon family as hereditary emanation bodies. Even though the KHri CHen usually married to carry on the family line, his religious status suggested that the officials with whom he came in frequent physical contact had to be pure according to the vows of the monastic order. Nevertheless, in the case of these officials, as well as those of the Government and Religious Establishment, taking monks from their life of meditation and religious observance and putting them in charge of secular matters was not quite consistent with religious belief. Part of the tolerance of this incongruity probably came from the advanced individualism of Tantric Buddhism and Tibetan mores, and part from the recognition that order in secular affairs often depended upon utilizing the talents of religious personnel. In Sa sKya, monks who had broken their vows were perfectly welcome to the highest official positions, and a monk who broke his vows while in office could remain without prejudice as long as he had presented a generous gift as an apology to his former monastery.

Both the government and the monks of Sa sKya seem to have shown no reluctance in individual cases to give the business of governing priority over the life of contemplation. Whatever justification was given for the offers of governmental positions and their acceptances, the principal reason for using monks in this way was the scarcity of administrative talent in Sa sKya. Of the eight monks who served the KHri CHen, three were from noble families, two from families of well-established subjects, and two from subject families in humble circumstances. Of the fifteen monks who were officials in the Government and the Religious Establishment, six were nobles, four were prominent subjects, and five began life with no advantages. From about 1937 until the Communist conquest, the office of ZHabs Pad of Sa sKya was occupied by two monks, one from a prominent noble family and the other from a relatively unknown family of subjects.

XII

With about 63 per cent of the total population of Sa sKya proper, the SHab Valley and the capital provided about three-quarters of the men who held the sKu Drag positions being discussed. Of the remaining quarter, about half came from noble or formerly noble families and half from obscure subject families.[33] All the subjects from all parts of the Sa sKya domain who held office came from families with allegiance to the Government or the Religious Establishment. Our respondents said that men with allegiance to a palace or a nobleman were fully eligible, but only one of them became an official during the period that was investigated. Since monks were conscripted only from Government and Religious Establishment families,[34] subjects of the nobility and the palaces did have less opportunity to become officials. There was, moreover, a feeling that a man with allegiance to a noble or a palace could not give his complete loyalty to a position in the Government or Religious Establishment. In this matter of loyalty, no distinction was drawn between subjects of the Government and subjects of the Religious Establishment. Finally, despite their higher standard of living and higher prestige, the isolation of the herders and their exemption from the monk levy prevented them from occupying office in the central government.

Twenty-eight of the fifty men identified as officials from the late 1920's until the middle 1950's came from twenty of Sa sKya's twenty-four noble families. Eleven of these twenty families produced one official and nine produced more than one official. The four noble families not represented in office during this period were a family of hereditary emanation bodies of the

[33] There were twelve men in this group. Seven were nobles or former nobles. Of the five from obscure backgrounds, one came from lHun aGrub sDings, two from dPal rTSe, one from rTSe gDong, and one from sPu dKar (Maps 1 and 3).

[34] See Chapter 11, section III.

Old sect, a family of hereditary medical practitioners serving the royal family, a family that had members serving as officials for the palaces and the monasteries, and a family that produced a ZHabs Pad. There was, therefore, virtually unanimous participation by the nobility in governmental affairs. The degree of each family's participation was determined by its interest in such matters, by its proximity to the capital—nobles who lived in the capital could simultaneously hold a governmental position and manage their estates—and to a great extent by the number of adult males it possessed. One noble family of the capital that was inclined to secular rather than religious affairs produced in these twenty-five years three sKu Drag officials and two Candidates. No noble family or group of families dominated Sa sKya officialdom, and the shortage of people qualified for official positions allowed only a very narrow scope for nepotism.

Eight men were identified as Candidates in the early 1950's. Since the Corps of Candidates usually had from five to thirteen members, these eight may have represented the full membership at that time. Six were from noble families, one was from a moderately prosperous former noble family, and one was the son of a subject who was a high official. Four were from the capital, one from SHab, and three from elsewhere. All were laymen.

XIII

Of the fifty-eight men identified as holding sKu Drag positions including candidacy, thirty-four (about 60 per cent) were from families of hereditary nobility and the rest were from subject families. Only one-third of the twenty-four subjects came from prominent families; the backgrounds of the rest gave them little or no aid in improving their social positions.

The policy of advancing commoners to high office in polities with hereditary nobles has been explained as a method designed to check the power of the nobles, to cause the common people to identify more closely with the regime by allowing some of them to rise to high status and by giving them officials drawn from their own ranks, or to draw upon all available sources of talent.[35] The motives for appointing subjects to high office in Sa sKya are not entirely clear, but the royal family apparently did not consciously intend to check the power of the nobility or to reinforce the loyalty of the subjects. The Sa sKya nobility had relatively few privileges and little solidarity of interest;[36] although KHri CHen NGag dBang mTHu THub dBang PHyug wished to accomplish certain reforms in governmental structure and policy and although he chose subjects as his highest officials, there is no indication that he saw the nobility as any special impediment to his plans. There is also no evidence that officials were drawn from subject families in order to make the subjects more favorably disposed toward the government; indeed, the theoretical presuppositions of the polity suggest the inconsistency of such a motive.

A nonpolitical device, the levy of monks (discussed in Chapter 11), provided the principal bond between the subjects and the capital and the principal reason for the subjects' identification with the fortunes of the Sa sKya religious sect and polity. Of the subjects who achieved sKu Drag standing, well over half were monks, most of whom had been conscripted into the monkhood. In a large proportion of the cases in which a subject was given the highest status, therefore, his advancement was more a result of the device that tied the status groups together than a calculated effort to produce such bonds. Nonetheless, the possibility for a levied monk to become a high official added to the average family's association with the regime. It was said that when a boy was conscripted into the monkhood, his parents speculated on his future, hoping that he would become a success-

---

[35] Pye, in *Politics, Personality, and Nation Building* (New Haven: Yale University Press, 1962), p. 73, says that having commoners as officials in traditional Burma provided a popular link with the god-king and helped to create a popular sense of identity with the ruler.

[36] See Chapter 8 and Chapter 12, section VI.

ful religious collector in eastern Tibet and even dreaming that he might one day be the ZHabs Pad of Sa sKya.

Our data strongly suggest that subjects were made sKu Drag officials principally in order to get able men for these positions.[37] There were only twenty-four noble families in Sa sKya proper, and seven of these, for one reason or another, were unable to supply governmental officials during the period from 1936 to 1950.[38] Of the seventeen remaining families, twelve lived at some distance from the capital, and hence at least one male member of each had to remain at home to manage his family's estate. Tibetan families, moreover, were rather small, and many men died in the prime of life. Consequently, subjects had to be used to fill the forty or fifty sKu Drag positions of the KHri CHen and the establishments. This search for governmental ability was clearly exemplified by KHri CHen NGag dBang mTHu THub dBang PHyug's making a relatively obscure subject his ZHabs Pad, a man from outside Sa sKya proper his Chief Secretary, three subjects from undistinguished families his Secretaries, and a nobleman whose personal loyalty he had some reason to doubt one of his Liaison Officers. Given the absence of any real threat to his power from an entrenched nobility, the KHri CHen of Sa sKya, with his ZHabs Pad, could incidentally demonstrate to his people the possibilities of rising within the system while trying to resolve his natural problem of finding the best men to operate the government.

XIV

The normal way for noblemen to enter governmental service was through candidacy. A young man's family applied to the

---

[37] This was the only reason acknowledged by KHri CHen NGag dBang mTHu Thub dBang PHyug.

[38] Members of two families had been discharged from office on a charge of disloyalty; one family provided the medical practitioners for the royalty; the members of another were emanation bodies of the Old sect; two other families had no eligible adult males; and the seventh had only one adult male who had to manage his estate at some distance from the capital.

ZHabs Pad through a Liaison Officer, and appointments were made with the approval of the KHri CHen. The noble families were also the first to be examined in the periodic searches for new Candidates made by the Government when the number of Candidates became low. Both these procedures were ways for subjects to enter government, but subjects also were occasionally appointed directly to sKu Drag positions after they had distinguished themselves in other walks of life. In the 1940's two subjects were appointed directly to high office without previous governmental experience. One was a man who had from very modest beginnings made a fortune in trade and had successfully accomplished a mission of some delicacy for the KHri CHen. He was made a Secretary after a token period as a Candidate and was subsequently made a lineage noble.[39] The other was a former monk from the Sa sKya territory of sPu dKar who had been an important religious collector in western Tibet for the Lhasa government. He was appointed Chief Secretary after only a brief acquaintance with the KHri CHen, who judged him immediately to be a man of great ability. He was not made a lineage noble, but (it was said) only because he had no son of his own and no opportunity to adopt one and thus no way to carry on his line.

Although subjects could enter government service at the highest levels, most of them first became Candidates or members of the Work Corps, and many of the monks had been junior officials in their monasteries. A young subject had some difficulty in getting appointed to candidacy. He could petition the ZHabs Pad, but this procedure required providing rather generous gifts for a number of high officials, and it might well have been considered presumptuous by the hereditary nobility and the sKu Drag officialdom, whose acceptance was necessary for ultimate success in office. When a subject did follow this procedure, his skill at letters and calculation was tested and the official records were consulted to determine the reliability of his family, meas-

[39] This man was Brag sPe, whose story is told in Chapter 8, section II.

ured by the amount of land it held and its promptness in meeting its revenue payments.

Young men from poor and undistinguished families nevertheless had a real chance of becoming sKu Drag officials, and about half of the sKu Drag who were subjects had this kind of background. Again, poor boys were able to get ahead principally through the monkhood and especially the conscription of monks; two-thirds of the men with unpromising backgrounds took this route to sKu Drag officialdom. Once in the North or South Monastery, an able young man received a free education, and he was in an excellent position and location to attract the attention of the ZHabs Pad or even the KHri CHen, who would take the initiative in making him a Candidate or an official. The members of the royal family, including the KHri CHen, could easily choose monks of no background as their personal attendants because they found them personally compatible. There was also a high official from a humble background who had succeeded in placing his son in the Corps of Candidates.

The other half of the subjects who became sKu Drag came from more promising circumstances. Half were from families that had formerly had hereditary noble status, and the rest were from well-established families of varying social positions. Even for subjects thus favorably situated, it was advantageous to be a monk: at least three-quarters of these men came to their offices from the monkhood.

There was an especially interesting case of a subject reaching sKu Drag status despite a very unpromising background. In the 1920's a monk from Khams in eastern Tibet broke his vows while a member of a capital monastery. He remained in the capital, married a woman who had some land, and became a servant in one of the palaces. He had a son who also became a servant in the palace. The son was a bright boy and managed to get an education; he attracted the attention of the KHri CHen, who put him in the Corps of Candidates in the late 1940's; and he subsequently became a member of the Work Corps. Unlike most subjects with few advantages, he was a layman, and he eventually married the daughter of a prominent and wealthy hereditary nobleman.

XV

In summary, the government of Sa sKya proper was rather centralized, a result no doubt of the principality's very small size.[40] The structure of the government was simple; it consisted essentially of the ZHabs Pad and the Steward of the Religious Establishment, aided by a number of assistants. These assistants had little authority to make final decisions or to innovate. The man in charge, on the other hand, had a very large number of small decisions to make; and although he could handle these details, his time was fully occupied in doing so. The whole system was designed to concentrate power and to make sure that the content of decisions and the methods by which they were made remained as stable as possible. The design prevented any dispersion of power and hence long tenures of office were quite acceptable. Any innovation in the political system had to come from outside this governmental apparatus, that is, from the KHri CHen himself, and he had time-consuming responsibilities for religious observance. Although the system was highly centralized and allowed for only a minimum of innovation, it was able to operate because of the modest function assigned to government.

Although the governmental organization was simple, men had to be drawn from every social stratum in order to staff it. The hereditary nobility participated in government as fully as it could; the monkhood was freely drawn upon; and, from the late 1920's until the middle 1950's, about one-fifth of the officials came from subject families with no apparent advantages. The use

---

[40] Carrasco, *Land and Polity in Tibet*, pp. 85–86, says that fragmentation was basic to the much larger political system of Lhasa; he estimates that 42 per cent of the land belonged to the religious establishment, 37 per cent to the government, and 21 per cent to the nobility.

of men from underprivileged backgrounds apparently had no effect upon the government's structure or policy. The belief that the basic function of government was to maintain order among subjects who were supposed to take care of themselves was strong enough to prevent any deviations by subjects who became officials. About three-quarters of these men, moreover, had been under monastic discipline from early childhood. Once a man became an official, he received substantial rewards in wealth and especially in prestige, and these no doubt sufficed to make him a contented supporter of the system. Indeed, subjects who became sKu Drag officials (reportedly) put on more airs than the hereditary nobility. The device of sKu Drag status was both a practical way to provide the government with an indispensable dignity and an effective method of bringing subjects into the governmental system without disrupting it.

Chapter 6

Legal Principles
and Practices

The government of Sa sKya had three sources of written rules and regulations that guided its activity: the "Thirteen Pronouncements" ascribed to a Tibetan king of the seventh century; a permanent code special to Sa sKya, dating from the thirteenth century; and special standing orders of the incumbent KHri CHen. These documents covered a number of topics, but their most important function was to provide standards for the several types of decisions made by the Law Officials.

I

The Thirteen Pronouncements were accepted throughout Tibet as the basis for governmental procedure in dealing with breaches of the peace,[1] but over the years Sa sKya came to have a version of the pronouncements that differed slightly from the version printed by the Lhasa government. Sa sKya's pronouncements were bound in a large, ornate volume kept in the courtroom of the Law Officials, who ceremoniously consulted it on occasions when they were in doubt about some complicated or delicate point of procedure.[2] There were no additional copies of

[1] The seventh-century Tibetan king credited with making the pronouncements was Srong bTSan sGam Po; they were supposed to be derived from the sayings of Me Long gDong, a mythical king of the time of the Buddha.

[2] The pronouncements were handwritten in cursive script. The ink and paper were of high quality, but the document was not lacquered. There was no indication that it had ever been amended.

the pronouncements, and only the highest officials had access to the original. According to Sa sKya tradition, the pronouncements had been compiled by aPHags Pa, but versions of the pronouncements are also attributed to Byang CHub rGyal mTSHan of PHag Mo Dru in the fourteenth century and to the fifth Dalai Lama in the seventeenth century.

The pronouncements deal with the reasons for governmental concern with certain undesirable acts, the proper responses to some of these acts, and the methods to be used in making these responses. They stress the importance of maintaining the proper religious observances and relate the prescriptions of religion to the maintenance of social harmony. They say that governmental officials must show no favoritism because of personal connections, loyalties, or grudges, that they should not delay in rendering justice, and that they should act so as to be models for all people. Officials are also warned against being greedy, but the pronouncements recognize that involvement with government is costly; it is said that although minor officials are especially rapacious, they are entitled to certain payments, which the pronouncements describe in some detail.

The Thirteen Pronouncements discuss how officials should sift and evaluate testimony, both in accusation and defense; they specify certain techniques of elicitation and verbal entrapment; and they explain when and how to produce results by bringing opposing witnesses together. Suspicion—an important concept, discussed below—is declared to be a valid basis for arrest and a guiding factor in investigation and the examination of witnesses. One of the pronouncements deals with the time when suspects should be seized, the necessity of binding them and how it is to be done, and the two purposes of imprisonment, to confine and also to flog, the flogging to be public in order to serve as a warning to all.

The pronouncements go on to state that punishments and restitutions must be proportional to the act committed and to the actor's degree of responsibility. Certain acts, especially killing one's parents, saints, teachers, and rulers, are so heinous that their perpetrators ought to be bound and thrown from heights or into rivers, or shot to death by arrows; bodily mutilation is also discussed as a punishment for other acts. Indemnity payments for homicide are declared to be proportional to the status of the deceased and the degree of responsibility of the person who did the killing. A homicide by a child under eight years of age or by a person judged insane and a death occurring in a fair fight all carried some obligation, if only to provide a token payment for religious services for the deceased. The seventh pronouncement says that the purpose of life-indemnity payments is to prevent revenge killings and blood feuds. The pronouncements also discuss wounds of several degrees of seriousness, defaulting on debts, theft, and adultery, and the kinds and amounts of restitution due in each case. Finally, the eleventh pronouncement deals with disputes within families and the ways to settle them.

II

The Sa sKya permanent code was called the gTan TSHigs, "gTan" meaning "permanent" and "TSHigs," a word also used to imply indisputability in logical discourse, perhaps translatable as "orders." The code was collected in a single volume containing at least two hundred separate "orders"; the definitive copy was kept in the Government's archives under the control of the ZHabs Pad, a number of handwritten copies being available to lower officials. The code probably originated with aPHags Pa, about the year 1280, and it had been revised three times: first by two of the dPon CHen during the period of Sa sKya ascendency in Tibet, next by KHri CHen sNGags aCHang dBang Po Kun dGaa Rin Chen, in the latter part of the sixteenth century, and finally by KHri CHen Gong Ma Kun dGaa Blo Gros, in the latter part of the eighteenth century. According to our respondents, KHri CHen NGag dBang mTHu THub dBang PHyug had drafted a revision of the code, but he had not promulgated it at the time of his death in 1950.[3]

The items of the code covered both general and specific matters. Some of them dealt with apportionment and remission of revenue, selling and buying among private parties, lending, borrowing, and interest, the "pawning" of land, inheritance and the division of property, and commercial practices. Homicide, theft, assault, and the other acts covered by the Thirteen Pronouncements were not dealt with in the Sa sKya code. Other items in the code stated specific policies that the government ought to follow, such as fixing interest rates and, in times of shortage, putting its own grain on the market and setting price ceilings. The code also dealt with the rules of the monastic order, such as the grounds upon which a monk was to be expelled from the monasteries.[4] Finally, the code contained expressions of the most general orientations in governmental policy. An interesting example was the statement that contacts with non-Tibetans must be kept to a minimum because these outsiders would offend the gods and sap the strength of Sa sKya.

The third set of written rules and regulations was the special orders—"bKaa gTSigs," or "important words"—of the reigning KHri CHen. These were promulgated as the occasion required, and they were circulated and then filed. Any topic could be covered by these special orders, and no doubt many of the orders became a permanent part of Sa sKya policy and governmental

[3] Unfortunately, we were unable to obtain a copy of the code, but our respondents had studied it and also the new draft by NGag dBang mTHu THub dBang PHyug; their memory of the code's general content was no doubt accurate.

[4] The basic rules for religious personnel, the canon law, was, according to the Tibetans, based on "the word of the Buddha," and it was distinguished from the rules applying to laymen, derived from "the word of the king." These secular rules were recognized as being based on the ethics of Buddhism, and as being influenced by custom, by the practices of the Mongols and the Chinese, and by a kind of primitive law antedating the Thirteen Pronouncements.

procedure. KHri CHen Kun dGaa bSod Nams Rin CHen (*c*.1700), issued a special order that recommended that the nobility be given responsibility for Government land as a means of better integrating them into the polity. KHri CHen NGag dBang mTHu THub dBang PHyug thought this such a good idea that he made the order part of the permanent code, of course being careful to cite the precedent.

III

The Thirteen Pronouncements, the Sa sKya code, and the standing orders of the KHri CHen all dealt with both general and specific matters of governmental policy and procedure. In these three documents, only two items were general enough to be called "constitutional": the emphasis on religious observance and the statement that life indemnities were to prevent feuds, both contained in the pronouncements. The power of government to punish crimes, settle disputes, and collect revenue was assumed, as were the two major structural principles, the power of the KHri CHen and the office of the ZHabs Pad. No one questioned these basic powers and principles.

The Thirteen Pronouncements dealt principally with the settlement of disputes and the punishment of crimes. Although they were never amended, at least some of their provisions fell into desuetude: under the influence of Buddhism both capital punishment and deliberate bodily mutilation were abandoned as reactions to "black" deeds. Most of the stipulations of the pronouncements, however, were followed by the Sa sKya government, and the pronouncements were clearly seen as somehow justifying this range of governmental activity. Our respondents were sure that the pronouncements provided standards that made the task of government much easier, for without them "everyone would have had his own idea of right and wrong," but they could not give clear reasons for the validity of the specific standards set by the pronouncements.[5] It seems clear, however, that the authority of the pronouncements came from their connection with the political tradition of all Tibet: they were supposedly promulgated in the seventh century by King Srong bTSan sGam Po, who also brought writing and religion to Tibet and who established a strong government in Lhasa, and he was supposed to have got them from a mythical Tibetan king of the time of the Buddha. The pronouncements were seen as an inseparable part of the essence of Tibetanness and to justify them was tantamount to justifying Tibetanness. This aspect of the pronouncements almost certainly explains why, in Sa sKya at least, they were never amended, even though some of their prescriptions had been abandoned. It will be recalled from Chapter 3 that this concept of Tibetanness had a powerful influence on the political ideas of Sa sKya.

IV

The two Law Officials were in charge of settling disputes and establishing criminal responsibility, and they heard their cases in a special courtroom of rather imposing dimensions and decor. They dealt with two different kinds of cases, those brought to them on the initiative of the parties involved and those referred to them by the ZHabs Pad. The court was almost always in session.

All disputes among the people of Sa sKya, both nobles and subjects of all allegiances, that the modern lawyer would call cases at civil law were brought to the Law Officials when other methods of resolving them had failed. A common source of dispute was the allocation of family property. The Law Officials always upheld written wills, but disputes rarely arose concerning them. In the absence of written wills, the Law Officials considered claims of the disinherited, agreements to allow a nonheir to

---

[5] One theory was advanced and then rejected: that the pronouncements were expressions of a kind of natural law, compliance with which brings man closer to the "gods."

use part of his family's land, and challenges to the right of an heir to give away private land. They also occasionally handled disagreements over division of property and custody of children resulting from divorce. An "unmarried" wife [6] who had children was usually given full rights to family property in cases of death or divorce. Upon divorce, the boys usually went with their father and the girls with their mother. The Law Officials would, if necessary, determine paternity; their method was to wait a few years and then decide on the basis of facial resemblance. The Law Officials also resolved disputes regarding ownership, such as those over boundaries, theft, trespass, grazing rights, allocation of water, and destruction of property. They dealt with problems arising from commercial transactions, such as lending and borrowing, payment of interest, pawning of land, and selling and buying. Finally, disputes arising from assault or disagreements that were likely to lead to violence could be referred to the Law Officials for definitive settlement.

In all these disputes, the decisions of the Law Officials were backed by the authority and coercive power of the Government. The only other officials who could make such definitive decisions were the District Officers and Headmen acting together, and they could do so only in cases involving assault or minor theft.[7] The severe limitations to this decentralization probably resulted in part from the belief that the expertise of the Law Officials was necessary to resolve cases of any degree of complexity. The Law Officials always upheld the formal joint decisions of Headmen and District Officers.

It was presumed, however, that even these relatively complicated cases should have been settled without reference to the Law Officials. The normal method was to use one or more mediators, who may have been members of the disputants' families, friends of the disputants, governmental officials such as District Officers, Headmen, and Group Officials, or important local

---

[6] See Chapter 8, section VI.   [7] Chapter 4, section V.

personages. All these people were usually anxious to keep disputes from being referred to the Law Officials: those personally interested in the disputants wanted to avoid the risks of formal litigation, and those who felt responsible for local communities wished to avoid reputations for disharmony. There were also people who sought personal prestige for their wisdom, eloquence, and *savoir-faire* from successful mediation of difficult disputes.

Even after a case had been brought to the Law Officials, it could have been referred to a private mediator. The Law Officials—and Headmen and District Officers, too—were willing and even anxious to be relieved of the task of trying to reach a settlement, and they welcomed, for example, a renewed attempt by the families of the disputants to settle out of court. Once the Law Officials had begun to consider a case, however, their written authorization was necessary for it to be referred to a private mediator. They also had to approve the terms of the settlement reached by the mediator, but this was little more than a formality, because the Law Officials' principal concern was to have the quarrel stopped and harmony restored and because their disapproval would have been a serious affront to the mediator. The conditions of the settlement of a case of this kind were made part of the Law Officials' records. If the mediator did not succeed in arriving at an agreement, the case went back to the Law Officials, usually with a statement that one or both of the parties had proved unreasonable. The mediator's ability to make this kind of statement no doubt aided him in his attempt to get the disputants together, for to be considered unwilling to compromise was a disadvantage to any party to a quarrel and in cases before the Law Officials might even earn him a flogging.

V

Despite all these efforts, many disputes were brought, on the initiative of either or both parties, to the Law Officials for settlement. In arriving at a settlement, the Law Officials were guided by the relevant general prescriptions of the Thirteen Pronouncements, by the items in the Sa sKya code that dealt with disputes, by the appropriate special orders of the reigning KHri CHen, and by previous decisions made in similar cases by themselves or their predecessors. The parties to the dispute could introduce as precedents the decisions of Headmen or District Officers acting in their official capacities—decisions, for example, that determined the payment due to someone who had been assaulted—and the Law Officials relied heavily upon these precedents. Decisions by private mediators could also be brought in as precedents by the disputants, and these decisions were also considered seriously by the Law Officials. Records of both types of decision were kept.

The acceptance of the decisions of local officials and private persons as precedents allowed for some development of the civil law in Sa sKya. These people probably knew little about the Thirteen Pronouncements, the code, and the standing orders of the KHri CHen; they probably acted according to their understanding of their small local community's concept of justice. This procedure probably led to standards that were more realistic, less harsh, and more acceptable to the subjects of Sa sKya than the standards devised solely by the noble officials of the capital. These locally created standards could also have changed as conditions in the villages changed. Unfortunately, none of the records of settlements of disputes were available; they would undoubtedly provide a fascinating picture of the degree and type of development of the civil law in a relatively unchanging society.

When a case was brought to the Law Officials, each party paid a standard fee of 20.4 Srang,[8] and of course there were usual gifts to the Law Officials and their assistants. In addition to the cost in goods and reputation, by bringing his case (or having it brought) to the Law Officials, a litigant came under the physical

---

[8] This was a fairly substantial amount, about a week's wages for a skilled artisan such as a carpenter (see Appendix D, section II).

power of the government. The Law Officials' decisions were, if necessary, enforced by physical means, and during the hearing of a case they could order a flogging for any party whom they judged unreasonably recalcitrant.

VI

Our respondents remembered the details of two interesting cases that were brought before the Law Officials. These illustrate the kinds of disputes that government in Sa sKya could concern itself with, the settlements it made, and the ways in which disputes were brought under its jurisdiction. The two cases were atypical in the uninhibited behavior of their principals, but it was this characteristic that brought them to everyone's attention.

Near the capital were three adjacent plots of farming land. Two were privately owned, by two prominent and relatively wealthy subjects, and the third was Government land farmed by a Government artisan of modest circumstances. The dispute began between the two prominent families over the strip of unfarmed land between their private plots, used by both for grazing animals. The head of one family claimed that his neighbor's animals were also using his fields for their grazing. His complaints were ignored, so one day he caught one of his neighbor's donkeys among his crops and he cut off its tail. Everyone soon heard of this amusing act, and the donkey's owner became the favorite butt of the local wits. After a time the teasing apparently became unbearable, and the owner of the donkey caught one of his neighbor's cows—who, reportedly, was not trespassing—and cut off her ears. The affair then achieved genuine notoriety, and the women of the capital made it the subject of several mocking calypso-type songs.

The KHri CHen and the ZHabs Pad knew the story as well as anyone else, and they were worried about the eventual outcome of the feud. They could have sent an official to order the disputants to stop their nonsense, or they could have arranged that the dispute be brought to the Law Officials, even though reference of a case to the Law Officials was supposed to come from a private person. The KHri CHen and ZHabs Pad, however, did nothing. The dispute had become the object of so much ridicule that they did not dare involve the government in it.

Throughout the early stages of the affair, the artisan had kept quiet, although his land was frequently enough visited by the animals of both his neighbors. As the dispute became more intense, he began to fear that the continuation of his much more powerful neighbors' policy of reciprocal destruction would result in his own suffering. To protect himself, he threatened to bring to the ZHabs Pad, through a Liaison Officer, the charge that the animals of his two neighbors were trespassing on his fields. This threat immediately prompted the relatives of the original antagonists to offer mediation. The artisan was willing to settle his complaint in this way, but the other two refused to accept mediation because they did not want to cooperate with one another and also perhaps because they considered the artisan too low in status to bargain with. The artisan thereupon petitioned the ZHabs Pad, who ordered all three of the parties to appear before the Law Officials. The entrance of the artisan into the case and his taking the initiative in litigation apparently relieved the government of its fear of looking foolish.

The Law Officials conducted a rather long and thorough investigation, the mutilated animals being among the evidence presented. Eventually everyone became very apologetic and harmony was apparently restored. To formalize this new spirit, the Law Officials drew up a written agreement to the effect that the two prominent families cease all actions and words against one another and that they stop abusing the artisan, who was to stop complaining. And to add some reinforcement to the settlement, the Law Officials stipulated that if the quarrel between the two prominent families recurred, the Government would take away their private plots of land over which the original dispute began.

Things went well for a time, but within a year the two were

quarreling again. The ZHabs Pad reacted by sending some members of the Work Corps to measure the two private plots, and he then ordered that they henceforth belonged to the Government. Both the disputants lost face by this action, but it did not damage them enough to prevent members of both families from later becoming rather important officials in the central government.

The second case involved two artisans of the capital, to be called A and B, who were great friends and drinking companions. It happened that during their celebrations A began to pay a great deal of attention to B's wife, a development that soon led to day-long picnics and similar activities. Tibetans take such matters relatively lightly, and B was indifferent to the relationship between his wife and his best friend. This was not, however, the attitude of Mrs. A. She was unhappy, and then she became very angry. One night when B was out of town, Mrs. A went to his house and surprised her husband in a rendezvous with Mrs. B. Apparently the lovers had taken few precautions, because Mrs. A burst into the house and attacked Mrs. B, raking her across the face with a comb. A, either frightened or confused, fled naked into the street. Not satisfied, Mrs. A summoned all the neighbors to be her witnesses.

When B returned to town and heard the news, he was most annoyed at Mrs. A for wounding his wife and creating such a scandal. He kept his own counsel, however, until one evening when A was away from home. B then went to see Mrs. A, and, in what must have been a masterful performance, persuaded her to go to bed with him. When the lady was undressed, B reacted rather unexpectedly by pushing her out into the street and locking the door.

These droll proceedings prompted relatives of the two couples to get together and draw up a written agreement to the effect that all drinking and other horseplay cease. The two men were willing to accept this resolution of their difficulties, but their wives thought themselves too aggrieved for such a simple settlement, and the efforts of the mediators proved fruitless. As in all such cases, the mediators were too committed to withdraw from the affair, and so the relatives of both couples together asked the ZHabs Pad through a Liaison Officer to refer the case to the Law Officials.

The ZHabs Pad, who no doubt had heard the details of the dispute and probably believed that its continuance would have been dangerous, accepted the petition, and the two couples were brought to court; each had to pay the court fee of 20.4 Srang (the cost of some seventy quarts of beer) and to distribute the usual gifts. The Law Officials required that Mrs. B receive compensation—the kind and amount were not recalled—for her bodily injury, but the remainder of their judgment concerned the future rather than the past. The two men were forbidden to drink more than a stipulated amount of beer—we were assured this was ten quarts a day—neither man was to be in the other's house after dark or in his absence, and all hostile words and actions were to cease. In the event of any further trouble, the family that began it would have to leave the capital forever. No further trouble occurred.

VII

In these two cases, the Law Officials, using common sense rather than following formal rules, stopped disputes that threatened to lead to violence. Although the ZHabs Pad could have interceded on his own initiative, he preferred to wait until he was requested to use the machinery of government. This machinery was available to any person who could not otherwise resolve his differences with his neighbors or business associates, provided that the ZHabs Pad considered the affair serious enough to warrant reference to the Law Officials. Most disputes over property, debts, and the like were considered to have this degree of seriousness: as a last resort, the government had to be available to provide a definitive settlement arrived at according to the standards contained in the Thirteen Pronouncements and the Sa sKya code. This arrangement assured the people of Sa

sKya that their contracts, property rights, and claims to inheritance could always be supported by the power of government,
and it represented a function of government usually called the
"maintenance of civil law." In another case to be described later,[9]
the ZHabs Pad refused to intervene in a disagreement over the
division of family property, but he did so only because he believed that a settlement could be reached by the mediation of a
Group Official. If the Group Official, who brought the prestige
of his governmental position to his attempted mediation, had
ultimately failed, the ZHabs Pad would no doubt have referred
the case to the Law Officials, since the responsibility for
paying governmental revenue, among other things, depended on
its resolution.

Although the government preferred that these disagreements
be settled privately, predictability in human relationships required the ultimate availability of its physical power and its
authority. Even in a society as small as Sa sKya, the force of
opinion and the prestige of mediators were not enough to guarantee the regularity necessary for property, contracts, and the
like. There was, moreover, always the danger that unresolved
disputes over economic matters would lead to violence, and
violence, as well as disrupting harmony, undermined the government's claim to be the only agency that could properly use
physical coercion.

The government did not take the initiative in these situations,
and it was willing to ignore them altogether, because it correctly
assumed that harmony and regularity could normally be restored
by extragovernmental methods. When it did intervene, on the
request of someone involved in the dispute who believed that
recourse to government was the only way to end it, its purpose
was not to punish anyone, but to obtain a just settlement between the people directly concerned. Justice was here less a
matter of abstract principle than something acceptable to the

---

[9] The case of the idol-maker, Chapter 10, section VIII.

disputants; social harmony was to be restored and future disputes forestalled. The physical power of government, however, was used either to guarantee the settlement or to guarantee that something unpleasant would happen if the settlement were not accepted.

VIII

In Sa sKya certain acts created situations of discord that were always resolved by the Law Officials and that could be resolved by no one else. These acts were, in the order of decreasing seriousness: killing an emanation body, a high religious official, or a high governmental official; killing one's parents; desecrating religious objects; other forms of homicide; arson and poisoning water; treason; and taking property belonging to monasteries, the Government, the Religious Establishment, or the palaces.

There were, however, two small exceptions to this rule. If in a desecration of religious objects the damage were not great or the object were of minor importance, restitution could have been effected through a mediator. Secondly, minor thefts from the North and South Monasteries and the palaces, sometimes of saleable religious objects, were dealt with by monastery and palace officials without reference to the Government; but in each case that we discovered, the person committing the act was under the jurisdiction of the organization in question, a monk in the monastery or a subject of the palace, and he received a flogging. If a subject of the Government were caught taking the property of the Religious Establishment, a palace, or a monastery, the officials of these organizations usually flogged him before turning him over to the officials of the Government, who were ultimately responsible for his behavior.

Upon the occurrence of homicide, major theft or desecration, arson, or water poisoning, the ZHabs Pad was immediately notified and given the available information. If the information did not indicate a suspect, the ZHabs Pad authorized an investigation by local officials or by officials of the central government. The ZHabs Pad was responsible for determining, on the basis of the original report or the subsequent investigation, that someone was under "suspicion" (Dogs Pa) for committing the act; this meant that there was enough evidence to arrest him and bring him to trial before the Law Officials. Determination of suspicion was a very serious decision, because the man under suspicion was bound, imprisoned, and flogged, all unpleasant experiences. If the homicide or other action was committed on the territory of the Religious Establishment, the Steward was immediately notified and, after consulting with the ZHabs Pad, conducted the investigation, determined suspicion, and handed the suspect to the Law Officials. When the act occurred on the territory of one of the palaces, the ZHabs Pad handled the affair, consulting with palace officials. When the act occurred on the territory of a nobleman, he notified the ZHabs Pad, conducted any necessary investigation under the ZHabs Pad's direction, and delivered the suspect to the Law Officials. When a monk committed one of these serious acts outside his monastery, he was first dealt with by his monastery's officials under the monastic code of rules. His punishment usually included expulsion from the monastic order, and then as a layman he came under the jurisdiction of the Government. Since he was usually flogged and often fined by the officials of the monastery, the Law Officials punished him relatively lightly when he came before them, but they maintained their full responsibility for arranging any restitutions, especially life indemnities in cases of homicide.

Arson and poisoning water supplies were considered extremely serious for obvious reasons and were not unknown in Sa sKya, although our respondents recalled no instances of either. Treason was also an obviously serious matter; it was dealt with by a special court consisting of the ZHabs Pad and the two Law Officials, who had to give a unanimous decision. This special court had not been convened in recent decades.

IX

The following case illustrates a number of interesting points in the Sa sKya government's attitude toward and treatment of theft. In the late 1940's, a Keeper of the Keys discovered that a window in the South Monastery had been broken and that some woolen cloth was missing from the Government's stores. Attention was immediately focused on a servant of one of the palaces who had recently shown signs of an unusual and unexplained prosperity. The ZHabs Pad notified the palace that the servant was suspected, but the palace officials replied that since a false accusation would embarrass the palace, they would release the man to the Law Officials only if the ZHabs Pad were positive that he was the thief. The ZHabs Pad could not meet this condition. Before too long, however, some old barley was taken from the stores. Soon barley of this type appeared in the capital; it was matched with the barley of the stores and then traced to the palace servant. On the basis of this evidence, the palace turned the servant over to the Law Officials.

The servant, under flogging, confessed to the theft and named four accomplices, who were also arrested and flogged. Each of the five had to pay the court fee of 20.4 Srang and some smaller fees, and they had to present the usual gifts to the Law Officials and their underlings. The value of the stolen material was determined, and the thieves were ordered to make full restitution. The four accomplices paid their shares and were released, but the servant was from elsewhere in Tibet, with no family in Sa sKya, and he could not raise the amount of his share. As a result, he was further flogged—to the point of permanent crippling, a not uncommon action—and then released. The Law Officials had the option of ordering a thief who could not make restitution to work off his debt or even to engage in a specified amount of physical religious observance, such as walking around a shrine. The servant in this case was not given these opportunities, perhaps because his act was considered quite serious or because he was judged the leader of the group of thieves.[10]

In pronouncing their judgment in this case, the Law Officials warned the five thieves that any further misbehavior would result in the loss of a finger or an ear. According to our respondents, this was only a bluff. Mutilation was not practiced in Sa sKya in recent decades. It was, however, apparently enough of a possibility to be a useful threat: in another case of theft, a suspect caught with the stolen goods had his arm fully prepared for amputation of the hand before he finally confessed.

In Sa sKya theft was considered undesirable, but it did not evoke much moral disapproval.[11] Most instances of petty theft— up to the value of a sheep or two—were dealt with by methods such as mediation. Large-scale theft—five sheep, for example— could usually not be resolved without the definitive judgment of the Law Officials regarding what was considered a dispute between private parties. Taking another's property to satisfy one's basic needs was much less serious than taking it for profit, and destroying property was even worse. Destruction of property could become a matter of automatic governmental intervention, as when crops or storehouses were destroyed by arson.

The principal concern in cases of theft was the restitution of the value of the stolen property. When any part of the governmental apparatus was the injured party, it naturally took the initiative in finding the thief and used its power to effect a restitution. The thieves in the above case were flogged as soon as they were arrested, but not to punish them or to get them to confess. The flogging was, instead, an expression of the power and majesty of government, an indication of what happened to people who came under the jurisdiction of the Law Officials,

---

[10] The servant had his allegiance to the Lhasa government, but the Sa sKya authorities tried and punished him without even notifying Lhasa. His low social status no doubt explains this.

[11] Cf. W. I. Thomas and F. Znaniecki, *The Polish Peasant* (Boston: Richard G. Badger, 1918), I, 188.

especially by being under suspicion. If the palace servant had been proved innocent of the theft, he would have been released but no amends would have been made for the floggings and other harsh treatment he received while under arrest. The use of physical discomfort to emphasize the status of government is even more clearly evident in cases of homicide, discussed below.

When it was discovered that the palace servant could not restore the goods he had taken, he was then beaten as a punishment, although, as said above, he could have been allowed to work to pay off his debt. His case nicely illustrates the ambiguity in treating theft, even theft from one of the establishments: in Sa sKya it was unclear whether theft was (in modern language) a crime or a tort.[12]

X

The functions of the Sa sKya government and the nature of its law are clearly illustrated in the treatment of homicide. There were one or two homicides a year in Sa sKya proper, a relatively low frequency for Tibet, and a number of cases were recalled in some detail. The methods and assumptions of governmental action can best be understood by following one of these cases.[13]

In the summer of 1940, two men of gYaa Lung quarreled over the distribution of irrigation water to their adjacent fields and began to fight with spades. The fight was stopped before anyone was hurt, but bad feelings between the two persisted. An uneasy peace was maintained until early in September, when beer began

---

[12] Victor Ehrenberg, in *The Greek State* (Oxford: Basil Blackwell, 1960), p. 79, points out that in the *polis* there was a logical inconsistency regarding which acts were the concern of government and which were left to private resolution.

[13] Homicide in Sa sKya is the subject of a manuscript being prepared by Ekvall for future publication. It treats of homicide in much greater detail than does our present account, and the case described below is drawn from it. For an introduction to this study, see Dan F. Henderson, "Settlement of Homicide Disputes in Sakya (Tibet)," *American Anthropologist*, LXVI (1964), 1099–1105.

to flow to celebrate the end of the harvest. The alcohol prompted abusive language between the two neighbors, and another fight occurred, this time with sickles. Again the two were parted before any injuries were inflicted, and everyone went home at the end of the day.

According to the story subsequently told by his wife, one of the men returned home that evening very drunk, and they went to bed early. Sometime during the night, "after the night was all black," she awoke to find him gone. He was not in the house, and after searching for him outside she finally found him lying dead in front of the house of his enemy, with his sickle in his hand and a girdle pulled tight around his throat. His shoulders and arms were bruised, but there were no wounds. The woman immediately raised the neighbors, and they all demanded that the dead man's enemy appear before them, but he was not at home. He later said that he was visiting at a relative's house, where he had arrived at about the time when the "six stars of the Pleiades became clear" and where he remained for some time drinking a medium-sized pitcher of beer.

The dead man had a younger brother who was also the cohusband of his wife.[14] On the evening of the death, the younger brother was away from home on governmental business, and upon his return he immediately accused the man with whom his brother had fought of murdering him. Two principles were now involved in the case: since it appeared to be a homicide, the government had to handle it, but since a close relative of the deceased had made a specific accusation, the case was treated in part as if it were a dispute between two private parties, to be resolved by an agreement between the parties based on an equitable payment, in the form of life indemnity, for the damage done by the killing.

When the local officials made their mandatory report to the capital, the ZHabs Pad decided that there was enough evidence

---

[14] On this type of marriage, see Chapter 8, section V.

to warrant suspicion of the accused, who, although he protested his innocence, was bound, brought to the capital, turned over to the jailers, and immediately given a formal and official flogging. Both the binding and the flogging were invariable steps in the procedure of bringing a suspect to trial, and their severity depended upon the degree of suspicion and the behavior of the suspect when being apprehended. As in the case of theft described above, this treatment was an expression of the power of government. When, in an instance of homicide, no one immediately came under suspicion, the ZHabs Pad usually sent members of the Work Corps or even higher officials out to investigate; and in case an arrest proved difficult, he sent out some or all of the policemen or floggers to make it.

Once a suspect was brought to the capital and turned over to the Law Officials, they took full charge of the case—with no interference whatever from anyone else, including the ZHabs Pad and the KHri CHen—until they pronounced a sentence. The Law Officials' courtroom was at the southwest corner of the Government Building on the north bank of the Grum River. The room was decorated with whips, chains, bar-shackles, cangues, and the instruments of torture no longer used. The official and ornate copy of the Thirteen Pronouncements was prominently displayed on a table.

XI

In the case at hand, the Law Officials had great difficulty in determining the times at which the key events were supposed to have occurred. In the absence of clocks, the dead man's wife could say only that she missed her husband "when the night was all black," and the relative of the accused could testify only that the accused had arrived at his house "at the time the six stars of the Pleiades became clear." There was no way to prove or disprove the possibility that the accused could have committed a murder either before or after he had gone visiting.

Other difficulties arose. The girdle around the dead man's neck turned out to be his own, and strangling oneself in this way is a common form of suicide in Tibet. The deceased, in a drunken frenzy, might have killed himself on his enemy's doorstep. Most disturbing of all, the accused persisted in maintaining his innocence. He frankly admitted his dislike of the deceased and their fights with spades and sickles, but he insisted that he had never been the aggressor and called attention to the fact that on the night of the death his rival had apparently come seeking him. When a suspect in Sa sKya refused to admit his guilt, the Law Officials ordered him to be flogged to see whether his story would change. The suspect in this case was flogged so often and heavily that he walked with a limp for the rest of his life, but his testimony and protestation of innocence did not change.

Throughout the trial, the younger brother of the deceased acted as a kind of prosecuting attorney in his roles as the accuser of the suspect and as the person to whom a life indemnity would be paid. The trial thus became, in part, a dispute between the accuser and the accused, with the Law Officials functioning as mediators. The accuser was as insistent in maintaining that the accused was the murderer as the accused was in denying it. He insisted on a full life indemnity and physical punishment as well. This handling of the case as in part a dispute meant that it could not be settled unless the accused admitted having done the killing, and hence agreed to pay the indemnity set by the Law Officials. A dispute could be resolved only if harmony were restored, and harmony required the overt agreement of both parties to the terms of the settlement.

The insistence on a "confession" may possibly have had other causes: both the lack of techniques by which to establish the occurrence of past events—illustrated in the present case by the Law Officials' inability to arrive at reasonably precise times—and the presumption that the fundamental significance in human relationships lay in overt behavior, with feelings and attitudes of little importance since they were not well understood, may have led the government of Sa sKya to be assured that someone had committed an act only when he acknowledged that he had done so.

Since the accused in the present case refused to admit his guilt and since his accuser persisted in maintaining he was guilty, the Law Officials ordered that the accuser be subjected to the "hot question," that is, that he be questioned while being flogged. The behavior of the accused had raised some doubts in their minds: after all, other people may have wanted the deceased out of the way, and the most likely other people were his wife and his younger brother and cohusband, perhaps working in collusion. Under flogging, however, the younger brother did not retract his accusation and his claim to a life indemnity.

This stalemate left the Law Officials powerless to proceed. The dispute over the claimed life indemnity could not be resolved without an agreement between the parties, and the guilt of the man under suspicion could not be absolutely confirmed without his confession. If the accuser had retracted his accusation, he would of course no longer have claimed a life indemnity, and the Law Officials would probably have pronounced the suspect innocent of the killing. The evidence against him was inconclusive, there were others who might well have committed the act, and he had always maintained his innocence. Since the accuser had not retracted, the issue of guilt was bound up with the issue of the dispute between the two men, and one could not be resolved without resolving the other. The Law Officials reported the stalemate to the ZHabs Pad and asked for advice.

The ZHabs Pad, who had originally determined the existence of suspicion, suggested that the issue be resolved by having the contestants throw dice. This was one of the three standard methods used in Sa sKya to resolve stalemates such as the present case; it involved a middle degree of psychological tension and hence was considered of medium seriousness. The simplest method, and the one involving least tension and apprehension for the contestants, was for them to draw pebbles from a jar of opaque oil.[15] Drawing pebbles and throwing dice were methods of indicating what really had happened in the past, because their results were believed to be signs connected with cause-effect relationships.

The third method of resolving a stalemate between accuser and accused was a direct appeal to the supernatural. Hair and fingernail-parings were taken from each man, put in separate packets labeled with the owners' names, and placed with suitable incantations before the images of the wrathful gods. Then everyone waited for the gods to make known their judgment by visiting the guilty party's person, family, or possessions with some kind of misfortune. This method was much feared, and to threaten its use was often enough to break a stalemate by a retraction from the accuser or the accused.

In the present case, following the suggestion of the ZHabs Pad but on their own authority, the Law Officials ordered that a yak be killed and its hide spread, bloody side up, on the courtroom floor. The accused, without clothes and with his hair let down, knelt on one edge and his accuser, normally attired, knelt facing him on the other edge. The accused had, as was his option, chosen to roll the two dice three times rather than once. Appealing to the supernatural, calling for vindication, and vilifying the opponent, the two men each threw the two dice once. The total of the accused's roll was higher than that of his accuser, and so he won the first round. He lost the second round, but won the third, and was thereupon declared innocent of the killing.[16]

The Law Officials reported to the ZHabs Pad that the case was closed. They had a document prepared that directed the

[15] The jar contained one white and one black pebble. The accused drew a single pebble and then replaced it; then his accuser drew a single pebble. The drawing continued until on one draw one man drew white and the other black. The issue was then incontrovertibly resolved in favor of the man who had drawn white.

[16] One of our respondents was an (unauthorized) witness of these proceedings.

accuser to apologize to the accused and to give him a token gift of beer and a ceremonial scarf, and that ordered both of them to keep the peace and engage in no reprisals. No further incident between the two occurred. The accused had acquired a permanent limp from his floggings, and the accuser probably considered himself fortunate not to be himself tried for the murder of his brother.

This case is a good illustration of the confusion in Sa sKya between homicide as a crime and homicide as an injury to a private party (similar to a modern tort). The killing had not been solved, but because the dispute had been settled no further attempt at solution was made. The crime, if one had been committed, went unpunished. The tenacity of both accuser and accused, may, however, have caused the government to become preoccupied with the contest between them and to forget the criminal aspect of the case.

Another case was remembered in which a man was found guilty of killing another man in a fight and was required to pay a life indemnity and to serve a term of imprisonment. He protested throughout his trial that he was innocent, but he finally agreed to accept the responsibility, saying that he would not go against the opinion of the Government. The dispute between private parties was resolved, but enough doubt remained among officials to cause them to continue the investigation. Some time later it was discovered that someone else had done the killing, and the condemned man was released from prison, where, on the order of the Law Officials, his treatment had been relatively mild, and the value of the indemnity was returned to him. In this case the government appears to have kept its attention on the problem of bringing a criminal to justice.

XII

After the Law Officials solved a case of homicide, they decided, according to two principles, that the act of the killer had a certain degree of seriousness. The first principle was that the higher the status of the slain man and the greater the difference between his status and the status of his killer, the more serious the act. The second was that the motives of the killer and the circumstances of the killing created different degrees of seriousness, ranging from killing for gain to killing in self-defense.[17] The Law Officials drew up a document that stated three alternative levels of guilt within the determined degree of seriousness and three corresponding types of punishment. This document was sent to the ZHabs Pad; he checked one of the alternatives and returned it to the Law Officials, who then ordered the application of the punishment.

The indemnity to be paid to the family or patron of the deceased was determined by a scale contained in the Sa sKya code, often modified to some extent by the demands of the family and the wealth of the slayer. The code listed three amounts corresponding to three status groups. Governmental officials, hereditary nobility, and monks who were officials of monasteries or considered especially pious brought the highest payment of about 400 rDo TSHad. Farmers and herdsmen of good standing and ordinary monks were rated at about 200 rDo TSHad. Artisans and farmers and herdsmen of little standing were valued at 100 rDo TSHad. If the man killed were a ruler, an emanation body, or a saint, there were no limits to the amount of indemnity required, although nine times the highest rate was often mentioned. A blacksmith or a butcher, on the other hand, might require an indemnity only half that of the lowest regular rate. In setting the scale of indemnity, the Law Officials were acting as mediators, although mandatory ones, and thus not even the ZHabs Pad could vary even slightly the amount fixed as a proper payment for taking a life.

---

[17] The different circumstances of a killing, in decreasing seriousness, were: to kill wantonly or for personal gain, as in a robbery; to kill upon provocation, where the killer can give a reason for his deed; to kill by accident; to kill a thief entering one's house; to kill in self-defense; and to kill in defense of religion.

These life indemnities were substantial amounts for most people. A subject of the capital whose living standard was rather high for Sa sKya spent about 43 rDo TSHad a year supporting a family of five,[18] so a killing meant almost permanent debt for the average family. Responsibility for making the payment was shared by all members of the threshold,[19] and when a man had committed homicide, it was time for his relatives and friends to prove their loyalty by coming to his financial aid.

Punishment for serious crimes such as homicide consisted of wearing shackles of varying weights, being imprisoned for different lengths of time, and receiving more or less severe floggings (in addition to the floggings administered upon arrest and during the trial). After the ZHabs Pad had chosen one of the three punishments suggested by the Law Officials, the guilty person began to serve his sentence. After a decent interval, his family or patron could appeal to the ZHabs Pad for his release, promising that he would cause no further trouble. If the ZHabs Pad considered the petitioners trustworthy, he could, on his own authority, have the prisoner released into their custody. A prisoner unlucky enough to have no one to stand bond for him had to serve his full sentence, and the conditions of the Sa sKya prison were so bad that an inmate was not likely to survive more than a few years.

Capital punishment had been abandoned in Tibet through the influence of Buddhism, but death could result from a long prison sentence or unusually harsh flogging. Once a religious collector returning to Sa sKya from eastern Tibet was killed by his servants for the wealth he was carrying. The murderers were captured in Lhasa territory, and the local official of the Lhasa government—horrified at the enormity of the deed, for the

[18] We calculate that 43 rDo TSHad per year was at about the eighty-fifth percentile of living standards in the capital. See Chapter 10, section VIII, and Appendix D, section III.

[19] This included natural sons living with their father, but excluded an "unmarried" wife (see Chapter 8, section VI) who neither had children nor was pregnant.

collector was considered a "substitute lama" and the wealth, of course, was for religious observance—ordered the killers beaten so severely that they died before the Sa sKya government was able to take charge of the case. Most of the wealth was recovered and sent to Sa sKya, and the case was considered resolved.

A long prison sentence could also result from the inability of a homicide to make the payment of life money required of him. If the man he had killed were an emanation body, a saint, or a ruler, the indemnity was so high that few men could raise the amount and the killer was in effect sentenced to death. In cases requiring a more modest indemnity, the slayer was kept in prison until he paid it. This policy seems to confuse homicide as a crime with homicide as an injury to the deceased's family or patron.

When a man had killed in self-defense, he received no punishment, but he was still responsible for a payment to the deceased's family. Since the Law Officials always determined life indemnities, the slayer was subject to the binding and flogging that accompanied all arrests.

XIII

Our respondents estimated that in about one fifth of the instances of homicide in Sa sKya no one appeared to claim a life indemnity and to act as a "prosecutor" of the suspected slayer. These cases could therefore not be treated as disputes between private parties; they were handled in the same way as other homicides, except that the Law Officials themselves took on the function of accusers and "prosecutors." If the Law Officials found the suspect guilty, he received the usual appropriate punishment, and half his wealth was confiscated if he had someone to act as his patron and all his wealth if he had no one to vouch for him. From this wealth the Government could at its discretion give up to one-half the regular life indemnity to the family or other sponsor of the deceased. If the deceased had no family or sponsor, the Government kept the entire amount. One-half a man's wealth was more often than not a smaller amount than the regular life indemnity.

An example of this type of case occurred when the husband of a servant in one of the palaces was killed in a fight. His wife was the only person who could have demanded an indemnity from his slayer, but she chose not to appear before the Law Officials. A lone woman of low status no doubt found it difficult to take the role of "prosecutor," and the cost of appearing in court was not negligible for one of limited means. The regular fee of 20.4 Srang, used to meet the court's operating costs, was required of both parties in a homicide case, and there were always the gifts to the Law Officials and their subordinates.[20] The woman received a settlement in cash and kind from the Government, and her husband's slayer received a prison sentence. She said she was quite satisfied with the resolution of the case, and she could hardly have complained, because she had foregone her rights to "prosecute" and to demand a full life indemnity. People who lacked the will to exercise these rights were unlikely to pursue a vendetta, even though they had not formally agreed to a settlement.

Since this type of case could not be treated as a dispute be-

---

[20] Only ceremonial scarves were openly given to the Law Officials; more substantial gifts were sent to their homes. To bring a case before the Law Officials, arrangements had to be made with their secretary, who naturally received a gift. Jailers, stewards, and floggers were always presented with gifts from the family of a prisoner. The winner in a case was expected to give another round of gifts, of lesser value, to the officials involved in it, and the loser had to pay a "guilt fee" to the court and a token "apology fee" to the winner. The officials no doubt considered their gifts as part of their regular salaries, but the government of Sa sKya did not use its judicial power as a source of income, as happened, for example, in medieval Europe. If proof that a decision of the Law Officials resulted from bribery was given to the ZHabs Pad, he would nullify the decision and probably suggest that one or both of them take an extended vacation. Our respondents maintained that bribery was rare in Sa sKya.

tween two private parties, the criminal aspects of the act took precedence in the government's reaction to a homicide. Sa sKya officials undoubtedly distinguished between murder and other kinds of homicide, even when a private "prosecutor" came forward, and they clearly intended to punish murderers. Our limited information suggests that the subjects of Sa sKya approved the punishment of murderers, or at least that they believed it proper for the government to punish them.[21] We can, however, only speculate about the reasons for this attitude toward murderers, arsonists, and the like. Perhaps Sa sKya had genuine rules of criminal law, rules based on the governed's recognition that they had an obligation to one another to refrain from acts such as murder and that anyone failing in this obligation deserved to be punished.[22] It seems unlikely, however, that law in this sense existed, because the individualism and absence of community feeling in societies such as Sa sKya are probably associated with a relative absence of this kind of social obligation.[23] Another possibility is that both the government and the governed deplored the murderer's willful taking of life and disruption of harmony and believed he should suffer some retribution, although the idea of retribution does not entail government as the agent of retribution. Finally, the punishment of murderers may have been implied by the basic responsibility of government—acknowledged by both governors and governed—to maintain harmony by the use of power. The Sa sKya concept of criminality may have involved all three of these ideas, but

[21] When the culprit was a relative or a friend and the victim a stranger, there was no doubt some resentment regarding the government's actions, but this probably was not intense enough to overcome the belief in the government's right to take these actions.

[22] For an analysis of criminal law in this strict sense, see C. W. Cassinelli, "Criminal Law: The Rules of the Polity," *Ethics*, LXXV (1965), 240–258.

[23] Daniel Lerner, in *The Passing of Traditional Society* (Glencoe, Ill.: Free Press, 1958), p. 50, stresses the low degree of empathy possessed by men he calls "traditional," men in economic and social situations similar to those of Sa sKya.

the use of power to visit deprivations upon those who created serious disharmonies as a means of deterring future acts of discord is the only idea directly connected with the theoretical foundations of the polity.

XIV

The Sa sKya legal system was quite fully developed regarding disputes that could arise among the people over property, debts, contracts, marriage, assault, personal affairs threatening violence, and similar matters. For these disputes to be handled by the Law Officials, one or more of the disputants had to request governmental action, and in this respect they resembled the civil law of the modern polity. The complexity of the Sa sKya economy and individualism of the Sa sKya society required that the authority and power of government be available to provide definitive settlements of these kinds of disputes. Some standards by which the Law Officials could make their judgments were also necessary; these were provided by the Sa sKya code, supplemented by standing orders of the current KHri CHen. These standards were revised only infrequently, an indication that Sa sKya's relatively high stage of economic and social development had remained relatively unchanged for some time.

Actions covered by the criminal law in a modern society were seen in Sa sKya as more than disputes between private parties, but they were probably not seen as the violations of rules to which everyone in the polity subscribed. A society's attitudes toward acts that it considers very undesirable and its beliefs about the ways these acts ought to be dealt with are best illustrated by its government's response to homicide. In Sa sKya, a man's death at the hands of someone else was seen as depriving his family or others who depended upon him of an important material asset and also, no doubt, as an affront to the honor of those most closely associated with him. To satisfy both the deprivation and the affront, a payment was necessary; and, as explicitly stated by the seventh of the Thirteen Pronouncements, the power of government was used to guarantee such a payment and hence to prevent those deprived and affronted from using their own resources in an attempt to obtain satisfaction. Clearly this was a sound method of dealing with homicide; every society should redress the material loss suffered by the dependents of a slain person. The device of allowing the sponsor of the deceased to serve not only as a plaintiff but also as a prosecutor was, however, rather unsophisticated, and it certainly encouraged the preoccupation with the contest between accuser and accused that in the homicide case described above apparently contributed to the government's failure to perform its function of identifying and punishing criminals.

The government of Sa sKya was clearly aware that certain acts by its subjects made them liable for punishment, although, in accordance with the restricted idea of the competence of government, fewer acts were considered punishable than in more "developed" societies. Theft from one of the establishments, as indicated above, was an act that resembled both a tort and a crime. The concept of criminality in Sa sKya seems to have been somewhat weaker than that prevailing in contemporary Western societies. The relatively light punishment received by murderers, who had, after all, committed one of the most heinous acts in Tibetan eyes, is evidence for this supposition. A "first degree" murderer, if he cooperated fully with the Law Officials, promptly paid the life indemnity, and had a sponsor to vouch for his future conduct, would probably have been free within a year or two of his conviction. The conditions of his confinement would have been unpleasant and unhealthful, but the proper gifts to his jailers would have eased his situation considerably.

The government of Sa sKya seems to have been successful enough in apprehending criminals, punishing them, and guaranteeing restitution to those whom they had harmed. Our respondents emphasized the preventive aspects of the criminal procedure in Sa sKya. The inhabitants of Sa sKya were more restrained in their behavior toward one another than were people elsewhere in Tibet,[24] a result, perhaps, of their awareness that the government would use its power to make sure they paid the very substantial life indemnities, served at least a minimal term in prison, and suffered some pretty rough treatment during the process. The goal of harmony and the emphasis on power—illustrated by the practice of flogging upon suspicion, described by the third of the Thirteen Pronouncements as a warning to would-be law-breakers—seem to suggest the use of punishment principally as a means to deter future serious breaches of the peace.[25]

[24] According to Ekvall's experience.
[25] See Cassinelli, "Criminal Law," where it is argued that prevention is at best only a subsidiary effect of "modern" criminal law.

Chapter 7

The KHri CHen and the ZHabs Pad

In the Sa sKya system of government, almost all important decisions were made by the KHri CHen and the ZHabs Pad. The KHri CHen had the only real power of initiative in the system, and his decisions were always final, but the ZHabs Pad had a great amount of autonomy in directing the daily business of government. The Steward of the Religious Establishment performed, for his smaller number of subjects, functions quite similar to those of the ZHabs Pad. Except for the judgments made by the Law Officials regarding degrees of guilt and amounts of indemnities, all actions of lower officials served to carry out the orders of these three men. The ZHabs Pad was formally the representative of the KHri CHen, and the Steward was his representative in fact. The system was very autocratic.

I

The KHri CHen had religious and political functions, and in both he was considered the representative of the aKHon family. The two types of functions were interrelated, but—as shown in Chapter 3—they were considered to be quite independent of one another.

The religious position of the aKHon family came from its status as hereditary emanations of the Bodhisattvas, a status following the bone line and propagated only by the men of the

[186]

family.[1] However the practice of linking emanations with the aKHon bone line began, Sa sKya legend gives its origin in the predictions of holy men, and Sa sKya doctrine teaches that a human being can be the emanation of more than one Bodhisattva and that a Bodhisattva can be emanated in two or more persons at the same time.[2] This second doctrinal point is logically necessary to the linkage of an emanation lineage with a family line.

The emanation bodies of the aKHon family were the focus of the attention of the Sa sKya sect. They had the power to aid ordinary mortals in the long progress toward liberation; they were worshiped, their advice was sought, and offerings were presented to them. The religious position of the KHri CHen was a device to create an even clearer focus for the attention of Sa sKya believers.

Although the governmental position of the KHri CHen was probably the direct descendent of the thirteenth-century position of Ti Shih, it seems that during the period preceding the split of the aKHon family into the PHun TSHogs and sGrol Ma palaces the principal reward of the KHri CHen was a prestige that was offset by heavy religious responsibilities. At the time of the split, the position of KHri CHen appears to have become more desirable, perhaps because of its income, or because of its increased political importance, or because of both. In any event, during the nineteenth and twentieth centuries the KHri CHen was able, within the Sa sKya system, to take any governmental action he desired.

The KHri CHen was the only one in the Sa sKya governmental system who could initiate policy, and the system allowed no effective resistance to any policy that a KHri CHen was determined to pursue. The KHri CHen was also able to make any

[1] The women of the aKHon family were called "rJe bTSun Ma" (revered females); they were designated as nuns, although they were free to marry.

[2] This means that no one need die in order for a male member of the aKHon family to be born an emanation, although aKHon males can be reincarnations of their ancestors.

decision normally reserved for any of his governmental officials or to change any decision made by any of them. The KHri CHen also had final control over the North and South Monasteries and over all appointments of abbots and religious collectors sent from the capital to other parts of Tibet. All promotions within the monasteries that did not follow the principle of seniority had to be approved by the KHri CHen, and KHri CHen NGag dBang mTHu THub dBang PHyug once expelled a monk from the North Monastery without consulting any of its officials. The KHri CHen could also quite autonomously introduce changes in the procedures of religious observance within the monasteries.[3]

The KHri CHen was an autocrat, but only in the sense that other individuals or groups within the polity could not consciously restrict his freedom of action as the principal governor of Sa sKya. He had always to be prepared for criticism from the other branch of his family, but if he chose to, he could ignore it.

The power of the KHri CHen was, however, subject to a number of severe limitations.[4] He was limited by the primitive state of Tibetan technology and by the absence of sophisticated forms of human organization. A KHri CHen could not, for example, mobilize his people for a "great leap forward," nor could he maintain a constant check on their activities and attitudes. Another restriction upon his freedom of action was the inability of the people of Sa sKya to comprehend or to accept marked departures from the usual ways of doing things. The KHri CHen's responsibilities for religious observance, especially for prayer and meditation, were demanding and time-consuming; they interfered with his attention to political matters and hence were a limitation upon his power. The KHri CHen was

---

[3] See Chapter 11 and Appendix E, section II, on the organization and procedures of the North and South Monasteries.

[4] On the theory of autocracy, see C. W. Cassinelli, "Autocracy," *International Encyclopedia of the Social Sciences* (New York: Macmillan and Free Press, 1968), Vol. I.

usually considered more a religious than a political figure, and most KHri CHen may have seen their responsibilities as predominantly religious, and thus have paid a minimum of attention to affairs of government.

The most important restrictions upon the KHri CHen's power came from the system of beliefs accepted by the KHri CHen himself as well as by everyone else. In the first place, as an emanation body, his function was to aid mortals in their striving toward liberation and also to give them practical advice about their mundane affairs. No matter how tenuous the connection between this religious function and the business of maintaining domestic order and collecting revenue, the KHri CHen's responsibility for showing compassion in his religious role prevented him from being a tyrant in his political role. Secondly, although the KHri CHen's governmental autonomy was justified by the power possessed by many generations of his family, this power was in turn justified as an instrument indispensable for the maintenance of harmony; hence, the KHri CHen could not take governmental actions that appeared disruptive of harmony. The concept of power, moreover, included a specific reference to the subjects of power—that is, land and people—and in the Tibetan environment power was maintained only as long as one's people did not "run away." Although the subjects of Sa sKya no doubt suffered occasionally from official highhandedness, their sparse numbers and territorial mobility prevented their governors from using the not uncommon technique of demonstrating governmental power by repeated acts of isolated arbitrariness.

In the third place, the emphasis upon outward appearances and overt behavior and the indifference to what people believed and how they felt were important limitations upon the power of the KHri CHen. Indoctrination and "thought control" were beyond the imagination of the Sa sKya government. Even a proposal to educate the children of subjects—although the extension of literacy would have increased the quantity and improved the quality of religious observance—was considered a rather startling innovation, and it was never implemented.

Finally, the KHri CHen's power was restricted by the basic metaphysical presuppositions of the Sa sKya belief system. The unreality of mundane existence discouraged schemes for changing social and economic arrangements, yet the belief that enlightenment was possible prevented the destructiveness that can result from a nihilist rejection of all cosmic meaningfulness. Although KHri CHen may have considered themselves less at the mercy of natural and supernatural forces than the average man, they shared the prevailing belief that history was cyclical, that conditions would repeat themselves quite independently of anything that men did or did not do, and that they were living during a period of degeneration. The KHri CHen, therefore, probably had a limited conception of what they could accomplish by governmental means.

In short, the KHri CHen of Sa sKya could not have been checked by the conscious action of any other person in the polity, but this freedom was limited to a range of activities circumscribed by the belief, shared by KHri CHen and subjects alike, that the functions of government were minimal.

II

The KHri CHen and the rest of the aKHon family were supported by the people of Sa sKya and the members of the Sa sKya sect throughout Tibet as specialists with superhuman powers to give both spiritual and practical guidance to ordinary mortals. Although the people of Sa sKya separated religion from government, the religious status of the aKHon family made it a natural nucleus of a polity, and increases in the KHri CHen's religious prestige served to augment his ability to accomplish things through the use of his government.

The KHri CHen of Sa sKya was a famous religious figure and as such was credited with supernatural powers. KHri CHen NGag dBang mTHu THub dBang PHyug, for example, while traveling in Nepal, was halted by a stream of water pouring across the road, but he cleared the way by causing the water to reverse its direction and flow uphill. He was once in western Tibet, three days from the nearest water, and by prayer he caused a spring to gush forth from the rocks. On another occasion, to avoid placing his shawl on a dirty floor, he hung it on a sunbeam entering the room. On the death of his father, he went into meditation and then disappeared for three days. When he reappeared, he had fresh fruit and flowers in his hands, although it was winter. He explained that he had been with his father, and the flowers and fruit were preserved in the PHun TSHogs palace. He was twice visited by the female divinities who appear to those who have reached high religious attainment,[5] and their visits were marked by the appearance of women on the mountains and rainbows in the palace. The KHri CHen also was able to predict future events.[6]

Although the Khri CHen and the other members of the aKHon family were august religious and political figures, Tibetan custom and the small size and population of Sa sKya made

---

[5] These beings are called "mKHaa aGro Ma" (sky go females).

[6] One of the more interesting anecdotes about clairvoyance concerned KHri CHen aDZam Gling CHe dGu dBang sDud. In preparing to go to Lhasa to pay his respects upon becoming KHri CHen—some fifteen years after the event—he insisted upon taking a tent. The other members of his party saw no sense in thus encumbering the voyage. Upon his arrival in Lhasa in February, 1910, he was visited by the thirteenth Dalai Lama, who had remained in Lhasa although he believed that a Chinese military force was close to the city. The Dalai Lama asked the KHri CHen to divine in order to discover what he should do. The KHri CHen divined and urged the Dalai Lama to flee immediately to India. The Dalai Lama took this advice. The KHri CHen then announced that he and his party were leaving for Sa sKya on the morrow. This decision was not too popular with his party, for they had just arrived, but the KHri CHen insisted. That night the Chinese reached Lhasa and the Sa sKya party was obliged to return home via the back roads through uninhabited country. There the KHri CHen was comfortable at night in his tent, and the rest of the party, including the ZHabs Pad, were miserable with the cold.

them very accessible to their subjects. The KHri CHen was supposed to make formal tours of Sa sKya proper that took him to each village about once in ten years. These trips were designed to check on the work of local officials, to aid families and communities in need, and generally to learn about conditions outside the capital. During such visits to a locality, the subjects, usually but not always through their Headman, could bring their problems to the KHri CHen, not directly but through a Liaison Officer and the KHri CHen's Butler. The answer was sent back through the same channels, but if the problem appeared serious, the KHri CHen referred it to the ZHabs Pad. Perhaps four problems were brought in this way to the KHri CHen at each of his stops, and although his contact with his subjects was indirect, it nonetheless was a clear indication of his interest in their affairs.

After these addresses had been taken care of, families or groups of families brought religious offerings to the KHri CHen and received his blessings. These offerings did not have to be elaborate or expensive, so even the poorest families were able to participate. The KHri CHen's blessing varied according to the status of those receiving it, but every blessing involved some personal contact with him.

It was not known how faithfully recent KHri CHen followed this practice of periodic tours. NGag dBang mTHu THub dBang PHyug departed from it by substituting a larger number of informal trips scheduled at short notice. He said that the custom of formal tours was too expensive, since it involved a large retinue and elaborate receptions. The KHri CHen's sons accompanied him on many of these trips, and perhaps once a year they also came in contact with the people outside the capital while traveling on their own business. This contact was, of course, only religious.

In addition to the KHri CHen's going to the subjects, the subjects came to the KHri CHen. Each summer and winter there was an important religious festival in the capital. Everyone who was free attended these gala affairs, and members of families took turns coming to the capital. It was estimated that each year 30 per cent of all the people of Sa sKya proper attended each of the two festivals, where the KHri CHen and aKHon family were on view to be worshiped. Many subjects also went to the capital on business, perhaps with revenue in kind or perhaps in attendance upon a nobleman or an official. Even the humblest subject had a right to an audience with the KHri CHen to present an offering and to receive a blessing, and the KHri CHen was supposed to be always available for such interviews. Obviously this right could not have been fully exercised, but NGag dBang mTHu THub dBang PHyug spent many hours talking to poor pilgrims from outlying areas, often to the annoyance of the ZHabs Pad, waiting to discuss pressing governmental business with his superior. Communication in Tibet was principally by word of mouth, and the KHri CHen was always anxious to get the latest news from any available source.[7]

Despite this accessibility of the KHri CHen, our respondents believed that he was relatively immune from popular criticism, his officials receiving the blame for any policy that went wrong or activity that was disliked. Although this separation of the monarch from his assistants usually depends upon his physical distance from the governed, the supernatural attributes of the KHri CHen probably gave him the necessary mysterious quality.

III

When a KHri CHen died in office, his next of kin—his brother, sons, daughters, and wife, in that order—automatically

[7] In the fall of 1966, Ekvall was in Switzerland interviewing Tibetan refugees for a work on pilgrimage. A woman from eastern Tibet had visited Sa sKya before 1950, and she stressed KHri CHen NGag dBang mTHu THub dBang PHyug's accessibility to pilgrims. "A very great lama and different from other lamas. He took time to talk with me, just a poor pilgrim woman, and asked me about my home, where I had been, and what I had seen and heard. He then ordered that my food bag be filled and told me to 'go carefully.' "

became KHri mJug, a kind of interim KHri CHen with the full powers of the office, until the end of the period of mourning. The mourning period lasted at least six months, and as long as a year if the palace of the deceased KHri CHen wished to make it a grand affair. For the first forty-nine days after a KHri CHen's death, social gatherings, the wearing of ornaments, and the slaughter of animals were prohibited in the capital. Seven days after his death, the body of the KHri CHen was cremated, although this treatment was not in accord with strict religious principle. Forty-two days later the ashes were mixed with clay to make two thousand images, which were placed in a stupa on the "life hills" (Bla Ri) of the aKHon family near the capital, and the bones were ground up to make eight thousand smaller images, which were placed in a stupa in the South Monastery.[8] During the period of mourning, the monks of the North and South Monasteries, working in shifts, said thirty million incantations of a Sanscrit formula of about twenty syllables.

At the end of the period of mourning, a big celebration was held in the capital. The ZHabs Pad then called a meeting of government and monastery officials,[9] and he and the Chief Secretary announced the order of succession to the KHri CHen-ship according to the principle of seniority. The assembled notables then ratified this order, and a statement declaring the man at the head of the list to be the KHri Ba (throne one) was written and sealed by the ZHabs Pad with the Government seal, by the Treasurers of the two palaces with the palaces' seals, the Steward of the Religious Establishment, the Abbots of the North and South Monasteries, the treasurers of the six subdivisions of the two palaces, and the sixteen District Officers.

[8] Each palace had a room in the South Monastery for the relics of all its members and for copper likenesses, copied from the corpses, of each member. Only the KHri CHen had stupas, and the wives of aKHon males had only likenesses. There was a room in the North Monastery for the relics and silver likenesses of the aKHon family before its division into the two palaces.

[9] This was a "Great Assembly Meeting" (see section IV below).

This document was then sent to the Dalai Lama, who sealed and returned it. This act of the Dalai Lama was explained as "giving his approval of Sa sKya custom," and it was said that he could not possibly find a reason for withholding his approval. In view of the history of internal dissensions within Sa sKya and of the attitude of Lhasa to the small principality, Lhasa had less interest in this act as a symbol of its superiority than Sa sKya had as a means of giving weight to the choice of KHri Ba in the event of a future disagreement or challenge. Since the choice of KHri Ba was not considered authentic until the declaration had been sealed by the Lhasa government, any delay by Lhasa left the matter of succession unsettled. As has been shown, the rivalry between the two Sa sKya palaces could lead to real trouble in the event of an unsettled succession, and evidence suggests that Lhasa did not take its responsibility too seriously.

When the declaration that one of the aKHon family was KHri Ba had been returned to the capital with Dalai Lama's seal, the ZHabs Pad held the document until the twenty-third day of the eleventh moon, when he formally announced the decision. On the twenty-ninth day of the eleventh moon, a thirty-day celebration began. At the end of this celebration, on the first day of the first moon, the KHri Ba ascended a two-layer throne: the lower part, of unfired brick, was reputedly the throne of Sa sKya Pandita and it symbolized religion; the upper part, of wood decorated with gold filigree, was reputedly the throne of aPHags Pa and it symbolized government. For three days the KHri Ba made religious offerings and delivered sermons from this throne, each offering ceremony lasting about three hours and each sermon about two hours. The sermons consisted of utterances of the Buddha, readings from the book of Sa sKya religious doctrine, and, at the KHri Ba's discretion, anything else he thought appropriate to say on the occasion. These ceremonies were attended by both branches of the aKHon family, all the governmental and monastic officials, representatives from Lhasa and Shigatse, and probably everyone in the capital and half of the remaining people of Sa sKya proper. When the ceremonies were completed, the KHri Ba became the KHri CHen.

According to custom, the new KHri CHen went to Lhasa to pay his respects to the Dalai Lama and his government, to receive their congratulations, and no doubt to remind them of the importance of the Sa sKya sect and the existence of the Sa sKya polity. Although this trip clearly indicated the superiority of Lhasa in the political affairs of central Tibet, it was apparently not considered very urgent in Sa sKya. aDZam Gling CHe dGu dBang sDud took about fifteen years to get to Lhasa after becoming KHri CHen, and NGag dBang mTHu THub dBang PHyug took about eleven years.[10]

The process of choosing and installing a KHri CHen had several obvious but important characteristics. It was, first of all, leisurely. A year or more could pass between the death of one KHri CHen and the installment of his successor. Although some member of the aKHon family always nominally headed the government, the KHri mJug and even the KHri Ba did not have full authority. The business of government proceeded, however, under the direction of the ZHabs Pad. The only power lacking in this interregnum was the power of initiative, and few situations in Sa sKya required this special power. When the succession was disputed, there was likely to be an even longer interval during which no one was clearly in charge of the Sa sKya sect and polity, but this delay did not seem to cause any serious inconveniences. Secondly, the symbolism of installing a KHri CHen referred clearly to both religious and governmental power, and the device of the superimposed thrones was nicely chosen to indicate his dual position. Finally, the mechanics of succession involved an impressive amount of pomp to emphasize

---

[10] There was also a position called "KHri TSHab" (throne substitute); the KHri TSHab acted as KHri CHen in the latter's absence. When KHri CHen NGag dBang mTHu THub dBang PHyug went to Lhasa in 1947, his father's sister was KHri TSHab during the eight months he was absent.

the significance of the KHri CHen-ship in the Sa sKya political and religious systems. The ceremonies were witnessed by a large proportion of the total population of the small polity, thus providing a remarkable opportunity—matched, perhaps, only by television—for the common man to associate himself with the regime.

When a KHri CHen was installed, the officials of the establishments and the monasteries took nothing resembling an oath of loyalty to him, even though in Tibetan monastic orders oaths to the Buddha and to one's teacher were standard practice. Tradition has it that aPHags Pa abolished the assemblies where allegiance was sworn to the ruler, a practice common in Tibet in his time. Any person accepting a position in any of the establishments also took no oath to it. We got the impression that every member of the polity was assumed to have a continuing allegiance to the aKHon family, and that the act of accepting sKu Drag status implied complete association with the governing group. If this assumption did exist, it fit very well with the basic justification of government in terms of continuity of power.

IV

KHri CHen NGag dBang mTHu THub dBang PHyug used to arise about three or three-thirty in the morning; he prayed and meditated until six, when his servants arrived to give him breakfast and prepare him for the day.[11] He wore the basic costume of a Sa sKya monk, but since he was not celibate he wore a white skirt instead of the regular red skirt. He carried a blessing wand, but he had no symbol of his secular position. The metal parts of his saddle and his stirrups were decorated with gold inlay or filigree, there was a red tassel hanging on the throat

[11] A written description of the daily activities of the KHri CHen was kept by the Archivist. A similar account was kept in Burma, to describe the "ideal of Buddhist kingship in action," an ideal that also required saying many prayers (John C. Cady, *Southeast Asia* [New York: McGraw-Hill, 1964], p. 388).

strap of his bridle and one on the martingale, and on top of the bridle were three peacock feathers or an iron piece made in the form of a peacock feather.

From eight in the morning until six in the evening, the KHri CHen attended to governmental and religious business, taking two hours for lunch. On five or six days of the month, however, the period from eight until noon was spent praying and making offerings, and on two or three days, the afternoon period from two to six was similarly spent. On these special days, the two-hour lunch period was used for any important mundane business. At seven-thirty in the evening, the KHri CHen ate dinner, the important meal of the day, with his family and perhaps some personal friends, and at ten everyone went to bed. In the winter, the KHri CHen's whole day was spent in the Government Building, and in the summer he lived in the PHun TSHogs palace and spent his working day from eight to six in the South Monastery. Governmental business did not fully occupy these working hours. NGag dBang mTHu THub dBang PHyug spent a large proportion of these periods editing religious texts for printing or manuscribing, assisted by monks from the North and South Monasteries.

During the daily periods devoted to governmental and religious affairs, the KHri CHen was contacted three or four times by a Liaison Officer on official business from the ZHabs Pad. These contacts were indirect, going through the KHri CHen's Doorman and Butler. If the ZHabs Pad, the Steward of the Religious Establishment, or the Chief Secretary wished a direct meeting with the KHri CHen, an appointment had to be made a day in advance; tea was usually served at the meeting. Despite the formality of these official contacts with high dignitaries, the KHri CHen was supposed to be always available to the humblest subject who had an offering and wanted a blessing.

Sa sKya subjects who had a grievance were allowed to make a written appeal to the ZHabs Pad if their attempts to get lower officials to act had failed; and, if dissatisfied with the results of this appeal, they had the right to address a further written appeal to both the ZHabs Pad and the KHri CHen. As long as the subject had exhausted the preliminary forms of appeal, he was in no danger (it was said) of getting in trouble from going over the heads of lower officials, but these preliminary forms were so complicated and expensive that the right to appeal to the highest figures in the polity was probably more formal than real. In any event, NGag dBang mTHu THub dBang PHyug reportedly tried to encourage his subjects to send formal complaints to him. He also sent secret agents throughout Sa sKya proper to discover what the subjects were talking about and how they were being treated by their officials.[12]

NGag dBang mTHu THub dBang PHyug was very interested in governmental affairs, and this interest led him to depart somewhat from precedent. He regularly called various governmental officials to personal meetings and asked their opinions on issues of policy. If he liked the official's opinion, he presented him with a gift. If the official was unable to produce an opinion, the KHri CHen would tell him to think about the matter and prepare a written report. This practice reportedly made the Sa sKya officialdom somewhat nervous; those who had lately been to see him were always asked what he was currently thinking about.

NGag dBang mTHu THub dBang PHyug's interest in government and his desire to introduce certain innovations led him to use great care in choosing his higher officials. For the first six years of his reign, he had only an Acting ZHabs Pad. He then found the man he wanted—PHun KHang, who is described below—but did not promote him from Acting ZHabs Pad to ZHabs Pad for five more years. The KHri CHen also had no

[12] KHri CHen aDZam Gling CHe dGu dBang sDud, the father of NGag dBang mTHu THub dBang PHyug, was reportedly very friendly with his subjects, both before and after he became KHri CHen. He kept a supply of food and drink for them on the lower floor of the PHun TSHogs palace and often joined them for tea. This behavior naturally prompted many remarks about the dignity of the KHri CHen.

Chief Secretary, acting or otherwise, for ten years; he then appointed a man from outside Sa sKya proper. And for twelve years he had only one Secretary. He was criticized for leaving these positions unoccupied, but he answered that the government would continue to operate until he found men of real ability. He was probably right; the government of Sa sKya could function for years without its highest officials as well as without its monarch.

According to his sons, NGag dBang mTHu THub dBang PHyug did not like to give orders, preferring to try to influence the people he was dealing with to arrive at a decision or action he himself approved. In 1945 the corner of the Great God House of the South Monastery collapsed, and the KHri CHen called a Great Assembly Meeting to discuss its repair. Although he preferred to make the repairs by drawing upon the treasuries of all the establishments and levying labor from the subjects, he made no suggestions to his officials. The largest group of these officials wanted to seek a loan from outside Sa sKya; the KHri CHen agreed, but he said that the loan must come from the Lhasa government and carry no interest. No doubt to his surprise, Lhasa agreed to an interest-free loan, and his failure to use his power frustrated his desire to repair the monastery without outside help.[13]

The Great Assembly Meeting mentioned above was a formal gathering of the officials of the several establishments and the North and South Monasteries.[14] Such meetings were called on important occasions, as when the ZHabs Pad reported who was to be KHri Ba and when the KHri CHen wished to announce an important policy. Whenever a ZHabs Pad was to be appointed, the KHri Chen was supposed to call a Great Assembly Meeting to ask for suggestions, but NGag dBang mTHu THub dBang

---

[13] The details on the repairs to the South Monastery are in Chapter 11, section IX, and Appendix D, section IV.

[14] The officials who attended these Meetings are listed in Appendix C, section II.

PHyug did not call one when he promoted PHun KHang from Acting ZHabs Pad. During his reign from 1936 to 1950, the KHri CHen called five Great Assembly Meetings: shortly after his enthronement, to announce certain policies he intended to pursue and to ask for the support of his officials; again shortly after his succession, to announce the punishment of a high official who had been found guilty of an act of treason; the 1945 meeting mentioned above; another meeting shortly thereafter, to announce the decision to seek the loan from the Lhasa government; and, last, in 1947, on the eve of his departure for Lhasa, apparently only to formalize the occasion. A KHri CHen never appeared in person at Great Assembly Meetings; the ZHabs Pad always spoke for him.

NGag dBang mTHu THub dBang PHyug believed that the KHri CHen should maintain his independence within Sa sKya in the same way that Sa sKya ought to maintain its independence within Tibet. This was the way of "harmony," the avoidance of creating discord by too frequent an exercise of power. Power should be carefully preserved; it had to be used sparingly. This principle of action seems wise in view of Sa sKya's position relative to the other governments of central Tibet, and it is a good indication of the limited nature of the KHri CHen's power.[15]

After the death of a KHri CHen, the Secretaries made a collection of all his statements regarding governmental matters, such as his special orders and his additions to the code. Some KHri CHen had said little about secular affairs, but NGag dBang mTHu THub dBang PHyug's collection weighed about seventy pounds.

V

The KHri CHen was an autocrat in the sense that he could make any governmental decision consistent with the beliefs and

[15] The more power a single man has, the more he must use it (see Cassinelli, "Autocracy").

customs of Sa sKya. The day-to-day business of government, however, was the responsibility of the ZHabs Pad,[16] and in the small polity this high dignitary himself made almost every governmental decision that was not made by the KHri CHen. The only exceptions were the independent decisions made by the District Officers, sometimes in conjunction with the Headmen, which were minor concessions to efficiency through decentralization, and the decisions of the Law Officials, which always gave some choice to the ZHabs Pad. Every official in the capital naturally had some discretion in the conduct of his office, but the important decisions connected with his function were made by the ZHabs Pad.

The ZHabs Pad was appointed by the KHri CHen, who was supposed to convoke a Great Assembly Meeting and ask it to send him a list of candidates, but who could select his own man without reference to anyone else. The method of selecting a ZHabs Pad no doubt depended upon the KHri CHen's interest in governmental affairs; anyone preferred by the KHri CHen was almost certainly on the Great Assembly Meeting's list of candidates.

A man was notified that he had been chosen to be the ZHabs Pad by the Acting ZHabs Pad, or by the Chief Secretary if he was himself the Acting ZHabs Pad. The new appointee selected an auspicious day upon which to present himself to the KHri CHen for an exchange of scarves and for congratulations. After this interview, the appointee went to the office of the ZHabs Pad, where the Acting ZHabs Pad or the Chief Secretary presented him with the Government seal, two eighteen-inch red

---

[16] "ZHabs Pad" means "lotus foot," an honorific; this title, with the appropriate additional honorifics, was used in addressing the ZHabs Pad by everyone from the royal family to the lowest subject. Letters to the ZHabs Pad used another title, Mi dBang CHen Mo (man power great one), and occasionally he was personally addressed by this title. Among themselves, the royal family called the ZHabs Pad the "mDZod Pa," or the "doer," a very descriptive name but not to be used in addressing him. "mDZod Pa" resembles the word "vizier," the bearer of burdens.

tassels for his horse, and the special hats of the ZHabs Pad.[17] The ZHabs Pad took no oath of office or of loyalty to the KHri CHen, who acted as the representative of the aKHon family in appointing him. Since the custom was that a ZHabs Pad remain in office until his death or retirement, he was viewed as the agent of the aKHon family and not of the KHri CHen who appointed him.

In appointing a ZHabs Pad, the KHri CHen exercised his governmental power, and the appointee became the personification of this aspect of the power of the aKHon family, its power to constitute a gZHung. The ZHabs Pad controlled the Government seal—the KHri CHen used the seal of his palace—and on occasions such as the announcement of a KHri Ba, the ZHabs Pad acted, as head of the Government, independently of the aKHon family. The letters from Lhasa reconfirming the principle of seniority regarding succession to the Sa sKya throne were addressed to the ZHabs Pad as head of the Government. There was no expression in Sa sKya comparable to "His Majesty's Government," but when a ZHabs Pad died in office, half his clothing, horses, and riding equipment became the property of the KHri CHen, a common way to symbolize a master-servant relationship.[18]

An Acting ZHabs Pad was also chosen by the KHri CHen. He had the full powers of the office, but he could not occupy the special chair in the ZHabs Pad's office, and his formal rank was lower rather than higher than that of a Retired ZHabs Pad,

[17] The summer hat of the ZHabs Pad was yellow, with a brim and red fringe on the crown. The winter hat was an old-regime Chinese official hat with an upturned black fur brim and a red crown with short black fringe. Each had a coral-colored button on the top. If the ZHabs Pad were a layman, both his hats had a bundle of the black hair-like feathers of the eared pheasant slanting backward from the crown like a plume.

[18] The KHri CHen also got from the ZHabs Pad's estate equipment for five servants. The other half of the clothing, horses, and riding gear went to the Government. Upon the death of a lower official, one of his suits of clothing went to the KHri CHen and one to the Government.

whose status was below only that of ZHabs Pad. One ZHabs Pad who was considered to have been disloyal to the KHri CHen was removed from office and denied the status of Retired ZHabs Pad.

The formal attire of the ZHabs Pad differed from that of other high officials by virtue of a coral-colored button on the top of his hat; the other officials wore buttons of other colors according to their rank. ZHabs Pad who were laymen dressed rather elaborately, but those who were monks wore only the usual monk's costume. The ZHabs Pad was always accompanied by a few lesser officials, but aside from this it was apparently not thought necessary to impress the subjects with the dignity of the office. The capital was small enough that everyone could recognize the ZHabs Pad. Upon encountering him the subjects were supposed at least to remove their hats and optionally to make other signs of deference. When we inquired what happened when someone omitted these acts of respect, when, for instance, a drunk just stood gawking, the answer was that if this drunken breach of manners occurred in the afternoon, the offender was probably only spoken to, but if it happened in the morning, some action was probably taken. Repeated instances of disrespect were punished.

The office of ZHabs Pad was well paid and it could make a poor man his fortune. The ZHabs Pad was assigned a generous amount of Government farm land to be used for his own profit; he received a regular income from the special monastery distributions and the religious collectors; and a varying proportion of the revenue in kind—one-third of the straw and fuel, and small amounts of grain, meat, cheese, and butter—were given him for his personal use. Although he was expected to be generous in his religious offerings and in contributions to celebrations and special public projects, the ZHabs Pad (unlike a few other high officials) had no regularly scheduled expenditures on such matters.

The largest part of his income probably came as gifts from

people who had business with the Government or who just sought friendly relations with its head. There was a rough dividing line between an appropriate gift and an attempted bribe. If someone wished to see the ZHabs Pad personally on some urgent matter, the discreet presentation of a side of prime beef and some fresh butter was within the bounds of propriety. In relation to the standard of living of most people in Sa sKya, this gift— worth perhaps 190 Srang—was substantial.[19] The last ZHabs Pad hired several men to use his wealth in trading ventures.

Subject laymen who became ZHabs Pad were normally raised to the station of hereditary noblemen.[20] A subject monk could not, of course, carry on a noble line, but his family would probably be given as their private land at least part of the Government land that went with the office of ZHabs Pad. They also had obtained a famous ancestor who would help their later claim to noble status, in the event that someone of a subsequent generation distinguished himself.

VI

The ZHabs Pad was usually a man who had had many years' experience in governmental positions, and once in office he usually remained there until his death or retirement. The appointment of a ZHabs Pad was a very important decision; as our respondents said, Sa sKya was governed well or badly depending upon the kind of man who was ZHabs Pad.

From some time before 1900 until about 1915, the ZHabs Pad was a monk from the noble SHab house of Bla Mags, who retired at the age of sixty. His previous governmental experience was not known. From about 1915 until 1936, the ZHabs Pad was TSHe Ring dBang rGyal, a layman of the noble SHab house of SHar ZHabs Pad. Before becoming ZHabs Pad, he had been a Liaison Officer and then a Secretary. From 1936 until 1942, there was an Acting ZHabs Pad, a monk from the noble SHab

[19] See Appendix D, sections II and III.
[20] The status of Drag bTSan (see Chapter 8, section II).

house of Nang bSam Pa. He had been Steward of the Religious Establishment, and he returned to this position in 1942.

In 1942 KHri CHen NGag dBang mTHu THub dBang PHyug appointed as Acting ZHabs Pad a monk, PHun KHang bKra SHis bZang Po. PHun KHang was from a well-established but not wealthy subject family of the SHab Valley that had previously not produced any especially distinguished men. He had advanced through the ranks of the South Monastery until he became a "doctor of theology." In 1936, as the story goes, PHun KHang was instrumental in preventing an act of violence against the person of the KHri CHen, and he was promoted to keeper of the Great God House in the South Monastery.[21] Shortly there-after he became Steward of the Religious Establishment, and in 1942 the KHri CHen arranged for Nang bSam Pa and PHun KHang to exchange positions—an exchange approved by Nang bSam Pa, who resumed his job as Steward. In 1947, PHun KHang was made ZHabs Pad. NGag dBang mTHu THub dBang PHyug wanted to choose his highest officials very care-fully, and he made PHun KHang Steward of the Religious Establishment in order to give him governmental experience and to test his ability. The five-year period when PHun KHang was Acting ZHabs Pad was a further test of his ability, but since he was from a relatively undistinguished family of subjects, the KHri CHen also wanted to see how he was accepted by both subjects and nobility. According to our respondents, PHun KHang possessed the natural dignity to impress all social strata.

The land given to PHun KHang as ZHabs Pad was near his family's home in Bar sDings. This land was managed by his brother, PHun KHang himself getting to Bar sDings only about once a year for a week or so. The ZHabs Pad traveled very little, virtually never having to leave the capital on governmental busi-ness. He bought a rather expensive house in the west village, hired a treasurer and a steward, and had several traders working

[21] On these monastic offices, see Appendix C, section II, and Appendix E, section II.

for him. Each morning about nine the two Keepers of the Keys met him at his home and, with two of his servants, escorted him to his office; they returned with him at five or six in the afternoon. In winter they all walked to the Government Building, and in summer they rode to the South Monastery. During festivals, the ZHabs Pad was accompanied by the Doormen as bodyguards. When moving about at night, the ZHabs Pad, like other high officials, went rather heavily armed. This precaution was taken, it was explained, not because he was unpopular, but because not even the most able ZHabs Pad could please everyone. Even in Sa sKya the strain of violence in Tibetan life was present.

PHun KHang owed his remarkable career to the faith in him possessed by KHri CHen NGag dBang mTHu THub dBang PHyug of the PHun TSHogs palace. As ZHabs Pad, however, he tried to maintain a strict neutrality in the rivalry between the two palaces. His loyalty was to the KHri CHen as the representative of the aKHon family, and in the dispute over the succession following the death of NGag dBang mTHu THub dBang PHyug in 1950, he was concerned only with getting some kind of settlement. PHun KHang remained in Sa sKya after it was occupied by the Chinese Communists, and in 1960 he was executed in a "people's trial."

VII

The dignity of the ZHabs Pad required everyone, except the Chief Secretary and the Steward of the Religious Establishment, to deal with him indirectly through a Liaison Officer. Indeed, whenever he left his office during business hours, he was accompanied by a Liaison Officer (and by some lesser officials to swell the entourage). Using an intermediary not only maintained the proper social distance between the ZHabs Pad and his subordinates and subjects; it also made his power appear less personal, avoided the embarrassment of a direct contact between the man who made the decision and the man who had to abide by it, and prevented the possibility of anyone's questioning the ZHabs Pad's decisions.

All formal governmental business with the ZHabs Pad was conducted through a Liaison Officer, but a lower official, or more rarely a private person of some importance, could contact him informally on matters considered delicate. This contact could have been personal, usually at the home of the ZHabs Pad, or by a letter taken to his home, for letters sent to his office were opened by the Secretaries.[22] For example, a District Officer faced with a complicated problem or under attack might have been anxious that the ZHabs Pad have a clear understanding of the situation. In a private meeting he could speak frankly and avoid distortions, and the ZHabs Pad was usually willing to grant this private interview as long as the District Officer had not bothered him with too many such requests in the past. The District Officer was sure to arrive with something expensive enough to be considered a handsome gift but not so expensive to be seen as an attempt at bribery. If any agreement was reached at these private meetings, it was later acted upon according to the proper formal procedures.

There was a presumption in Sa sKya that the ZHabs Pad was somehow to share his responsibilities with the Chief Secretary. Since the Chief Secretary had no authority over subjects or lower officials (except the three Secretaries), in practice he could serve only as a consultant. Because of the presumption, however, and because the two officials shared the same office, the ZHabs Pad no doubt usually wished to be on good terms with the Chief Secretary and may even have informed him of the important or delicate matters that he dealt with in his private meetings with lower officials or prominent subjects or noblemen. KHri CHen NGag dBang mTHu THub dBang PHyug was very careful in his selection of a Chief Secretary, leaving the

---

[22] The Tibetans call a private meeting bypassing the regular channels an "inner" meeting; the formal method brought about an "outer" meeting.

office vacant for about ten years until he found a man to his liking.

According to our respondents, the job of the ZHabs Pad was difficult and arduous, and the man who undertook it deserved all the wealth that came to him. Much of his time was spent resolving disagreements among his subordinates. On some mornings the ZHabs Pad arrived at his office to find a queue of officials waiting to contact him, and "he had to have an answer for each one." Unfortunately we could get little information on the specific problems typically presented to the ZHabs Pad, but he unquestionably was subject to many pressures and requests for special treatment. The system's centralization meant that only the ZHabs Pad could make adjustments. He was unavoidably preoccupied with the myriad details of the daily operation of the government.

VIII

The ZHabs Pad had impressive formal powers. He authorized the choice of Headmen, and if the subjects could not agree on a Headman he could appoint one for them. He appointed all District Officers. He appointed all officials of the Work Corps, with the KHri CHen's approval only in the case of the Sedan Officer, and all lower officials of the Government in the capital. He approved all the appointments to the staff of the Religious Establishment made by the Steward, and he had the power to resolve any disputes between the Steward and his subjects over the appointment of Religious Establishment Headmen. He appointed, with the express approval of the KHri CHen, the two Group Officials, the Candidates, and all officials above the rank of the Work Corps. He could dismiss any of the officials for whose appointment he was solely responsible, and he may have been able to dismiss for cause even those officials whose appointments were expressly approved by the KHri CHen.

The ZHabs Pad controlled all the Government's supplies. He had the only full inventory of the Government's stores, and all withdrawals from them had to have his approval. He authorized withdrawals of grain or other food for distribution to subjects at times of severe shortage. All material drawn from Government stores for the maintenance of public buildings, roads and bridges, and the capital's irrigation system needed his consent, and he also fixed and allocated the labor for this maintenance. He decided how the annual requests from the Lhasa government for military supplies were to be met, and he authorized the conscription of men for the Lhasa army. He authorized and organized the levy of monks for the South Monastery.[23] He approved all requests for animals and men under the transport levy and sent them to the KHri CHen for final authorization. The document certifying a traveling official's right to the levy of transport was sealed by both the ZHabs Pad and KHri CHen.[24]

The ZHabs Pad had control of all matters concerning revenue in kind. Any adjustments in the revenue schedules had to have his approval, but permanent changes could be approved only by the KHri CHen.

The ZHabs Pad had the only index to the Government's archives, which contained vital statistics and revenue schedules and which included a copy of the records of the Religious Establishment and information on the families owing allegiance to the nobility. Definitive copies of the Sa sKya code and of all the KHri CHen's special orders were also in the archives. Access to the archives required the ZHabs Pad's approval. He controlled the seal of the Government, and at the Great Assembly Meetings he spoke for the KHri CHen. He also dealt directly with important people who came into Sa sKya on business—for example, a district commissioner of the Lhasa government come to discuss a quarrel between subjects of the two governments. He also welcomed important guests who were passing through Sa sKya.

The ZHabs Pad was in charge of the governmental process

[23] See Chapter 11, section III.

[24] This document was called a "Lam Yig" (road letter).

that dealt with acts by subjects considered to be serious breaches of the peace. All such acts were immediately reported to him, and he determined the suspicion that led to an arrest. If an arrest proved difficult, he sent some of the policemen or floggers to effect it. His jurisdiction included all subjects of the Government, the nobility, and the palaces, and when the act had been committed by a subject of the Religious Establishment, the Steward consulted with him. The Law Officials determined ranges of guilt and punishment, but the ZHabs Pad made the exact decisions within these ranges. He also had the power of pardon. If it were proved to the ZHabs Pad that the Law Officials had been bribed, he could declare their decisions invalid.

The ZHabs Pad authorized the reference of all private disputes to the Law Officials. All their decisions were sent to him, and he spent a large portion of his time reading them. The ZHabs Pad had no power to change any decision in which the Law Officials had acted as mediators, but all other decisions needed his approval. Important matters like declarations of bankruptcy also needed his approval. He could order that an unusually disruptive quarrel be brought to the Law Officials, or he could himself order the disputants to stop quarreling. The ZHabs Pad and the two Law Officials constituted a special court to handle charges of disloyalty or treason.

All these decisions within the power of the ZHabs Pad could also have been made by the KHri CHen, but a KHri CHen could obviously not overrule his ZHabs Pad too frequently, and probably he was usually too busy with his religious responsibilities to follow any but the most important matters very closely. We discovered cases in which the ZHabs Pad sought the opinion of the KHri CHen regarding matters that proved difficult to resolve and cases in which the ZHabs Pad privately disagreed with a decision the KHri CHen was determined to make. Every subject or lower official had the right to appeal a decision of the

ZHabs Pad to the KHri CHen by sending a letter addressed to both of them, but this right was no doubt exercised very infrequently.

IX

Sa sKya was governed by the ZHabs Pad. He had about two dozen assistants of one kind or another, and in all his actions he was directly responsible to the KHri CHen.

Every decision to use the coercive power of government was made by the ZHabs Pad: the settlement of disputes at civil law, actions to preserve the peace, the punishment of criminals, the collection of revenue in kind and labor, and the draft of soldiers and monks, all took place upon his initiative and authorization. His decisions were taken within the framework of the Thirteen Pronouncements, the Sa sKya code, and the standing orders of the incumbent KHri CHen. Although the ZHabs Pad had no power to alter this framework, by his actions he created the routine of the governing process, and he could always depart temporarily from this routine. Only the KHri CHen could make permanent changes in the routine, but they had few reasons for introducing innovations.

The ZHabs Pad made every type of governmental decision except those reserved for the Law Officials, namely, the decisions that an illegal or serious antisocial act had been committed and that its perpetrator was to make a restitution or suffer a punishment or both. These decisions concern two of the most elementary functions of government—indeed, having a recognized agency to decide that an antisocial act has occurred may define a polity—and it is significant that the government of Sa sKya, a minimal government in a literate society, exhibited this single instance of a "separation of powers."

The Sa sKya governmental system appears to have been reasonably efficient. The ZHabs Pad had to supervise the work of sixteen officials—the Work Corps, the Archivist, the Keepers of the Keys, and the Liaison Officers; he had to review and approve the work of the Law Officials; and he had to cooperate with the Steward of the Religious Establishment and the Chief Secretary (who supervised the Secretaries). The system also seems to have been tolerably effective: the small apparatus of government, more or less indifferent to its subjects and relying upon the presumption that almost all problems should be resolved by nongovernmental means, had relatively very little to do.

Chapter 8

The Hereditary Nobility

The hereditary nobility of Sa sKya apparently dates from the thirteenth century, when aPHags Pa gave noble status to his military and civil officials, including Headmen. From the thirteenth to the twentieth century, new noble lines were periodically added, created by the KHri CHen as a reward for services to himself or to the government.

The original intention was probably for the nobility to provide all the officials of the central government and to help hold the polity together through a decentralized "feudal" arrangement.[1] By the twentieth century, the nobility had lost its monopoly of governmental office, probably because it could not supply enough men, and the small territory of Sa sKya proper could be governed from a single source.[2] Some noblemen had a few subjects as late as the mid-twentieth century, but this arrangement had little political or economic importance.

I

Despite its reduced circumstances, the Sa sKya nobility is interesting for several reasons. Even though it shared govern-

---

[1] Pedro Carrasco, in *Land and Polity in Tibet* (Seattle: University of Washington Press, 1959), p. 105, says that the existence of nobility in Tibet was connected with the greater economic productivity and greater population of the agricultural areas. Herding and nomad communities had no nobility.

[2] The nobility did not help bind the other parts of the Sa sKya domain to the capital, since of the outlying areas only rTSe gDong (Map 1) had resident nobility.

mental office with a large number of subjects, there was a presumption that office-holding was to be hereditary; this was manifested in the selection of Candidates from noble families and in the frequent succession of sons to their fathers' Jo Lags positions.[3] The standards and style of behavior of the sKu Drag officialdom were set by the hereditary nobles. Our respondents insisted on numerous occasions that the hereditary nobility had the self-confidence, the pride, and the gracefulness in religious practice and social intercourse that enabled them to be effective as officials charged with the responsibility of directing and protecting the subjects. sKu Drag officials from subject families were said to have copied the demeanor of their noble colleagues. This self-conception of being "natural rulers" perhaps accounts for the persistence of the nobility; the royal family accepted the nobility, while realizing that ability and heredity had no special connection, and the subjects probably did the same.

At times our respondents' interest in the efficiencies of centralized governmental power led them to the judgment that the hereditary nobility of Sa sKya was at least dispensable, but they never abandoned the idea that the status of sKu Drag was necessary to maintain the proper dignity and prestige of the governmental officialdom. In a place as small as Sa sKya, however, the abandonment of the presumption of heredity might have undermined the august nature of the sKu Drag official. In a larger polity, an official's association with the government, headed by a king or emperor, may by itself suffice to evoke the proper awe; but if all the Sa sKya officials had come from subject families, the governed might have resented men from their own station giving them orders.

Although the political system of Sa sKya no doubt required a rather large social distance between the governors and the governed, the existence of heredity officials diluted the power of the KHri CHen and thus had a decentralizing effect. The hereditary nobility could not frustrate a determined KHri CHen, but an

[3] On Jo Lags status, see Appendix C, section I.

official who came from a family with a history dating from aPHags Pa would hardly have been awestruck in the presence of royalty. In addition, the hereditary nobility was recognized as one of the establishments. Although it showed no solidarity on specific political issues, its awareness of its status as an establishment must have given it some feeling of independence. Our respondents reflected that, although the hereditary nobility was useful as a source of governmental personnel, the political system of Sa sKya would have been improved if the nobility had not had the status of an establishment, with subjects and immunity from paying revenue. There is sense in this speculation, because the hereditary nobility could have been defined in other ways and because, as will be seen below, it had been gradually losing the special privileges of an establishment.

II

The status of sKu Drag, held only by governmental officials, was the highest in Sa sKya, save for the royal family and the highest officials of the North and South Monasteries. The hereditary nobility dating from the thirteenth century was called "brGyud Pai sKu Drag," which means "sKu Drag of the line." These brGyud Pai sKu Drag families were supposed to supply the highest governmental officials; their members who were not in office did not, however, have sKu Drag status, but a lower status entitling them to wear formal costumes similar to those of Jo Lags officials.[4] The hereditary noblemen created by the KHri CHen from time to time after the thirteenth century were called "Drag bTSan," both words meaning "fierce" or "might."[5] They had the same relationship to the status of sKu Drag as did the older noble families, and they wore the same costume.

Both types of nobility had the same opportunity to become

[4] See Appendix C, section I.

[5] Under the Lhasa government these nobles were called "sGer Pa," with the basic meaning of "fragmentation," and sometimes this title was used in Sa sKya.

sKu Drag, but neither had an inherent right to high office. There was a presumption that both would produce qualified young men, and hence they had a kind of obligation to do so. Whenever the number of Candidates was reduced to four or five, the ZHabs Pad, on the authorization of the KHri CHen, first examined the members of all noble families. The ZHabs Pad was not obliged to recommend every young nobleman for candidacy, nor did the KHri CHen have to accept every nobleman that he recommended. This search for new Candidates also included a survey of the North and South Monasteries, so the subjects had an opportunity to overcome part of the nobility's advantage in prestige and contacts with people in power.

Before the ZHabs Pad recommended a nobleman for candidacy, he obtained the assent of the young man's family. The family could refuse, but it was expected to have a good reason; for example, if it lived outside the capital, it could claim that the young man was needed at home to manage its estate and subjects. Although some noblemen disliked the life of a governmental official, most were pleased with the power and wealth resulting from service with the government.

The status of Drag bTSan was conferred by the KHri CHen as a reward for special merit in governmental affairs; it carried a little more prestige than the status of brGyud Pai sKu Drag. The Drag bTSan family perhaps had higher standing because it had received its specific recognition by the KHri CHen in recent times, rather than relying upon the exploits of a distant ancestor of the thirteenth century. Occasionally a brGyud Pai sKu Drag family was also given Drag bTSan status when one of its members distinguished himself. The slightly higher prestige of the Drag bTSan resulted in some small advantages over the brGyud Pai sKu Drag.

The creation of a Drag bTSan was formalized in a document sent to the head of the family and sealed by both the KHri CHen and the ZHabs Pad. These letters were carefully preserved by the Drag bTSan families, although they probably never had occasion to produce them. brGyud Pai sKu Drag families also kept documents that proved their status.[6]

Drag bTSan status was rather sparingly conferred. During his fourteen-year reign, KHri CHen NGag dBang mTHu THub dBang PHyug elevated only one family to this status, the family of Brag sPe from dPal rTSe. This family of Government subjects had not previously participated in governmental or monastic affairs. During the 1930's and 1940's, the head of the family, TSHe Ring rDo rJe, and his two sons made a fortune in trade. Somehow they managed to get capital—they borrowed grain or money from the PHun TSHogs palace early in their business career—and entered the trade that took grain and manufactured goods to the nomads north of Sa sKya proper and animal products south of the Himalayas. They prospered remarkably. They began to make loans in money and kind; they purchased land that became available and let part of it to sharecroppers. Eventually their wealth was second only to that of the richest nobles. The father had somehow obtained an education, and he sent his two lay sons to the capital and paid the monks to educate them. As often in Tibet, the Brag sPe made no large donations for religious purposes while all its members were active in worldly affairs.

TSHe Ring rDo rJe, among his other accomplishments, gained a reputation for forthrightness, and he was selected by KHri CHen NGag dBang mTHu THub dBang PHyug to go to Lhasa and negotiate for the return to Sa sKya control of the small area within the city of Lhasa.[7] This task required both the greatest delicacy and the greatest perseverance. It was successfully accomplished, and Brag sPe was made a Drag bTSan.[8] His

---

[6] See Appendix A, section 3, for a list of both kinds of nobility.

[7] See Chapter 2, section V.

[8] His sons believe that NGag dBang mTHu THub dBang PHyug would have ennobled his Chief Secretary, not just because the man held such a high position but because he did an outstanding job in this office. The Chief Secretary, however, had no one who could carry on his family line. See Chapter 5, section XIV.

sons made good marriages, and one became, through adoption, the holder of the title of a very old and prominent noble family.[9]

Drag bTSan status was normally conferred upon a man and his descendents for an indefinite period, but in one case it was given for a definitely specified period. The reasons for this action were not remembered; but since the family in question was already of brGyud Pai sKu Drag status, it probably was a way to express a limited appreciation of some service to the KHri CHen, the polity, or the religious sect. Occasionally a brGyud Pai sKu Drag family was given the additional status of Drag bTSan for an indefinite period. Four families with this highest possible degree of prestige were identified. One of them was very wealthy, another fairly well off, the third tolerably comfortable, and the fourth quite without capital.

Both brGyud Pai sKu Drag and Drag bTSan status could be taken away by action of the KHri CHen. A number of families were identified as being former nobility, and there were probably many more. Unfortunately, our respondents were not familiar with any case of the reduction of a nobleman to a subject. Presumably this action was taken only when the family had somehow seriously displeased the KHri CHen, who made the decision quite autonomously. During his reign, KHri CHen NGag dBang mTHu THub dBang PHyug only once considered demoting a family, because he believed that its head had committed treason. He finally decided against demotion: the accused died shortly after the event, a man who was not his blood relative became head of the family, and the sGrol Ma palace intervened on behalf of the family.

III

Both types of Sa sKya nobility had two privileges that made the nobility an establishment, comparable to the Government

---

[9] This family was Lug Rags (see Appendix A, section III). On the nobility's family structure and marriage practices, see sections V and VI below.

and the Religious Establishment, but much less important. Hereditary noblemen could have subjects, and they had no responsibility to provide labor for the Government.

At the time of aPHags Pa, all noblemen of brGyud Pai sKu Drag status were probably given subjects. By the twentieth century, sixteen families of this status remained, but only seven of them had subjects. Acquisition of Drag bTSan status did not automatically result in the acquisition of subjects, but in creating a new nobleman a KHri CHen probably gave him subjects to make his prestige comparable to that of the old nobility. In the twentieth century, only three of the twelve Drag bTSan families in Sa sKya had no subjects and so (presumably) had in some way lost them. The Drag bTSan's better record in retaining their subjects was probably connected with their later origin, and it may have contributed to their slight edge in social standing over the brGyud Pai sKu Drag.

The twenty-four noble families of Sa sKya proper had a total of about seventy-seven families of subjects, about 3 per cent of all subjects.[10] Nine had no subjects at all, only three—all Drag bTSan—had approximately ten families, and the rest had from three to five families. Eleven of the noble families, nine of whom were Drag bTSan, were classified as "very wealthy"; they had fifty of the seventy-seven subject families and only two of them had no subjects. The older nobility tended to be less wealthy and to have fewer subjects, an indication of the weakness of the nobility in the Sa sKya political system.

The subjects of a nobleman were responsible to him in the way all subjects were responsible to their respective establishments. They worked land that belonged to him, paid him a fixed

---

[10] The total of noble families in the preceding paragraph is twenty-eight because four families had both kinds of noble status. The nobility also had an undetermined number of herder families, probably less than 3 per cent of all such families. Our respondents explicitly stated that "in a small place like Sa sKya the system would not have worked if the nobles had had too many subjects."

revenue in kind, and were obliged to provide him with labor. Each nobleman was free to require any amount of revenue in kind, but he could not take more from his subjects than the Government took from its subjects without evoking their protests and perhaps even causing them to ask the Government to relieve them of their allegiance to him. The nobleman was also free to determine the precise amount of work owed him by his subjects, and this responsibility for work seems to have been the source of constant bickering. It was said that a brGyud Pai sKu Drag received less work from his subjects than a Drag bTSan received from his, but neither the specific difference nor the reason for it was known. Perhaps the greater prestige of the Drag bTSan made it more difficult for his subjects to argue with him. All the subjects of noblemen also had to provide labor for the Government.

Noblemen had difficulty in acquiring new subjects. The more powerful establishments would not give up their own subjects, and they were anxious to obtain people new to Sa sKya. Before Brag sPe was ennobled, he had three families sharecropping on his private land. These people may have come from other parts of Tibet, or they may have split off from Sa sKya families, and they had no responsibility for establishment land. Upon his ennoblement, these sharecroppers were given the choice of becoming subjects of the new Drag bTSan or being given Government land and becoming Government subjects. They chose to become subjects of the nobleman. There is no reason to believe that any pressure was put upon them, for the Government would have been glad to gain new subjects. If they trusted Brag sPe, they had reason not to leave their homes for possibly inferior land. (Good unoccupied land was usually scarce in Sa sKya.) In any event, giving subjects to the new nobleman did not require taking them from another establishment or causing any other disruption.

It was not so difficult, on the other hand, for noble families to lose subjects. When noble status was taken from a man for displeasing the KHri CHen, he could no longer have subjects; in one such case, the former noble retained his private land and his subjects became sharecroppers upon it. An aging nobleman in a burst of piety could donate part of his land and the subjects upon it to the Religious Establishment. Inept management sometimes required noblemen to sell land farmed by subjects. Harsh treatment or neglect sometimes prompted subjects to leave Sa sKya or to appeal to the Government. The head of one prominent noble family was an inveterate litigant, who (rumor had it) often woke up at night and wrote down new arguments. His sons tended toward prodigality and unsound business practices. About 1935, half of their numerous families of subjects, complaining of neglect, petitioned the Government to be relieved of their allegiance. Their appeal was successful, and the Government also took the private land of the nobleman that they had been farming.

IV

The second privilege of the Sa sKya nobility was its freedom from the obligation to provide revenue in the form of labor to the Government. This immunity symbolized the political independence of the noblemen, because such "outer revenue," as the Tibetans called it, was always the mark of political subordination, whether or not it was useful to the recipient and whether or not he had any real control over the man who paid it.[11] A wealthy Sa sKya subject could live solely on the returns from his private land, paying no revenue in kind to anyone, but he still was the subject of some establishment and had to supply it with labor (which he probably hired). The nobleman's status was acknowledged by his freedom from this responsibility, but the practical effects of this privilege were slight. The revenue in labor lost by the Government and saved by the nobility was insignificant, and many noblemen paid revenue in labor because,

[11] See Chapter 2, section I.

for one reason or another, they farmed land belonging to the Government. Nonetheless, being exempt from the "outer revenue," in conjunction with being able to have subjects, formally qualified the nobility to constitute a genuine establishment.

A nobleman could hold four types of land. The first was land occupied by his subjects, his establishment land. The second was private land not occupied by his subjects.[12] This land was worked by the nobleman's family, by his servants, by hired labor, sometimes by sharecroppers, and also by his subjects, whom he was supposed to pay at the same rate as hired labor. It was said that at least some noblemen tried to get their subjects to do this kind of work without pay, and that when the subjects were paid it was always below the standard wage. A third type of land was Government land held as the principal remuneration for service as an official; the nobleman had to pay the Government revenue in labor proportional to the size of this land. Finally, a nobleman might have taken on the responsibility for working Government land on the same basis as an ordinary subject, and on this land he paid revenue both in kind and in labor. A nobleman might have asked for land of this last kind because he needed to increase his income, but the KHri CHen could assign such land to the nobility, even when they had not asked for it, and thus bring them under some supervision by the Government.[13] The most significant result of this kind of assignment seems to have been only a slight reduction in the nobility's prestige. The responsibility for farming this last type of land was not passed on to the nobleman's heirs.

[12] The private land of a nobleman had a formal title, gZHis CHung, literally "country small" and perhaps equivalent to "estate" or "manor." This title suggests the special status of the nobility within the polity.

[13] The KHri CHen's right to do this was said to be based on a special order of KHri CHen bDags CHen Kun dGaa Blo Gros, who reigned in the latter part of the eighteenth century. KHri CHen NGag dBang mTHu THub dBang PHyug reportedly used this power rather frequently, but no specific cases were discovered.

V

Tibetans did not follow a rule of primogeniture, and all families from the royal aKHon to the lowest subjects could split, each branch having a claim to the original family's property and social position. Fragmentation of the royal family was always a threat to Sa sKya political stability, and a split in subject families could reduce the size of farms and complicate the pattern of government revenue.[14] The problem of maintaining its inheritance intact was critical for the noble family, because the nobility as a whole would have been seriously weakened by the proliferation of impoverished brGyud Pai sKu Drag and Drag bTSan. The nobility used a number of methods to prevent the division of families—methods also used by the royal family and the subjects—but all these methods ultimately depended upon the continuing cooperation of siblings.

The head of a noble house usually tried to settle the inheritance before his death, by choosing one of his sons as heir to his title and land—daughters could not be heirs—and by making other arrangements for the other sons, all of whom had the special right and the special duty to serve as sKu Drag officials. If the parents attempted to make such a settlement, they usually, but not always, chose the oldest son as the heir.[15] To try to make this choice effective, all remaining sons could be put into monasteries, usually entered by boys at the age of six. Another arrangement was to have two or three sons share the title and property and carry on the line by means of a polyandrous marriage.[16] A

[14] On the royal family, see Chapter 1; an example of the division of a subject family is given in Chapter 10, section VIII.

[15] During the generation dominant during the 1930's and the 1940's, in at least five of the twenty-four noble families the oldest son was not the heir. In one prominent subject family, the third son was the heir and in another the fourth.

[16] At least two noble families adopted this device during the 1930's and 1940's.

younger brother, upon reaching adulthood, might have been asked by an older brother to marry the older brother's wife.[17] Another arrangement was for one or more lay sons with their own wives to live on the estate with their brother who was the heir. Since this arrangement provided many opportunities for quarrels, a lay brother who was not the heir usually went into government work or trading.

If a family had no sons, it usually brought a male from outside to be heir and carry on the family line. There were a number of arrangements, sometimes involving changes in establishment allegiance: the outright adoption of a male relative or nonrelative as a son; the designation of a consanguine relative, most frequently a brother, as heir; the designation of an affinal relative, usually a son-in-law living in his extended family or as head of a nuclear family, as heir; and the provision of an heir by arranging an uxorilocal marriage of a daughter whereby her husband became a "called-in son-in-law." [18] If the family had a number of daughters, the called-in son-in-law might marry the two oldest, as happened in the case of a noble family whose adopted heir and son-in-law came from a subject family and had been a monk and a sKu Drag official. (Polygyny could also occur when the first wife had no children, and a combination of polygyny and polyandry when the first childless wife was married to two brothers.) In a second noble family, the heir became incapacitated; his sister's husband, the younger brother of the heir of another noble family, became the adopted heir. In a third case, a wealthy

---

[17] This relationship was not too stable, for the younger brother might later have wanted a younger wife of his own and have been unwilling to share her with his brother in a polyandrous, polygynous marriage.

[18] The called-in son-in-law was called a "Mag Pa," the equivalent of Chinese concept of "chao hsia tih nü hsü." He did not have the full rights of a real or adopted son; he could not, for example, divorce his wife and remain in possession as heir. He could, however, bring his own family's bone name into the marriage if his wife's family had no bone name.

nobleman died without issue, and his wife's brother became the heir. This case is interesting because the brother and sister were from an undistinguished subject family, and the brother owed his remarkable rise in life to his sister's striking beauty. Another nobleman had an older daughter and a young son. His daughter married a man who had a rather high status under the Lhasa government, and the noble made him the family heir. This was a poor arrangement, because the son, upon obtaining his majority, could easily have legally contested the heirdom.

Parents usually arranged for the succession when their sons were quite young,[19] and they often gave force to their choice by retiring in favor of their chosen heir, giving the religious reason of withdrawal from worldly affairs.[20] Although the parents' decision was normally respected by their family, a contest for the heirdom was always possible. A son put in a monastery as a child might leave the monkhood as an adult and contest the inheritance. A polyandrous marriage might break up. The heir might die prematurely and the heirdom be contested by his son and his brother.[21] Whenever two or more contestants proved adamant, the Sa sKya Government enforced a division of the property and the noble line. Only one noble family had so split in the twentieth century.

Contests for the heirdom were probably avoided in many instances by another arrangement for dividing family property. Any brother or sister of the heir of a noble family had a right to use for his own purposes a part of its private land not farmed by subjects; upon his death or retirement this land reverted to the control of the family's current heir, and his children became part of the heir's household. Usually the heir retained control of at

---

[19] One of the considerations that affected their choice was the resemblance of their children's characters to those of ancestors who had been successful as monks or as laymen.

[20] Upon retirement, the parents usually remained in the main household or set up separate living quarters, usually on the estate.

[21] In such cases preference usually went to the older generation.

least three-quarters of this kind of land. If the issue were brought before the Law Officials in the capital, his portion might have been reduced to one-half; but this would have been done only in the unlikely event that more than one sibling were asking for a share. Every male and female member had a right to a small portion of property such as jewels, money, and livestock, which he could then pass on to his own children. Monks had no right to claim any part of the estate for their own use, but a monk who left the monkhood had the same rights as everyone else.[22]

Inheritance had to be settled before the death of the head of the family, or the line was considered ended. Sometime early in the twentieth century a brGyud Pai sKu Drag nobleman and his only son were killed in a riot. The man had no daughters, his wife was dead, and his son had not married. He naturally had made no arrangements for someone such as a nephew to carry on his family, and so the noble line was declared ended and the Government took the entire estate.

It was obviously very important for the Sa sKya nobility to maintain a single line of succession, and according to our information in recent times they were pretty successful in doing so. The membership of twenty-one of the twenty-four families was known to our respondents. Two had no sons, four had only one son, and fifteen had from two to five sons. Only one of the last divided into two separate noble families.

VI

In these efforts to maintain an undivided family line, considerable pressure was probably put upon both male and female offspring. The men, at least, had ways to relieve an unpleasant marital situation. Taking another wife was one response, for all

[22] Former monks claimed part of their family's land in two prominent subject families during the period of our study. In one of the noble families, the eldest son broke his vows and then devoted his full time to trading. His younger brother, who was the heir, became incapacitated, but the former monk was not interested in the heirdom, and an adopted heir was brought in.

offspring of polygamous marriages were considered equal members of a single nuclear family. There was also the response of the youngest of three brothers all married to a single woman: he joined the Tibetan army.

Marriage in Sa sKya, among all social strata, was as often a practical matter as it was a romantic alliance. The nuclear family was an economic and legal unit, but it was otherwise rather loose. A number of important men had mistresses, and some husbands took their natural children into their households. Divorce was a matter to be negotiated by the families of husband and wife, but the division of property and the custody of children could be effected by the Law Officials. Although the men seem to have had more freedom, women were far from totally dependent upon their husbands.

The act of getting married involved no governmental procedure or religious ceremony. The symbolic act of marriage, comparable to placing the wedding ring, was placing a turquoise in the bride's headdress. On the occasion of a marriage, the wealthier families spread a large feast for their friends and invited a number of religious dignitaries to provide the proper blessings. It was said that about 30 per cent of the marriages of the nobility did not begin even with these formalities, and among the subjects the proportion was one in three. This informality resulted from the reluctance of either partner to make the commitment, and from a mild bias against marrying women who were "widows" in the special sense of having gone through the above procedure, a bias that did not apply to "widowers." An "unmarried wife" and her children had a slightly lower social standing and a slightly weaker legal claim to property.

Sa sKya noblemen, like all Tibetan males, had an eye for beauty, and they often took as wives women from subject families or from outside Sa sKya. Our respondents were unable to identify the families of the wives of most of the noblemen whom they knew very well. Alliances through marriage appear to have had little importance in the politics of the principality.

The oldest families in Sa sKya had "bone" names—"aKHon" is an example—but these names were rare. Families of some standing, including subjects, had "house" names—"Nas Og Pa" was the house name of the wealthy Headman.[23] The lower strata of subjects generally had only given names.

When a son was born to a wealthy family, it invited the highest available religious personage—a monastery official or a very pious monk—to a celebration during which he chose a personal name for the baby, cast its horoscope, and performed a religious ceremony seeking a long life for the new arrival. A less wealthy family took a gift to an important monk and asked him to name the child. The poor dispensed with ceremony, or if they were brazen enough, they would accost a man of religion, gift-less, and wheedle a name from him.

VII

According to our respondents, the Sa sKya nobility was much weaker than its counterparts under Lhasa and Shigatse.[24] Whether or not the comparison is correct, it is clear that the KHri CHen could, if he so desired, remove almost all the privileges of his nobility. He could relieve a nobleman of his subjects and even of his nobility, or he could allow the man to retain his nobility but bar him or his sons or both from holding governmental office. During the 1930's two generations of one family were barred from office on the charge that the family had plotted against the KHri CHen. The KHri CHen could also confiscate any or all of the private land and other property of an errant nobleman. Confiscation was also contemplated in the incident of the 1930's, but never put into effect. Finally, the KHri CHen could lessen a noble's prestige by making him pay revenue to the Government.

The lack of a firm principle of succession gave the KHri

[23] "Rus" is translated "bone," and "TSHang," "house."

[24] See Carrasco, *Land and Polity in Tibet*, pp. 215–218, on the strength of the Lhasa nobility.

CHen some opportunity to encourage dissension within noble families for the purpose of weakening the nobility or keeping it in check. There was no evidence of such interference in recent times, but the apparent turbulence of affairs involving noble standing in Sa sKya makes it reasonable to suppose that at one time or another a KHri CHen took advantage of an uncertain inheritance to increase his own power.

From time to time the Government called upon noblemen to perform special services, such as looking out for Sa sKya interests in other parts of Tibet. It was difficult for a nobleman to refuse to comply with such a request, although it was said that a Drag bTSan was in a better position to excuse himself than a brGyud Pai sKu Drag. The Government took a direct interest in the personal affairs of two of the noble families because their fortunes were believed to be linked with the fortunes of Sa sKya as a whole: "it was a Sa sKya tradition that these families not be allowed to die out." In one case, when the head of one of these families unexpectedly died, the Government made sure that his younger brother left the monkhood to carry on the line.[25]

The formal power of the KHri CHen over his nobility was virtually unlimited, and considerable indirect evidence suggests that his actual power came very close to equaling it. The frequency with which families lost their noble status; the fact that there were so few brGyud Pai sKu Drag families compared to the number of governmental posts—including, it must be remembered, that of Headman—that existed during the time of aPHags Pa and immediately thereafter, combined with the fact that many of these families traced their nobility to relatively insignificant officials of the period;[26] the relative poverty, lower prestige, and fewer subjects of the older nobility; the reported freedom with which KHri CHen NGag dBang mTHu THub dBang PHyug dealt with some nobles he considered disloyal;

[25] This family was PHu SHar bKra SHis sGang. The other was Lug Rags. See Appendix A, section III.

[26] See Appendix A, section III.

and the ability of the KHri CHen, and only the KHri CHen, to take the initiative in governmental policy—all these facts indicate political turbulence and the continuing ascendency of the KHri CHen.

Chapter 9

Property, Land, and Government Revenue

Sa sKya had a rather well-developed set of regulations regarding the disposition of material things among individuals and families, regulations that were interpreted and enforced by the Law Officials, backed by the power and authority of the Government. Standard arrangements also existed regarding the division of material things between the subjects and the establishments. The establishments themselves had final power over these arrangements, but their freedom of action was limited by custom—by what both they and their subjects considered proper —and by the requirements of the Sa sKya economic system. In all these matters, Sa sKya did not differ fundamentally from any other polity.

The present chapter will describe the regulations among private parties and between them and the government regarding both the material goods of consumption and those of production. The concept of ownership need not be used in this discussion. Ownership can be defined (in the case of Sa sKya) only as a certain degree of power over material objects, and there is little value in trying to determine the precise degree. No society allows an entirely unrestricted use of any material object, and no government lacks the power, under certain circumstances, to relieve anyone of any power he may have over material things. In discussing property, the goal should be to describe the specific powers possessed by specific types of people over specific kinds of material things. In Sa sKya, the specific people were the subjects, the nobility, the governmental officials, the monks and monastic officials, the royal family, and the KHri CHen. The most important specific material things were agricultural land and its crops, which sustained the population of the principality.

The establishments of Sa sKya had effective claims to a number of things created by the labor of their subjects. Some of these claims resembled taxation, some were of the nature of tariffs, some appeared more like tribute, and others are difficult to name. Since there are few useful concepts applicable to governmental income in this type of polity,[1] throughout our study we refer to this income by the somewhat awkward but hopefully neutral word "revenue."

Our principal concern in this chapter and the next is to show that Sa sKya economic structures and processes were integral parts of the political society by virtue of their congruence with the belief system, the patterns of social stratification and distribution of power, the structure of government, and the content of governmental policy.

I

Small movable articles were almost completely under the control of the individual. Clothing, jewelry, furnishings, tools, utensils, money, and animals could be disposed of by the person who had accumulated or inherited them in any way he saw fit, as long as his action did not cause injury in the usual sense to other people. A man was responsible, for example, for any damage that his animals might cause to another person's crops. If someone took one of these articles from someone else, the latter had a claim to restitution that the Headman would support. Usually

[1] On the difficulties of the concepts of ownership, revenue, property, rent, and taxation, see Walter C. Neale, "Reciprocity and Redistribution in the Indian Village," in Karl Polanyi et al. (eds.), *Trade and Market in the Early Empires* (Glencoe, Ill.: Free Press, 1957), pp. 218–236. The terminological difficulties in the study of European "feudalism" are well known.

the affair was settled at this level in an informal way, but if either party proved recalcitrant, the Law Officials could make a definitive settlement. If the article taken were food and its taker could show that he was short of food, no basic right was violated, and the original possessor did not always recover the value of the food. When the material was taken for the profit of the taker or when it had a rather large value—five sheep, for example, were considered a large amount and one sheep a small amount—the original possessor had a right to restitution.[2]

Monks had the same rights as laymen over these kinds of valuables. A monk could freely will the articles he possessed outside the physical limits of his monastery, and if he died without leaving a will, his family could claim them. Each monastery had its own regulations regarding the disposal of its monks' private goods stored within its walls. When a monk was alive and maintaining his vows, he could use these goods at his own pleasure. In most monasteries, when he died, his possessions went to the monastery unless he had a nephew in the same monastery. In the North and South Monasteries, however, this wealth was always given to the deceased monk's family. Monasteries also differed in their treatment of the possessions within the monastery of monks who broke their vows. The South Monastery, for example, did not allow a conscripted monk who broke his vows to take any of his wealth with him, but the goods could go to a brother or nephew who took his place. A volunteer monk who broke his vows could take all his possessions with him, provided that he admitted his transgression, apologized for it, and gave his erstwhile fellows a "big tea." The monastery confiscated the possessions of volunteer monks who tried to hide the fact that they had broken their vows.

Valuables of this kind could be freely borrowed and lent, usually with interest, by all people. Debts were upheld by the

[2] Cf. W. I. Thomas and F. Znaniecki, in *The Polish Peasant* (Boston: Richard G. Badger, 1918), I, 188: taking necessities might have been unfair but it was not theft; taking material to sell was full-scale theft.

Law Officials and the ZHabs Pad. The heirs of a family took on its debts, but monks were never responsible for the indebtedness of their relatives. Each individual member of a family, including monks, could lend and borrow in his own name. In lending and borrowing, monks operated "under royal law"; the regulations of their monasteries did not cover such transactions.

The government had certain fixed claims on portions of some of these material possessions. When a subject of any establishment died, his best suit of clothing went to the KHri CHen. This was described as a religious offering, but it was such a "hard custom" that the act was not voluntary.[3] This loss was mitigated somewhat, at least for the inhabitants of the capital, because at religious festivals these clothes were placed on great racks in the capital marketplace and sold at bargain prices.

In addition to the establishments' claims to material and labor for their principal revenue, discussed below, the Religious Establishment each year received 1 per cent of all sheep and goats possessed by its own subjects and by subjects of the Government. This was an important fixed claim with the full weight of government behind it.

All these material goods could be freely sold, purchased, and willed according to their possessors' wishes. Written wills were upheld by the Law Officials, who also settled disputes over inheritances, and relatives of the deceased had the right to request the government to enforce their claim to material when they had been "disinherited."

II

Anyone in Sa sKya could own and inherit houses. Houses could be freely sold to people of the same establishment, and the

---

[3] In medieval Europe, when a serf died, the lord of his manor claimed his best beast or best movable possession, and the priest often took the second best. According to G. G. Coulton, in *The Medieval Village* (Cambridge: Cambridge University Press, 1925), p. 75, this was a most burdensome claim upon the serf.

sale included the land upon which they were located and yards of varying sizes surrounding them. When houses were situated in the midst of establishment land, selling them to subjects of establishments other than that of their possessor involved complications, including the precise determination of the amount of land that went with the sale, and the establishments at least discouraged such sales. There were, however, few reasons why anyone would want to buy a house in the middle of someone else's farm land. When a private house was in a village, its owner could sell it to anyone he chose. A man was also free to donate his house and site to any establishment but the nobility, which could then rent it, either for a fixed payment or, more usually in the capital, for the responsibility of doing chores for the establishment upon apparently rather irregular call.[4] Houses and sites were retained by their possessors in the rare cases when they changed their allegiance from one establishment to another.

Houses in Sa sKya were made of bricks of earth or clay dried in the sun or of tamped earth, and this composition had an interesting influence upon a man's power over his dwelling. He could alter his house by adding or removing a section, but he needed the Government's permission to demolish it or to build a new one. Such a major disturbance of the earth might offend the earth gods and hence the signs had to be right before governmental permission was given. A man from aKHril sPe once wanted to build himself a new house, an operation that did not involve destroying an old one. When he asked the capital for permission, he was told to wait until the crops had been harvested. He was, however, something of an expert himself on these matters, so he made his own divinations and discovered that it was quite safe to proceed immediately with his project. He did so, but unfortunately shortly thereafter a sudden sharp hailstorm damaged some crops in his neighborhood. The builder thereupon felt obliged to distribute gifts to those who had suffered

----

[4] The imprecision of this responsibility is reminiscent of medieval Europe (see Coulton, *Medieval Village*).

from the hail. No governmental action was taken, but it was said that if the affair had involved destroying a house the man would certainly have been fined.

III

The great proportion of the farming land in Sa sKya belonged to the establishments, but perhaps 40 per cent of all families had some land of their own, although few had more than very little. The individual, whether noble or subject, had full control over this "private" land and all its produce. He could use it for crops or for grazing or let it lie fallow, and he could burn at will, but he was of course responsible for any damage done to neighboring fields or buildings. He also had full "subsurface" rights to his private land, despite the taboo against mining, although clay for pottery was the only thing of any value.

A man retained control over his private land when he changed his allegiance from one establishment to another. He could will it to anyone, including the Government, the Religious Establishment, the palaces, or a monastery, and if necessary his decision was enforced by the Law Officials. If he made no will, his sons equally shared control over this land, or they divided it into equal portions if they could not agree upon joint management, and the Government resolved all disputes that could not be settled by private mediation. Daughters had equal rights to this kind of land and to the other types of private possessions described above. When a daughter married, she could take the value of her portion of the inheritance in the form of movables, and if she were divorced she got back the wealth she had brought into the marriage. Monks and nuns had no claim whatever to land or to houses. A brother who went into another family as an adopted heir had a right to his share of the movables, but had no claim on his family's house or land. No one had to pay anything to government as a result of possessing or inheriting this land, or as a result of possessing or inheriting houses and sites.

Anyone could sell his private land to anyone with allegiance to Sa sKya, no matter what the buyer's establishment and even if the buyer lived outside Sa sKya proper, but he could sell it to no one else. He was, however, not allowed to offer it as collateral for a loan, to be forfeited if the loan were not repaid. The only explanation for this prohibition is that the government believed it more tempting to pledge land than to take the irrevocable decision to sell it, and it did not want private land to become concentrated in too few hands. Although this land could not be pledged, it could be used to raise liquid assets according to an arrangement whereby, for a sum below that which the land would have brought if sold, the full free control over it was transferred to someone else. At any time the original owner could regain control by returning the sum without interest. This apparently was a rather frequent practice, and the Law Officials handled many cases involving it.

Holdings of private land probably came originally from the establishments as rewards for unusual service. (Under no circumstances would any establishment have sold any of its land.) Three prominent families who lived south of the capital were known to have retained private land given to their ancestors by aPHags Pa himself. The case of PHun KHang, the last ZHabs Pad, illustrates the way subject families acquired private land.[5]

The Government took away a man's private land only if he committed a very serious crime such as treason, and when there were no heirs to private land it came under Government control. These conditions applied to the private land of everyone from the most obscure subject to the hereditary nobility, including the land worked by subjects of the nobility. The Government had the right of eminent domain, but no instances of its exercise were discovered. The males of the aKHon family were considered the

[5] On PHun KHang, see Chapter 7, sections V and VI. See F. L. Ganshof, *Feudalism*, trans. Philip Grierson (London: Longmans, Green, 1952), p. 42, on the tendency in medieval Europe for land originally used as "salary" for an office to become private land.

owners (bDags Po) of all the land of Sa sKya, no matter who actually controlled it, and the KHri Chen was thought of as their representative. This theory was a natural answer to the abstract but understandable question of who had ultimate control over the territory of Sa sKya; one of its concrete implications was the prohibition against selling land to people without allegiance to the aKHon.[6]

IV

By far the largest part of the farming land "belonged" to the several establishments. Since the nobility and the palaces had only a small percentage of this land, and since the power of the Religious Establishment over its land was the same as that of the Government, the following description focuses upon the relationships between the Government and the people who farmed its land. The nobility and the palaces had similar arrangements, but they were less formal and less rigid.

Government land was divided into carefully delineated plots more or less randomly located throughout Sa sKya proper. In order to work one or more of these plots, a man had to accept certain specific economic and political responsibilities. When a sharecropper, a former monk, or a new arrival to Sa sKya had no establishment land, and Government land happened to be unoccupied, the Government usually wanted to get the person and the land together, for it was anxious to have all its land under cultivation and to have everyone in Sa sKya responsible for establishment land. The farmer, for his part, obtained some security and stability from having allegiance to an establishment, but his principal motivation for taking Government land was that it

[6] Our respondents were unclear whether the aKHon family could give up control of land and people. The theory of government as power suggests that it could, and part of TSHa Zur, the Sa sKya area in the city of Lhasa, was sold to the Chinese in the 1950's. The idea of the "inalienability of the royal domain" is basically modern (see Hans Kohn, *The Idea of Nationalism* [New York: Macmillan, 1961], p. 113).

was a better arrangement than sharecropping. To be given Government land, a newcomer had to have some collateral or, more usually, a sponsor who had known him for a couple of years and who would vouch for his integrity. Men without land occasionally agreed to take Government land and then absconded with the seed grain. Once a man had accepted the grant of land, he and his heirs were thereafter responsible for it, with few opportunities (other than leaving Sa sKya permanently) for relieving themselves of this responsibility.

An unusual case concerned a subject of the PHun TSHogs palace who lived in the capital. His father had acquired a considerable number of sheep, which were pastured in the high country south of the capital, and he had continued to add to the flock. One day he asked the palace officials to be freed from his responsibility for palace land so that he could devote his full time to herding. He argued that by doing this he would be more productive and thus better able to meet his responsibilities to the palace and to Sa sKya. The palace gave its permission, and it had no difficulty finding someone else to take over responsibility for its land. Nonetheless, establishments did not usually allow their subjects to leave the land. Very few families had the skill and capital to start a successful herding operation, and those that did usually sent one or more sons to the pastures while others remained upon the family's farming land. The only other profitable business was trading, which also required unusual amounts of skill and capital. Sa sKya proper was quite fertile by Tibetan standards and produced grain for export. The government had some economic reason for insisting that its subjects remain on the land.[7]

The establishments required only that some member of the subject family take responsibility for the land. The family itself, using the methods described above,[8] determined which of its

[7] Farming, herding, and trading are discussed in more detail in Chapter 10.

[8] Chapter 8, section V.

offspring was to be the heir to the land's returns and responsibilities. Sons who were not heirs were free to go into any occupation they pleased, or even to leave Sa sKya, but again herding and trading were difficult and sharecropping and agricultural wage-labor were not very desirable. All our evidence suggests that most subjects were glad to have establishment land.

V

An establishment took land away from a family only on the grounds of political disloyalty, and then only after repeated warnings. The attachment of people to the land was not only an economic arrangement, advantageous to both government and subject; it also symbolized the basic political relationship between the government's power, on the one hand, and the elements of that power, land and people, on the other.[9] On the practical level, our respondents said that removing a family from its establishment land only created the problem of finding something else to do with it.

Another illustration of the political nature of the subjects' relationship with the land appeared in the following context. Farming plots in Sa sKya were very fragmented, and when we asked our respondents if the establishments ever traded some of their land for the private land of an individual in the interest of consolidation of holdings, the answer was emphatically in the negative. If such trading had been allowed, "everything would have fallen to pieces." The belief seems to have been that the introduction of such flexibility would have undermined the traditional and fundamental relationships among government, people, and land by raising some question about their immutability.

Some concessions, however, were made to economics in the allocation of land. In the 1940's there lived in the capital a very poor man who had no establishment land and who lived by begging from the monks, doing odd jobs, and giving an occa-

---

[9] See Chapter 3, section X.

sional street concert with his nine children. He was a favorite of the KHri CHen, who used to ask him when he was going to take some Government land. The man always managed more or less gracefully to parry the question, but it was not meant seriously, for, as the ZHabs Pad said, he would probably eat the seed grain given him or, if he did plant it, would always claim, truthfully or otherwise, that he could not meet his revenue payments.

An establishment could always temporarily redistribute its land among its subjects according to their short-term needs, but the Government and the Religious Establishment rarely did so. The PHun TSHogs palace—and perhaps the other smaller establishments as well—made more or less regular adjustments. When the needs of the palace's families changed sharply, because of an increase in children or a decrease in labor, or when the revenue from its land was not up to expectations, the palace officials took land from one subject and gave it to another, but only for what was considered a period of emergency. The action was justified to the subjects by saying that the palace was the "owner" (bDags Po) of the land, and that they were only being allowed to use it. The following case was handled by our respondents.

A family consisting of a widow, her son, his wife, their two small children, and a younger idiot son incapable of work approached the wife of the palace and, with the argument that on their holdings they could not make ends meet, requested either a loan or more land. The family's plea was considered valid, and the palace decided to help. The palace treasurer opposed giving a loan because the family seemed to be a poor risk and because their obvious poverty made it difficult to charge them interest. The suggestion that they be given some of the palace's land that was not being worked by subjects was rejected because the result would have been a net reduction in the palace's income. The head of the palace then ordered an examination of the records describing all the land held by all the palace's subjects. This examination revealed only one source of land for the widow's family. Another family, consisting of a man who was a trader for the palace and received an income from this work, his wife, and two children of working age, had more palace land than the first family. The trader was called in, reminded of his relative affluence, and told that some of his land was to be given to the widow. He was not very happy to hear this, but (it was said) he could hardly protest because the inequity between his situation and the widow's was so obvious. The land was reallocated so that both families had the same amount.

A subject always had the right to ask his establishment for a better piece of land even when he was living comfortably enough in his present location. Occasionally good land did become available, but to have a chance at getting it, a subject had to provide the usual gifts to a number of officials, including the ZHabs Pad himself in the case of Government land. The land did not necessarily go to the highest bidder, but a man without the means to follow the custom would not have been considered.

The allocation of establishment land could also be changed by marriage. If the bride and groom were from the same establishment, two holdings could be combined into one and thus into a single responsibility. The wife had to be the only child in her family, and her land had to be close to the land of her husband. Given the additional factor of at least some mutual personal attraction, this kind of consolidation was not frequent. The establishments, moreover, were usually rather unwilling to approve such combinations since they involved changing the records—one can imagine the officials' reluctance to alter the neatly written and carefully filed records—and since, if the couple were divorced, the wife could take back her original land, and once again the records would have to be altered. This retention by the wife of her right to use the land originally granted to her family is an excellent illustration of the claims of the subject to land "belonging to" an establishment.

Between all plots of land, both establishment and private, there were usually boundary strips six to twelve feet wide. The land in these strips "belonged" to no one; it was used for grazing and even crops on a kind of squatter's rights basis. No one had to be paid for the use of this land, and it was in effect the private property of anyone who could reach a stable agreement with his neighbors. Disputes over any kind of boundary could be referred to the Law Officials in the capital, and quarrels over the use of these "unowned" strips occasionally came before them.

The best and most accessible pasture land was under the control of the several establishments, but any subject was free to put his animals in any pasture of his establishment. Just south of gYaa Lung (Map 2) there was a large pasture open to everyone except noblemen and their subjects. Apparently overgrazing created few problems, but any needed priorities were set by establishment officials and many disputes naturally occurred over the boundaries of pastures. Some of the pasture land was kept closed by establishment officials until the grass reached about a span in height. Each establishment also had hayfields, and after its subjects had cut the hay for its own use, they could let their animals graze on the stubble. A subject could also rent grazing land from an establishment not his own at the market price based on the number of his animals. In the very high country—and it must be remembered that the elevation of the capital was about 12,000 feet (Map 2)—the pastures were under no one's control, and anyone could use them. The difficulties of herding in these areas, however, restricted their use to the most hardy and skillful.

VI

Once a man took the responsibility for establishment land, he could use the land in any way that he chose.[10] A Government subject always had the right to receive from the District Officer the seed required to sow his Government land, but he was under no obligation actually to sow it. If he had a store of grain, he

[10] See Melville J. Herskovits, *Economic Anthropology* (New York: Alfred A. Knopf, 1960), p. 351, for other examples of this type of arrangement.

could put in plants bearing oilseeds. If he were very prosperous, he could let the land lie fallow for a season. Probably 90 per cent of the subjects, however, had no surpluses and each year they had to plant the seed issued to them. The subjects could use any farming methods, and they could allocate their time in any way between their establishment land and their private land, if they had any. The annual payment that each subject owed to his establishment was a fixed amount to be met out of his total resources.

This annual payment was the principal economic responsibility accompanying the use of establishment land. The arrangements for Religious Establishment subjects were the same as those for Government subjects, with the Steward performing the functions of the ZHabs Pad. The arrangements between the palaces and nobility and their respective subjects were similar but more flexible.

The amount due to the Government depended upon the extent and quality of the land held by the subject. In the capital there were records of all pieces of Government land, the families that held them, and the revenue due from each piece. The amount of revenue due was not calculated in terms of the actual yield of any land but apparently according to what the land could be expected to yield. How this expectation was determined was not known to our respondents, but it must have been based on some past experience of what were considered normal yields. Our estimate is that during the 1940's those families that met their revenue obligations—and they were only about half of all families—paid the Government about one-quarter of the actual gross yield of their Government land.[11]

[11] Unfortunately all the records regarding land and revenue were left in Sa sKya. Our estimate of 25 per cent of actual gross yield is based upon our estimate of the annual income and expenditures of the establishments (see Appendix D, section IV), the population's standard of living (see Appendix D, section III), and the normal yield in barley of this type of land, supplemented by what a number of subjects told our respondents about their revenue obligations. Pedro Carrasco, in *Land*

The amount due to the Government from each portion of its land did not depend upon the costs of production of the man who worked it nor upon his personal expenses. The amount due was rarely changed, not even when land was temporarily reallocated among families in response to pressing needs. A family could, however, plead that changed circumstances—such as births, deaths, illness, and accidents—made it unable to meet its payments for the year, and the Government could lower or waive these payments. Entire communities often asked that their payments be lowered because of damage to their crops, especially by hail. In all these cases, the request came to the capital through the Headmen and District Officers; it was approved by the ZHabs Pad after he had checked with the local official or, in the more important cases, had sent an official from the capital to verify the circumstances. The Government also occasionally permitted a subject to sign a promissory note for revenue currently due.

The Government rarely took the initiative in revising the payments expected from those who worked its land. It would make the adjustments described above, but only for a temporary period. Not even a prolonged inability on the part of a family or a locality to meet its payments prompted the Government to reflect upon the workability of the system. Our respondents estimated that each year about half the families in Sa sKya proper failed to produce enough grain to have seed for the next season, to feed themselves, and, as the last priority, to pay the Government the full amount it expected. It is reasonable to suppose that a large proportion of all families were permanently in arrears. KHri CHen NGag dBang mTHu THub dBang PHyug initiated a periodic review of the revenue schedules, to be conducted at three-year intervals, in order to lessen the amounts due from those who had consistently failed to meet their payments and to raise the amounts due from the more

and Polity in Tibet (Seattle: University of Washington Press, 1959), p. 88, says that in prosperous years the Lhasa government took as much as 40 per cent of the gross yield.

affluent. This policy was explained as an attempt to prevent the poor from getting poorer and the rich from getting richer. "People who become too poor may move away, and it is not desirable to have only a small number of rich families." The total amount of revenue was apparently to be the same and the share of each family was still to be determined before the harvest. Although a family owed payments to the Government only on its holdings of Government land and although barley was the principal material collected, the Government regularly asked for its revenue in a variety of materials. Other grains, vegetables, animal products, manufactured articles, and building materials were requested as substitutes for barley, according to the Government's current needs and the specialties of the several sections of Sa sKya.[12]

The Government collected this material from its subjects once in the summer and once in the winter, according to the products available at these times. The Headmen were responsible for notifying each family of the amount expected from it and for collecting and storing the material,[13] and with the District Officers they could use force against any subject suspected of double-dealing. In the capital two members of the Work Corps were appointed each year to supervise the collections, and requests for adjustments were made through them. The records of the schedules were kept in the capital, and every subject had the

---

[12] The following goods were regularly collected: barley, wheat, buckwheat, and peas; meat, usually mutton, with one goat acceptable with seven or eight sheep; edible oil and oilseed, eggs, fruit, butter, and cheese; wool, felt, sheepskins, hides, homespun cloth, and animal droppings for fuel; saddles, straw, hay, prepared charcoal, and leather and hair rope; and slate roofing slabs and brush for decorative borders on public buildings, particularly from the herders. The people from Ding Ri sTe Sa, outside Sa sKya proper (Map 1), supplied black sugar and "Chinese" and "Indian" salts, apparently welding flux and borax respectively, all procured through trade. Cf. Carrasco, *Land and Polity in Tibet*, p. 90.

[13] There were storage facilities at the District Offices and the capital, and elsewhere there were granaries that were checked and sealed by neighboring District Officers or officials sent out from the capital.

right to see his own.[14] When a man inherited Government land from his father or otherwise took on the responsibility for it, his name was placed on these records; this authorized him to act for his family in such matters as the selection of a Headman and the organization of work levies.

In collecting its revenue, the Government was careful to leave each family enough seed for the following season. In the districts outside the capital, each family at harvest time gave the District Officer the seed it needed for planting in the spring. Families in the capital retained their own seed, and the Group Officials were responsible for ensuring that everyone kept enough. Where there were no Headmen, revenue was often collected by "tax farmers," who may or may not have taken seed into account.[15]

The herding families in Sa sKya proper also had regular payments in kind to make to the Government; these were animal products in amounts proportionate to the number of animals they possessed. The exact size of these payments was not remembered, but they were much less burdensome than the demands made of the farmers. The herders, moreover, had many ways to avoid revealing the real size of their flocks. They also had to supply building materials found in their high areas, and they were liable to occasional special requisitions of material and levies of labor. The revenue system, however, was not devised to draw on the resources of this approximately 6 per cent of the population.

VII

The establishments of Sa sKya received from their subjects revenue in labor as well as in material. All subjects of the Government, the Religious Establishment, and the nobility were

[14] Cf. Carrasco, *Land and Polity in Tibet*, p. 95.

[15] See Chapter 11, section II, on revenue within the Religious Establishment.

obliged to work for the Government. A nobleman's subjects consequently had a double responsibility for work,[16] but the Religious Establishment made no demands of its own for work from its subjects. The subjects of the palaces were exempt from all the Government's levies of labor, except those for repairing the capital's irrigation system.

The amount of labor due from Government and Religious Establishment families was directly proportional to the amount of material in kind they owed their respective establishments. In the case of noblemen's subjects, the Government requested from the noblemen a specific amount of labor based upon the number of his subjects and the extent of their land, and the nobleman then apportioned the responsibility among his subjects. Any nobleman who himself held Government land became eligible for labor levies on the same basis as an ordinary subject, and so did palace subjects who rented or sharecropped Government land. People who did not hold land of any establishment were not formally eligible for labor levies, but they were periodically asked to perform some task for the Government, a request that they could rarely refuse. Their labor responsibilities were usually lighter than those who held land, but occasionally one of these people would draw an expensive assignment, such as a trip outside Sa sKya proper to conduct Government business.

The ability to demand labor from the subjects symbolized the political superiority of the Government among the Sa sKya establishments. (Palace subjects were excepted because of their special relationship to the royal family.) In the two eastern areas of the Sa sKya domain, revenue in kind was collected by Sa sKya officials, but the power to levy labor was possessed in one area by the government at Lhasa and in the other by the Chinese government, a recognition that they were politically superior to

[16] On the work owed a nobleman by his subjects, see Chapter 8, section III.

Sa sKya.[17] Our respondents gave no reasons for this symbolic superiority of the right to command labor—indeed, they had not fully recognized it. It may have come from the previously explained dependence of political power upon land and the people who work it.[18] For example, in the early period of Sa sKya, decentralization of the governmental function by using a scheme of local noblemen depended upon their being given land and people. The land was thus "theirs" and they had a right to part of its produce. Their governmental superior, it may be speculated, was left with the only other valuable that the people could supply, that is, their labor.

The levy of labor—like the very important levy of monks, to be described—was connected with the possession of establishment land, another manifestation of the political system's preoccupation with the land. The informal demands made upon the labor of people who had no land naturally had to be based on another principle, the somewhat inconsistent principle that everyone with an allegiance to Sa sKya owed something to the Government.

The Government received labor from the subjects on the following projects: constructing and maintaining roads, bridges, public buildings, and systems of irrigation; supplying building material by making adobe bricks and quarrying stone; haying; decorating the capital for festivals; and, especially for those without land, making trips on governmental business.[19] Other than the seasonal chore of haying, these levies of labor occurred at irregular and not especially predictable intervals. The usual

[17] See Map 1 and Appendix B. The levy of labor was called "outer revenue" (PHyi KHral), and the collection of material "inner revenue" (Nang KHral). "Outer" suggested a greater degree of formality.

[18] See Chapter 3, section X.

[19] The people of the area of Mus (Map 1 and Appendix B) had a special responsibility. Mus was the only source of gold in the Sa sKya domain, and each year its District Officer instructed his Headmen to organize parties to dig and wash until they had the amount regularly requested by the capital.

practice was for the capital to notify District Officers or Head-men that their people were to perform a particular job and leave it to these lower officials to allocate the labor. This process of allocation often involved meetings of the heads of the relevant families at which the Headman, or Group Official in the capital, was always present. Any subject could meet his labor responsi-bilities by hiring someone to take his place, but only the most wealthy did so.

VIII

The principal levy of labor in Sa sKya provided transporta-tion for officials of the Government, the Religious Establish-ment, and the North and South Monasteries when they went on official business within Sa sKya proper or to points outside. This levy applied to all subjects, save those of the palaces, and the amount due from each family was closely proportional to the amount of establishment land that it held. There were three schedules on which every family was listed; these were applied on a basis of strict rotation, although by mutual consent families could exchange their positions on any schedule. As in the case of other levied labor, anyone could hire other people to perform his transport labor, but few could afford to do so. The first schedule was for mounts, the second was for pack animals, and the third was for attendants to carry the traveling official's credentials and symbols of office, to perform chores, and generally to add to the impressiveness of the entourage. Even the poorest families had some donkeys and could provide pack animals—at the rate of two donkeys for one pack horse—but providing riding animals was often a problem. When the levy for a mount fell on a family that had no horse, it usually had to rent one. Some of the poorer families jointly purchased a horse in order to meet this responsi-bility.

All transportation levies were authorized by the ZHabs Pad and approved by the KHri CHen, who, if he were interested in such matters, could always check the amounts of animals and men authorized and change them. The traveler then received his authorization in a formal document, sealed by both KHri CHen and ZHabs Pad,[20] which he presented to the Transportation Official, who with the Group Officials and the Headman of aKHril sPe organized the levy from the capital. The people of the capital took the traveling official to another point in Sa sKya proper, where the responsibility of transporting him was assumed by the people of that area. The people on the periphery of Sa sKya proper, especially those of the SHab District, transported officials bound for places outside Sa sKya proper some distance beyond the borders. At these points outside the capital, the transport levy was organized by District Officers, Headmen, and local noblemen in areas such as Ga Ra and gYaa Lung.[21] If the traveler were someone as important as the Chief Secretary, these local officials received advance notice of his arrival. Travelers of lesser status arrived unannounced and presented their authorizations for levied transport.

Transport levies could occur at any time, and our respondents acknowledged that they frequently enough interfered with the business of farming. The people of some areas of Sa sKya had much heavier responsibilities than those of others—Ga Ra and SHab, on the route to Shigatse, Lhasa, and the east, had an especially large number of travelers—and the people of some areas, such as Ko CHag, had practically no trips to pay for (see Map 3). No adjustments in the payments in kind due to the Government were made to balance these irregularities in the levy of labor, but the people of the capital—whose transport levy was relatively light in comparison with that of the people of SHab, the other major area of Sa sKya—were more frequently called upon by the Government for other kinds of labor.

Writers on Tibet have said that under the Lhasa government the transport levy, similar to that in Sa sKya, was a heavy and resented burden on the people and that the traveling officials

[20] This document was a Lam Yig (road letter).
[21] See Chapter 4, section XIII.

acted in a most haughty and highhanded way. The Communists have also stressed the transport levy as a principal example of the tyranny from which the Tibetans have been liberated.[22] Whatever the situation was under Lhasa—and the reports may well be exaggerations—the people of Sa sKya do not seem to have been seriously exploited, and they probably were not bitterly resentful. We made a rough calculation of the annual cost to the average family, and although in some cases it was far from negligible, it was never a crushing burden.[23]

The behavior of traveling officials toward the local subjects was discussed by our respondents at some length. It was acknowledged that they were undoubtedly inclined to be demanding, insisting on eggs, meat, butter, and other delicacies, an inclination no doubt equaled, in the best traditional way, by the skill at evasion possessed by their hosts. It was, however, pointed out that, at least in recent years, those officials about to set out on journeys were cautioned by the ZHabs Pad not to take advantage of the subjects along the way, and that the small size of Sa sKya made it possible for the ordinary man to protest to the capital if he were unduly mistreated by the lower officialdom. The consensus was that officials traveling within Sa sKya proper probably behaved well enough, but that they may well have been less restrained when traveling in other parts of the Sa sKya domain. This conclusion is consistent with our information on the relationships between the government and the governed and between the higher and lower officials. Government in Tibet had to be relatively sensitive to the expectations of the governed because of the presumed ability of dissatisfied subjects to leave

[22] According to Carrasco, *Land and Polity in Tibet*, p. 91, the transport levy was the heaviest single requisition upon the average Tibetan. On the highhandedness of the officials, see George N. Patterson, *Tibetan Journey* (London: Faber and Faber, 1954), pp. 101, 126, 127, 154, 155, 195, 196. The Communists' position is expressed by Susan Warren, *The Real Tibet* (New York: Far East Reporter, 1959), p. 4.

[23] See Appendix D, section I, for this cost and our method of calculating it.

the polity. The short physical distance between the government of Sa sKya and its people did allow tolerable communication between the two. And, finally, the ZHabs Pad and the KHri CHen were able to maintain a rather close supervision over their relatively few subordinates.

The movement of officials from one place to another was considered by both the government and the subjects of Sa sKya as a normal cost of government. When we questioned the wisdom of interrupting the harvest to transport an official, the inconvenience was admitted but it was considered inevitable: "officials with their retainers, baggage, and supplies had to be moved from one place to another." No doubt the subjects who, however reluctantly, provided the means of this movement would have responded in the same way. Regarding the attitude of traveling officials, the subjects can be imagined as saying "it was ever thus," and perhaps secretly approving arrogance as the mark of a truly important man. Neither the government nor the governed had considered that paying for hired labor from a slightly increased governmental revenue in kind would have been a more efficient way to transport officials. This method presupposes a degree of specialization and even a degree of political equalitarianism unknown to Sa sKya. Such a "rational" method, however, would probably not have resolved the principal inconvenience of disrupting the agricultural process, for at harvest time no unoccupied labor was available for hire.

IX

Every political society has a pattern of control over material valuables backed by the power of its government and representing the government's understanding of the personal relationships among its people required for the proper style of consumption and the most effective method of production. In Sa sKya, this pattern was quite consistent with the attitudes and beliefs that defined the social order and the role of government within it. Its elements were a minimal protection of personal possessions, an emphasis—as much political as economic—upon agriculture and an indifference to other occupations, and a fixed claim by the government to the material and labor necessary to meet its operating expenses, a claim based on the assumption that the levels of production and consumption would not vary.

The government of Sa sKya quite fully supported an individual's claim to his personal possessions, but it provided little physical protection of these possessions. It was indifferent to the amount of goods a man could accumulate by his own efforts; although it tried to discourage the concentration of private land, it did not prevent anyone from buying as much as he could. The few subjects who became very wealthy and showed an interest in political affairs were easily absorbed into the hereditary nobility. There were few pressures to donate excess wealth to religious observance, and those that existed were not mandatory. It was expected that a rather sizable proportion of the wealth obtained by a religious collector be returned as a religious donation upon his death, but his family was not obliged to make this offering.[24] The usual Tibetan practice was to make a more or less substantial donation for religious observance upon death or retirement, but the gift was freely given and its value determined by the giver. When the wealthiest nobleman in Sa sKya died, his family gave a religious donation worth about 100 rDo TSHad, the value of fourteen or fifteen yaks. The government was concerned that the rich might get richer at the expense of the poor, but no continuing policy was designed to prevent this development. Perhaps the frequent loss of noble status described in the preceding chapter resulted in part from a desire to prevent the concentration of wealth.

Although the government also did not want the poor to become poorer, it did little to help them, aside from an occasional temporary redistribution of land and the provision of aid in serious emergencies.[25] Sa sKya had, of course, no concept of a

[24] On religious collectors, see Chapter 11, section VI.
[25] See Chapter 10, section VII, on governmental aid in emergencies.

person's right to any minimal standard of living; the concern with the poor came from the government's concern with its own power.

The government of Sa sKya made sure that its agricultural land was occupied by more or less responsible people, but beyond this it was quite indifferent to the whole process of production. It insisted that most people stay on the land, but farming was by far the easiest way to make a living and undoubtedly almost everyone was glad to have a plot of establishment land. The maintenance of an apparently rather severe fragmentation of plots seems to have been the only government-created impediment to production.[26]

The portion of his crop that each man owed the government and the labor that it levied from him were essentially neither a tax upon what he produced, nor a rent paid for using the land, nor a tribute to his superiors. These payments are probably best interpreted as his contribution to the maintenance of government; this contribution was expected because he not only enjoyed the stability provided by government but also was in charge of the polity's greatest resource, the land that gave it a surplus of grain.[27] In assessing this portion from the farmer, the government did not consider his competence as a producer, or the possibility that another man might do the job better, or whether there were other methods of extracting value from the land. It only reasoned that the land was the most valuable asset in Sa sKya and that the government had a right to support itself from the produce of the land. It took advantage of this right in

[26] See Chapter 10 on the process of production.

[27] According to our estimates, the people of Sa sKya paid less of their goods and their labor in order to maintain government than did the people of medieval Europe (see Coulton, *Medieval Village*, chs. 7 and 8). To say that the government received a portion of the crops because it "owned" the land is only a redundancy, for the claim to this portion was the only control it had over the land, other than the ultimate power possessed by most governments to take land in the event of some pressing need or emergency.

the simplest way, by demanding a fixed portion of what the land could be expected to produce.

Despite the fact that each year as many as half the families failed to pay their establishments the full amount expected of them, the government was not too disturbed, for its total revenue almost always more than covered its total expenses. Underlying this approach to the problem of paying for government was the belief that the only really proper political bond between the government and the governed existed when the subject was committed to farming land on which the government had the right to exercise the above claim. This belief was based on the realization that stability and permanence were best obtained when everyone was settled on his own plot of land and convinced that this was by far the best way of life for himself and his descendants.

Chapter 10

The Economy

A number of excellent descriptions of economies similar to that of Sa sKya have recently appeared. These economies occur in a variety of geographical and cultural contexts and, despite a number of differences, they have some common fundamental elements, especially an unquestioned reliance upon unvarying methods of agriculture and a standard of living well below that found in "developed" societies. Although these basic characteristics are well enough known, few theoretical concepts have been devised to explain these "backward" or "undeveloped" economies and to make them comparable to "modern" economies.[1] It is generally recognized that relatively unproductive processes of economizing are accompanied by unexperimental attitudes of mind and an acceptance of the economy's meager output without speculating on how it could be increased. Some writers have suggested that these attitudes are the principal reason for the static economy, rather than being results of or reactions to the low level of productivity.[2]

The economy of Sa sKya was based on a nonexperimental agriculture and provided a low standard of living. We have

[1] See, for example, H. Myint, "An Interpretation of Economic Backwardness," in A. N. Agarwala and S. P. Singh (eds.), *The Economics of Underdevelopment* (New York: Oxford University Press, 1963), pp. 112–118.

[2] For example, J. L. Sadie, "The Social Anthropology of Economic Underdevelopment," in David E. Novack and Robert Lekachman (eds.), *Development and Society* (New York: St. Martin's, 1964), pp. 218–219.

already shown how the Sa sKya belief system, from its metaphysics to its conception of government, implied an acceptance of things as they were. In the present chapter, we describe the economy in some detail in order to show that its principal features were congruent with the other main features of the small principality: its structure of government, its law, its governmental policy, and its patterns of power and prestige. We make no attempt to decide whether the economy was the cause or the effect of any or all of these other features.

I

Agriculture was the basic occupation of Sa sKya proper, with almost 90 per cent of the 3,200 families depending for their support solely upon the land and most of the rest deriving part of their income from farming. The basic crop was barley. Some wheat was grown in the milder areas such as the SHab Valley, and other minor crops were buckwheat, oats, mustard and rape for oilseed, peas for both human and animal consumption, and a limited amount of vegetables. Sa sKya produced a surplus of barley, which was used in external trade, and it had a smaller proportion of full-time herders than was usual in Tibet.

The lowest valleys were at an elevation of about 12,000 feet (Map 2). Above the limits of agriculture were hayfields and grazing lands of the establishments and above these was unowned land frequented by musk deer, roedeer, stag, blue sheep, foxes, leopards, snow leopards, brown bears, and wolves. Only the most intrepid herders utilized these areas. In the present century Sa sKya was poorly forested, with some scrub or brushwood, such as scrub willow, juniper, and tamarisk, and a few meager stands of small evergreens, probably firs. Ko CHag, however, had some forests of birch and fir or spruce. The tradition is that in the eleventh century much of the country was covered with scrub forest.

The productiveness of the several areas of Sa sKya varied according to their vulnerability to hail, the fertility of their soil, and the ease with which they could be irrigated. The SHab Valley was the only region favorable on all three counts, and its people grew about one-third as much wheat as barley. The concentration of population at the capital resulted from its importance as the religious and governmental center of Sa sKya; its principal crops were barley and peas, with not more than 5 per cent of the land in wheat. There were fewer wealthy people in the capital than in the fertile SHab Valley, but it was said that there was also less acute poverty, perhaps because the poor of the capital could more easily get aid from their establishments and because they had access to religious distributions by the palaces and monasteries.

Water for irrigation was drawn from all the principal rivers, except those running through the districts of dPal rTSe and dPal lDan rTSe (Map 2). The methods of irrigation varied according to the relative locations of the streams and the farming land. Where the land was at the same elevation as the rivers, water was taken directly by means of small ditches; each farmer built his own irrigation system, and he was subject to no control over the amount he drew or when he drew it. Where the land was higher than the rivers—as in the Grum Valley below the capital, the PHu Valley, and gYaa Lung—there were occasional dams across the rivers and ditches supplying a number of farmers. The capital had taken no part in the construction of these projects, which were "owned" by the people who built them. Disputes over use of the water were sometimes settled by Headmen or District Officers, who intervened not as men in charge of the irrigation systems but as men responsible for maintaining harmony among individual subjects. The pool system of irrigation used in the capital is described in Chapter 4.

Sa sKya apparently never experienced serious shortages of water. The capital's storage pools were tapped about seven years in ten, and the remainder of the country relied upon irrigation a similar proportion of the time. Hail was always a threat, but no instances of flooding were recalled. Rodents posed a special problem. Field mice and pikas were plentiful and destructive, but to save one's crops meant taking a large number of lives. Sorcerers were often consulted on how to control these pests, and monks were usually willing to give advice. Some farmers surreptitiously smoked out the rodents and drowned them. An artful method (and one religiously more acceptable) was to secure a diseased mouse or pika and introduce him into the local pack.

To complicate the problem of rodents, the Government ordered periodic prohibitions against taking life of any kind. A standing order prohibited killing on the eighth, fifteenth, and thirtieth days of every month; and on special occasions—for example, the thirteenth birthdays, and all subsequent birthdays at twelve-year intervals, of the KHri CHen and the Dalai Lama—no one was supposed to kill anything for periods of a year or more. During these last prohibitions, farmers were known to claim (successfully) that they could not meet their revenue payments because so much of their crops had been destroyed by the rodents.

The fields were fertilized by ashes, especially from sod used for cooking and heating, and by a compost from stables and cattle pens, but the use of animal droppings as fuel reduced the amount of fertilizer available. According to our respondents, the ideal methods were to leave one-third of the land fallow and to rotate crops, but only the wealthiest people could afford to be this farsighted. The normal yield of barley was about six times the amount of seed sown, with the ratio increasing to ten to one in very good years.[3]

Areas of farm land were measured in Tibet by the amount of seed required to sow them. In Sa sKya the basic unit of area was a KHal, which was sown by one KHal, or about one-third of an

[3] This estimate was the result of much discussion. Pedro Carrasco, in *Land and Polity in Tibet* (Seattle: University of Washington Press, 1959), p. 88, says that the ratio around Shigatse was twenty to one. All our estimates of government revenue and living standards have been based on this six-to-one return.

American bushel, of barley.[4] The average family had about twenty KHal of land, usually divided, at least in the more heavily populated areas, into several noncontiguous plots. One man in the capital, for example, had one "large" field of about ten KHal and four "small" fields each of about two to three KHal. Some capital families farmed land as far away as gYaa Lung, some ten or fifteen miles from their homes. When a farmer had land so far away that he could not work it, he leased it to someone closer for a fixed amount of grain for a period not exceeding three years; the lessee met the revenue payments on the land and kept the surplus. Farmers usually lived on their private land, when they had some, or in their own or establishment houses on establishment land or in the villages. If a farmer's plots were contiguous, he could plant the border strips between them and perhaps add a KHal or two to his total crop land. In the capital, he needed the approval of the Group Officials, but they rarely refused. The farmer carefully marked off these strips because he owed no revenue on them to his establishment. Although the separation of land into several plots was an insurance against hail or some other natural disaster, the Sa sKya farmer seems to have been principally aware of the inconvenience of traveling from one of his plots to another. The fragmentation of land did not prevent the construction of systems to supply water, although it may have kept down their number and reduced their size.

The farms were worked by all members of the poorer families. Even some of these families, however, had to rely upon hired labor, which was usually available. The plow was wooden

---

[4] We estimate that a KHal of area was about one-tenth of an acre. This estimate is very crude, but accuracy here makes little difference. The important figure is that one KHal of land in Sa sKya proper normally produced six KHal of barley. According to United States government standards, a KHal of barley in Sa sKya, at three KHal to the bushel, weighed about sixteen pounds. See Appendix D, section II, for units of measurement and the methods of estimating them. See Carrasco, *Land and Polity in Tibet,* ch. 2, for estimates of KHal in other parts of Tibet.

and edged and tipped with cast iron. It was drawn by two animals, the wealthy farmers using yak-cattle hybrids, the less wealthy oxen, and the poorest their milk cows. Horses were used only as mounts and pack animals, and they were too expensive for most of the farmers. Donkeys were the principal carriers of goods and people, and everyone had to have at least a few. Most of the families seem to have had a cow or two, both for plowing and for butter, and perhaps some goats, which were not milked. Mutton was the principal meat, but yak, cattle, and hybrid meat was preferred to mutton.

Milk came from yaks, cows, and hybrids. The yaks gave the richest milk, but in very small quantities. The hybrids gave richer milk than the cows and in much greater quantity than the yaks, so they were the preferred source of milk for making butter and cheese. No mules were bred in Sa sKya, and no hogs were raised. Most families had some chickens—they were very numerous in the SHab Valley—which were used only for eggs. Dietary habits and religious taboos kept chicken and fish off Sa sKya menus, although some of the poorest people could not afford to be too fastidious.

If a farmer had about twenty KHal, he needed about thirty rDo TSHad worth of equipment: two cows for plowing, a few donkeys, a plow, a harrow, two pack saddles and gear, three spades and shovels, three hoes, three sickles, four haircloth grain sacks, a rake, a fork, and a winnowing basket.[5]

Horizontal direct-drive mills were located on the principal streams; they were usually built and operated by private persons. When the mills were on establishment land, they could be constructed only with the establishment's permission, and most of the land bordering the larger, all-year streams was under establishment control. A considerable outlay of capital was required to set up a mill, but the milling fee was 10 per cent of the flour and some millers did rather well, although probably none could make

[5] See Appendix D, section II, for monetary units and prices.

a living from milling.[6] Herders, isolated farmers, and the poor ground their own flour by hand on querns. Oil was extracted from mustard and rape seed by means of presses working on a leverage principle, with stones used to weight the beam. The fee was also one-tenth of the seed to be pressed.[7]

The hereditary nobleman Nang bSam Pa, of the southernmost part of the SHab Valley (Map 3), was one of the richest men in Sa sKya. He was a Drag bTSan, a status conferred on his family in the seventeenth or eighteenth century, and his wealth was principally from agriculture. His land was probably at an elevation lower than the capital, and the SHab Valley in his area was wider than the valley of the Grum near the capital. He never was short of water, which he obtained by simple riparian irrigation. He grew barley, wheat, peas, and oilseeds, rotating his crops and always leaving one-third of his land fallow. He had his own oil press but no mill. He had many sheep and larger animals which he placed with herding families in the higher country, perhaps as far away as Ga Ra. In addition to meat and milk products, the herders supplied him with plenty of fertilizer. About ten members of his family lived on his estate, and the active members supervised the agricultural and domestic work. This work was done by people from his ten subject families, who were fed but not paid; by hired hands who received both food and wages; and by three or four domestic servants, who came from his subject families and lived in his house—they received full support including clothes but no wages, and they were allowed to leave this service only with his permission.

KHri CHen NGag dBang mTHu THub dBang PHyug was always concerned with the conditions of agriculture in Sa sKya.

[6] There were three mills in the capital (Map 5). The westernmost was owned and operated by a family of at least five generations of millers. The central mill was owned by a capital nobleman. The eastern mill was built by the Government after 1945, when the workers came to the capital to repair the Great God House of the South Monastery (see Chapter 11, section IX, and Appendix D, section IV).

[7] There were two oil presses in the capital, both privately owned.

Among other measures, he kept a weather-eye on the skies above the capital, and whenever a threatening black hailcloud appeared he sent a monk or one of his sons to the top of the PHun TSHogs palace to sound a trumpet made by KHri CHen mTHu CHen dBang sDud sNYing Po (r. 1783–1806) from the thigh bone of a sixteen-year-old girl. For areas out of the sound of the trumpet, he prepared many small images made of herbs and relics in the form of rabbits. He also had prayer wheels containing special incantations placed in the streams throughout Sa sKya. These were to attract rain clouds.

II

About two hundred families in Sa sKya spent their full time tending animals. Only a few of these families were truly no-madic; most of them moved much less frequently than true nomads, and hence they may have lived in houses rather than tents. These herders always maintained a close functional rela-tionship with the agricultural community from which they orig-inated as a form of transhumance. These relationships included the frequent exchange of food and fuel, an interchange of per-sonnel, and a seasonal movement of livestock from one commu-nity to the other.[8] Since these herders were much less mobile than the true nomad, they were easier to control politically. Not more than 10 per cent of the farming families in the capital and the PHu Valley had herding branches, and the ratio was about one in six in the agricultural areas close to good grazing land. No

[8] This type of herder was called a "Sa Ma aBrog," neither a farmer (Sa, soil or fields) nor a nomad (aBrog, wilderness or grazing grounds). See James F. Downs, "Livestock, Production, and Social Mobility in High Altitude Tibet," *American Anthropologist*, LXVI (1964), 1115–1119, for an example of how Sa Ma aBrog come into existence and an account of their relationships with the farming communities. The true nomads—aBrog CHen, or "great wilderness"—lived in tents the year round, had high spatial mobility, and came in contact with agri-cultural communities only through selective barter once or twice a year.

herding families originated in the rich SHab Valley; the people of SHab consigned their many animals to herders from other areas.

About 6 per cent of the total Sa sKya population was engaged in full-time herding, in contrast to perhaps 15 per cent in Khams and elsewhere in Tibet, because in Sa sKya proper good grazing land was relatively scarce and conditions for agriculture relatively good. Sa sKya proper was, moreover, able to complement its grain with animal products from the Sa sKya territory of Mus and from the nomads of Byang THang (Map 1).

Our respondents knew little about the daily life of the herder in Sa sKya. His standard of living was higher than that of the average farmer, but it was difficult to initiate a herding operation and few people attempted it. To become a herder of substance, the very high land not controlled by an establishment had to be used, and this required bold and adventuresome men with experience in handling animals. The weather was bitter, the terrain was rough, and wolves and thieves were to be discouraged only by firearms. A more modest operation based on establishment-owned grazing land was easier, but these lands seem to have been pretty thoroughly exploited.

The 1 per cent tax on animals was much lower than the 25 per cent expected by the establishments from their agricultural subjects, but a considerable amount of capital was needed to set up a profitable herding operation. The minimal requirements to justify the effort of going into animal-herding were estimated as one hundred sheep, forty yaks, a second-hand tent, one cheap rifle and three matchlocks, and four horses, for a total investment of about 465 rDo TSHad (about fifteen times the capital required for farming twenty KHal).[9] A profitable trading venture cost much less to set up (see section IV) and required less skill and effort, but the returns from herding were much greater. The

[9] See Appendix D, section II, on prices and Appendix D, section III, on living standards. A six-year religious collector made a profit for himself of about 780 rDo TSHad (see Chapter 11, section VIII).

government preferred to keep its people on the land, but it did not discourage those who were likely to become successful herders. One drawback to herding was that it required slaughtering many animals for meat and skins or selling them for slaughtering by others. To the Tibetan Buddhist this was a sin, or complicity in a sin, and it evoked strong feelings of guilt.[10]

III

The skilled craftsmen of Sa sKya were the tailors, bootmakers, hatters, and saddlers; the blacksmiths; the smiths working in copper, brass, bronze, silver, and gold; the stonemasons; the carpenters; the artists who specialized in making idols and painting idols, scrolls, and murals; and the rug-makers. There were also people who specialized in butchering, tanning, and weaving. The ordinary subject occasionally dealt with the blacksmith, the tanner, the butcher, and perhaps the shoemaker, although he could have done the work for himself. All families spun wool and wove a coarse woolen cloth from which they made their clothes. The other artisans and specialists worked for the wealthy and especially for the establishments.

In the capital there were about forty tailors, bootmakers, saddlers, and hatters, about thirty smiths of all kinds, about thirty carpenters, about twenty-five stonemasons, and about twenty makers of idols. All these men, except about ten of the tailors, had a special connection with the Government whereby they were obliged to work for it when it called them and for only a token wage. This relationship was formalized by organizing the artisans into five groups, each headed by a Jo Lags official of "orange" rank; one group, the tailors, had two "brown" Jo Lags subordinate leaders.[11]

[10] See Chapter 9, section IV, for the case of the farmer who became a herder. On slaughtering animals, see Robert B. Ekvall, *Fields on the Hoof: Nexus of Nomadic Pastoralism in Tibet* (New York: Holt, Rinehart and Winston, 1968).

[11] On Jo Lags rank, see Appendix C, section I.

The payment an artisan owed to the Government because he held Government land was, however, reduced according to the length of time he worked for the Government, a period varying from about to 75 to about 120 days each year.[12] Our respondents described this arrangement as the payment to the Government of "inner revenue" in skilled labor rather than in farm produce. Since these artisans were always on call, they had to get the Government's permission to leave the capital area. All of them held Government land, and they were not allowed to give it up to concentrate on their crafts. Other than the men who worked with precious metals and were relatively highly paid, the most successful artisan could make no more than half his living from his special skill.

The artisans had workrooms in their own homes, and sons learned the skills from their fathers. Each Government artisan was expected to train at least one son to succeed him, but if a man had no sons he was not required to adopt one or to teach someone else. Some of these men apparently felt it very important to preserve their skills in their offspring. Although the crafts of Sa sKya involved a considerable investment in the time spent learning them, they required very little investment in tools and other equipment, and Tibetan houses were usually large enough so that the provision of a workroom involved no extra outlay.

Outside the capital, there were fewer artisans in proportion to the total population because there was no demand for their work comparable to that made by the establishments and the North and South Monasteries. Certain areas by custom specialized in certain skills. The SHab Valley, for example, was noted for fine woolen cloth and the dMigs District for tanning. There were a number of workers in brass near the monastery of gDong dGaa CHos sDe. A small foundry and cutlery employing four or five men was located at CHu aDus, where there were also smiths working in copper, silver, and gold (Map 3). Except for a

[12] On the usual number of days worked for the Government by each type of artisan, see Appendix D, section IV.

famous goldsmith at CHu aDus, probably none of these special-ists made more than half his living from his craft.

As in many other societies, the blacksmith was held in low repute. The regular life indemnity payment for a blacksmith was about one-quarter of that for a farmer or herder, and members of blacksmith families were not accepted in the monkhood. Our respondents explained this bias by saying that smiths disturb the earth gods and make the instruments of killing, but these expla-nations are not very convincing. As far as we could tell, black-smiths were accepted, without discrimination, as useful members of the community, and some managed to become moderately wealthy. In fact, the only manifestations of a prejudice were the low life indemnity rank and the inability to become monks, and these are best explained as "being the custom."

Gold was the only metal mined in Tibet, and Sa sKya proper got its gold from the Sa sKya territory of Mus. There was some fear of offending the earth gods by extracting silver, copper, iron, and even coal, but the principal reason for importing these things seems to have been that no one had considered it profita-ble to produce them domestically.

Butchers were perhaps even lower on the social scale than blacksmiths, although they were in the same life indemnity class. They, too, were not allowed to enter the monkhood. In addition to the usual reasons for holding butchers in low repute—that they have a bloody, dirty, and callously brutalizing job—Bud-dhism is strongly opposed to taking life of any kind—one must if possible avoid killing even insects. There were fifteen or twenty butchers in the capital, and perhaps one of them made enough from slaughtering and cutting to support himself.

Sheepskins, made into garments and robes, provided the basic protection against the bitter Tibetan cold. The hides of yak and cattle were used for shoe soles, rope, bags, saddlery, and so forth. All hides and skins were tanned by chamoising them with rancid butter bought from the monasteries when the religious idols made of butter were dismantled. Fine lambskins were similarly prepared by using a mixture of buttermilk and brains. The only tool needed was a tanning saw, a simple device of hardwood.

Unlike elsewhere in Tibet, women did all the spinning and weaving in Sa sKya. If one wanted either coarse or fine thread, he gave the proper grade of raw wool to the spinner, who kept half as her fee.

The only printing in Sa sKya was done by about twenty monks of the North and South Monasteries working with paper brought from Mus and wooden printing blocks imported from eastern Tibet or made by itinerant carvers.

The nobility and the wealthy subjects sent their sons—and, on rare occasions, their daughters—elsewhere in Tibet to be educated or hired tutors within Sa sKya. Retired monks were a natural source of this skill, and they often lived in the homes of their patrons, being supported and then given a generous gift when the course of studies was completed. Active monks were free to use their spare time as they chose, and people often brought their sons to the monasteries to be tutored. An active monk was paid on the same basis as a retired monk.

The most interesting craft was rug-making. Rugs were not made in Sa sKya proper until the late 1930's, when KHri CHen NGag dBang mTHu THub dBang PHyug sent to Gyangtse for information that enabled about ten families to go into the business. These rug-makers, like the other artisans of the capital, did most of their work for the Government, but they were paid the market price for their work rather than having it treated as government revenue. Most of the ten families supported themselves by their craft, and although some of them farmed Government land, others had no land at all.

The customer was always wise to have craftsmen work in his own house, where he could, for example, guard against adulteration of precious metals and make sure that his rugs contained the agreed-upon quantity of knots on the cross threads (determining the thickness and closeness of the nap). He had, moreover, to be courteous and generous with these skilled workers, especially the gold and silver smiths, for they were easily offended and the quality of their work invariably reflected their feelings toward the customer.

IV

A daily market for the people of the capital was held in the official square next to the Government Building (Map 5), where regular merchants and others who had something to sell could, without cost, display their goods. Larger trade-fairs were held periodically in various places in Sa sKya, and they attracted people from some distance. Large fairs occurred in the capital during the religious festivals of the seventh and eleventh moons and at the New Year.

In the capital there were about ten full-time merchants and about twenty taverns selling beer which the tavern-owners brewed themselves. Some Sa sKya subjects who traded regularly with the outside—in addition, of course, to farming establishment land—set up daily displays in the market place, and some of the taverns were owned by Sa sKya subjects, including a nobleman or two, but most of the retailing was handled by the "Nepalese." The government of Sa sKya would not allow its subjects to give up their land in order to become merchants.[13]

Sa sKya proper had a surplus of grain, and the foundation of its trade was the exchange of this grain for salt, animals, and animal products with the nomads of Byang THang north of Sa sKya (Map 1). The people of Sa sKya took their grain, and other goods obtained south of the Himalayas, to the nomads and returned with salt, sheep, cattle, yaks, cheese, butter, tallow, wool, and yak hair and tails. Most of the meat and butter was consumed in Sa sKya; the other goods were taken to the south to be exchanged for raw sugar, dried fruit, tea, rice, tobacco, hardware, and cloth, some of which was returned to Sa sKya with the remainder going into the trade with the nomads. One-half a

---

[13] See Chapter 3, section VI.

rupee's worth of plastic bracelets from India purchased a sheep from the nomads. A similar pattern of trade existed with Shigatse and points farther east, but it was less important.

A north-south trading operation required a substantial investment, considerable initiative, and the ability to leave one's farm for some length of time. The trader needed at least twenty yaks, which he had to purchase at a cost of 140 rDo TSHad, and at least ninety KHal of barley, worth 25 rDo TSHad. With this large a caravan, he also had to hire animal handlers at 1.5 rDo TSHad a month. When the cost of his pack saddles and other gear is included, the whole venture probably required an investment of close to 200 rDo TSHad. To engage in a profitable trading venture to the east, slightly over 100 rDo TSHad was required; animals could have been hired for this trip. A trading operation within Sa sKya proper required at least six donkeys and 10 rDo TSHad worth of goods, a total investment of about 35 rDo TSHad. The basis of trade within Sa sKya proper was also the exchange of animal products and grain, with the herders taking meat, wool, skins, milk, butter, and animal droppings to the farmers.

There were relatively few full-time traders, for the establishments would not allow their subjects to give up their responsibilities for land to go into trading and few families had both the capital and the personnel for such ventures. The Government, the palaces, and wealthy but busy men such as the ZHabs Pad hired men on a full- or part-time basis to trade for them. Only a few cases were discovered of families that became wealthy through their trading operations. On the other hand, a large number of people engaged in part-time, small-scale trading within Sa sKya proper.[14]

---

[14] This may have indicated underemployment, at least during the winter months. See Raymond Firth and B. S. Yamey (eds.), *Capital, Saving, and Credit in Peasant Societies* (Chicago: Aldine, 1964), p. 233.

V

All material goods had a monetary price in Sa sKya and could be purchased for money. Small transactions usually involved money; large deals were often on the basis of barter, but the value of the goods exchanged was based on their monetary price. Sa sKya did not issue any money. The paper and copper Srang, and the ZHo, worth 0.1 Srang, both issued by the Lhasa government, were the only currency in common use in Sa sKya proper.[15] Neither Lhasa nor Sa sKya attempted to control the value of the currency.[16] The Sa sKya Government, however, put ceilings on interest rates, and in times of scarcity set maximum prices for grain or put its own grain on the market at the normal price.

The entire twentieth century was a period of inflation. An old woman in the capital used to complain about modern times by pointing out that in the days of KHri CHen aDZam Gling CHe dGu dBang sDud (r. 1895–1915) one could get dead drunk on 0.15 Srang worth of beer. This amount purchased only a pint in 1947. After 1947, influenced by inflation in neighboring countries and occupation by the Chinese Communists, inflation proceeded more rapidly.

Hired labor was common in Sa sKya, and in the capital work was always available, at least during the farming season, for those who sought it. The labor market was perfectly free, although the Religious Establishment and the nobility were expected to get the *pro forma* permission of the Government or the palaces before hiring Government or palace subjects. Working for

[15] Our estimates of governmental income and expenditures and other large amounts have been given in terms of the rDo TSHad, a Lhasa-issued unit worth fifty Srang. Some of the wealthy in Sa sKya had rDo TSHad, and they also had other coins, paper money, and bars of precious metals.

[16] See Melville J. Herskovits, *Economic Anthropology* (New York: Alfred A. Knopf, 1960), p. 238.

wages was socially quite acceptable: if a man needed a little extra income, seeking employment was one of the possibilities that immediately occurred to him. Men often helped their neighbors on the implied or express understanding that the help would be returned, but assistance was more usually arranged on a straight wage basis.[17]

In seeking work, one always first approached one's family, neighbors, and friends. If they had no suggestions he could, in the capital, inquire of the groups of women who sat spinning and weaving in the sunshine; prospective employers sometimes used the same source of information. There were always twenty or thirty drifters from outside Sa sKya in the capital, and they frequently sought employment through these "sunshine channels" of information. Although local labor was given preference, drifters received the same wages and apparently they could always find work. Full-time employees were, however, very difficult to obtain. The nobility got most of their servants from their own subject families, and wealthy subjects usually had some poor relatives willing to work for room, board, and perhaps clothing.

Large trading ventures to the outside needed hired handlers of pack animals; this kind of labor was very scarce because the job required skilled and experienced men to leave their homes for months at a time. The job was also very hard on clothing, but it was well paid—the wages in the spring were only half as high as those in the fall—and the men received superior food.

The people of Sa sKya had only fourteen holidays a year. In the city of Lhasa, there were about sixty holidays from work each year, and elsewhere under the Lhasa government there were more than fourteen but fewer than sixty. Our respondents

---

[17] Wages paid by a private person to an agricultural worker or to an artisan were called "Nag Gla," which connoted a transaction among subjects. The token wages paid by the Government to its artisans were called "gSol Ras," which connoted that the payment was made by the grace of the Government.

considered fewer holidays in Sa sKya an indication of the Sa sKya government's better control of its subjects.

VI

Loans could be obtained from wealthy individuals, from the two palaces, and from monasteries other than the North and South Monasteries, whose concern with a reputation for piety prevented any involvement in business affairs. The Religious Establishment spent all its income, and the Government, although it had regular surpluses, virtually never made loans. The Government usually saved for the sake of saving; it withdrew material from its stores only to meet emergencies, such as the threat of starvation.[18] The palaces also kept reserves, but they were not reluctant to lend grain or money to people of all social and political statuses. All the wealth that came to the individual members of a palace went into a single fund managed by the palace treasurer and the wife of the palace's head.

All the monasteries of Sa sKya proper, other than the North and South Monasteries, regularly made loans to the laity. These loans were usually handled by the monastery's business manager, but individual monks occasionally had enough wealth to lend from their own resources. Every monastery used as much wealth as it could spare in this way, and hence the religious donations made by the people of Sa sKya and the donations collected from outside Sa sKya by the monks of CHos aKHor lHun Po were put to use.[19]

People borrowed from these sources to meet their living ex-

---

[18] It was estimated that in the 1940's the Government had about 3,000 KHal of barley, worth 840 rDo TSHad, and substantial amounts of wheat, rice, salt, and tea stored in the South Monastery. It also had granaries in many of the districts and other outlying areas (see Chapter 12, section IV).

[19] On these donations, see Appendix E, section III. On such donations and the quasi-banking operations of monasteries, see Robert B. Ekvall, *Religious Observances in Tibet* (Chicago: University of Chicago Press, 1964), pp. 190–198.

penses or to invest in business enterprises. A loan in order to go into animal husbandry was easy to get, but as said above the possibilities for such ventures were limited. Most loans for business were utilized in the trade that exchanged the surplus grain of Sa sKya for the products of the northern nomads, an enterprise that brought a sure, high, and quick profit. There was no indication that anyone even contemplated seeking a loan to invest in agriculture.

A large proportion of the people of all social strata were in debt because they had borrowed to meet their normal living expenses. A man might have borrowed to purchase a plow or a donkey, to buy food, clothing, tools, and utensils, and to meet the expenses of marriages, funerals, and the like. This kind of borrowing was a response to accidents such as damage to crops and loss of animals, to bad luck or bad management in trading ventures, and particularly, as so often in economies of simple technology, to the inability of a considerable number of people just to make ends meet. The Government set a ceiling of 12.5 per cent on the interest that could be charged for loans needed for subsistence. This maximum was stated in the Sa sKya code, but there is no way of knowing how effective it was in practice.

Interest rates ranged from 10 per cent to 25 per cent annually, with the normal rate being about 16 per cent. Most loans were for short periods; three-year loans were common and five-year loans unusual. Many creditors, however, were willing to let debts continue indefinitely as long as they received their annual interest.[20]

The borrower was required to furnish the creditor with collateral, usually worth half the value of the loan, or to obtain a

[20] High interest rates in peasant societies, it has been said, may be commensurate with the risk taken by creditors, and when the creditor depends upon informal sanctions, the community may not support him if it considers his interest exorbitant (see Firth and Yamey, *Capital, Saving, and Credit in Peasant Societies*, pp. 31, 248).

co-signer of sufficient wealth and reputation.[21] The collateral or pledge was usually movable valuables such as jewelry, armor, weapons, images, furnishings, clothes, and animals; it was held by the creditor, who was not to use it. A man could pledge his standing crops, but his establishment required that he leave un-pledged an amount sufficient to meet its revenue claim. The creditor could keep the pledge if the loan were not repaid at the end of the specified period, and he usually took the word of the borrower regarding the value of the pledge. If the prospective borrower appeared unsound, the creditor could require both a co-signer and a pledge. Even small loans necessary for subsistence were supposed to be backed by a pledge, but if the man in need had none, he could appeal—perhaps with help from his Headman—to the compassion of the man of means.

The debts of the head of a family were assumed by his heir. A monk had no responsibility for his family's debts, and he could not be required to take over its land in case the heir died prematurely. A man who became an adopted heir was held responsible for half his original family's debts in the event that its heir died prematurely. When there was no one to succeed a deceased heir, his establishment had full control over its own land that he had been working, but his creditors could claim all his personal property, including his house and his private land. If a debtor refused to meet his obligations, his creditors could claim his belongings to the total amount of his debt, less the value of any pledges in their possession. All these rights and responsibilities were ultimately definable by the Law Officials and enforced by the ZHabs Pad.

Bankruptcy could be declared, but this action required the personal approval of the ZHabs Pad, who always first had the case investigated. When a declaration of bankruptcy was approved, the creditors kept their pledges and divided the bank-

[21] The collateral or pledge was called "gTe Pa" or "gTaa Ma," and the co-signer, "KHa bDags" (part owner).

rupt's personal property; the signed loan agreements were returned to the debtor.

The Government prohibited pledging private land for loans, although it did not prohibit its sale. It did, however, allow private land to be used to secure a loan under an arrangement in which, for advancing an amount less than its market price, the creditor could use the land as if it were his own private land. He could not, of course, sell it, and at any time the debtor could regain control of the land by returning the amount borrowed without interest. There was no time limit on such arrangements, and many cases involving them came before the Law Officials.[22]

When we asked our respondents if the wealthy were considered to have a responsibility to help the less fortunate, they answered that definitely no such attitude existed in Sa sKya. They interpreted the question as referring to aid to those in straitened circumstances, rather than to investment in the productive process, and the answer was consistent with Sa sKya's strong individualism. Despite this individualism, destitution created disharmony, and the Headmen and others put pressure on the wealthy to help the poor. KHri CHen NGag dBang mTHu THub dBang PHyug reportedly broke precedent by giving the poorer subjects loans that carried no interest and required no pledges. He was concerned with their poverty, but his loans were so small—from three to twenty KHal of barley—that they did no more than provide temporary relief.

VII

Most of the people of Sa sKya had a low level of consumption. Standards of living were expressed in terms of the KHal of barley rather than in monetary terms. The monks of the North

[22] Cf. F. G. Bailey, "Capital, Saving, and Credit in Highland Orissa (India)," in Firth and Yamey, *Capital, Saving, and Credit in Peasant Societies*, p. 113. Much of our information on indebtedness was corroborated by the history of a prominent subject family of SHab, told to our respondents by a member of the family who was an official in the PHun TSHogs palace.

and South Monasteries, for example, were described as living at a
sixty-KHal level, which meant that each monk annually consumed the value of sixty KHal of barley (or about seventeen
rDo TSHad in monetary terms). It was estimated that an adult
could manage to live to a normal age in an average degree of
health at an annual level of eighteen or twenty KHal. About 15
per cent of the subject families of the capital had a standard of
living of at least thirty KHal and the remainder had standards
below this figure.[23] The situation outside the capital was no
doubt similar: the SHab Valley, because of its fertility, was said
to have a larger proportion of wealthy people than the capital,
but it also had more destitution because its poor did not have
access to the special "charities" described below.

The people of Sa sKya were not faced with the problem of
reaching a point in the accumulation of wealth where they could
no longer consume this wealth themselves. There were always
better foods, household furnishings, clothing, riding animals,
firearms, and the like, that could be purchased and utilized by a
sedentary population, and servants were usually available for the
well-to-do. No potlatch was needed to dispose of surplus goods
of consumption, and no one gave half his wealth to a monastery
because he could find no other way to spend it on himself.
Accumulation of personal wealth was, however, an infrequent
occurrence in Sa sKya, where probably not more than 10 per
cent of the families had any surplus beyond the minimum for
what was considered a tolerable standard of living.

By a rough guess, about 1,000 people in all Sa sKya proper had
a standard of living lower than eighteen KHal a year. Malnutrition, however, was apparently less frequent than might have
been expected; only one death from malnutrition in the capital
was remembered, a six-year-old whose father was incapable of
regular work. It seems that if he could have worked, jobs would

---

[23] For examples of different standards of living, see Appendix D,
section III.

have been found for him, but as it was there were no procedures to resolve his serious situation.[24]

The monasteries provided the poor of the capital with a special source of income. Whenever there was a regular religious celebration or a special distribution to the monks, the poor people stood with bowls in hand outside the monasteries and the monks gave them food. These alms were part of the calculated cost of religious distributions, and they gave the poor of the capital an advantage over those living elsewhere in Sa sKya proper. In eastern Tibet, people who could not fully support themselves used to leave home for a month or two and wander about begging. Such tours were not practiced by the people of Sa sKya, because, among other reasons, their government did not approve.

A large amount of petty theft took place in the capital. It will be remembered that the man who took someone else's food because he did not have enough to eat was not treated as a thief; official tolerance of this behavior constituted a rudimentary kind of welfare policy. A poor subject was once helping to prepare his establishment's barley for roasting, and in the process he also helped himself to about a month's supply. He was apprehended, but not punished, because he successfully claimed that he could not have lived without it.

Probably as many as nine-tenths of the families in Sa sKya, hereditary nobility and governmental officials as well as ordinary subjects, were in debt. Borrowing was a common way to meet necessary expenditures, and most families could find something to use as a pledge; a good sheepskin coat, for example, could be pledged for six or seven KHal of barley. When a man had borrowed as much as he could and was still short of the necessities of life, he approached his Headman or, in the capital, a Group Official, who tried to arrange a loan and perhaps acted as a co-

[24] One problem in identifying malnutrition was that swollen extremities, a symptom of malnutrition, are also a symptom of circulatory difficulties caused by the weakening of the heart in very high altitudes.

signer. If unsuccessful, the Headman could refer the case to the District Officer, who had the authority to make small loans of from five to ten KHal of grain without interest from Government stores, but who usually also tried to arrange a private loan. These loans, according to the Sa sKya code, were to carry no more than 12.5 per cent annual interest. In the capital, a subject who believed he could not get his family through the year went to one of the Group Officials, who first verified the man's story by talking with his neighbors. If the Group Official were unable to arrange a loan, he reported the matter to the ZHabs Pad, who authorized an investigation to determine the most feasible solution—for example, an interest-free loan or reallocation of land. There was, of course, always the possibility of reducing or postponing the payment a man owed the Government for working its land in order to allow him to live until the next harvest. The Group Official was supposed to prevent situations of this kind developing to the point where they had to be referred to the ZHabs Pad.

The Government also helped people who found themselves in difficulties because of natural disasters such as destruction of their crops by hail. After the loss was verified by an on-the-spot investigation, the Government could remit all or part of the revenue due it for one or two years, give the people free seed for the following year, or present them with free grain—the oldest edible grain in its stores—to enable them to live until the next harvest.[25] We estimated that the annual average of gifts from the Government amounted to about nine KHal of barley for each of 250 people, a cost of about 630 rDo TSHad. Most of these gifts seem to have been given to meet emergencies caused by acci-

[25] In 1941, crops in rMa Bya, aKHril sPe, and parts of the capital were heavily damaged by hail. The Government was reluctant to deplete its stores of grain—the revenue had not yet come in—so it gave the people whose crops had been damaged about half the amount of grain they needed for subsistence and made up the difference in animal products. This action resulted in an increase in the price of grain, so the Government set a ceiling price for grain.

dents of weather. The Government was generally indifferent to families that were very poor because they lacked land or skill; this kind of poverty was to be handled by nongovernmental methods, by the unofficial aid of Headmen and the charity of neighbors.

VIII

A capital subject family well known to our respondents had a standard of living of thirty KHal and thus spent about 8.5 rDo TSHad each year for the consumption of each adult. This standard was better than that of 85 per cent of the subjects in the capital.

The head of the family, who will be called lHa bZo Pa, was an idol-maker about thirty years of age in 1947. His first responsibility was to make and paint idols, images, scrolls, and murals for the Government when it requested his services, about 120 working days each year. He also had some Government land, and in his spare time he worked for private employers, making religious objects, decorating interiors, and repairing almost anything that was broken.

lHa bZo Pa was the youngest of the four sons of a capital tailor. The oldest son followed his father's occupation, the two middle brothers became monks, and lHa bZo Pa became an idol-maker and stayed at home. He and his lay brother took a common wife, but the arrangement broke down because, among other reasons, the lady much preferred the elder brother. lHa bZo Pa thereupon left the family home—no formal divorce proceedings were required—and soon got a wife of his own. He then began to negotiate for his portion of the Government land held by his family and his share of the family's movable valuables; the family had no private land.

The two brothers were on good terms and they amicably agreed to divide everything equally, but the wife of the elder—who was formerly the common wife of both—objected strenuously. She maintained that since she was a member of the family before it divided, she and the elder brother should retain two-thirds of the property rather than half. lHa bZo Pa then took his case to one of the Group Officials, but the Group Official's attempts to mediate were fruitless. The dispute was eventually referred to the ZHabs Pad, but he was most annoyed at being bothered by such trivia and referred it back to the Group Official. With this extra incentive, the Group Official managed to secure an agreement dividing the property half and half. Before this agreement was made formal and binding, however, lHa bZo Pa's new wife began to say some very unpleasant things in public about his former wife, with the result that the latter resumed her insistence on receiving two-thirds of the property. She had a better case this time, and eventually she prevailed. The idol-maker consequently began his independent life with less than thirty KHal of Government land.

lHa bZo Pa's new wife bore him no children. After a few years he took a second wife, who had a boy and a girl, and relationships within the family were apparently quite amicable. (Whenever he was too busy to attend a public meeting, and he often was, he made sure to send his second wife as his representative.) In answer to comments on the wisdom of poor men having two wives, lHa bZo Pa replied that he had wanted a son who could carry on his skills.

The land that lHa bZo Pa worked was divided into three plots of about three KHal each located between the two palaces and three plots of the same size just east of bDe sKyid (Map 5). The first plots were about two miles from his home in the east village and the second about four miles. He also had a few small plots in gYaa Lung, about fifteen miles away, which he and his family worked themselves. Finally, he had some small plots in KHra U, about twenty-five miles from his home (Map 3); these the family could not work. lHa bZo Pa worked on the average about 120 days a year for the Government as an idol-maker, for which he received only token wages of 0.3 Srang per day but all his meals including two quarts of beer. A call from the Government could come at any time, and its artisans had to answer it at once. In his free time, lHa bZo Pa worked for anyone who would hire him—but usually only the nobility could afford to do so—making religious images and masks, decorating interiors, and making and repairing furniture. He could work in any material. He fit false teeth that he had carved from ivory. He once went to India and watched radios being repaired. When he returned to Sa sKya, he took an old broken-down radio he found in the PHun TSHogs palace and put it in working order.

When working for private employers, the idol-maker received three Srang in cash per day and three very good meals with the usual two quarts of beer and tea of good quality throughout the day. For breakfast, he probably ate tsamba, a dish made of parched barley flour mixed by hand with tea, butter, and cheese, and some boiled mutton; for lunch, tsamba, fried bread, and perhaps some sweet bread; for dinner, rice or wheat noodles with cheese, meat, and yoghurt; throughout the day he received tea churned with butter, milk, and salt; and during the afternoon he had his two quarts of beer. If the food and drink were of lesser quality, the idol-maker and the other artisans of Sa sKya expected larger wages in cash. lHa bZo Pa's young son assisted him, often receiving for his work two Srang a day from private employers. With all this time spent on their crafts, the family occasionally had to hire men to work in its fields. Trading ventures of any size were beyond its capacity, and it had no way to acquire the capital to buy sheep to be placed with herding families.

The family had three cows, only two of which gave milk, about five donkeys, and a half-dozen chickens. Their cows did not give enough milk, and they had to purchase butter for their tea and tsamba. The cows were bred at two-year intervals, and the calves were usually butchered early. The family ate meat once or at most twice a week, usually buying a quarter of mutton of five or six pounds. Their staple food was barley tsamba; rice was a delicacy that the very wealthy ate only two or three times a week, and wheat in the form of noodles, the usual dinner food of the wealthy, was beyond the idol-maker's means. Everyone ate barley tsamba for breakfast and lunch, supplemented by what he could afford; the poorest people mixed dried peas with their barley. Vegetable oil was readily available, but lHa bZo Pa could rarely afford yoghurt. His family drank the cheapest grade of Chinese tea, mixed in equal parts with a substitute called Seng lDang, a red wood cut in shavings or splinters. Beer was plentiful in Sa sKya, and it was served on the same formal or ceremonial occasions when tea was served elsewhere in Tibet.[26]

lHa bZo Pa's house in the east village was owned by the Government, but because he was a Government artisan he paid no rent. It was a single-story house of medium size, with a stable built into the house, and consisted of a room of about twelve feet by eighteen feet used for living, sleeping, cooking, and eating and three smaller rooms, one a workroom for the artisan, one a workroom for the women, and the third used as a storeroom. The house was furnished poorly and the household equipment was inferior. Heat was used only for cooking. Since their animals did not provide enough fuel they purchased peat and sod, which were cheaper than animal droppings, but gave less heat and burned with an unpleasant odor, although the ash made good fertilizer.

lHa bZo Pa had one good garment of lambskin worn with the fleece on the inside and faced with broadcloth. When he worked for the Government—about four months each year—he felt obliged to wear this garment rather than the trousers, shirt, and robe of undyed woolen homespun that constituted the normal garb of the poorer people of Sa sKya. In the 1950's he became the head of the Government image-makers, a post of "orange"

---

[26] Each of the palaces had a family of subjects that made its beer; the palace supplied the ingredients, and for its work the family kept the lees.

Jo Lags rank.[27] For every celebration or official meeting he had to borrow an orange satin robe from the PHun TSHogs palace.

The family of three adults, one youth, and a small girl were usually only barely able to make ends meet. As a Government artisan, the idol-maker did not owe the Government any payments in kind for working its land, but his family was eligible for the work levies. When he became head of the image-makers, his family's responsibility for work levies was reduced, but this did not make much difference in their standard of living. He probably was in debt for about a hundred rDo TSHad. It will be remembered that lHa bZo Pa and his family were reckoned to have a higher living standard than 85 per cent of the people in the capital.

IX

The low level of innovation in the Sa sKya economy did not result from the absence of a desire to increase production. All but the most wealthy were perfectly aware of a large number of desirable consumer goods that were available but beyond their means, and all would no doubt have been glad to escape their perpetual indebtedness. The wealthy, for their part, fully appreciated the advantages of wealth, and they were usually interested in acquiring more. They lived well; they enjoyed their prestige and power; and they invested their wealth in trading and making loans. There were, moreover, no restrictions placed by government or custom on the accumulation of wealth, for even religious donations were not required except at the time of a man's death and then they were relatively modest.[28]

The government of Sa sKya also appreciated the advantages of material wealth, and it too was usually interested in increasing its own income and that of its people. Its principal concern, as

[27] See Appendix C, section I.

[28] See Manning Nash, "The Social Context of Economic Choice in a Small Society," *Man*, LXI (1961), 190, for devices to limit the accumulation of wealth.

described in the following chapter, was to maintain as many monks as it could in enough material comfort to allow them to devote their full time to religious observance and to keep them happy and thus disciplined; and more books, images, offerings, and other religious objects would always have been welcome as additions to the supernatural and mundane reputations of the North and South Monasteries. From a political point of view, the government was always worried that its people might become so poor that they would abandon their nonmovable possessions and leave Sa sKya.

Despite these reasons for wishing to increase production, nothing was done to rationalize the methods of production and the basis of governmental revenue. There was nothing to stimulate a revision of the Sa sKya manner of economizing: there was no pressure from within and no example accepted from without. Imperial control, so often a force for modernization, came only in the 1950's, and then it was so drastic that the Tibetans were left with practically no autonomy. Life in Sa sKya was apparently pleasant enough by Tibetan standards, and consequently no one was dissatisfied enough to seek new ways of doing things. Those who had capital, as our cases show, were in a position to make the most of farming, herding, and trading—the traditional ways of accumulating wealth—and hence had no reason to innovate. The attitude of the government was similar. It maintained its independence, supported one of the most famous monastic establishments in all Tibet, and kept its people. It had no reason to prompt its people to innovate, nor to revise a scheme of revenue under which only half the families could meet their quotas.

Although hired labor was usually available and often used in Sa sKya, the scope of farming, trading, and herding operations was limited by the supervisory ability of the members of a single nuclear family. Our information shows rather clearly that one of the principal factors in a family's prosperity was the number of adult males upon whose labor it could draw. The atypical man who could keep several grown sons within his household, or who could arrange a partnership with his brother, could make better use of his land and could diversify his operations by engaging in herding and trade. Coordinated economic activity beyond the nuclear family did not go beyond the most rudimentary levels. The absence of larger voluntary economic organizations corresponds rather well to the excessive individualism implied by the otherworldly orientation of the Sa sKya belief system. In addition to being the basic economic unit, the nuclear family raised children and provided companionship. Although marriage in Sa sKya implied a more limited involvement than marriage in "modern" society, the relationships it created were much more intense than those that existed outside it. The members of the family relied rather heavily upon one another; it can be inferred that one reason for this reliance was the mistrust of other people, whose motives were unknown and actions uncontrollable.[29]

The presuppositions underlying the polity were no doubt the most important single correlate of the static nature of the Sa sKya economy. The traditional union of land and people was fundamental to the whole political system, and any innovation in the method of production would have disturbed the pattern of obligations existing between the government and its subjects defined by their respective relationships to the land. The methods of production and the patterns of allocation in Sa sKya were those to be expected among a people with an otherworldly, individualistic belief system, a rudimentary structure of government, a minimal governmental policy, and a division of population into rulers and ruled.

[29] Cf. Clifford Geertz, *Peddlers and Princes* (Chicago: University of Chicago Press, 1963), p. 126, on the limited scope of voluntary association. Cf. Manning Nash, *The Golden Road to Modernity* (New York: John Wiley, 1965), p. 16, and Herbert A. Phillips, *Thai Peasant Personality* (Berkeley: University of California Press, 1965), ch. 1, on the function of family ties.

Chapter 11

The Sa sKya Monasteries

The North and South Monasteries in the capital were both the headquarters of the Sa sKya sect of Tibetan Buddhism and important parts of the polity of Sa Kya proper. In conjunction with the government, they created the centripetal force of the capital within Sa sKya proper; they received respect and donations from all parts of Tibet and from some neighboring countries; their maintenance took a sizable proportion of Sa sKya's resources; they enabled men from the most humble backgrounds to attain wealth and prestige; and through the conscription of monks they provided the strongest single bond among the social strata and the localities of Sa sKya proper.

I

The size of the North and South Monasteries fluctuated according to Sa sKya's economic prosperity and to the religious zeal of the incumbent KHri CHen. The total number of monks varied from about four hundred to about six hundred; for our study we have assumed a constant total of five hunderd during the period from 1936 until 1950, two hundred monks in the North Monastery and three hundred in the South Monastery. Virtually all these monks were in good standing, and our respondents said they had an excellent reputation for discipline and piety.[1] The monasteries were rather small by Tibetan standards,

---

[1] There were no more than ten to fifteen monks who had broken their vows—the so-called Ban Log or Grwa Log, "rebel monks"—attached to the two monasteries, and probably not more than seventy-five connected

[289]

and the monks were a relatively small proportion of the total population of Sa sKya proper. There were also fourteen other monasteries and eight nunneries in Sa sKya proper, but they had no significant connections with the North and South Monasteries and no significant effects upon political and governmental affairs. They are briefly described below.

In 1073 the capital was founded by the construction of a small religious building that became, with later additions, the North Monastery and Government Building (Map 5). Protective fortifications were put up during the chaotic period after the death of aPHags Pa in the thirteenth century. The building contained the winter offices of the KHri CHen, the ZHabs Pad, and other officials, the courtroom of the Law Officials, and the winter living quarters for both branches of the royal family. The two hundred monks of the North Monastery lived in many small units on the hill behind the east and west villages; the three hundred monks of the South Monastery lived within the monastery itself.

The construction of the South Monastery (Map 5 and Plate 5) began when, after 1260, aPHags Pa was able to send wealth back to Sa sKya and his regent could levy labor and material from the thirteen myriarchies of central Tibet.[2] When the monastery was completed, each of its outer walls was about 260 feet long and its interior was divided into several buildings and sections. During the summer months the KHri CHen and the ZHabs Pad had their offices in parts of the South Monastery.

One of the largest units in the South Monastery complex was the Great God House, a large hall whose ceiling was supported

---

with all the monasteries of Sa sKya proper. The strict standards of the North and South Monasteries were not congenial to a monk who had broken his vows. The principal function of the rebel monk in other Tibetan monasteries, to look out for his monastery's mundane affairs, was performed by the Government and the Religious Establishment. There were also no emanation bodies other than the aKHon family. See Robert B. Ekvall, "Three Categories of Inmates within Tibetan Monasteries," *Central Asiatic Journal*, V (1960), 206–220.

[2] See Chapter 1, section VI.

by a number of pillars. Four of these were single tree-trunks of about five feet in diameter, and interesting legends were attached to each. The southeast pillar was called the "tiger pillar." It was brought to Sa sKya from India on the back of a tiger, which died upon arrival and whose skin, measuring eighteen feet from nose to tip of tail, was fastened to the pillar. This animal was a magical manifestation of an Indian "defender of religion" (CHos sKyong) by the name of Bram bZugs. The tree was probably cedar, and all its bark was left on it. Over the years the lower bark completely disappeared because it was believed effective against animal sickness; regulations against taking bark did not deter the pilgrims. The only observance appropriate to this pillar was to touch one's hands and forehead to the floor.

The southwest pillar was the "pillar of the wild yak." It was brought from India on the back of an enormous black male yak, the manifestation of a defender of religion called Nag Po CHen Po. Just south of gYaa Lung was the Pass of the Yak's Tears, where on his trip the yak wept and created a spring which became an attraction for pilgrims. The skin of the yak was preserved, stuffed, and put on display in the North Monastery. Children were passed under its belly to prevent their crying at night. The pillar's wood was darker than cedar, with the bark also remaining; it, too, was recognized by the "three-point salutation."

The northeast pillar was the "pillar of Kublai Khan," a gift from the emperor to aPHags Pa. It was carried by hand from China, and the marks of the iron spikes that held the carrying racks remained visible. This pillar clearly symbolized the governmental function; it was presented as a gift by the Chinese emperor, who thus recognized the special political status and power of Sa sKya. Each New Year's day the ZHabs Pad, as the representative of the Government, hung a scarf on the pillar; and the monks hung a scarf on it whenever they received a large donation, either from a private party or from one of the establishments. The pillar physically resembled the southwest pillar, and it was religiously recognized in the same way.

The northwest pillar was the "pillar of dripping black blood." This tree, of light color and without bark, came from India, but the legend regarding its mode of transport was not remembered. The tree was originally the dwelling of a Klu, or Naga (serpent spirit), and when it was cut it dripped blood. There were also many Klu in Tibet, and prayers to this pillar were effective in dealing with diseases that they caused.

II

About half the means of support of the monks of the North and South Monasteries came from the revenue collected by the Steward from the subjects of the Religious Establishment. The other half came from the Government, the palaces, the religious collectors, the 1 per cent levy on sheep, and private donors.[3] All this income was managed by the Steward, who paid himself with a portion of it that varied according to what was available but that apparently was always rather generous. The capital monks had about a sixty-KHal standard of living, a handsome standard compared to that of the average subject.[4]

An increase in the revenue of the Religious Establishment often meant an increase in the number of monks in the North and South Monasteries, and so the Steward never had any surplus. In supporting the monks, the Steward was always faced with the problem of conserving his supplies, which were never as plentiful as he would have wished, and (as a consequence) raising complaints from the monks about his niggardliness. All the revenue from Religious Establishment subjects throughout Sa sKya was brought by them directly to the capital.

The formal relations between the Religious Establishment and its subjects were the same as those between the Government and its subjects, but the actual relations were said to have been more relaxed. The Steward was more inclined to be lenient than the

[3] The Steward also helped support some of the other monasteries of Sa sKya proper. On all this material, see Appendix E, section I.

[4] See Chapter 10, section VII, and Appendix D, section III.

ZHabs Pad, who operated from the position of highest power in
Sa sKya and who dealt with many more people. In addition, the
subjects of the Religious Establishment could always appeal to
the Government if they thought they were being badly treated.
As a result, the subjects of the Religious Establishment tended to
be less evasive in dealing with their officials than the subjects of
the Government with theirs. The subjects of the Religious Establishment also paid a slightly smaller percentage of their crops
in revenue than did the Government subjects.[5] Since the Religious Establishment subjects paid their revenue in labor to the
Government, whenever the Steward needed transportation for
any of his officials, he had to request it from the ZHabs Pad.
Copies of all Religious Establishment censuses and revenue records were kept in the Government's archives.

The Steward of the Religious Establishment had no part in the
internal management of the North and South Monasteries. The
abbots and their subordinates maintained discipline and were
responsible for all religious affairs.[6] If the abbots had any kind of
serious problem, they consulted with both the Steward and the
ZHabs Pad. The Steward was always consulted by the ZHabs
Pad when monks were to be levied, for he had to provision the
new monks, and they were, moreover, chosen from Religious
Establishment as well as Government subjects. He was also consulted upon the conscription of soldiers and levies of supplies for
the Sa sKya contingent in the Lhasa army because these, too,
affected the subjects of the Religious Establishment.

The abbots and other officials were concerned only with internal procedures, organization, and discipline of their monasteries. This was a rather demanding job because the monks were
allowed only minimum participation in worldly affairs and had

[5] The same situation occurred under the Lhasa government (see
Pedro Carrasco, *Land and Polity in Tibet* [Seattle: University of Washington Press, 1959], p. 98).

[6] See Appendix E, section II, for a list of officials of the North and
South Monasteries.

to be kept occupied and happy by their religious responsibilities.

The South Monastery was given formal precedence over the North Monastery. If the KHri CHen were a monk, as he occasionally was, he was also the abbot of the South Monastery. If the KHri CHen were married, he could not even enter the confines of the monastery; but he was free to visit the North Monastery, where a less rigorous traditional orthodoxy was maintained. Again, the abbots and other officials of the South Monastery were seated ahead of their counterparts of the North Monastery at affairs such as the Great Assembly Meetings, and in the regular distribution of rations by the Steward of the Religious Establishment the abbot of the South Monastery received five shares and the abbot of the North Monastery only three. (All other officials of both monasteries received two shares, and ordinary monks one share.) Despite this advantage in prestige, the South Monastery served as a kind of induction center, receiving the bulk of the new recruits and sending the most promising to the North Monastery, from whose members the important religious positions both inside and outside Sa sKya proper were filled.

III

The description of the South Monastery in military terms as an induction center to receive, train, and screen new recruits is more apt than it might have appeared, for most of the three hundred monks in this monastery were conscripted into monkhood by the Sa sKya Government. This draft or levy of monks was unquestionably one of the most important characteristics of the small polity.[7]

The monk levy applied to all families that held Government or Religious Establishment land, including any noblemen who, by his own choice or by that of the KHri CHen, took the responsibility for Government land. People who sharecropped,

[7] Only rTSe gDong (Map 1) of the other areas in the Sa sKya domain had a monk levy. It was for local use only, and we did not investigate it.

the "Nepalese" of the capital, full-time traders and artisans, and the subjects of the palaces and the nobility were never required to give a son to the monkhood. The levy of monks, which was so important to both the religious sect and the polity, was based exclusively upon the relationship of the people to the land of the two principal establishments. About two-thirds of the monks of the South Monastery and virtually all the monks of the North Monastery were levy monks. (The remainder were volunteers, or what were called "faith monks," in distinction to the "revenue monks," who were conscripted.[8])

The purpose of the monk levy was not to assure a supply of monks from a reluctant people; even if more than enough volunteers to fill the North and South Monasteries had been available, the levy would have been retained, and there is no indication that the people of Sa sKya would have preferred it otherwise. The levy of monks was a device that involved all the people of Sa sKya in the society's principal manifestation of religious observance and in the government's principal object of concern. The levy was based on the schedule for revenue in kind. Since most single families did not pay enough revenue to be solely responsible for providing a monk, the Government often notified a number of families that they were jointly responsible for producing a boy for the monk levy, and they had to decide among themselves from which family he would come. This process meant a collective involvement in the problem of staffing the North and South Monasteries, and the government was quite aware that such an involvement strengthened the cohesiveness of the polity. In addition, the levy of monks enabled the government to make sure that all areas of Sa sKya proper and all types of families were represented in the monkhood; and it allowed the government to maintain a proper balance between men in the monkhood and men in economic production. If the levy worked as planned, it provided the South Monastery with a tolerably representative sample of the subjects of Sa sKya.

[8] Respectively, Dad bTSun and KHral bTSun.

Levy monks had certain advantages over volunteer monks, especially the opportunity for attaining personal wealth. This opportunity—and the general advantages of monkhood, such as education, high prestige, material comfort, proximity to the sources of power and authority, and the chance to become a sKu Drag official—apparently made the levy of monks a quite bearable institution. Moreover, the family that produced a boy upon call had its revenue lowered in compensation. It must also be remembered that the average Tibetan family felt a kind of duty to provide at least one son to the monkhood.[9]

Levies of monks usually occurred at intervals of from three to five years. The initiative was taken by the abbot of the South Monastery, who notified the ZHabs Pad and the KHri CHen that the number of his monks had been lowered by promotion to the North Monastery, retirement, and the breaking of vows. The Steward of the Religious Establishment was then consulted to determine how many monks he could afford to support. When a number was decided upon, the ZHabs Pad assigned two members of the Work Corps to analyze the geographical representation of the levy monks currently in the North and South Monasteries, and then to examine the revenue schedules and the birth records of those areas with lesser representation. It was said that the Government also took into account the availability of agricultural labor. In the unlikely event that not enough boys were available in Government and Religious Establishment families, monks could have been conscripted from families with allegiance to noblemen, but under no circumstances could they have been levied from subjects of the palaces.

When the final determinations were made, the individual families or groups of families were notified and they selected the boys to become monks. The ZHabs Pad then sent officials to

[9] Proxies could be purchased for levy monks, but the practice was very infrequent. The usual price was eighteen rDo TSHad, but cost apparently was not a principal factor in the infrequency of proxies. In Sa sKya, proxies for volunteer monks were not allowed.

examine the prospective monks; if they were physically or mentally inferior, they were rejected and the families involved had to
provide substitutes. The officials then brought the boys to the
South Monastery for induction into the order.

There was also a levy of nuns to staff the two nunneries near
the capital, Sa bZang and Rin CHen sGang (Maps 3 and 5),
with a total of about 110 nuns, of whom not more than 10 per
cent were volunteers. The nun levy was also based on the schedule of revenue in kind, and a family that gave up a little girl also
had its revenue lowered. The levy of nuns, like the levy of
monks, no doubt helped tie the polity together, but in a much
less significant way. The life of a nun had few attractions.
Monks always served as abbots of the nunneries and hence only
lesser positions were open to the nuns. No nuns were sent out of
Sa sKya proper, and the most a nun could aspire to was becoming a personal servant of the royal family, usually of its unmarried daughters. Ordinary nuns, moreover, usually had to spend
about half their time in physical labor outside their nunneries.
The levy of nuns was probably the only way to keep enough
nuns in the capital nunneries in order to maintain the religious
prestige of the sect.

IV

About one-quarter of the three hundred monks of the South
Monastery were from outside Sa sKya proper, most coming
from Khams in eastern Tibet. Of the two hundred twenty-five
from Sa sKya proper, probably not more than 10 per cent were
volunteer monks.[10] An even higher proportion of the two
hundred monks of the North Monastery were levy monks from

---

[10] Parents usually offered a son when he was about six years old. He
was sent to a monastery as soon as possible after an official ceremony in
which he received a new, monk's, name. It was said that many little
boys may well have liked the prospect. Youths as old as twenty could on
their own enter monkhood, provided they could prove that they were
sexually pure and had not taken life. The physical and mental standards
for volunteer monks were lower than for levy monks.

Sa sKya proper. Officials of the North and South Monasteries and the smaller monasteries of Sa sKya proper were almost always either levy or volunteer monks from Sa sKya proper.[11] A monk from another part of the Sa sKya domain might have become a monastery official if he had received his training in the North Monastery, but there was a conscious attempt to keep all positions in the hands of natives of Sa sKya proper. Our respondents justified this policy on the grounds that these critical posts had to be occupied by men associated as closely as possible with Sa sKya: "It was necessary to have our own at the top of the monastic organization." It was also said that reserving these offices for men from Sa sKya proper was designed to increase the subjects' association with the regime.

This emphasis on getting people from Sa sKya proper in monastic office clearly expressed a recognition that the religious sect and the polity were interconnected and especially that members of the polity could best be trusted to promote the interests of the sect. It is thus curious that there was no such prohibition against outsiders, laymen or monks, serving as sKu Drag officials in any of the branches of government, although in practice there were very few of them. This difference might be explained by the greater symbolic importance and the higher status of the sect and the monastic organization over the polity and the government.

No distinction was made between levy monks and volunteer monks in appointments to offices in any of the monasteries or in the governmental apparatus of Sa sKya proper, but monks who were sent out from Sa sKya proper to administer monasteries or to collect religious offerings were always levy monks.[12] One explanation for this monopoly is that these positions usually brought the incumbents considerable personal wealth and the

[11] Only one exception was discovered: an abbot of the South Monastery during the late 1920's and early 1930's was from Srad (Map 1).

[12] Only one exception was discovered, and it was considered an improper appointment.

levy monks were given this opportunity as a means of keeping up their morale.[13] It was also suggested, in an unclear way, that sending only levy monks abroad was another way to ensure the loyalty of these men, who represented the religious sect and looked out for its interests away from home. Although the Sa sKya government itself may not have fully understood the reasons behind this suggestion, perhaps its recognition that the sect and the polity were mutually dependent led it to emphasize this interdependence by sending abroad only men who had come into the monkhood by means of governmental action. In addition, the very fact that the monks were conscripted into monkhood may well have made them more loyal to the sect and the polity than men who were monks entirely by their own choice. The acceptance by the people of Sa sKya of the levy of monks as a proper function of government indicates that they took service in the sect's principal monasteries quite seriously. Reliance upon the government to guarantee this service may easily have been an indication of the strength of the bonds that held the people of Sa sKya together rather than, as might superficially appear, a mark of their unwillingness to volunteer. A man who felt himself a part of this institutionalization of religious observance might have been more loyal and enthusiastic than a man who had enlisted to serve his religion solely as an individual. Whatever may have motivated the government and the individual monks, only levy monks were sent out from Sa sKya proper. What they did and its importance to the principality are discussed in section VI.

The most able monks of the South Monastery were promoted to the North Monastery, and once there they progressed from lower to higher positions according to seniority. From the rank

[13] It was said that since volunteer monks did not have this chance for personal wealth, they entered the monkhood less fully committed to it as a lifetime career. This may have been one reason why breaking vows, or "rebellion," was more frequent among volunteer monks than among levy monks.

of an ordinary monk, a man was promoted to a kind of candidacy from which were made all appointments to important positions both inside and outside Sa sKya proper. Exceptions to the rule of seniority were possible: at the level of entering candidacy, exceptions were recommended by the official in charge of the candidates, and at higher levels by the highest officials of the monastery acting collectively; both types of recommendation had to be approved by the KHri CHen himself.

This principle of seniority was another device that involved the whole polity in the affairs of the monasteries and the religious sect, because it involved a random selection of monastery officials from among the monks who had been successful in their studies. Of the twenty-nine officials of the monasteries of Sa sKya proper who were identified, fifteen were from SHab, eight from the capital, four from other parts of Sa sKya proper, one from Srad, and the origin of the last was not recalled.[14] Four of the twenty-nine officials were from noble families, eight from prominent subject families, seven from well-established but undistinguished subject families, and ten from quite obscure backgrounds. Although the upper strata had some advantage, a boy from anywhere in Sa sKya proper clearly had a real opportunity to go from the humblest to one of the most exalted stations in life. The possibility of rising in the world through the monkhood, and especially the levy of monks, will be seen again when the men sent out from Sa sKya proper as monastic officials are examined in section VII.

The abbots of the North and South Monasteries usually had progressed by seniority to high monastic office before their appointments. There was, however, no regular progression to these abbacies, and upon a vacancy the monastery's officials sent two or three names to the KHri CHen, who made the final selection.

[14] The high percentage from SHab, Sa sKya's most fertile region, was perhaps a result of basing the monk levy on revenue schedules rather than on population. Many of the 7,000 people of the capital were not eligible for the monk levy.

KHri CHen NGag dBang mTHu THub dBang PHyug used a chance method to select the abbots from the lists submitted to him. This method "left the decision to the gods," and it also helped get a representative cross-section of Sa sKya involved in monastic affairs. In the case of one appointment, however, the KHri CHen selected a man in whom he had great confidence without resorting to the chance method and without even receiving a list of nominees; he relied on the fact that some years earlier this man's name had been submitted for the abbacy but had not been drawn in the random selection.

V

The monasteries of Sa sKya outside the capital contained about five hundred monks (Map 3). About fifty of them were elderly monks retired from the North and South Monasteries, and about fifteen were monks who had failed to meet the scholarly standards of these monasteries. The remainder were volunteer monks, and about half of them were in the large monastery of CHos aKHor lHun Po. In addition to the two nunneries in the capital, there were six nunneries in Sa sKya proper with a total of somewhat less than one hundred fifty volunteer nuns. Only a very small number of these monks and nuns received any support from the Religious Establishment.[15]

The monastery of CHos aKHor lHun Po was in every way quite different from the North and South Monasteries. Its approximately two hundred monks were all volunteers, and probably two-thirds of them came from outside Sa sKya proper, mostly from the western parts of the Sa sKya domain. The discipline was lax, the monks spent little time in religious ceremonies and observances, and consequently the monastery had a low religious reputation. As many as one-third of the monks who entered this monastery eventually broke their vows. The entire body of monks was in residence at the monastery only

[15] These monasteries and nunneries are described in more detail in Appendix E, section III.

during the summer and winter convocations. Sometimes there
were as few as thirty monks at the monastery, the remainder
being engaged in collecting religious donations and in business
ventures for the monastery or for themselves. Like the monks in
the less politically stable parts of Tibet, the monks of CHos
aKHor lHun Po had horses and firearms. Both the monastery
and its individual monks were wealthy and made a practice of
lending grain and money to the laity. The monastery's low
religious reputation was matched by its renown for business
acumen.

CHos aKHor lHun Po, unlike many of the monasteries outside the capital, had no private land of its own. In compensation,
it was the only monastery allowed to send out monks regularly
to collect religious donations, principally from the nomads to the
north of Sa sKya proper. About sixty monks, traveling in pairs,
went out for a period of six months each year. They were not
required to return with specific amounts of donations, but they
were supposed to give everything they had collected to the
monastery.

Four of the other monasteries outside the capital each had
forty to fifty monks. Two of the four had good religious reputations, and they were no doubt religiously influential in their
localities. These four monasteries had private land of their own,
which was worked by hired or donated labor or let out to
sharecroppers.[16] The monks lived on the returns from this land,
payments they received for religious services, donations from the
local people, and occasional trading and lending. A monastery
had to obtain special permission from the Government to solicit
support from the laity. Having to ask for this permission was a
sign of poor management or a poor religious reputation or both,
and in the memory of our respondents only one relatively small
monastery of twenty-four monks was reduced to such so-
licitation.

[16] This private land of the small monasteries is to be distinguished
from the land worked by the subjects of the Religious Establishment.

The remaining monasteries and the nunneries supported themselves in the same ways, except for a few small monasteries of
retired monks that received all or part of their support from the
Religious Establishment. None of these small monasteries and
nunneries had any significant effect upon the political or economic life of its locality.

VI

From the North Monastery of the capital a sizable number of
monks were sent on official assignments to Sa sKya areas outside
Sa sKya proper, to other areas of Tibet, and even to Nepal and
Bhutan. It was estimated that there were fifty-six offices of this
kind; we were able to identify forty-four offices and to get
biographies of fifty-nine men who held one or more of these
forty-four positions.[17] There were three types of officials: those
sent abroad for an indefinite tenure to serve as abbots of Sa sKya
sect monasteries and to have only administrative duties; those
sent out to a monastery or group of monasteries for a period of
six years to supervise the administration of the monastery and
also to collect religious donations to be brought back to Sa sKya
proper; and those sent out for a period of six months each year to
districts of Tibet, rather than to specific monasteries, who also
were to return with religious donations but who had no administrative responsibilities.

The principal purposes for sending out these officials were to
hold together the administrative apparatus of the Sa sKya sect, to
supervise its widely dispersed interests, and to maintain its reli-

[17] The total of fifty-six was estimated by Byams lDing Sangs rGyas, a
Sa sKya monk now in India, who also identified many of the monasteries in and out of Sa sKya proper and the men who held positions in
them. We are grateful to him for this information. There may, however, have been more than fifty-six such positions. The locations of the
monasteries are given on Map 1 and are only approximate. There were
also a considerable number of Sa sKya sect monasteries in Tibet that
appointed their own chief administrators and that did not contribute
religious offerings to Sa sKya proper.

gious reputation. Even those officials who only traveled around in search of offerings to be returned to Sa sKya proper kept the people of their assigned areas aware of the presence and the vigor of the Sa sKya sect. All these officials brought wealth into Sa sKya proper, both for the several establishments and for themselves; the opportunity to be sent abroad was an opportunity for a great increase in personal prestige and material well-being; and the health of the Sa sKya religious "empire" and the respect that it evoked from Tibetans of other sects were no doubt major factors that enabled the small polity to resist the pressures of its much larger neighbors.

When a vacancy occurred in one of these positions, the abbot of the North Monastery, in consultation with three of his highest subordinates, selected someone from among the lower officials or candidates of the monastery.[18] When the four of them agreed, they sent a single name to the ZHabs Pad, who had the authority to veto it but who usually approved, and he sent it to the KHri CHen, who also could veto but rarely did. If the North Monastery officials could not agree or if no one wanted to take the job, they sent a list of three or four names to the ZHabs Pad, who could eliminate any of them before sending the list to the KHri CHen, who made the final choice.[19] KHri CHen NGag dBang mTHu THub dBang PHyug also introduced a chance method for choosing among the names on such a list. All the monks eligible for these appointments had been promoted from the South Monastery to the North Monastery on the basis of their abilities, but once in the North Monastery, they had advanced by seniority. Only levy monks were eligible for these positions outside Sa sKya proper.

[18] The three high officials were the chant leader, the Grwa TSHang mCHod dPon, and the beadle. For these offices and the lower officials and candidates, see Appendix E, section II.

[19] The same procedure was followed in making appointments to the monasteries in Sa sKya proper outside the capital.

When an important appointment was to be made, much discussion and argument took place regarding who was most suitable, a considerable amount of promotion of potential appointees occurred, and not a few gifts were quietly presented to the monastery officials who made the recommendations. The family of a monk who had a chance to be appointed was wise to come to his aid with gifts at this point, because the gifts were investments that could bring handsome returns were the monk appointed to a good post. Although the need to present gifts was a handicap to monks from poor families, the gifts were not meant to change any official's mind or to get him to act against his better judgment. They were expressions of the proper thing to do under the circumstances, and they were responses to the monastery officials' right to receive such favors. The ZHabs Pad could veto any appointment he believed suspect or any man he thought unfit; and, as shown below, a large number of monks from humble backgrounds received these highly desirable appointments.

In addition to the ZHabs Pad's participation in the selection of all these administrators and collectors, their formal title expressed the connection between the Tibet-wide religious organization and the Sa sKya polity: they were the representatives (TSHab) of the Sa sKya "polity" (Gong Ma). The monk levy, the induction and screening by the South Monastery, and the training by the North Monastery all served to prepare a group of men responsible for maintaining the prestige and the independence of the small principality. They apparently met this responsibility rather well, and their success must be balanced against the cost of the monastic establishment within Sa sKya proper.

VII

We were able to identify thirteen positions outside Sa sKya proper filled by men from the North Monastery who were in charge of both religious organization and procedure and the material interests of their monasteries.[20] These officials had an indefinite term of appointment, they went to small monasteries located in or near the realms of the Dalai and Panchen Lamas, and they were not expected to bring any religious donations back to Sa sKya proper.

Six officials, all of whom were identified, traveled in specified areas, five in western and one in central Tibet, for a period of six months each year collecting religious donations, which they brought back to the capital. A seventh official spent nine months of each year traveling extensively throughout central Tibet, often overlapping territory assigned to other collectors, in search of donations to bring back to the capital. He was not a supervisor; he tried to tap sources missed by the other collectors.

We identified twenty-four positions outside Sa sKya proper occupied by men sent from the capital to Sa sKya monasteries—or to areas with several monasteries—for six-year terms to serve as the representatives of the emanation bodies of the Sa sKya sect and thus to be the focus of religious observance in these monasteries. They preached, bestowed blessings, held initiations, and presided at graduations. They also supervised the work of the permanent administrative staffs chosen by the monasteries. At the end of their six-year terms, these officials returned to Sa sKya proper with wealth they had collected as religious donations. They went to relatively large monasteries in eastern Tibet, and they were the most important of the officials who held the Sa sKya religious empire together.

Both the six-month and the six-year religious collectors had to produce fixed amounts of wealth upon their return to the capital. Any collector who had not accumulated his required amount had to make up the deficit from his own pocket, but the requirements were low enough that probably no one ever returned without enough to meet them. The collectors were allowed to keep for themselves anything they had accumulated beyond

[20] All the forty-four positions identified are listed in Appendix E, section IV.

these required amounts, and a six-year term in eastern Tibet virtually guaranteed its incumbent a lifetime of material comfort.

When a collector served a six-year term in the east, he was completely free to handle the donations he collected as he saw fit; he was required only to meet his quota upon his return. Collectors therefore treated what was given them as their working capital, to be invested in any venture that might prove profitable, and many collectors took with them someone, usually a relative, to act as manager of this capital. At the expiration of his appointment, the collector turned all his goods into movable form and brought them home. On an average each six-year collector probably came back with half again as much as was required to meet his quota. The surplus was his private property; he could keep it with him in the North Monastery, invest it in his family's farm or flocks, give it to his family, or lend it at interest. He could will all his property, and his family could claim it if he had made no will.[21]

In 1947 the value of a six-year collector's quota was about 1,650 rDo TSHad, and the average collector thus had a surplus of about 825 rDo TSHad in currency and goods to keep for himself. He was expected to provide a celebration for the monks of his monastery, an expenditure of about 45 rDo TSHad, leaving him with 780 rDo TSHad. In Sa sKya one could live quite well on 20 rDo TSHad a year, a profitable herding operation could be set up for about 465 rDo TSHad, a viable trading venture to the nomads north of Sa sKya could be initiated for 165 rDo TSHad, and 100 rDo TSHad was enough to buy the equipment for a rather substantial farm. The six-month collec-

---

[21] In the less politically stable parts of Tibet, the monasteries were often the safest places to keep personal wealth; in Sa sKya, a monk need not have been so cautious. Except for the North and South Monasteries, the monasteries of Sa sKya proper confiscated property under their jurisdiction unless the deceased monk had a nephew in the same monastery.

tors had a quota of 120 rDo TSHad, and thus had for themselves
60 rDo TSHad each year, but they usually returned to their
collection areas year after year.[22]

The religious collectors did very well for themselves. Most of
them helped their families, but some did not.[23] Probably over half
of the collectors' families declined in wealth after the death of
the collector, partly because of lack of skill in investing or
trading, the principal sources of wealth, but also because there
was a strong social pressure for the family to make a large
religious donation upon the death of the collector or even of his
father. Religion had a claim upon this wealth because religion
was the source of it.

VIII

The monk levy and promotion by seniority in the North
Monastery provided an opportunity for men from the humblest
origins to rise to high social and material levels. We identified
thirty-two men who had been six-year collectors, seven who had
been six-month collectors, and eighteen who had served as administrators on indefinite appointments. Of the fifty-seven,
twenty-seven came from SHab, twenty from the capital, seven
from other areas of Sa sKya proper, and three from rTSe
gDong. Three were from noble families; nine from prominent
subject families; twenty-one from subject families who, although
sometimes poor, were well established and known as "solid citizens"; twenty-one from families with no status at all in the
society, some having drifted into Sa sKya and become sharecroppers before taking the responsibility for Government or Reli-

[22] On monetary values, see Chapter 10 and Appendix D, section II.
Six-year collectors were not usually reappointed. For a collector to have
a second term, he had to have a petition from the people of his
collection area. Perhaps 5 per cent of the collectors managed this, and
one case of a second reappointment was cited. One six-month collector
told our respondents that he made for himself 100 rDo TSHad each
year; this amount seems excessive or at least unusual.
[23] See Appendix D, section III, for examples.

gious Establishment land; and the backgrounds of the three from rTSe gDong were unknown, but in all likelihood they were quite humble. Of the thirty-two men identified as occupying the most lucrative positions of six-year collectors, one was from a noble family, six from prominent subject families, twelve from established subject families, ten from very obscure families, and three from rTSe gDong. Three success stories follow.

A levy nun in Sa sKya once broke her vows. In a rather unusual decision, the ZHabs Pad ordered that her fatherless son enter the South Monastery as a kind of replacement for her. Somewhat later a monk who was a sKu Drag official in the Work Corps, but who came from an obscure family, broke his vows and entered into an "informal" marriage with the former nun.[24] After some years the son was appointed to a six-year term as a religious collector, and his stepfather resigned from the Government in order to accompany him to the east as his business manager.

In the SHab Valley lived a very poor couple who never could meet their revenue payments. Their only son was chosen in the monk levy, and although he was needed at home, they had no money for a proxy. Fortunately, the boy did very well in the North and South Monasteries and eventually was sent as a six-year collector to Khams. His personal property gained on this tour of duty changed his parents' poverty to prosperity.[25]

The most interesting, although somewhat ironical, success story concerns the levy monk from a very poor family in the capital who became the interpreter of the oracle at the famous monastery of bSam Yas, south of the city of Lhasa. In this position he received many gifts, and he returned to Sa sKya a wealthy man. It happened that a noble family of the capital found itself in reduced circumstances and, moreover, without a

[24] On this kind of marriage see Chapter 8, section VI.
[25] The collector was robbed and murdered on his way back to Sa sKya, but his goods were recovered and his parents were given the surplus over his quota.

son. This family asked the monk to join the laity and marry the family's two daughters as a called-in son-in-law and heir. He accepted the proposition, and later the new nobleman became a sKu Drag official as a member of the Work Corps. Unfortunately, however, his marriage produced no sons.

The monk levy and the position of religious collector undoubtedly offered the ordinary Sa sKya family a real possibility of rising in the world, but too much should not be made of this opportunity. A full 90 per cent of the families were very poor indeed, having barely enough to eat by Sa sKya standards. There were about 2,550 families in Sa sKya proper, of which about 2,240 were eligible for the monk levy. There were at least fifty-six positions available outside Sa sKya proper, and with the turnover in the six-year collectors perhaps 115 appointments were made in a single generation. Hence, omitting the bias against families that were not well-established, which may have resulted from their inability to produce the expected gifts when a position was open, only about 5 per cent of the 2,240 eligible families realized any sudden increase in their prestige and wealth. This one in twenty ratio may have sufficed to keep up the spirits of the average man of Sa sKya. When the desirable positions in the monasteries within Sa sKya proper are added to the outside jobs, the ratio improves to almost one in eleven. Each advancement, however, involved the early separation of a son from his family.

The possibility of spectacular advancement for a few combined with hopeless poverty for the many is found in a number of "traditional" societies. Unsophisticated people seem to focus on the possibility of such strokes of luck rather than upon the infrequency of their occurrence.

IX

The monasteries of Sa sKya proper were maintained at a sizable cost to the economy, a cost that can be estimated with fair accuracy. They also brought some economic benefits to the polity, which again can be estimated; but their principal contributions were to the independence of the principality, the religious prestige of the sect, and the psychological or spiritual satisfaction of all strata of the population. There is no way for us to estimate the value of these returns.

The first item in the cost of the monasteries was manpower. Of the approximately 985 monks, about 230 came from outside Sa sKya proper. The remaining 755 were about 9 per cent of the male population of 8,000; it has been said that other parts of Tibet had one-third of their male populations in monasteries.[26] About 400 monks were levied from the approximately 2,200 families of the Government and Religious Establishment, and hence at any time about 18 per cent of these families had one male member out of the household. There were about 250 nuns in Sa sKya, 100 of whom were levied. Since most nuns did ordinary work outside their nunneries about half of the time, only 125 women, or 1.5 per cent, of the 8,000 women in Sa sKya were withdrawn from the process of economic production.

This withdrawal of manpower was a real cost to the people of Sa sKya, but it was not as large as it might appear. Although the monastic officials levied only those boys who were physically and mentally sound, they did not take all the best boys nor was there any guarantee that the ones they took would retain their superiority in adulthood. The economy of Sa sKya, moreover, was not especially short of labor, and labor was not particularly productive. Our limited information suggests that if the monks and nuns had been returned to the laity they would have done little more than support themselves.

The two hundred monks of CHos aKHor lHun Po were self-supporting. They had no land and received only a minimum of offerings from the people of Sa sKya; they lived by collecting donations from outside Sa sKya and by trade, loans, and other

[26] See Carrasco, *Land and Polity in Tibet*, p. 121. When questioned about the relatively few monks in Sa sKya, our respondents said it was not wise to take too many men away from the land.

business enterprises. The other monks outside the capital, about 285 in number, and the equivalent of 125 nuns who did not support themselves by working lived on the land of their monasteries and nunneries and on donations and payments for religious services. They probably suffered no material deprivations, but their standard of living was below that of the North and South Monasteries and probably not too much above that of the average layman. The North and South Monasteries were well known to our respondents and hence we know how much the five hundred monks consumed and the sources of their support.[27] These monks had a standard of living that seems to have been almost three times as high as that of the average layman. The Sa sKya economy, consequently, had to support approximately 1,700 religious personnel, or about 11.5 per cent of the total lay population. The annual cost in money can be estimated at about 13,000 rDo TSHad.

A third cost was the outfitting and movement of the collectors and administrators sent out from Sa sKya proper. The Religious Establishment provided them with objects to be used in religious rituals, barley flour for themselves, and feed for their animals. The Government gave them tea, meat, butter, cheese, mules, horses, saddlery, bags, and boxes, and part of their journeys to and from the capital were accomplished by means of the transport levy. Every collector was also given, at Government expense, a number of pellets of magical powers. The pellets contained herbs and bezoars, imported by the Government, and relics of the aKHon family. Each palace maintained its own store of these relics, and the Government kept the relics of family members before its division into two palaces. The pellets were effective against illness, especially anthrax, they prevented wounds, and when placed in the mouth of a dying man they insured against his arrival in the infernal regions. A two-year supply of these pellets took the monks of both the North and the

---

[27] See Appendix D, section IV, and Appendix E, section I.

South Monastery about a week to make; during this period the Government fed them handsomely and provided them with beer. (Pellets of special potency were made by the KHri CHen himself: in addition to herbs, bezoars, and relics, they contained ground gold, silver, and iron; and in addition to the powers of the regular pellets, they were effective against dropsy, leprosy, cancer, and strokes.) The total annual cost of provisioning these religious officials was about 350 rDo TSHad.

The maintenance of the buildings of the North and South Monasteries cost the Government about 200 rDo TSHad a year in wages, but the cost of material was no doubt negligible. These buildings also housed the officials of the Government and the Religious Establishment, and the royal family spent half a year in the North Monastery; hence only about half the cost of maintenance should be charged against the monastic establishment. In 1945, however, one of the pillars supporting the Great God House of the South Monastery gave way, causing extensive damage that cost about 19,500 rDo TSHad to repair. More than a quarter of this amount was raised by a special religious collection outside Sa sKya.[28] By 1950, when the repairs were almost completed, 3,600 rDo TSHad of the cost had been met, but nothing had been repaid on an interest-free loan of 10,000 rDo TSHad advanced for the repairs by the Lhasa government. The actual expense of the five years of work was thus about 700 rDo TSHad a year; and if the loan had been repaid at this rate, the yearly sum of 700 rDo TSHad would have been spent for a period of nineteen or twenty years. This 700 rDo TSHad can reasonably be included in the annual cost of maintaining the North and South Monasteries.

The total annual cost of the monastic establishment was about 14,150 rDo TSHad, plus the withdrawal of about nine hundred people, or slightly over 5 per cent of the total population of Sa sKya proper, from the process of economic production.

[28] See Appendix E, the end of section V.

X

On the credit side, the regular religious collectors brought about 13,400 rDo TSHad into Sa sKya proper each year, and the collections of the monks of CHos aKHor lHun Po more than made up the difference between this amount and the cost of 14,150 rDo TSHad. These collections may have covered even the cost of withdrawing people from the productive process.

The wealth brought in by the monastic establishment was concentrated in the hands of a small group of religious collectors, the capital monks, a few government officials, the establishments, and the royal family. This concentration made the wealth available for use as investment capital, but unfortunately it was impossible to calculate the amount put into the productive process. All we know is that the monasteries outside the capital, many individual monks, and the palaces lent money and grain to the laity. The monastery of CHos aKHor lHun Po, which got its basic wealth outside Sa sKya and engaged in and financed many business ventures, must surely have had an impact upon the economy, but no details of the operation of this organization of two hundred men were available.

Laymen in Sa sKya by custom gave only minor donations to the monasteries during their productive years; the most common practice was to invite a number of monks—usually only a few, although the wealthiest laity sometimes asked as many as one hundred—to a few days' entertainment at one's home. The most substantial donation was presented upon a man's retirement, or more usually by his family upon his death. This custom encouraged saving, and no doubt made some contribution to the accumulation of capital. These donations brought an immediate reward to their givers, however, in the form of religious merit. Such satisfactions cannot be measured in rDo TSHad or KHal of barley.

A subject once came to the Steward of the Religious Establishment and announced that he intended to give a "big tea" (Mang Ja) for the monks of the capital. This man worked for one of the palaces as a custodian of a building high in the mountains; the palace gave him a small wage and he supplemented his income by hunting musk deer and blue sheep. The Steward, knowing the man was very poor, asked him what he proposed to give to finance the big tea. "Five sheep" was the answer. Since the Steward was pretty sure that the man possessed no more than ten sheep, he refused the donation. But the hunter was so persistent that the Steward finally referred the matter to the KHri CHen. The KHri CHen said that since the man wanted so strongly to make the donation it should be accepted.

One form of religious donation was called a "great assembly distribution." It was sponsored by successful traders, religious collectors, wealthy established families, and sometimes by entire communities, and it involved a distribution of goods to the KHri CHen, the palaces, and all governmental officials. These dignitaries gathered in a large hall of the South Monastery, where a member of the Work Corps saw that everyone got his share according to his rank. Some of the lower officials were usually glad enough to get these gifts, but to those of higher status the amounts received were not impressive. These distributions occurred two or three times a year, and the day of the distribution was a great one for the sponsor—it was "his day." He had dealt with the ZHabs Pad in arranging the distribution; he was admired by his peers and lesser folk; and he had personally and directly given something to the highest clerics and governors in the land.

Even the nonvoluntary contributions made by the people of Sa sKya to the maintenance of a large number of monks cannot be evaluated solely in terms of the capital they made available or the tea they brought into the country. The Tibetan considered it very important that large numbers of men were free to spend their time in performing the several types of religious ob-

servance.[29] The monks verbalized religion by reading and re-
citing religious texts and prayers and activating them by means
of prayer wheels; they made religious offerings, carefully observing all the minutiae of ritual; they performed the proper
salutations to images and shrines; and they circumambulated
shrines, monasteries, stupas, and sacred mountains and lakes. The
average man of Sa sKya may well have congratulated himself on
having five hundred monks with high reputations devoting
themselves exclusively to the critical chores of religious observance.

Finally, the cost of maintaining the monasteries must be balanced against the contribution they made to Sa sKya's political
independence. The incident of the damage to the South Monastery is most instructive. When the government of Lhasa was
approached for help, it provided a large loan without interest—
something quite extraordinary in itself—and the labor of thirty
men working nine months a year for five years. The rulers of Sa
sKya were clearly aware of the connection between the reputation of the North and South Monasteries and the skill of their
emissaries, on the one hand, and the independence of their principality on the other. Their response to this realization can undoubtedly be judged effective.

XI

The Sa sKya political system allowed little initiative in the
governmental process to anyone except the KHri CHen. The
KHri CHen, however, was obliged by his religious and political
positions to restrict his initiative to what he considered improvements in the traditional way of doing things, and in taking any
such action he obviously could not be completely indifferent to
the opinions or presumed opinions of various important groups

---

[29] These observances were called "CHos Las" (religion works). For a
full discussion, see Robert B. Ekvall, *Religious Observances in Tibet*
(Chicago: University of Chicago Press, 1964), *passim.*

and individuals. The attention he paid to these people was a measure of their political power.

The small monasteries and the nunneries had virtually no political power. The KHri CHen and the central government probably never considered what the men and women of these institutions thought about any issue that arose in the capital. These monasteries also had little power in the local governmental process; they seem to have divorced themselves from local affairs. For example, the officials of the monastery THub bsTan dGe aPHel in Mang mKHar, where there was no District Officer, would mediate disputes but only when specifically requested to do so.

The monastery of CHos aKHor lHun Po was characterized as politically influential because in their business ventures its monk came in constant contact with the laity, but no instances of their influence were given. Any opinions the monks might have had were undoubtedly communicated to the subjects with whom they had contacts, but there is no reason to believe that all two hundred of them shared the same opinions. Even if they had had a single point of view strongly held on an important issue, there is little likelihood that they could have so aroused the laity that the government had to consider "public opinion." The monastery's lack of religious prestige probably meant that the government did not ask itself when arriving at a decision what the opinion of the officials and monks of CHos aKHor lHun Po might be.

The North and South Monasteries were, of course, one of the government's most important concerns, and the morale and discipline of their monks were critical to the health of the Sa sKya sect. The monks had to be kept happy—Tibetan monks were not known for their docility—and one of the marks of a good abbot of the North or South Monastery was that he kept his monks from grumbling and even from criticizing him. Little anonymous notes of protest could at any time appear upon the monastery walls. In the early 1930's, to emphasize their support for certain religious practices that the government had failed to introduce, about thirty monks from the North and South Monasteries went on a kind of strike by leaving their monasteries and going to a monastery outside Sa sKya. This action must have been very embarrassing to the government, and its subsequent institution of the practices in question must have been at least in part a response to the walkout. The monks, incidentally, did not originate the policy they were supporting; they followed the lead taken by a member of the royal family.

The officials of the North and South Monasteries presumably favored any measures that strengthened or enlarged the monasteries and opposed measures with the opposite effects. In this they agreed with the governors, but differences of opinion regarding the effects of specific measures may well have occurred. The abbots were regularly consulted on matters that concerned the upkeep of their monasteries and the welfare of their personnel, but there is no evidence that they ever took the initiative and suggested new policies to the government. Of the ten former abbots about whom we have information, only one was characterized as interested in governmental policy, and he was made an abbot by KHri CHen NGag dBang mTHu THub dBang PHyug expressly because he supported certain reforms of interest to the KHri CHen.[30] The abbots were kept busy with day-to-day procedures in their monasteries, and it was unseemly for them to concern themselves too much with governmental affairs.

It can be concluded, perhaps contrary to expectations, that the officials of the North and South Monasteries had less political power than the body of ordinary monks, and that together they had relatively little power in the political system of Sa sKya.

---

[30] An abbot of the monastery of gDong dGaa CHos sDe, personally well known to our respondents, was described as a very able man in an important position, but also indifferent to matters of policy and power.

XII

The Tibetan is preoccupied with his religion, which for him comprehends the riddle of existence and offers the keys of mystical power as a solution. It summarizes all the best of what the human spirit may think, desire, and feel. It embraces everything in his culture that marks it as something more than a way of subsisting. The treasures of his mind, the resources of his language, the fruit of his body, and the gains of his toil are devoted to religion; for him it signifies all that is worthwhile.

The Tibetan is especially concerned with physical acts that express the proper attitudes toward the divine and the supernatural, the acts of religious observance. These acts give him what might be called "supernatural credit," and he usually believes that some men have special capabilities enabling them to be more effective than the average person in dealing with the supernatural and that the task of proper religious observance is so time-consuming or complicated that some men must devote their full time to it. In both cases, he himself benefits from what the specialists do.

In Sa sKya the KHri CHen and the whole aKHon family were the specialists who had religious powers beyond those of ordinary mortals, and the polity itself was organized around them. The monks were the specialists who, because they were relieved of normal worldly responsibilities, could devote their full time to religious observance that benefited everyone. It was only natural that the government, the most effective and efficient device available, supported both groups of specialists.

Chapter 12

Policy and Power

The basic reason for studying any polity is to understand why its government acts as it does. Examining a polity's economic, communal, and social structures, its history, traditions, and beliefs, and its governmental organization and procedure is significant, in the final analysis, only to the extent that it helps explain why government is used to deal with certain issues and why it responds in specific ways to these issues.

The government of Sa sKya maintained the peace, defined and protected property, collected revenue in labor and in kind, and promoted religious observance. In the present chapter, several additional types of governmental policy will be described, the government's allocation of its resources will be examined, and the pattern of power in relation to specific policy decisions will be analyzed.

I

The policy pursued by any government includes not only the actions it takes but also those that it does not take. The government of Sa sKya was indifferent to many things that modern governments of all kinds are almost preoccupied with, especially the expression of ideas and the operation of the economy. This indifference was not accidental, but an integral part of the small political society.

All the people of Sa sKya, no matter what their status, had almost unlimited freedom of movement. As far as the government was concerned, only the responsibility to meet payments of revenue in kind and in labor restricted a subject from going anywhere at any time he pleased. Any subject could leave Sa sKya, on business or religious pilgrimage, for a year or more as long as he satisfied his Headman or other official directly over him that he had the material to meet his payments to his establishment and had arranged for someone to take over his responsibility for the transport and other work levies. This freedom from governmental interference was, of course, meaningful for only those few affluent enough to provide the officials with such a guarantee. There were, however, few occasions on which a man would want to be away from home for an extended period. In other parts of Tibet entire families frequently took extended tours of various holy places, but for members of the Sa sKya sect the most important religious places and people were not more than a few days away, and for any short trip no official had even to be notified. Any family that could afford a trading venture that took it away from home for some time had its farming operations well under control.

These governmental and economic impediments to movement applied only to the heads of families that had establishment land. Everyone else, including the heads of families that lived exclusively by herding, sharecropping, trading, or retailing, was completely free to go wherever he wanted. The government did not worry about smuggling, intrigue, disloyalty, ideological contamination, citizenship, and other similar matters that modern governments consider problematic.

There were no restrictions in Sa sKya on the possession of weapons. The subjects had an estimated three or four thousand firearms of varying efficiency, most being matchlocks, but our respondents gave no indication that these arms represented power that might threaten the government. They stressed the necessity of having a completely loyal official in charge of the government's horses; [1] they were very alert to the possibility of

[1] Chapter 5, section II.

political challenges from noblemen, perhaps with assistance from other noblemen outside Sa sKya; but they did not see the subjects as a source of possible challenge to the regime or even as a possible support for others making a challenge. This judgment was probably correct. There is absolutely no reason to suppose that the subjects had any motives for becoming involved in any struggle to control the government. It is reasonable to infer that they believed a change in governmental personnel would not result in any basic change in policy and that the possibility of changing the form of government had never occurred to them. Any nobleman or official who attempted a rebellion would have used the methods of assassination and coup d'état. He would not have considered enlisting "popular" support in his venture, because he could see no need for it and because, moreover, it was not proper to involve the subjects in such matters. Anyone in Sa sKya therefore could have a firearm to guard his flocks from thieves and wolves, to do a little hunting, and maybe to provide himself with some personal protection.

In Sa sKya, as throughout Tibet, there were people who, in moments of ill-temper or inebriation, uttered the greatest impieties, attacking the most basic tenets of the faith by heresies such as cursing all emanation bodies as frauds. Any unorthodoxy of this or other types was not considered a matter of governmental concern; the response was left to supernatural forces. This indifference was an implication of the principle that no one could be forced to have the proper religious faith, but it also probably came in part from a recognition that the intensity and comprehensiveness of the Tibetan's faith required the release of an occasional irreverence.[2]

As a corollary to the principle that people could certainly be required to do what their government told them to do, criticisms of the Sa sKya government, in the form of attacks upon the men

[2] See Robert B. Ekvall, *Religious Observances in Tibet* (Chicago: University of Chicago Press, 1964), pp. 65–66.

who personified it, were not allowed. Anyone who said that the KHri CHen was unjust or that the ZHabs Pad "ate wealth" would have been accused of disloyalty. All lower officials, however, with the possible exceptions of the Steward of the Religious Establishment and the Chief Secretary, were fair game for criticism by the subjects. The subjects' opinions were expressed openly in conversations, clandestinely by nocturnal devices such as spreading leaflets around the streets or posting large placards on the dwelling of the official in disfavor, and impersonally in calypso-type songs describing the official and personal shortcomings of the man under attack. The Liaison Officers, who were usually hereditary noblemen, were natural targets of criticism; and the songsters of the capital were especially active on one occasion when a monk who was a sKu Drag official broke his vows.

The government of Sa sKya provided education only for the monks, but it had no objection to anyone's getting an education. Laymen subjects could learn to read and write by hiring tutors, and even the poorest could occasionally attend classes at a neighboring monastery. Tibetan Buddhism implied that the extension of literacy was beneficial because it enabled more people to participate in an additional degree of religious observance.[3] The government, however, apparently ignored the problem of education until KHri CHen NGag dBang mTHu THub dBang PHyug proposed to institute a free school for one hundred children from subject families, later to be extended to include all the children of Sa sKya. His proposal represented an innovation in governmental policy by its introduction of a new idea of governmental responsibility, but it did not depart from the presuppositions underlying the political system. The KHri CHen saw his school as a means of reinforcing religion and, consequently, the culture of Tibet.[4] His project was never initiated.

[3] *Ibid.*, p. 125.
[4] Cf. Manning Nash, *The Golden Road to Modernity* (New York: John Wiley, 1965), p. 95.

II

Diseases of human beings and animals were a rather serious problem in Sa sKya, and our respondents were sharply aware of the primitive nature of the means available to combat them. There were at least three families of hereditary medical practitioners who treated human beings; one of these provided the official "doctors" for the aKHon family. The practitioners had establishments like clinics where people went to get purgatives, febrifuges, and remedies for headaches and indigestion, to be bled, to have sores lanced and wounds cauterized, and to have broken bones set. The practitioners received payment for their services and gifts upon the recovery of their patients. These practitioners had the status of Jo Lags, thus being recognized as performing a governmental function. A number of people also specialized in treating diseases of animals.

Outbreaks of communicable human and animal diseases were to be reported to governmental officials. If the outbreak did not appear serious, Headmen and District Officers dealt with it by calling in the proper medical practitioners and imposing quarantines. When the outbreak looked serious, the capital was notified. A case was recalled of a death from leprosy in rMa Bya. Upon being informed, the Government ordered the deceased's body and all his possessions including his house to be burned and then covered with packed earth. This method of disposing of a corpse was not in accord with orthodox Tibetan religious precepts.

Smallpox was very prevalent in Tibet. In 1941 the KHri CHen decided to take some action; he sent to India for vaccine and the directions for its use. Some of the more conservative people of Sa sKya objected to the use of "foreign medicine" and argued that vaccination was not "the Tibetan way." The KHri CHen had divinations performed, and these unsurprisingly supported the plan to vaccinate all the people of Sa sKya proper. Officials and others with manual dexterity, including members of the royal family, were taught to perform the operation. They then vaccinated the entire population of Sa sKya proper, collected by Headmen and District Officers at convenient spots. The campaign apparently met no serious resistance from the subjects, and it was a success.

KHri CHen NGag dBang mTHu THub dBang PHyug was concerned about problems of health and the inadequacy of Sa sKya's medical facilities. He once sponsored a convention of all the practitioners of medicine in the hope of improving their methods, but it had few results. The Chinese Communists were not especially welcomed to Tibet, but most people appreciated their medicine, including one of the hereditary practitioners of Sa sKya. Modern medicine can be recognized as not only clever but of immediate use. The Tibetans probably did not realize that the pragmatic spirit of medicine, like that of all science and advanced technology, would eventually have come in conflict with the otherworldly orientation of their most fundamental beliefs.

III

Although the polity of Sa sKya probably owed its existence to the existence of the Sa sKya sect of Tibetan Buddhism, and although the preservation of the sect was the most important responsibility of the Sa sKya government, the belief that no man could be commanded to have faith was strictly observed in governmental policy. The inhabitants of Sa sKya proper adhered to at least five religious persuasions. The Sa sKya sect was heavily predominant, with probably 95 per cent of the population following its doctrines and procedures. Perhaps 2 per cent were members of the Yellow sect, headed by the Dalai Lama in Lhasa. A number of people belonged to the rNYing Ma Pa, or Old sect, the ancient Buddhist sect from which the Sa sKya sect emerged in the twelfth century. There were also some followers of the pre-Buddhist Bon religion, particularly in Ko CHag, and a few of the so-called Nepalese of the capital retained their Hinduism. Finally, there were perhaps fifteen or twenty men who claimed to be Sa sKya monks but who were recognized by the government as only rather questionable lay practitioners. Each of these four small groups was completely free to follow its own observances and maintain its own beliefs.

The Yellow sect, as the most important sect of Tibetan Buddhism, was considered fully respectable in Sa sKya. Although its tenets and practices were slightly different from those of the Sa sKya sect, the similarities between the two sects were considered more important than their differences. The people of Sa sKya who were members of the Yellow sect were assumed to be less committed to the polity of Sa sKya than members of the Sa sKya sect; they were probably mildly discriminated against in matters such as appointment to governmental office, but they seem to have had no other disadvantages.

The people of the Old sect, on the other hand, were fully accepted members of the polity. One of the most prominent families of hereditary nobility in Sa sKya, the SHar ZHabs Pad family of the SHab Valley, adhered to the old beliefs and practices. One member of the family was always instructed in the rituals of the sect, which were performed in private. In public the family followed Sa sKya religious practices, and occasionally Sa sKya monks were invited to the family home to perform their rituals. As the family name indicates, its ancestor was a ZHabs Pad of Sa sKya, and one head of the family in the twentieth century was also a ZHabs Pad. The wife of KHri CHen NGag dBang mTHu THub dBang PHyug came from a non-Sa sKya family of the Old sect. Males of the aKHon family frequently married women from outside the Sa sKya domain who were of this sect or the Yellow sect; these women then became members of the Sa sKya sect.

Several establishments (called Bla Brang) were devoted to the religious observances of the Old sect. The KHa Gung Bla Brang and the aGro mGon Bla Brang of Ko CHag (Map 3) were the most prominent. The family of aGro mGon was a family of hereditary emanation bodies of the Old sect, and they had the noble status of Drag bTSan. The family line was traced back to about A.D. 800, and in the seventeenth century a daughter of the family married a Sa sKya KHri CHen.[5] The aGro mGon family had some Government land and a larger amount of private land. It had the same kind of allegiance to Sa sKya as the secular hereditary nobility, but it had a higher social status because of its religious characteristics.

The people who still maintained the beliefs and practices of the pre-Buddhist Bon religion were not interfered with, because Bon, although not a variety of Tibetan Buddhism, was recognized as genuinely Tibetan.[6] Many of its features, moreover, had been incorporated into Tibetan Buddhism. Most of the so-called Nepalese of the capital were Buddhists and followed the rules of the Sa sKya sect. Some, however, were Hindus, but they too were free to follow their religion.

Perhaps the most interesting example of religious tolerance was the government's attitude toward a rather odd institution humorously called "Bo brDZus" (imposter). This was an establishment in the high country of the dMigs District (Map 3), operated by about fifteen men who claimed to be Sa sKya monks and maintained that their institution was a genuine monastery. These claims were easy enough to dispute, however, for all the men had families. At one time this may have been a real monastery and then degenerated, or it may have been started by deserters from a nearby monastery.[7] These spurious monks performed religious services, divinations, and black magic for the orthodox locals. Occasionally they provided themselves with forged papers and, posing as genuine Sa sKya religious collectors, tried to pick up something from the unsuspecting. This imposture the government would not tolerate: when apprehended in such activities, they were soundly beaten. Otherwise, they went their

---

[5] On these noble families, see Appendix A, section III.

[6] See Chapter 3, section V.

[7] The monastery of sGra aDrai (Map 3), which was once very large (see Appendix E, section III).

way and made their claims quite freely. They were considered to be Buddhists, but somewhat unorthodox, and they were rather illogically classified as "lay practitioners" (Ser KHyim Pa), a standard Tibetan religious category. The families of Bo brDZus specialized in trading, and their religious festivals were the occasions of trade fairs attracting people from some distance.

Although these religious diversities were tolerated, everyone had to contribute goods and labor to the maintenance of the dominant Sa sKya sect. There is no reason to believe that any religious minority objected to this obligation.

This tolerance of different religious beliefs was a practical policy because the overwhelming majority of the people belonged to the official sect. The government of Sa sKya, however, does not seem to have tolerated the unorthodox because it knew they posed no threat to the proper beliefs and practices. The maxim that "the government cannot tell the people to have faith" means exactly what it says, that the religious beliefs of the members of the polity are outside the proper sphere of governmental concern. This attitude was a logical extension of the individualism of Sa sKya and its limited appreciation of the possibilities of organized action. The religious homogeneity of the population of Sa sKya, however, enabled the government to follow its natural inclination and devote a large proportion of its resources to a specific kind of religious observance.[8]

IV

Although Sa sKya was very small and the activity of its government was limited, the cost of government is difficult to estimate because the governmental function was divided among

[8] Lucian W. Pye, in *Politics, Personality, and Nation Building* (New Haven: Yale University Press, 1962), pp. 74–77, says that in traditional Burma, Buddhist individualism led to many divergences in religious beliefs and "a host of different religious groupings, with overlapping memberships." All were tolerated because all had some representation and respectability in the highest political circles. This was probably a secondary reason for toleration in Sa sKya.

the several establishments, with the KHri CHen having his own separate income and expenditures, and because governmental income was obtained by a number of rather irregular methods. We have, nevertheless, made rough estimates of the value of governmental revenue and of the ways in which it was spent. The nobility was omitted from these calculations because its relations with its subjects were so informal, but it probably received about the same proportion of its subjects' crops as the larger establishments. Religious donations were often used for governmental purposes, and their value could not be estimated; they were, however, not revenue but voluntary contributions.

We made our estimates for a typical year during the period from 1945 to 1950 and we used 1947 prices. The incomes of the principal establishments varied from year to year, according to the harvest, but an average year was one in which about half the scheduled revenue in kind was actually collected. By the method described in Appendix D, section IV, we estimate the annual cost of the governmental apparatus to the 16,000 inhabitants of Sa sKya at about 17,000 rDo TSHad.

Slightly over half the expenditures of the several branches of government went directly for religious purposes such as maintaining the North and South Monasteries, making religious offerings, and equipping religious officials sent out from Sa sKya proper. About 23 per cent of the total expenditures went to maintaining the royal aKHon family, which had at least as much religious as political significance. As we have said before, in matters of religious observance there is no reason to suppose that the people of Sa sKya believed that their wealth was being misspent.

About one-quarter of governmental expenditures was absorbed by the maintenance of government buildings and personnel, and perhaps half the cost of supporting the royal family can be taken as a purely governmental expense. Hence about 6,000 rDo TSHad was taken from the people for these purposes, an average of about 0.37 rDo TSHad per person. Since this amount was collected roughly according to the ability to pay, it does not seem to have been an excessive price for the organizational prerequisites of "law and order."

According to our respondents, KHri CHen NGag dBang mTHu THub dBang PHyug made a special effort during his reign to save a portion of his own and the Government's income so that he could make certain purchases, set up some new institutions, and invest in a trading program. A desire to accumulate wealth for its own sake, with little thought of its use as capital for investment, was, however, typical of Sa sKya. Tibetans considered the liquidation of reserves to be a loss of face, and people borrowed before they sold their grain or animals. The Sa sKya Government apparently was upset when its yearly budget did not show a surplus.

In addition to what must have been a fairly substantial amount of durable valuables—it was said that some precious metal in the Government treasury had been there since the time of aPHags Pa—the Government kept in storage large amounts of perishables, especially grain. The approximately three thousand KHal of barley in the large Government granary near the South Monastery was constantly inspected and grain that had begun to deteriorate was removed.[9] Deterioration began after about eight years of storage, but the price of barley began to decline after about three years—and that of wheat even sooner—because the grain began to acquire a bad taste. Occasionally deteriorated grain was sold to the poorer people, but at times as much as half the grain removed was unfit for human consumption. If every family in Sa sKya had fully met its revenue obligations, the income of the Government would have been over twice the amount of its normal expenditures.

Storing or hoarding quantities of commodities and goods—rolls of cloth, entire hides of leather, stocks of grain, rows of cauldrons and pots, and so forth—was a marked feature of Ti-

[9] There were also other grains in the capital granary, and barley in granaries at District Offices and elsewhere throughout Sa sKya proper.

betan economic behavior. This hoarding had a number of possible reasons. There were no banks and safety deposit vaults where money could be kept securely, and although precious metals were stored, goods could be used as well as traded. Since merchandise was seasonal in supply, sometimes being available at reasonable prices and at other times being in short supply and expensive, it was desirable always to have some on hand. The cold, dry climate minimized damage from mildew, moths, and the like. Prestige was also a reason for hoarding. Having material to use or to lend added to a man's standing, but often prestige was sought by nonfunctional hoarding. Even when stocks of goods were used in trade, the result was often a barter that only replaced one hoarded good for another.[10]

Whatever the reasons for hoarding, the Sa sKya government did not make full use of its capital resources.[11] It did not, however, entirely neglect its opportunities for investment. Every year the Government gave from twenty to one hundred rDo TSHad in money or in grain to each of from ten to twenty private individuals. These men—called "grain and money merchants"—invested the money or grain, and at the end of the year they returned the original capital and any profit they had made. The Government paid their expenses—they turned in full written accounts of their dealings—and gave them something for

[10] In areas of eastern Tibet where there are forests, firewood was sometimes accumulated year after year, walls and dykes of corded log sections being built up around the house or in the courtyard. The lowest level might have been rotted to uselessness, but each year new logs were added on top. The owner sold this wood only when he was in financial straits, and he tried to do it surreptitiously. Quite meager fires were often kept going with cow dung and bits of brushwood in houses surrounded with walls of corded firewood (Robert B. Ekvall, *Tibetan Skylines* [New York: Farrar, Straus and Young, 1952], p. 184).

[11] J. L. Sadie suggests that traditional society's failure to use capital is connected with its absence of concern about the future ("The Social Anthropology of Economic Underdevelopment," in David E. Novack and Robert Lekachman [eds.], *Development and Society* [New York: St. Martin's, 1964], p. 215).

themselves. In a good year the investor might double his capital and get 30 per cent of the original amount for himself, but if he lost any of the capital, he had to make up the difference from his own pocket. The Government had to exert some pressure in order to get people to engage in the enterprise. In a typical year, the Government might have invested in this way 900 rDo TSHad, the equivalent of 3,200 KHal of barley, and have received a profit of 250 rDo TSHad.[12] No sustained attempt was made to utilize fully the Government's resources in trade, and very little was invested in agriculture, the source of the surplus.

Part of the Government's surplus, it will be recalled, was given to subjects threatened with starvation. In an average year perhaps 2,250 KHal of barley, worth 630 rDo TSHad, were expended in this way.[13]

V

The income of the establishments of Sa sKya took several forms, which were often complicated and usually somewhat inefficient. The division of governmental functions among the establishments, the payment of revenue in both kind and labor, and the irregularity of the labor levies are previously discussed examples. The method of paying governmental officials is another interesting case of how Sa sKya financed its operations and the reasons for its procedures. About 15 per cent of the cost of government was absorbed by these "salaries."

The principal means of paying officials, both laymen and monks, was to give them the use of amounts of establishment land proportionate in size to the importance of their offices. They paid no revenue in kind on this land, but they were responsible for the revenue in labor that went with all Government and Religious Establishment land. The officials usually did

---

[12] See Appendix D, section IV.
[13] See Chapter 10, section VII, and Appendix D, section IV.

not have time to supervise the cultivation of this land; it was often divided into rather small plots, and most of it was at some distance from the capital. They left it in the hands of relatives or sharecroppers. When we told our respondents that this seemed an inefficient method of paying officials and asked them why it was used, they acknowledged the inefficiency but said that it was "the Sa sKya custom."

From thirty to thirty-five of the sKu Drag officials also received some income from acting as "collectors of revenue" (bsDus Pa).[14] Each year at the time of the collection of revenue in the late summer or early fall, about one-third of these officials left the capital to visit certain District Offices. One-half of the group went east to the SHab and rTSe gDong District Offices, and the other half went west to the District Offices at Gru bZHi, rMa Bya, dPal lDan rTSe, dPal rTSe, CHu aDus, Mus, Yul CHen, sPu dKar, Ding Ri sTe Sa, AH Po, and PHyogs dKar (Maps 1 and 3).

These trips were considered official business and hence the travelers received animals and men under the transport levy and were provided with quarters and food along the road. The officials did not, however, conduct any business for any of the establishments. They arrived at a District Office at the time when revenue was being collected, and they remained there, living off the local population, until they had been given enough gifts to prompt them to move on. Our respondents estimated that an official usually received gifts of cash and kind worth about twelve rDo TSHad on each "collection" trip, either to the east or to the west.

The officials anticipated their turns at going on these trips with great pleasure, and if for some reason an official was unable to leave the capital, his turn was not lost but postponed until a future year. Each year before the two groups left, the ZHabs Pad assembled them and gave a brief warning against the

[14] For a list of the officials who went on these trips, see Appendix D, section IV.

several tricks, such as becoming ill and thus unable to move on from a District Office, used to increase their mild extortions from the subjects. In recent years, at least some people in Sa sKya had recognized that this method of providing income for governmental officials was inefficient and burdensome for the subjects, but nothing was done about it. No doubt at one time the "collectors" had some responsibility for seeing that the revenue was properly paid and stored. When this responsibility was taken over by the District Officers, the officials from the capital must have been most reluctant to give up their profitable vacations, and probably to keep them quiet they were allowed to continue as if they were doing something useful.

Approximately thirty days a year the officials of the Government had to work beyond dinnertime; on these days they received meals of high quality. The Government usually did not provide any lunch—although it made the best tea available throughout the day—and the officials were supposed to remain on the job during the lunch-hour. Those who could not afford to have servants bring their lunches supplied themselves, in the most inconspicuous possible manner, with the Tibetan equivalent of the brown paper bag of sandwiches.

VI

The general scope of the activity of every stable political system is set by the value premises of its environment. The disagreements that arise over policy—the political "issues" as they are often called—concern the means of realizing these goals. More differences of opinion regarding policy are possible, and thus more political factions are likely, when the goals are ambitious than when they are minimal. There are, for example, many more possible interpretations of how "to promote the general welfare" than of how to maintain social harmony or to engage in religious observance. In Sa sKya a minimum of debate occurred about how things ought to have been done, and most disagreements and factions concerned matters peripheral to the basic functions of government.

Of all the officials in the government of Sa sKya, only the ZHabs Pad had the formal power to introduce innovations of any consequence, and only he (and perhaps the Chief Secretary) had the perspective necessary to conceive of reasonable changes. The burden of his daily work, however, and the culture's presumption in favor of retaining the goals and methods of the past prompted the ZHabs Pad to follow the path of his predecessors, making *ad hoc* and individual adjustments when these were required to maintain the system.

Even the formal power of the ZHabs Pad, however, was so dependent upon the political and religious power of the KHri CHen, the representative of the aKHon family, that he could have done nothing new without the KHri CHen's express approval. Although the majority of KHri CHen were probably content to let methods and policies follow the traditional patterns, from time to time a KHri CHen took a stronger than usual interest in governmental affairs and, prompted by his appreciation of domestic inefficiencies or foreign examples, decided to introduce certain innovations. These decisions no doubt always met with varying responses from the people of Sa sKya, but since the KHri CHen's own position and bases of power did not allow him to depart sharply from precedent, usually no social or economic stratum was threatened and thus approval or disapproval of the innovation was based on individual interests and preferences and did not correspond to any economic or status groups in the polity. The only possible exception to this kind of individualistic response was in the case of the action reportedly taken by several KHri CHen to limit the power and prestige of the hereditary nobility,[15] but the nobility could do little to resist; and, at least since the split of the royal family into the sGrol Ma

[15] See Chapter 8, sections IV and VII.

and PHun TSHogs palaces, the nobility (as will be suggested in section VII) may well have been divided against itself.

Sa sKya, of course, contained no organized interests that could support or oppose any actions of the KHri CHen. Even the bonds of the extended family were missing as a result of Buddhist beliefs and the structure of the economy.[16] Opinions were, however, expressed informally and in private by individuals regarding any departure by the KHri CHen from established routine. The nature of the political system prevented anyone with lesser status than the KHri CHen from overtly criticizing him, but his own family, especially after the split, was rarely of one mind and hence always a potential source of criticism.

A number of departures and proposed departures from routine occurred during the twentieth century. When KHri CHen aDZam Gling CHe dGu dBang sDud of the PHun TSHogs palace (r.1895–1915) proposed to construct the irrigation storage pools in the capital area,[17] he met with some criticism. Although the project was unusual because of its size and because storing water for irrigation was a technique very rarely used in Tibet, it was only an extension of the normal governmental function of providing and maintaining some basic "public works." The proposal met with two highly predictable criticisms: such a major disturbance of the topography was a serious affront to the earth gods and an invitation to misfortune, and the religious status of the aKHon family made it improper for them —indeed, forbade them—to engage in such mundane affairs.

The fear of the earth gods was firmly fixed in the Sa sKya belief system, and it was only natural that it prompted many people to oppose the pools, even when some of them stood to benefit directly from the increased regularity of their supply of

---

[16] On family ties among the nobility, see Chapter 8, section VI; on Buddhist beliefs, Chapter 3, section II; and on the economy, Chapter 10, section IX. The disappearance of the extended family as a basic social unit may be connected with the growth of a strong government.

[17] Chapter 4, section XV.

water. This fear was expressed by people from all social strata; it came from personal characteristics such as timidity, lack of imagination, and dogmatism. The story, incidentally, is that in answer to the argument based on the possible reaction of the earth gods, aDZam Gling CHe dGu dBang sDud reminded his people that he was himself not completely lacking in supernatural power.

The argument about the impropriety of the aKHon family engaging in mundane affairs may also have been based on undue religious conservatism. In Tibet, however, emanation bodies were usually expected to concern themselves with practical affairs, and some previous KHri CHen of Sa sKya had been rather active in governmental matters. This argument, therefore, may have been used by those who opposed the scheme on other grounds. Since opposition on the grounds of feasibility seems to have been unlikely—the KHri CHen was going to pay for construction out of his own pocket—the grounds may very well have been only personal. According to our respondents, the sGrol Ma palace opposed the scheme, at least at its inception, and this seems reasonable enough given the rivalry between the two palaces.

Before his accession, NGag dBang mTHu THub dBang PHyug of the PHun TSHogs palace suggested that two religious practices be revived. One was a summertime retreat of forty-five days during which the monks remained in their monasteries, refrained from eating meat, and performed special rituals. The other was a school for training monks in rhetoric and religious dialectic or logic. Although these practices would have increased religious observance and would have involved no significant expense or inconvenience, the proposals met with opposition. Again this opposition could have been based only on personal grounds.

KHri CHen NGag dBang mTHu THub dBang PHyug once bought some waterpipe to be used for irrigation in the capital. When the news of this purchase got about, the older nobles, monks, and subjects were very upset, for such a foreign device was sure to infuriate the earth gods. There was no public protest, but so many people were so obviously disturbed that the KHri CHen abandoned the project, and the pipe remained rusting in storage. This incident is reminiscent of the thirteenth Dalai Lama's automobiles. Whenever one went onto the streets of Lhasa, it caused people to break into tears, and so he was obliged to stop using them.[18]

NGag dBang mTHu THub dBang PHyug announced his intention to effect a number of other innovations that he was never able to accomplish. He proposed to organize a great trading venture using the grain of Sa sKya as investment capital; he wished to institute a system of free universal education, to be started with one hundred selected children from subject families; and he intended a thorough reorganization of the structure of the central government. This reorganization was eventually to divide governmental personnel into four sections, all under the ZHabs Pad. The first was to deal with economic affairs; the second was to handle the affairs of the Religious Establishment; the third was to conduct Sa sKya's relations with other governments; and the fourth was to be responsible for the education of Candidates, religious personnel, and subjects, including the preservation and promotion of handicrafts. The KHri CHen believed that this reorganization would eliminate red tape and other inefficiencies, with a "few officials doing much work rather than many officials doing little work." The status of sKu Drag was to be maintained for the more important offices.

Apparently none of these suggested innovations met with serious opposition within Sa sKya, although many people seem to have privately disapproved of them. They were all designed as improvements in the methods of pursuing the time-honored goals of political independence and religious pre-eminence; the KHri CHen could not innovate in any other way without un-

[18] Cf. Richard H. Pfaff, "Disengagement from Traditionalism in Turkey and Iran," *Western Political Quarterly*, XVI (1963), 79–98.

dermining the beliefs upon which his power depended. Although some foreign devices may have frightened the more timorous, none of the innovations violated any basic norms or threatened any of the vested interests of any segment of the population.

The proposed innovations did violate the presumption that the methods of the past are not to be lightly abandoned, but the power of the KHri CHen was too great to permit anyone to oppose him on the grounds of this presumption. As we have repeatedly emphasized, real opposition to a KHri CHen could come only from the other branch of his own family. But after 1935 and 1936, when NGag dBang mTHu THub dBang PHyug had successfully overcome a challenge by the sGrol Ma palace to his accession as KHri CHen,[19] his position was unassailable.

VII

Despite the personal involvement of our respondents in the response to the innovations proposed by KHri CHen NGag dBang mTHu THub dBang PHyug, we believe that, by careful checking of their statements, certain generalizations can be made about the pattern of approval, disapproval, and indifference regarding these proposals. The important people, both noblemen and subjects, who had local followings or unusual prestige, exhibited no significant differences of opinion corresponding to the division between the hereditary nobility and the subjects, to the residence of the family, or to the manner in which it derived its wealth. Most of the less wealthy families seem to have supported the KHri CHen's proposed innovations, but the more wealthy showed no pattern of opposition. Families living in the capital tended to support the KHri CHen, but those who lived elsewhere did not tend to oppose him. This evidence suggests only that those who wished they were more prosperous tended to

---

[19] Chapter 1, section XIII.

support change, and that people who were physically close to the KHri CHen probably found it expedient to express their support of his policies. Neither of these reasons implies any evaluation of the merits of the proposals.

The differences of opinion over the KHri CHen's suggested changes in method apparently arose principally from considerations other than whether these changes would better accomplish the purposes accepted by everyone. Except for the possibility that a few people were so farsighted that they saw the reforms as marking the end of their traditional way of life or so insecure that they could not tolerate the slightest deviation from the customary way of doing things, the support and the opposition to the KHri CHen were based on considerations other than the merits of his proposals—on "personal grounds," as it is often said. Two characteristics of Sa sKya reinforced the tendency to respond to the proposals not on their merits but upon their source: the very small size of the polity and the split in the royal family.

When NGag dBang mTHu THub dBang PHyug made his proposals, everyone who considered himself competent to have an opinion on governmental affairs immediately understood them as the policies of the PHun TSHogs palace. A handful of nobles and prominent subjects had reasons for being loyal to the KHri CHen himself—because they had worked closely with him in the past or, especially, because they served as his personal attendants—but most were in one way or another aligned, through their families or on their own account, with one of the palaces. Because of the standing rivalry between the two palaces, a man aligned with PHun TSHogs probably had a favorable opinion of the KHri CHen's proposals and a man aligned with sGrol Ma probably disapproved of them. A few people, however, were flexible enough to be enthusiastic partisans of whichever palace was currently providing the KHri CHen.

A man might have aligned himself with one of the palaces

because it had done him some favor or service. A rather large proportion of the Sa sKya nobility was frequently somewhat short of cash, and the palaces were a usual source of loans. An anecdote was told of one nobleman who went seeking a loan to the palace with which his family was aligned and met with a refusal. He then applied to the other palace, was granted a loan, and became one of its partisans. Although no examples were given, it is reasonable to assume that a Drag bsTan nobleman would be a partisan of the palace of the KHri CHen who granted the family's noble status. As has been pointed out, relationships by marriage were of little importance in Sa sKya, but one case was cited of a man who favored one palace until he married a woman related to the other palace.

Another reason for being a partisan of one palace or the other was peculiar to Tibet. Every monk in Sa sKya proper was initiated into the monkhood by a member of the aKHon family. The current KHri CHen usually performed these initiations, but a monk could request any other male member of the family. The relationship between teacher and pupil is so important in Buddhism that a monk has a personal loyalty to the man to whom he made his vows, a loyalty he very often retains even if he breaks his vows and leaves the monkhood. This kind of loyalty may have led the monks and former monks in the offices of the several establishments and in the monastic hierarchy to incline to one palace or the other, and it may also have influenced their families.

To align himself with one of the palaces, a man had to have a certain amount of standing so that he could withstand pressures from those of the other preference, or he had to have no standing at all so that he had nothing much to lose or even might not be taken seriously. The Group Officials in the capital maintained a strict neutrality, since they were so close to the powerful and because they were themselves of modest means and status. Probably most Headmen were similarly discreet, but one Headman, who lived at some distance from the capital and who was very rich, was an open partisan of one of the palaces. The story was also told of the man who led a nomadic existence in one of the higher areas of Sa sKya proper. He was so partisan to one palace that upon the accession of a KHri CHen from the other palace he left Sa sKya with his family and possessions, returning, however, some twenty years later when "his" palace once again supplied the KHri CHen.

VIII

Governmental office is usually considered so important that its occupants are rewarded by unusual wealth and prestige, and in Sa sKya these rewards also served as a principal means to differentiate the rulers from the ruled. The wealth, prestige, and psychological satisfactions that accompany governing are often the objects of ambition and the subjects of disputes and rivalries. So-called power-seeking, however, must always be seen in the proper perspective. Self-seeking and intrigue among powerful individuals and groups often appear more important than they are because in certain "pre-modern" systems those with power have few disagreements regarding the methods and means of carrying out governmental policy. Personal rivalries flourish in the absence of policy alternatives.

(The power accompanying governmental office is also commonly used to augment the formally designated rewards of office. Dealing with the governed in an unnecessarily high-handed and humiliating way, which apparently gives some kind of satisfaction, and using one's position to enrich oneself, perhaps by dipping directly into the treasury, are obvious examples. This behavior, too, must be seen in the same perspective.)

Although rivalries, intrigue, and struggles for power are only by-products of stable political systems, the frequency and manner of their occurrence can be correlated with the basic principles of the system. The small size of Sa sKya proper and its governmental apparatus afforded relatively little scope for official in-fighting, but some did occur and after the pattern one would expect.[20]

Occasionally the competition for governmental power in Sa sKya became violent, a result not only of the relatively uninhibited Tibetan personality, but also of the structure of government. Appointment and promotion were completely controlled by the ZHabs Pad and the KHri CHen, there were few criteria of expertise for any position, men remained in the higher offices until their death or retirement, and differences in policy were absent or irrelevant. There was thus always a temptation to use violence to open up a position or to eliminate a rival. In the early twentieth century, an official was stoned to death by a mob; although it was never proved, there was reason to believe that the mob had been instigated by another official who had seen the deceased as a competitor for promotion to a very high office.

The KHri CHen and other members of the aKHon family were also vulnerable to acts of violence. The principle of hereditary rulership allows for changes in incumbency only upon the occasion of resignation or death, and the lack of a firm principle of succession within the Sa sKya ruling family added to the temptations of assassination. The political system was so designed that the fate of anyone who assassinated a KHri CHen was solely in the hands of the man who by this act became the new KHri CHen. Assassinations of members of the royal family were frequent in its early history, and attempts at assassination (at the least) were not unknown in the last one hundred years.

The KHri CHen had an interest in preventing cliques or factions within his officialdom, but certain KHri CHen took little interest in governmental affairs, devoting as much of their time and energy as possible to their religious responsibilities. Under these circumstances, the ZHabs Pad had a free hand in

[20] Our method of obtaining information on Sa sKya did not allow us to get an unbiased account of individual and factional rivalries, but such an account would have contributed little to an understanding of the political system.

running the government and some ZHabs Pad may have had reasons for favoritism or have been too weak to prevent factions. For example, a ZHabs Pad with expensive tastes and not too many scruples could have created a clique that assured itself of generous portions of government revenue.

IX

The great majority of the subjects had no effect upon and were unaffected by the disagreements over methods and the struggles for office described above. Their concern was with the concrete application of the standard policies—the labor levies, the conscription of monks, the allocation of revenue responsibilities, and the behavior of the officials who came in frequent contact with them. They often enough sought reductions or other adjustments of the claims made upon them, and they had several methods of exercising influence. They could petition the ZHabs Pad through a Liaison Officer, or they could address a written petition to both the ZHabs Pad and the KHri CHen. They often came to the capital in groups to petition in person; the officials often started their working day by the casual remark, "Well, I wonder what group will show up today."

The effectiveness of these formal methods depended upon the government's desire to avoid unpleasantness, additional work, and "disharmony," and the ruling class's mild fear of the subjects. The government probably believed, perhaps unconsciously, that if the specific grievances of the subjects were not met they would react in some wild and unpredictable way.[21]

The informal methods used by the subjects to try to influence the government gave some substance to this uneasiness. Campaigns of gossip and slander were deliberately started, and the anonymous letters, placards, and songs described above were also used as methods of protest. Outside the capital, the subjects sometimes refused to cooperate with the local officials, requiring the central government to explain and justify its decisions. These

[21] See Chapter 3, section XIII.

methods of influence were similar to those available to the ordinary monks of the North and South Monasteries.[22]

The possibilities of popular action are illustrated by the following anecdote. In 1943 about ten families in aKHril sPe suffered serious damage to their crops from a hailstorm, and they found themselves without the means to subsist for the year. In such an emergency, they could have applied to the Government for relief, but this was not their style. Two or three members from each family equipped themselves with drums and began a tour of neighboring settlements, where they sang and danced and then passed the hat. If the leader of the entertainers was satisfied with the amount that had been donated, he waved a white yak's tail; if he believed that the contributors had been somewhat niggardly, he waved a black yak's tail. The black tail was not merely an expression of disapproval; it strongly suggested that the audience was to experience some kind of misfortune. This tour by the aKHril sPe people naturally attracted much attention, and the ZHabs Pad ordered them to terminate it. (Among other things, he believed it was bad publicity for the Sa sKya government, suggesting an inability to handle its affairs.) The minstrels protested this order so vigorously that the ZHabs Pad referred the matter to the KHri CHen, who compromised by allowing them to continue, but only for two weeks. He also ordered that they be given grain from the Government's stores.

Within the limited range of action that the poorer subjects believed properly open to them, they were able to exert some influence upon governmental decisions. Their influence was, however, sporadic and limited to protests against specific grievances.

X

Although we secured little direct evidence on local patterns of power and influence, extra-governmental relationships in Sa

[22] Chapter 11, section XI.

sKya were undoubtedly dominated by the wealthy. The power of wealth came from the ability to extend credit and from the natural desire of the poor man to be on good terms with those who could come to his assistance in emergencies. The presumption that government was to be used as sparingly as possible added to the informal power of wealth. Headmen and District Officers were naturally anxious to remain on good terms with the wealthy people in their localities, but in performing any of their functions that had the direct backing of the capital they could act quite independently of local notables. At most four of the eight District Officers were themselves from wealthy families, and about half of the Headmen we were able to identify were personally fairly wealthy.

The KHri CHen and the ZHabs Pad, who dominated the central government, had too much prestige, wealth, and authority of their own to be subject to much influence by the wealthy. One of the Liaison Officers in the 1940's was a very wealthy man, and a number of the less affluent sKu Drag officials clustered around him to enjoy his largesse, but he was described as having little political power.

Wealth in Sa sKya, however, brought a number of small but genuine political advantages. It enabled one to educate his children, thereby increasing their prestige and making it possible for them to enter governmental service. The gifts and other expenses involved in doing business with the government also made personal wealth convenient. Wealth by itself, however, brought little prestige.

Personal wealth in Sa sKya depended ultimately upon the land, and private land seems to have been almost always necessary for the accumulation of private fortunes. This private land originated in gifts from the aKHon family for services performed; and, although once granted it was free of governmental control, the royal family always had the power to take it back. And the KHri CHen, at least, could always find some excuse for removing the source of the personal wealth of anyone who opposed him.

XI

The belief system of Sa sKya was otherworldly and traditional. The people of Sa sKya believed that life had little intrinsic value and that it was to be spent accumulating merit through religious observances; they took only limited action to control their environment and themselves. Their theory of history presented the past as a golden age; their lack of understanding of natural phenomena prompted them to retain traditional modes of behavior; and their concept of government as power led them to justify their own government by reference to the past.

Government was seen as a device external to usual human relationships serving to guarantee their harmony. A ruling class was thus required, and its existence prevented the development of a political community. The view of government as the maintainer of harmony was correlated with a relative indifference to the thoughts and behavior of the subjects, and both were correlated with the belief that the maintenance of governmental power necessitated its concentration and required that it be used only sparingly. The actions of the Law Officials neatly illustrate this political theory: they dealt with as few cases as possible; the cases they handled were usually treated as disputes between private parties; when they intervened everyone was strikingly reminded of the power of government; and their treatment of criminals can best be understood as warnings to others rather than as reactions to breaches of a community's rules.

Since government had relatively little to do and since power received so much emphasis, struggles for position and prestige within the ruling class unsurprisingly constituted most of the action. The government was naturally not concerned with solving problems or designing policies to improve society, nor did "society" want it to be so concerned. The political system was naturally held together by the cooperation of a ruling class in order to maintain its privileges, and the ruled class expected and approved of this arrangement.[23]

[23] Cf. Pye, *Politics, Personality, and Nation Building*, p. 78.

The autocratic power of the KHri CHen, as the representative of the aKHon family, was a correlate of the theory of government as power. His power was circumscribed by the presumption for following tradition, by the restricted sphere of proper governmental action, and by the simple organization of the governmental apparatus. The political system was absolutely dependent upon the principle of hereditary power and upon the continuity of the royal family. Although the rivalry between the two palaces occasionally became rather fierce, the aKHon were always aware of their common descent. Current struggles for succession could not efface the memory of a common "glorious history" going back to aPHags Pa and beyond. This solidarity was exhibited in a number of small ways: for example, the medical practitioner who served the sGrol Ma palace was the brother of the medical practitioner who served the PHun TSHogs palace, and when NGag dBang mTHu THub dBang PHyug became KHri CHen, he retained as one of his personal attendants of sKu Drag rank a man who had served his predecessor from the sGrol Ma palace.

The KHri CHen of Sa sKya "controlled the means of production" and the pattern of distribution because he had the power to allocate land; but his allocations seem always to have been motivated by considerations of his personal political advantage. He did not participate in any important decisions regarding the actual process of economizing, and he probably could not have made any significant changes in the methods of production and distribution. His ability to alter the schedules of revenue owed to the establishments probably did not suffice to alter the manner in which the people of Sa sKya supported themselves. Political and economic power in Sa sKya were, in a limited sense, combined, but it would be absurd to argue that the KHri CHen's political power resulted from his economic power, nor can his political power best be understood by reference to his economic power. Sa sKya's concept of the functions of government included control over the land, and this concept was rooted in its total world view. The distribution of economic power was an integral part of the complex of factors constituting the polity, and had it been different there would have been a different distribution of political power. This relationship between political and economic power, however, gives no support to the theory that government exists to maintain a division of labor.

The KHri CHen was a very high religious figure as well as a governmental autocrat, and he also had ultimate control over the North and South Monasteries, the headquarters of the Sa sKya sect. Sa sKya was not, however, a "theocracy," and the common question about the relationship between "church" and "state" is not applicable. Tibetan Buddhism did not enable anyone to claim a monopoly of correct interpretation of a divine will, and no one had the sole power or right to deal correctly with the supernatural. The government did not consider itself responsible for the religious beliefs and practices of its subjects, and there were no religious qualifications for governmental office.

XII

The last act of Sa sKya as a polity was its response to the Chinese Communists after 1950. In accordance with the theory of government as power, when Sa sKya recognized the overwhelming force of the Communists, it was prepared, no matter how reluctantly, to adjust to it. Its sentiments were no doubt those expressed by the Indian poet Tagore, wistfully comparing modern politics with those of an earlier age: "Through all the fights and intrigues and deceptions of her earlier history India has remained aloof . . . her thrones were not her concern. They passed over her head like clouds. . . . Often they brought devastation in their wake but they were like catastrophes of nature, whose traces are soon forgotten." [24] The Communists, however, were not interested in "occupying a throne"; their goal was revolutionary. Although our evidence is inconclusive, we can

[24] Quoted in Elie Kedourie, *Nationalism* (New York: Frederick A. Praeger, 1960), pp. 110–111.

make a number of suggestions regarding the reactions of the people of Sa sKya to this unprecedented challenge.

The technology of the Chinese seems to have impressed everyone who experienced it, and the money that the Chinese spent rather lavishly in their first contacts with Sa sKya was appreciated by all. Chinese officials organized meetings of Sa sKya officials to explain Communist goals and methods; they attempted to enlist the support of anyone who was amenable and to take advantage of any disagreements and grievances among the Sa sKya ruling class. Reactions to this phase of the Communists' program seem to have depended upon individual personalities rather than upon wealth, status, or background: those Sa sKya officials with "open minds" tended to react favorably, and those who were "conservative" tended to reject the Communists' arguments. We did, however, discover one Sa sKya official who was persuaded to collaborate. He came from a very undistinguished subject family, and he had got ahead solely on his personal ability and by the use of his wits.

At first the Communists paid little attention to the subjects of Sa sKya. They gave them some interest-free loans, which were appreciated, and they proclaimed that communism was the champion of the downtrodden, a theme that the subjects probably did not understand. The District Officer who championed the subjects, for example, reported that the Communists were talking about something quite different.[25] The Communists' rejection of the concept of a ruling class was foreign to the attitudes and experiences of the subjects of Sa sKya.

Before too long, however, the Communists' adamant stand against religion made the Sa sKya officialdom realize that adjustment to the new source of power was impossible. This was not to be a transfer of power and privilege that, in the fashion of traditional empires, left customs, beliefs, and social relationships intact. The Chinese then resorted to physical force and put

[25] See Chapter 4, section X.

everyone of importance in prison or in work gangs where they were humiliated and subjected to "re-education" to get them to embrace communism and denounce the "Tibetan way." When the ruling class was incapacitated, the subjects could offer little resistance.

Appendix A

Royalty and Nobility

I. Genealogies of the PHun TSHogs and sGrol Ma Palaces (PHo Brang)

The founders of the palaces, Yab CHen Kun dGaa Rin CHen and Padma bDud aDul dBang PHyug, were the sons of mTHu CHen dBang sDud sNYing Po, who was born about 1763, became KHri CHen about 1790, and died in office about 1806. sNGags aCHang aJam mGon rDo rJe Rin CHen, the common son of the founders, became KHri CHen in 1806, reigned for a brief period, and then resigned. He was succeeded by his elder father, Padma bDud aDul dBang PHyug of the sGrol Ma palace, who was succeeded by his son (by a second wife), bKra SHis Rin CHen.

The PHun TSHogs Palace

Yab CHen Kun dGaa Rin CHen = sDe Ba Rang Byon (in common with Padma bDud aDul dBang PHyug)

sNGags aCHang aJam mGon rDo rJe Rin CHen (KHri CHen, c.1806–?)

= rTa Ba Pa (second wife)

sKyabs mGon PHyogs Kyi Glang Po (died at age 28)

NGag dBang Kun dGaa bSod Nams = sNYing Ri Ba (?–1887) (KHri CHen, 1866–c.1887)

aDZam Gling CHe dGu dBang sDud = Sa dBang THon Pa (1855–1919) (KHri CHen, 1895–1915)

aJam dPal lHun Grub rGya mTSHo (or dNGos Grub dPal aBar) (died young)

1922

NGag dBang mTHu THub dBang PHyug = Mi SHang Bya Rig Pa = THub bsTan mKHas Grub rGya mTSHo (1900–1950) (c.1906–c.1933) (KHri CHen, 1936–1950)

divorced common wife, then = lHa rTSe sKyid sBugs

NGag dBang Kun dGaa PHrin Las (1934–) (monk)

five daughters

NGag dBang Kun dGaa bSod Nams = sGrol dKar lHa Mo (1929–)

divorced, then = bSod Nams TSHe aDZom

five sons (oldest b.1953)

The sGrol Ma Palace

Padma bDud aDul dBang PHyug = sDe Ba Rang Byon (in common with Yab CHen Kun dGaa Rin CHen, then divorced)
(KHri CHen, ?–?)

sNGags aCHang aJam mGon rDo rJe Rin CHen
(KHri CHen, c.1806–?)

= Mus Pa (second wife)

bKra SHis Rin CHen = ?
(?–1865)
(KHri CHen, ?–1865)

aJigs Med dBang rGyal rDo rJe = lHa Rigs rTSe Pa = gSang bDag dPal CHen Od Po
(?–1894)   (died in his 20's or 30's)
(KHri CHen, 1887–1894)

aJam dByangs THub   NGag dBang lHun Grub   Grags Pa Blo Gros
bsTan bZang Po   (rebel monk) =   (monk)
(monk)   daughter of Sikkim king   (died young)

two sons (whole family died young)

Drag SHul PHrin Las Rin CHen = SHab rDo Zur
(1871–1935)   (?–c.1938)
(KHri CHen, 1915–1935)

NGag dBang Kun dGaa Rin CHen = two daughters of gZims Bon SHod = NGag dBang Kun dGaa rGyal mTSHan
(1902–1950)   (elder, 1906– ;   (c.1903–c.1940)
                               younger, ?–c.1946)

four daughters

two daughters   NGag dBang THeg CHen dPal aBar
                       (1945–)

II. The Organization of the Palaces

As described in Chapter 1, in the fourteenth century the Sa sKya domain was divided among a number of branches of the aKHon family, each of which had lands, property, and people. The division of the family into the sGrol Ma and PHun TSHogs palaces in the eighteenth century followed this precedent. Whatever the original division of subjects between the two palaces, by the twentieth century each palace had only about 4½ per cent of the families of Sa sKya proper as its subjects, or Mi Ser; these subjects worked land "belonging" to the palaces in the sense described in Chapter 9, section IV, and each palace also had its own grazing lands. The palaces were thus "establishments" and further fragmented the small polity, especially at the lower levels of the governmental apparatus.

The subjects of the palaces provided the royal family with some income, especially in the form of free domestic and other labor, but their principal significance was symbolic. They symbolized the importance of the royal family and its independence of the Government. Except for work on the capital's irrigation system, palace subjects were exempt from the Government's levy of labor, the indication (as seen in Chapter 3) of that establishment's ultimate authority. They were also exempt from conscription as soldiers (Chapter 2) and as monks (Chapter 11). They were tried as criminals by the Law Officials only with the consent of the palace officials.

Each palace had three Bla Brang (religious houses), allocated to unmarried daughters, who were considered to be nuns, and each Bla Brang was given its own subjects and treasurer. In the 1940's each Bla Brang of the PHun TSHogs palace had eight subject families. All three Bla Brang buildings of the PHun TSHogs palace were located near the Government Building; one Bla Brang of the sGrol Ma palace was in the east village, one was near the palace, and one was in aKHril sPe (Maps 3 and 5). When there were more than three unmarried daughters, two or more shared the same Bla Brang; when there were fewer than three, one or more Bla Brang buildings were closed down.

Each palace had about fifty subject families in the area of the capital, about seventy elsewhere in Sa sKya proper, and an undetermined number in the other western territories of the Sa sKya domain. About fifteen farming families lived within the walls of the PHun TSHogs palace; they were allocated in equal parts to KHri CHen NGag dBang mTHu THub dBang PHyug's two sons. In the capital area, the land of the palaces was scattered about.

Each palace had a set of sKu Drag officials (in addition to those of the KHri CHen described in Chapter 5, section IX). They were all formally appointed by the ZHabs Pad, but the palaces themselves usually made their own choices, from the Corps of Candidates, from the lower government officialdom, or from the populace at large. All these officials were supposed to be monks, but occasionally a layman or former monk was appointed. The palace officials received their board and room and two complete suits of clothing each year and occasionally were given palace land for their own use.

The most important palace official was the treasurer, who appointed his own staff of from twenty to thirty people. He was responsible for the treasuries, land, livestock, trade, and subjects of his palace. The wife of the head of the palace handled the interior finances of the palace, and she and the treasurer consulted frequently. The treasurer organized and supervised the frequent levies of work from the palace subjects living in the capital, and he was immediately informed of and investigated any trouble that palace subjects became involved in anywhere in Sa sKya proper.

Each male of both palaces was entitled to a butler and a valet. The butlers attended to the food, drink, and person of an adult male, and always accompanied the male children; every male aKHon seems to have had a butler. The valet attended to garments, ceremonial robes, bedding, and so forth. Only a palace wishing (and financially able) to be elegant had a full contingent of valets. Each palace had an offerings official, who was always a monk in good standing. He was responsible for religious offerings and received a portion of the material so used. Finally, the palace from which the KHri CHen did not come had a chef, who ranked with the Government's Work Corps. (In the 1940's the PHun TSHogs palace also had a man in charge of six traders, who took palace goods throughout western Tibet, working on a percentage basis.)

All the other officials of the palaces ranked just above the Liaison Officers, and all were entitled to attend the Great Assembly Meeting, although only the treasurers did so (Appendix C, section II). There were also medical practitioners in the service of the royal family who had sKu Drag rank, the most prominent being the house of sKu Drung of the dPal rTSe District (Map 3). The rank of these practitioners was the same as that of the Work Corps. In addition, certain Government officials—especially the Equerry, the Building Official, and the Fuel Official—also served the palaces.

The sKu Drag positions connected with the palaces and with the KHri CHen were about 40 per cent of all sKu Drag positions, a clear indication of the importance of royalty.

III. List of Noble Families

Because there were no central records of noble status, each noble family keeping its own papers, the following information is based on our respondents' memories of what was said about the families listed. The list probably includes all the nobility in Sa sKya proper and no one without noble status, but the precise status—brGyud Pai sKu Drag or Drag bTSan—and the reasons for and duration of the status are all subject to some doubt. The approximate location of the residence of every family except SHar ZHabs Pad and dPe rGyal sDe Pa Lags, both of the SHab Valley, is given on Map 3. The twenty-four families were:

dBon mDaa, of the capital; brGyud Pai sKu Drag, given to a secretary of a high official of aPHags Pa.

Klu Pa, of SHab; brGyud Pai sKu Drag, given to an Equerry of aPHags Pa.

KHro mGar, of SHab; brGyud Pai sKu Drag, given to a mounted retainer of aPHags Pa.

rGya U sPugs Pa, of the capital; brGyud Pai sKu Drag, given to a spearman of aPHags Pa.

dPal aByor sGang, of the capital; brGyud Pai sKu Drag, given to a mounted retainer of aPHags Pa.

dPe rGyal sDe Pa Lags, of SHab; brGyud Pai sKu Drag, given to a Headman in the period 1268–1338.

SHar ZHabs Pad, of SHab; brGyud Pai sKu Drag, given to a ZHabs Pad in the period 1268–1338.

Zur KHang Nub Pa, of SHab; brGyud Pai sKu Drag, given to a guardian of valuables under aPHags Pa.

Rang Byon, of SHab; brGyud Pai sKu Drag, reason for status not remembered; family pre-dated aPHags Pa.

Con Pa, of SHab; brGyud Pai sKu Drag, reason for status not remembered.

Lug Rags, of gYaa Lung; probably brGyud Pai sKu Drag, given to a steward of aPHags Pa; also Drag bTSan, reason for and duration of status not remembered.

Zur Drug sDe Pa Lags, of the capital; brGyud Pai sKu Drag, given to a headman probably during the time of aPHags Pa.

Byang aGo, of rMa Bya; probably brGyud Pai sKu Drag, given to a secretary in the period 1268 to 1338; also Drag bTSan, reason for and duration of status not remembered.

Nang Pa, of the capital; probably brGyud Pai sKu Drag, probably given during the period 1268–1338.

CHu Mig Nang Pa, of the capital; brGyud Pai sKu Drag, reason for status not remembered; family pre-dated aPHags Pa; also Drag bTSan, reason for and duration of status not remembered.

bDe Legs Pa, of the capital; brGyud Pai sKu Drag, reason for status not remembered; also Drag bTSan, reason for and duration of status not remembered, although it automatically ended with the death of a head of the family during the period 1915–1935. The family subsequently split, thus creating a new brGyud Pai sKu Drag line.

Bla Mags, of SHab; probably Drag bTSan dating from seventeenth century; reason for status not remembered.

Brag sPe, of dPal rTSe; Drag bTSan, given in 1948 for negotiating return of TSHa Zur area of city of Lhasa to Sa sKya control.

lCam Mo Grwa TSHang, of SHab; Drag bTSan dating from nineteenth century, reason for status not remembered.

aGro mGon, of Ko CHag; Drag bTSan, status perhaps connected with marriage of a daughter to KHri CHen NGag dBang bSod Nams Rin CHen during seventeenth century.

sKu Drung, of dPal rTSe; Drag bTSan, status probably connected with appointment of family as official medical practitioners for the aKHon family during the period 1783–1806.

Ma Ba TSHogs, of Gru bZHi; Drag bTSan, reason for and duration of status not remembered.

Nang bSam Pa, of SHab; Drag bTSan since seventeenth or eighteenth century, reason for status not remembered.

PHu SHar bKra SHis sGang, of Ga Ra; Drag bTSan, status perhaps connected with an ancestor who served as a butler to the KHri CHen during the period 1728–1783.

In addition, a number of formerly noble families still living in Sa sKya proper in the twentieth century were identified. Some time between 1900 and 1915, a Liaison Officer and his son, who was a Candidate, were killed in a riot in the capital. These deaths ended a brGyud Pai sKu Drag family, whose name was not remembered, that derived its status from an ancestor who was a Secretary during the period 1268 to 1338.

The families Bar Pa, rMon mDaa, and rTa Ba Pa, living just

south of the capital, were formerly brGyud Pai sKu Drag. All three had got this status from ancestors who were spearmen for aPHags Pa.

The family Bar sDings sDe Pa Lags, of SHab, was formerly brGyud Pai sKu Drag because of its status as hereditary headmen. The family Ha Ma sDe Ba, of the capital, may also have been in this position.

The family gZims dPon, of KHra U, were of Drag bTSan status at least during the nineteenth century, but at some later date and for a reason not remembered it lost this status. It then had the title "Drag bTSan aDul rGyul" (roughly "demoted Drag bTSan").

This list of formerly noble families was recognized by our respondents as most incomplete.

Appendix B

Sa sKya Territories
outside Sa sKya Proper

Since the Sa sKya territories outside Sa sKya proper (Map 1) were not closely related to the government located in Sa sKya proper, little time was spent on them in the interviews. The following information was provided by our respondents, who naturally had less knowledge of these outlying areas.

The territory of Mar KHams rGya KHag was located south of Markham Dzong between the Mekong and Yangtse Rivers. Its population was not known, but it was principally an agricultural region. Its chief Sa sKya official was called a "dPon," in contrast to the title "gZHis KHa" (District Officer) used in the western Sa sKya areas. He was appointed by the government in the capital, but it had very little knowledge of what he did and no doubt usually appointed a local man. The dPon collected revenue in kind from the people and had legal jurisdiction over them; but the Lhasa government could levy work from the people of the enclave (it "collected the outer tax," as the Tibetans say), and this symbolized the priority of the Lhasa government. This arrangement may have been a rudimentary kind of federalism, but more possibly represented a tribute to a superior power.

The territory of aDam THog was located on the southwest bank of the Yangtse River, about 32° north latitude. It contained about six hundred families, not all of which belonged to the Sa sKya religious sect. There were three monasteries in the territory, with a total of about four hundred monks, to which were sent from Sa sKya proper two six-year religious collectors (Bla Ma TSHab) (see Chapter 11 and Appendix E, section IV). The chief official was a dPon. He was appointed by the capital, but again there was probably little real control over him. For example, in the early 1950's the dPon was a Lhasa nobleman who had married a Sa sKya woman. He was appointed by the sGrol Ma palace and was concurrently a military official (Ru dPon) of the Lhasa government. NGag dBang Kun dGaa bSod Nams was in this territory in the 1950's and had occasion to check its revenue system. He reports that the system was in poor shape, with some families paying no revenue at all. The levy in labor from this area went to the Chinese.

Although revenue from these two eastern areas was never brought to Sa sKya proper, the capital occasionally allocated some of it for various religious projects in eastern Tibet.

In reference to the above two areas, it must be remembered that eastern Tibet had a reputation for political instability and governmental impotence.

The area rTSe gDong was located on the north bank of the Tsangpo River to the east of Shigatse, about seventy miles from the capital. It was the outside area most closely connected with Sa sKya proper: its District Officer (gZHis KHa) was called sKu TSHab (representative of the body), referring to the KHri CHen, and formerly a branch of the aKHon family had a palace (PHo Brang) in the territory. Serious crimes such as homicide had to be referred to the capital from rTSe gDong, and the District Officer had the option to refer lesser cases. In contrast, if a serious crime such as homicide occurred in the other western territories, the District Officer in charge informed the ZHabs Pad, who decided whether or not the case should be brought to the capital. If both families involved in a homicide agreed, the ZHabs Pad could send a member of the Work Corps or a Candidate to the territory to assist the District Officer in resolving the case. The District Officers in all these areas had prisons.

There were about a hundred families living near the rTSe gDong District Office, which was the former palace, and about a hundred others scattered throughout the territory. A number of Sa sKya monasteries were located in the enclave: one of about one hundred monks, one of about fifty monks, and several smaller ones. All the officials of these monasteries were chosen by the monks themselves, with the approval of the capital. rTSe gDong had a warmer climate than Sa sKya proper, and its soil was sandy. It was noted for its fruit and the skill of its artisans.

People from rTSe gDong had a better chance of becoming important in religious and governmental affairs in Sa sKya proper than people from other outside areas, but still only a handful in lower positions were identified. The people of this area, like the people of all the western enclaves, were subject to the transport levy (see Chapter 9, section VII); but since they were located on the route from the capital to Lhasa and the Sa sKya monasteries in eastern Tibet, their burden was considerably greater. Revenue in kind from the stores of the District Officers of the western territories was brought to the capital whenever the ZHabs Pad was in need of the available material. According to what they produced and their distance from the capital, they made such shipments from two or three times a year to once in three years.

Our respondents expressed a mild distrust of the people from rTSe gDong, saying that "they talk sweetly but are hard on the inside." This may express a normal misunderstanding of strangers, or it may indicate that the people of rTSe gDong were not especially enthusiastic about their political relationship with the capital.

The territory of Mus was located on the north bank of the Raga Tsangpo River about sixty miles from the capital. Its total population was unknown, but it contained a high proportion of herders and its people were rather prosperous. The people of Mus spoke a dialect somewhat different from that of Sa sKya proper and had slightly different customs. They were characterized as creating little trouble for the government. The territory provided coarse paper, meat, felt, and butter, and it was the sole source of gold for Sa sKya proper.

The District Officer (gZHis KHa) of Mus was appointed, apparently with some real control, by the capital. He reportedly had many disputes with the governments of Lhasa and Shigatse over boundaries. The abbot (mKHan Po) of the rTa Mo Gling monastery in Mus, with about seventy monks, was appointed for an indefinite tenure by the government in the capital.

The territory of Yul CHen was located on the south bank of the Tsangpo River about one hundred miles due west of the capital. This rather large area was said to have contained only about seventy-five families, a large proportion of whom were herders. The District Officer (gZHis KHa) was appointed by the capital. The monastery in Yul CHen, with about twenty-five monks, was headed by an abbot (called a Bla Ma TSHab) appointed for an indefinite tenure by the capital.

The following smaller territories were less known to our respondents. In contrast to the territories already mentioned, which are represented on Map 1 on a true scale according to our respondents' estimates, these smaller territories are exaggerated in size on Map 1 so that they can be more clearly seen.

The territory of sPu dKar was part of a larger area of western Tibet also called sPu dKar. It was located about sixty miles southwest of the capital, and contained about a hundred families principally engaged in agriculture. Its District Officer (gZHis KHa) was appointed by the capital.

The part of the Sa sKya domain called Ding Ri sTe Sa consisted of about seventy families who were interspersed with families under the governmental control of Lhasa. This was the only case we found where the principle of territorial contiguity was not followed in defining a Sa sKya political unit. The Sa sKya District Officer (gZHis KHa), appointed by the capital, performed the normal legal and revenue functions regarding these noncontiguous families and he kept careful records of who they were. The District Office was located about twenty miles due west of sPu dKar, near Tingri Dzong.

The territory of Srad was located about forty miles southeast of the capital. It contained few people, most of whom were herders; there was little good farming land; and the area was noted for its felt. The District Officer (gZHis KHa) was appointed by the capital. There also was a Lhasa dzong in the area. Srad was the only Sa sKya territory in the west that was not visited by the so-called "revenue collectors" (Chapter 12, section V).

Almost nothing was known about the territories of AH Po and PHyogs dKar. AH Po was located about halfway between Sa sKya proper and Yul CHen, and PHyogs dKar between Yul CHen and Mus. Both had District Officers (gZHis KHag) appointed by the capital.

In addition to these enclaves throughout Tibet, there were at least two other special political arrangements. The small area in the heart of the city of Lhasa, called TSHa Zur, occupied by only a handful of families, belonged to Sa sKya, but was used (and could be used) only as a place where visiting Sa sKya officials could stay. There may have been other such areas in Tibet under Sa sKya governmental control. Sa sKya monasteries located in the territory of non-Sa sKya governments may have had land and peasant families under a feudal-type arrangement.

Appendix C

Governmental Officials

I. The Rank of Jo Lags

Lower officials of the Sa sKya government had the rank of Jo Lags, which entitled them to a special regalia and associated them with the KHri CHen, the ZHabs Pad, and the function of government. "Jo" is literally "older brother" and "Lags" is an honorific; a younger brother can call his older brother "Jo Lags," and the term is also used to address servants and attendants of some standing. Its governmental meaning was, however, quite specific, even though it was related to its literal meaning and to its usage as a term of address.

All Jo Lags officials wore the same insignia, but there were several grades of Jo Lags designated by the color of the outer garment. The standard insignia were: a long outer garment, with its lowest edge within about nine inches of the ground (ordinary people wore thigh-length outer garments); a long left earring and a turquoise-colored button in the right ear; a bowl-bag hanging from the girdle over the left buttock and a case-knife with matching chopsticks in the case hanging over the right (ordinary people could wear the knife but not the chopsticks); a large yellow hat like that worn by sKu Drag (Jo Lags wore their hair long and gathered behind rather than in a topknot); and a red crossband over the right shoulder.

The formal outer garment of Jo Lags officials was of satin, a material reserved for governmental officials and hereditary nobility. The color of this garment indicated the rank of the Jo Lags official: in decreasing rank, yellow, red, orange, and brown.

Only one official, the assistant to the Treasurer of the KHri

CHen, was entitled to wear yellow. Only one official was entitled to wear red: the assistant to the Sedan Officer.

The officials who wore orange satin outer garments were: the sixteen District Officers (gZHis KHag and dPon); the heads of the Government artisans; the twelve lowest officials on the permanent staff of the Steward of the Religious Establishment; and the male valet of the wife of the KHri CHen. The Government once appointed a representative to Lhasa, and he was given this rank.

The officials who wore brown satin outer garments were: the Headmen (dZaa dPon, SHe dPon, sDe Pa Lags); the two Group Officials; the two Hospitality Officials, in charge of greeting and housing guests; and the two subchiefs of the Government tailors.

One official, the chief of the servants in the Government building, was entitled to wear all the Jo Lags insignia, but he could not wear a satin outer garment. Temporary appointees, like tax-farmers, could wear long outer garments but nothing else to indicate their official status.

Certain people, who were not ordinary subjects even though they had no governmental status, were allowed to wear part of the Jo Lags costume or other items of clothing usually reserved for government officials. The hereditary nobleman who was head of his family wore on formal occasions the full Jo Lags regalia with brown satin. The same arrangements applied for the hereditary medical practitioners.

Sons of hereditary noblemen were allowed to wear any color satin save yellow in the "dragon pattern," which was reserved for very high officials, and they could wear no insignia. Families that once had had noble status were by courtesy allowed to dress as the nobility.

II. Ranking of Sa sKya Officials

The Great Assembly Meeting was called by the KHri CHen or the ZHabs Pad (or Acting ZHabs Pad) and was held in the Government Building. It was attended by officials of the Government, the Religious Establishment, the KHri CHen, and the North and South Monasteries, who were seated and served tea according to their status ranks.

The meeting-hall was rectangular with the unoccupied throne of the KHri CHen in the center of a shorter side. There were two facing banks of seats, of about eight rows each, parallel to the longer sides of the hall. The officials of the North and South Monasteries sat on the right hand of the throne, the higher position, and the other officials sat on the left. The seat closest to the throne in the front row of the right bank was ranked highest, and the ranking continued along the front row, with the seat closest to the throne in the second row following the last seat in the first row. The same scheme applied to the left of the throne.

The highest monastery officials were ranked as follows:

the abbot of the South Monastery (mKHan CHen, or KHri Ba)

former abbots of the South Monastery (mKHan Zur)

the abbot of the North Monastery (brGya TSHo dPon Slob)

the chant master (or leader) of the North Monastery KHri CHen's College (dBu mDZad CHen Mo)

the chant master of the South Monastery (dBu mDZad CHen Mo)

The remaining seats on the right side were occupied by the following monastery officials, alternating between the North and South Monasteries (a grand total of seventy-four, plus any retired abbots):

South Monastery:

the business manager (sPyi CHen dPon Slob)

the work manager (Las THog Pa)

the two thousand-offerings officials (sTong mCHod aGo Ba)

the religious law official (CHos KHrims Pa)

the keeper of Great God House (dKon gNYer CHen Mo)

the heads of the sixteen Gling (Gling dPon)

the eight assistant chant masters (bsKul CHung Pa)

the eight conch-blowers (Dung mKHan)

the twenty doctors of theology (bKaa Rab aByams Pa)

North Monastery:

the three assistant chant masters (dBu mDZad)

the two offerings officials (mCHod dPon CHen Mo and Grwa TSHang mCHod dPon)

the two assistant chant masters (bsKul CHung Pa)

the beadle (dGe bsKos)

the dGe aPHel dPon Slob and dGaa lDan dPon Slob

the members of the bDe CHen Gling

the religious law official (CHos KHrims Pa)

The governmental officials were seated as follows (a total of seventy-six, plus the Candidates and any retired ZHabs Pad):

the ZHabs Pad

retired ZHabs Pad

the Acting ZHabs Pad

the Steward of the Religious Establishment

the Chief Secretary

the three Secretaries

the Butler to the KHri CHen

the Valet to the KHri CHen

the Offerings Official of the KHri CHen

the Treasurer of the KHri CHen

the assistant to Treasurer of the KHri CHen

the two Keepers of the Keys

the two Law Officials

the two Palace Treasurers

the two highest officials of the Religious Establishment

the four Liaison Officers

the Chef of the KHri CHen

the Archivist

the six middle officials of the Religious Establishment

the ten members of the Work Corps

the Candidates

the assistant to the Sedan Officer
the twelve Jo Lag officials of the Religious Establishment
the sixteen District Officers (gZHis KHag and dPon)
the five chief artisans
the two Group Officials
the two Hospitality Officials

In addition to the order of seating, there were other ways in which rank was indicated. The number of cushions upon which the official sat varied from one to five (the KHri CHen had seven), and they were made of satin or cotton. All abbots, retired abbots, true, acting, and retired ZHabs Pad, the Steward of the Religious Establishment, and the Chief Secretary had backs to their seats; all other seats were without backs. The seats of the monastery officials were superior in quality to those of other officials. Tea was served to the highest officials in china bowls with elaborate metal lids and stands; the next highest officials got only the stand; the next only the lid; the next only the china bowl; and the officials at the bottom brought their own undecorated wooden bowls. There were other signs of rank, but they were not investigated.

Not all sKu Drag officials attended the Great Assembly Meeting, and not all who attended were sKu Drag. sKu Drag officials were ranked as follows, with the numbers indicating rank and the order of listing indicating priority within the rank.

1. the ZHabs Pad
   the Steward of the Religious Establishment
2. the Chief Secretary
3. the three Secretaries
4. the Butler to the KHri CHen
5. the Valet to the KHri CHen
6. the Offerings Official of the KHri CHen
7. the Treasurer of the KHri CHen
8. the two Keepers of the Keys
9. the two Law Officials
10. the palace butlers (indefinite number)

the palace valets (indefinite number)
the two palace offerings officials
the two palace treasurers
the Body Servant of the KHri CHen
the two highest Religious Establishment Officials
the four Liaison Officers

11. the Chef of the KHri CHen
12. the Archivist
13. the chef of the palace "out of power"
the remaining six Religious Establishment officials
the ten officials of the Work Corps
medical practitioners in the service of the royal family
    (indefinite number)
the two Doormen for the KHri CHen
14. the Candidates (indefinite number)

Appendix D

Economic Affairs

I. The Transport Levy

The Tibetan levy of transport has been the subject of so much discussion that our detailed information on Sa sKya should be of interest to many readers. In addition, it was from this information that we arrived at our estimate of the cost of this levy to the people, as will be made clear below.

For every traveling official, the subjects (and others who held Government land) had to supply pack animals and riding animals. The amounts of both varied according to the official traveler's importance and the amount of material he had to take along: for example, a six-year religious collector (Chapter 11, sections VI and VII) normally received five mounts and ten pack animals; a trip of congratulations to Lhasa (Chapter 2, section V) required two mounts, three pack animals, and one retainer. The provision of retainers to carry credentials and symbols of authority (called Mi Hreng, man force or man urgent) was required only when the traveling official was very important. On longer trips, the subjects had to provide the officials and their servants with food and lodgings, and they had to provide fuel and animal-feed for certain travelers going beyond the boundaries of Sa sKya proper. All these expenses can be estimated in terms of market prices for goods, labor, and rental of animals, and thus the average cost to the families of specific areas can be calculated. It was the custom for the local people, prompted by their District Officers or Headmen, to bring gifts to the traveling officials. The value of these gifts cannot be estimated. The people of rTSe gDong also had to transport officials from the capital going to the east, but we did not figure the cost of this service.

The trips were always by stages, the people of one locality taking the officials to another place, from which they were moved on by the local people (see Maps 1 and 3). Trips within Sa sKya proper had shorter stages than those that went to the outside. Officials going to the east were moved by the people of the capital and aKHril sPe to the SHab District Office, a trip lasting two days with the night spent in Ga Ra; the people of the SHab District took them in two days to Shigatse; the people from rTSe gDong picked them up in Shigatse and moved them in four days to Rinphung Dzong; and from there they were on their own, with some help from the Lhasa government, for three days until they reached the city of Lhasa. Going south, the capital people took officials to aKHril sPe (only a few miles), and the aKHril sPe people took them to gYaa Lung, the whole trip taking from one to two days; the people of gYaa Lung took them in two days to rMa Bya; the people of rMa Bya took them to CHu aDus in one day; and the people of CHu aDus took them to the east or the west for one day. Going west, the schedule was one day from the capital to the District Office at lHun aGrub sDings, with a change in aKHril sPe; thence to gDong dGaa in one day; and then two days to Lhatse Dzong. Officials going north took one day to Ga Ra, where there was a change; two days to the SHab District Office; and two days to the dMigs District Office. There was no transport north from dMigs.

In a normal year, four trips were made to Lhasa, three for the routine congratulations and one on special business; seven trips on special business were made to Shigatse, rTSe gDong, or Gyangtse; one group of five officials went east through SHab and another group of five went west through CHu aDus on the annual "collection" tour (Chapter 12, section V); one short-term religious collector (Chapter 11, sections VI and VII) went east through SHab and five went west through gDong dGaa; five six-year religious collectors went east through SHab; one

outside abbot (Chapter 11, sections VI and VII) went west
through gDong dGaa and one went east through SHab (this
assumes an average tenure of nine years for these abbots); and
there was one trip to Lhasa with military supplies, which required only twenty to forty pack animals. Also in a normal year
officials went out from the capital about four times to other parts
of Sa sKya proper to investigate various disturbances and emergencies. Officials of the Lhasa government received bargain
prices for riding and pack animals when traveling through Sa
sKya, which they did at least twice and at most five times a year.

Whenever a riding or pack animal was levied, someone had to
accompany it to get it to its destination and then back home. One
man could take care of his own and others' animals, so probably
only three men went on the trip to care for ten animals. On these
trips no one was in a hurry. The officials were under no pressure
to get to their destinations, and they might have enjoyed traveling and picking up gifts from the local people en route. The
subjects, for their part, were anxious to prevent their animals
from losing too much flesh. If the subjects were interested and if
they could afford it, they were free to take along goods on their
own additional animals and do some trading on the trip. The
return trip was made more rapidly, probably taking about 75 per
cent of the time spent going out. Only in the SHab District did it
take an appreciable length of time to move oneself and one's
animals from one's home to the District Office to pick up the
travelers (Map 3). Hence one day was added to the average cost
of the transport levies to the people of this district.

The accompanying table gives the figures derived from this
information, assuming that two of the internal trips went to
SHab and two to CHu aDus and combining the costs for the
people of the capital and for the people of aKHril sPe (which
included the village of CHos aKHor lHun Po). The market
price for renting a riding animal was 15 Srang per day (50
Srang = 1 rDo TSHad); for renting a pack animal, 7.5 Srang
per day; and for hiring an animal-handler, 2.5 Srang per day.

The people of areas not listed paid no transport levy except when an internal trip was made to their areas. The people of dMigs had to transport a Lhasa official or a religious collector south to the SHab District Office.

The costs to the people at stopping-points of providing rooms, fuel, and feed for the officials' animals were too small to be worth calculating. The same was true of the fuel and animal feed

Annual Cost of Transport Levy

Area	Animal-days per year		Man-days per year	Total cost (rDo TSHad)	Average cost per eligible family (rDo TSHad)
	mount	pack			
Capital	475	838	431	290	0.29
SHab	835	1498	732	510	1.30
gDong dGaa	116	194	93	67	0.39
rMa Bya	63	106	51	37	0.80
Ga Ra	14	73	26	16	0.42
gYaa Lung	105	177	85	62	2.13
lHun aGrub sDings	121	205	98	72	0.80
CHu aDus	22	35	17	13	0.26

provided by the people of SHab, gDong dGaa, and CHu aDus to officials traveling to points outside Sa sKya proper.

The total annual income to the government from the transport levy in monetary terms was about 1,067 rDo TSHad. The average annual cost to the families involved was about 0.60 rDo TSHad, the price of two KHal of barley (see sections II and III below). The average annual cost to all the families of Sa sKya was about 0.43 rDo TSHad. These costs were no doubt always met, for few could claim (as in the case of payments in kind) that they could not meet their transport responsibilities and still feed their families. It must be remembered that the amount of transport facilities required from a family was proportional to the amount of establishment land that it held.

II. Monetary Units, Units of Measurement, Prices, and Wages

Monetary Units

The monetary units current in Sa sKya, all minted or printed by the Lhasa government, were the Kar Ma, the ZHo, the Srang, and the rDo TSHad. Their equivalencies were:

$$10 \text{ Kar Ma} = 1 \text{ ZHo}$$
$$10 \text{ ZHo} = 1 \text{ Srang}$$
$$50 \text{ Srang} = 1 \text{ rDo TSHad}$$

In 1947, 1 rDo TSHad was worth about 3.33 Mexican silver dollars or about 2.4 Chinese taels, or ounces of silver.

Units of Measurement

Units of measurement were apparently not standard throughout Tibet. The units of measuring volume used in Sa sKya were the Bre and the KHal:

$$20 \text{ Bre} = 1 \text{ KHal}$$

It was estimated that a Bre of grain filled a man's cupped hands, and thus that a Bre approximated an American pint.

The units of weight were the sPor, the NGag Ga, the rGya Ma, and the KHal:

$$4 \text{ sPor} = \text{NGag Ga}$$
$$4 \text{ NGag Ga} = 1 \text{ rGya Ma}$$
$$5 \text{ rGya Ma} = 1 \text{ KHal}$$

A "medium" load on an animal was about 140 pounds, and 14 KHal of butter was a "medium" load. Hence one KHal was

about 10 pounds. Also, 6 Chinese catties (1⅓ pounds each)
equaled 4 rGya Ma, which makes a rGya Ma equal to 2 pounds.

Prices

The following is a list of typical prices in Sa sKya proper in
1947, all in Srang:

barley (1 Bre)	0.7
wheat (1 Bre)	0.9
rice (1 Bre)	2.0–2.5
dried peas (1 Bre)	0.6
butter (1 sPor)	0.5
dried cottage cheese (1 Bre)	0.7
mutton (1 rGya Ma)	3
beef, prime (1 rGya Ma)	5
suet and tallow, unrendered (1 rGya Ma)	5.33
vegetable oil (1 sPor)	0.37
tea, coarse brick (1 sPor)	0.5
Seng lDang (1 sPor)	0.5
eggs (capital only), each	0.75
dried tubers (Gro Ma) (1 Bre)	1.4
salt (1 Bre)	
pure	0.93
impure	0.7
beer (1 Bre)	0.15
wool (1 rGya Ma)	5–6
woolen homespun (1 fathom—8″ wide) [1]	0.5 (weaving fee) plus 2 rGya Ma of wool
dyed woolen cloth (1 fathom)	14–17
sheepskin (1) [2]	
tanned	6
untanned	3
goatskin (1)	
tanned	3
untanned	1.5

[1] A full garment of shirt, trousers, and robe required nineteen fathoms.
[2] A winter coat required seven or eight skins.

yak hide (1) [3]	
tanned	20
untanned	10
animal droppings for fuel, for 1 day	0.12–0.15
hay, for 1 animal for 1 day	0.5
greeting scarf, smallest	2
firearms (1)	
highest quality British Enfield with 200	
rounds	3,000
cheapest rifle	1,000
Mauser pistol	1,000–2,500
matchlock	100–150
pots (1)	
rough, locally made	0.5
imported	20–30
plow, yoke, harness	125
harrow	20
spade or shovel	15
hoe	10
sickle	4
wooden rake	2
wooden fork	1
winnowing basket	1
haircloth grain sack	5
pack saddle and gear	30
riding saddle	250
second-hand haircloth tent	1,800
sheep	
local	30
nomad	20
lamb	5–10
yak	350
barren yak cow	400
hybrid ox	600
DZo Mo (best milker)	600
milking cow	250
horse	750–1,500
mule	1,500–5,000
donkey	150–250
rental of animals, 1 animal for 1 day	
riding	15
pack	7.5

[3] One yak hide made one pack bag and a few boot soles.

Wages

The working day was from sunrise to sunset throughout the year. Artisans usually worked more in the spring and summer. In addition to their wages, all workers got three meals a day and beer; the quality and quantity of food varied with the skill of the worker and the quality of work expected from him. When an artisan worked in his own house, he received the price of his food in addition to his wages. Wages varied, but the following were normal. All are given, in Srang, for a day's work for a private employer.

silver, gold, and copper smiths	10–15	blacksmiths	10
rug-makers	2–4	tailors, etc.	3
image-makers	3	carpenters	3
stonecutters	3	stonelayers	2
drovers	2.5	weavers (always women)	1.5
spinners (always women)	0.8–1.0	agricultural laborers	1

Butchers received 2.15 in cash and internal parts for each sheep, 12 for each larger animal.

III. Illustrations of Living Standards

The following are brief biographies of Sa sKya families that illustrate several levels of consumption. Family A was described as the most wealthy subject family in the capital that had no connection with governmental offices. Family B was estimated to be at the ninety-ninth percentile of wealth, and family C at the ninety-second. (lHa bZo Pa, described in Chapter 10, section VIII, it will be remembered, was at the eighty-fifth percentile.) Family D is an example of the poorest stratum in the capital. (The widow's family in the reallocation of land case in Chapter 9, section V, is another example of the very poor.)

Family A

The family of PHu Nub Pa lived about ten miles south of the capital (Map 3), where it had been located for at least three generations. In the 1940's it consisted of the father and mother, two married sons and their wives, and an undetermined number of children. Two other sons had married into other families, and still two more sons were monks.

The father had accompanied his brother, a religious collector in Khams, as his business manager. The collector had done well and had put all his profits from collecting and trading into the family estate.

The family worked Government land, but it had much more private land of its own. This private land was probably acquired during the father's generation, principally by purchasing all the private land available from other people as far north and west as the monastery of CHos aKHor lHun Po, although this generation had also inherited a small amount of private land around the family house. The family did not rely upon hired help for farming its scattered portions of land. Water was plentiful in the vicinity of the family's residence, and good grazing land for cows and goats was close by. They had two or three hundred sheep and an undetermined number of yaks, cattle, and hybrids placed with herders higher up the river. They had five horses and at least fifteen donkeys. Their house was large, they ate well, and they had three good firearms.

Each year the family took grain to Phari Dzong near the border of Sikkim—a trip of perhaps two hundred miles—where they exchanged it for wool to take to India. From India they returned to Sa sKya with manufactured goods such as cotton cloth, pressure lamps, mirrors, and pots and pans. These articles were displayed in a free stall in the market place in the capital (Map 5). The goods that were not sold here were hawked throughout Sa sKya proper. In these trading and marketing ventures the family relied on its own labor.

This family was more wealthy than a large proportion of the hereditary nobility. It took, however, no interest in governmental or religious affairs, contenting itself with accumulating wealth. Although the family's business acumen was acknowledged, our respondents did not consider this to be an especially laudable quality.

Family B

The family of rTSab rGyas—the father, the mother, a married son with his wife, and a younger son—lived a few miles south of the capital (Map 3). Another son was a monk. The father's brother had been a religious collector, but apparently he did not invest as much in the family estate as did the collector brother of PHu Nub Pa. The family farmed Government land and had a smaller amount of private land of its own. They had two horses, about fifteen donkeys, perhaps three hundred sheep, and an undetermined number of yaks, cattle, and hybrids. The family's grazing land was only fair. It did some trading and had no debts. rTSab rGyas, in short, profited from the same advantages of location, land, and labor enjoyed by PHu Nub Pa, but his profits were less because his advantages were inferior.

Family C

This family consisted of a man, his wife, and their grown son. The father was a Government artisan of "brown" Jo Lags rank (Appendix C, section I), and the son was also a Government artisan. They had about thirty KHal of Government land and about four KHal of private land "given" to the father's father for some service he had performed for one of the palaces. All this land was in (or very near) the capital. The three of them worked in the fields, but because of the men's responsibility to the Government and because the two artisans could work profitably for private employers, the family hired labor rather frequently. They had four cows, about seven donkeys, and good clothing and personal ornaments. They ate well, with wheat perhaps three times a week and rice once. Each year they bought a few lambs from herders and fattened them for their own meat. As artisans, they paid the Government no revenue in kind; they paid the work levies on thirty KHal of land. The family was at approximately the 50-KHal-of-barley annual living standard. It had perhaps 50 rDo TSHad of debts.

Family D

The father of this family was the man who had no establishment land and was considered too irresponsible to farm it (Chapter 9, section V). He, his wife, and their nine children, two of whom died fairly young, lived in rather picturesque destitution. The entire family lined up with their bowls at every religious celebration, and the father said he could get as much as four days' food from the monks on a single occasion. Occasionally, it was said, he went as far as Shigatse to receive these religious handouts. He also played a musical instrument known as a "Chinese violin," and the entire family periodically gave street concerts. The father made very rough earthen pots and the mother wove baskets, both of which were sold at low prices. The man had obtained an old matchlock of Tibetan manufacture. With this he killed marmots, whose skins he sold for 5 Srang and whose meat he fed to his family, despite the strong Tibetan avoidance of such fare. Unlike many of the poor of the capital, he never helped himself to others' property.

IV. Governmental Income and Expenditures

The following estimates of government income and expenditures are for a typical year from 1945 to 1950 and they are expressed in the prices of 1947. Once again, although the items are given in monetary terms, they should be understood as only approximations. The general pattern of income and expenditures should, however, be accurate enough.

The Government also received revenue in kind from the other western parts of the Sa sKya domain. This material was not regularly delivered to the capital; when the Government's stores were short of specific materials, special deliveries were called for from these areas. According to an area's distance from the capital and the kind of goods it produced or obtained through trade, it made such deliveries as frequently as three times a year or as infrequently as once in three years. There is no way to estimate the annual value of this income, but it was probably rather small. Revenue from the two easternmost areas of the Sa sKya domain was never brought to the capital. The Government or the KHri CHen could allocate part of it to various projects in eastern Tibet.

A sizable proportion of the income of the several establishments came from religious offerings from the people of Sa sKya and from outsiders, including important patrons (Yon bDag) of the sect such as the King of Derge. There was, unfortunately, no way even to guess at the value of these gifts.

There are many duplications in the budgets of the several establishments, and not all their expenditures were paid for by the people of Sa sKya proper. The total governmental expenditure and the total cost to the people will be calculated later. We will first give the estimated income and expenditures of each establishment.

Government Income

The Government's income in cash and kind came from two principal sources: first, the revenue in kind from about 1,600 subject families, equivalent to about 23,000 KHal of barley and worth about 6,400 rDo TSHad: second, the payments from the religious collectors, calculated in Appendix E, section V, as about 1,150 rDo TSHad. To this total of 7,550 might be added 250 rDo TSHad got from the Government's "grain and money merchants" (see Chapter 12, section IV), on the supposition that fifteen men were each given the value of 60 rDo TSHad and twelve made a profit for the Government of 35 per cent.

The Government's revenue in kind from its subject families was calculated as follows: The Steward of the Religious Establishment provided food worth 4,200 rDo TSHad to contribute the value of 30 KHal of barley to each of his 500 monks each year. Of this, 2,000 rDo TSHad came from the 1 per cent tax on sheep and goats. The remaining 2,200 rDo TSHad came from the revenue in kind from subjects of the Religious Establishment. There were about 530 such families, and thus the average payment for a family was worth 4.15 rDo TSHad, the equivalent of 14.8 KHal of barley. The Government, for its part, spent about 5,300 rDo TSHad that in all likelihood came from its revenue in kind, and our respondents estimated that in the 1940's the Government was collecting an annual surplus of from 16 to 20 per cent. If it received 20 per cent more than it spent, its income was about 6,400 rDo TSHad. There were about 1,485 farming families and about 128 herding families with allegiance to the Government. If a herding family paid half as much in revenue as a farming family, the average payment of the farming family was about 4.13 rDo TSHad, an amount very close to the 4.15 rDo TSHad calculated for the average Religious Establishment family.

If the average family in Sa sKya had three adults and two children, it needed about 20 KHal of barley per adult and 10 per child in order barely to make ends meet. If it netted 75 KHal, it paid 31 KHal in revenue according to the ideal of about 25 per cent of gross paid to its establishment, if it avoided the milling charge of 10 per cent for the grain it consumed. Since it was said that at least one-half of Sa sKya families could not in normal years fully meet their payments to their establishments, this average of 14.8 KHal seems reasonable enough.

The Government also received from several sources income the value of which could not estimated. The District Officer at dMigs collected a tariff of about 1 per cent of the wool and salt coming into Sa sKya. These were principally transit taxes on material that went south of the Himalayas. The military supplies to Lhasa amounted to about twenty "half-loads" in a normal year; this income was, of course, directly and entirely spent, and, although it was a net charge to the people, it was very small. The Government operated some mills, but the quantity of grain these handled could not even be guessed at. And, of course, there were always gifts from both within and outside Sa sKya.

Government Expenditures

Most of the Government's regular expenditures were recalled, and it was not too difficult to estimate the amounts involved:

1. Equipment for religious collectors: about 65 animals (50 per cent of transport-levy schedule), with a work-life of about six years; about 42 pack saddles, with a life of two years, and 23 riding saddles, with a life of six years; food for three months for 10 men on six-year terms and for one month for 14 men on short terms, at 2.5 Srang per man-day; and ingredients for the magic pellets (estimated at 80 rDo TSHad) and food for 500 monks, at 3 Srang per monk-day, for three and one-half days (during the fourth moon) while they were constructing the pellets. Total cost, about 447 rDo TSHad.

2. Annual renewal, during the twelfth moon, of all offerings and images (made of butter and grain) in the North and South Monasteries, and supplying butter for the constantly burning lamps. These constituted the largest single governmental expenditure, and we took the maximum estimate of 2,000 rDo TSHad as their cost.

3. Annual subsidies to the aKHon family: to the KHri CHen, 115 KHal of barley and 70 pounds of tea; to the other four males, 46 KHal and 28 pounds each; to the ten females and the rGyal Yum, the wife of the KHri CHen, 23 KHal and 14 pounds each; and to the three bDags Mo, wives of other aKHon males, 12 KHal and 7 pounds each. Total cost, 193 rDo TSHad.

4. Annual memorial services on the anniversaries of the deaths of all male members of the aKHon family prior to the split between the palaces and of all KHri CHen since the split, a total of about 47. These observances took the form of providing a three-day feast each month for the 200 monks of the North Monastery, the food costing about 3 Srang per monk per day. About 80 per cent of the cost was met by the Government, the

remainder by the two palaces. Total cost to the Government, about 345 rDo TSHad.

5. Annual five-day religious service during the first moon: food for 500 monks at 2 Srang per day, and the gift of 6 Srang cash and a small scarf to each monk. Total cost, 180 rDo TSHad.

6. Food for Government officials on overtime work: 35 officials for 30 days at 2.5 Srang per man-day. Total cost, 52 rDo TSHad.

7. Week-long feast for all Government officials: 80 men at 4 Srang per man-day. Total cost, 45 rDo TSHad.

8. Incense, 40 rDo TSHad, and paper (35 half-loads), 10 rDo TSHad.

9. Food for workers on building maintenance: 20 men for 9 months at 2 Srang per man-day. Total cost, 216 rDo TSHad.

10. Food (at 2.5 Srang per man-day) and token wages to artisans working for the Government: 15 blacksmiths for 90 days at 0.6 Srang daily wages; 15 other smiths for 90 days at 1 Srang; 30 carpenters for 90 days at 0.3 Srang; 25 stonemasons for 75 days at 0.3 Srang; 22 idol-makers for 120 days at 0.3 Srang; 40 tailors for 120 days at 0.3 Srang. Total cost of food and wages, 833 rDo TSHad.

11. Religious celebration during the fifth moon: 5 Srang in cash and one small scarf to 40 winners of horseraces, and 2 Srang apiece to 70 riders; one-day feast for 500 monks and 100 governmental officials and menials, at 2.5 Srang apiece. Total cost, 40 rDo TSHad.

12. A small feast for the 16 Gling of the South Monastery during the sixth moon. Cost, 4 rDo TSHad.

13. Thirty-day feast for the 200 North Monastery monks in the seventh moon, at 1 Srang per monk-day, plus a gift of 2.5 Srang to each monk. Total cost, 130 rDo TSHad.

14. A nine-day chanting service during the ninth moon for the founder of the Sa sKya sect: 500 monks at 1 Srang each per day. Cost, 90 rDo TSHad.

15. A thirty-day service for 100 selected monks during the

tenth moon, at 0.75 Srang per monk-day. Cost, 45 rDo TSHad.

16. During the eleventh moon, a six-day feast for the 200 North Monastery monks and a one-day feast for all 500 monks, at 1 Srang per monk-day. Cost, 34 rDo TSHad.

17. Gifts to the people of Sa sKya to relieve the distress of disasters or extreme poverty: roughly estimated at the value of 9 KHal of barley for each of 250 people. Cost, 630 rDo TSHad.

Items 1–17 total 5,334 rDo TSHad.

The total income in cash and kind of the Government was 7,800 rDo TSHad and its total expenditures came to 5,334 rDo TSHad. We have assumed an expenditure of 80 per cent of collected revenue, which would be 6,240 rDo TSHad, so about 900 rDo TSHad of expenditure was not accounted for. It is difficult to believe that any major regular item of Government spending was not remembered or that the estimated costs for the listed expenditures were greatly in error. Hence this 900 no doubt went to the Religious Establishment.

The cost of the Government to the people of Sa sKya proper includes the 6,400 rDo TSHad of revenue in kind plus labor in various forms. The transport levy was worth 1,067 rDo TSHad as calculated in section I above. Laborers working on public buildings received the usual food but not the normal wage of 1.4 Srang per day; they thus paid the Government these wages, which totaled about 151 rDo TSHad. Artisans also received their usual meals, but only token wages: the usual wages for blacksmiths were 10 Srang per day; for other metalworkers, 15 Srang; and for the remaining artisans, 3 Srang. The difference between the token wages the Government paid them and the wages they received in the market totaled 1,185 rDo TSHad. Labor levies for road repair, decorating the capital for special occasions, repairing public buildings outside the capital, repairing irrigation systems, haying, and other such tasks could not be described in enough detail to estimate their value. The total of the calculable costs of the Government to the population was about 8,800 rDo TSHad.

Religious Establishment Income

The income in cash and kind of the Religious Establishment came from three sources: revenue in kind from its subjects equivalent to about 7,860 KHal of barley, or 2,200 rDo TSHad; 2,000 rDo TSHad worth of animals from the 1 per cent tax; and payments from the religious collectors totaling about 420 rDo TSHad (see Appendix E, section V). This income totaled about 4,620 rDo TSHad.

Religious Establishment Expenditures

The annual expenditures of the Religious Establishment were these:

1. Half the living expenses of 500 monks. Total cost, 4,200 rDo TSHad.

2. Clothing for about 70 monks under sixteen years of age: about two and one-half outfits for a ten-year period, at 600 Srang per outfit. Total cost, 210 rDo TSHad.

3. Subsidies to the aKHon family: to the KHri CHen 30 sheep and 70 pounds of butter; to the four males, 12 sheep and 28 pounds each; to the ten females and the rGyal Yum, 6 sheep and 14 pounds each; and to the three bDags Mo, 3 sheep and 7 pounds each. Total cost, 120 rDo TSHad.

4. Salary and expenses of the Steward, 200 rDo TSHad.

Total expenditures of the Religious Establishment, 4,730 rDo TSHad.

The approximately 110 rDo TSHad that the Religious Establishment spent in excess of its regular income no doubt came from gifts and from the Government and perhaps also the KHri CHen. The Religious Establishment never had a surplus.

Income of the PHun TSHogs Palace

In the 1940's the KHri CHen was of the PHun TSHogs palace, so his income and expenditures have been combined with those of the palace. From the religious collectors was received a total of 5,046 rDo TSHad (see Appendix E, section V); revenue in kind from about 117 subject families (at 14.8 KHal of barley per family—see above) amounted to 485 rDo TSHad; subsidies from the Government and Religious Establishment (see above) amounted to 190 rDo TSHad; the outfits of clothing given the KHri CHen on the death of each person over twenty years of age (Chapter 9, section I) were worth about 30 Srang apiece—assuming a death rate of 1 per cent per year, their total value was about 97 rDo TSHad. This income adds up to 5,818 rDo TSHad.

The PHun TSHogs palace also engaged in trade, which brought it some income, and its members, especially the KHri CHen, received many gifts and religious offerings. There is, as we have said many times, no way to estimate the value of these types of income. The palace also received domestic help from its subjects in the area of the capital, for which no wages were paid. This work was a cost to the people of Sa sKya; it probably did not exceed the value of 50 rDo TSHad per year.

Expenditures of the PHun TSHogs Palace

The expenditures of the PHun TSHogs palace and the KHri CHen for the year 1947 were remembered and estimated as follows: the regular memorial services for the four PHun TSHogs males other than the KHri CHen (see Government Expenditures, item 4), costing 30 rDo TSHad; celebrations of the birthdays of three living male members of the palace, involving a one-day feast for the 500 capital monks, at 3 Srang per monk, totaling 90 rDo TSHad; and the annual religious services during the second moon (see Appendix E, section I), costing 300 rDo TSHad. There were also the following special expenditures: the celebration of the thirteenth birthday of NGag dBang Kun dGaa PHrin Las, costing 100 rDo TSHad; a renewal of the offerings at some shrines in the capital area, at a cost of 50 rDo TSHad; the repair of two god houses about a mile north of the capital, costing 170 rDo TSHad; and the renovation of the nunnery bGon Pa rGyas, at a cost not exceeding 100 rDo TSHad. The support of the 50 monks in the "school of rhetoric and dialectics" (bSHad Grwa) (Chapter 12, section VI) cost 4 Srang per monk per day for nine months; the total cost was 1,080 rDo TSHad.

It was said that KHri CHen NGag dBang mTHu THub dBang PHyug was very generous in aiding Sa sKya monasteries in western Tibet to renovate and refurnish, and that he made himself unusually accessible to beggars seeking largesse on days of religious significance. There is no way of knowing how much he spent annually on such matters.

The living expenses of the people of the palace were quite high. It was judged that 180 rDo TSHad was spent each year on the food for each member. An outfit of clothing for a special occasion could cost as much as 250 rDo TSHad. The sKu Drag officials attached to the palace also had to be fed and clothed. It might thus be supposed that about 3,500 rDo TSHad were spent in a year on such domestic items.

These estimated expenditures total 5,420 rDo TSHad. If it is also assumed that the palace and KHri CHen were saving about 20 per cent of their income during this period, they had about 4,654 rDo TSHad of their income to spend, minus the 50 that was in the form of labor. The difference of some 800 rDo TSHad no doubt came from religious offerings and gifts.

Income and Expenditures of the sGrol Ma Palace

Naturally less was known about the income and expenditures of the sGrol Ma palace. Certain fixed items can be given: the palace received 2,249 rDo TSHad from the religious collectors, 485 rDo TSHad from its subjects, 57 rDo TSHad from the Government, 35 rDo TSHad from the Religious Establishment, and 50 rDo TSHad in work from its subjects. It spent 300 rDo TSHad on a five-day religious service during the second moon, 58 rDo TSHad on memorial services for eight deceased male members of the palace, and 60 rDo TSHad on the birthdays of its two living male members. The palace also spent about 50 rDo TSHad for special renewal of the offerings at some shrines in the capital area. The palace that did not have one of its members as KHri CHen was always at a financial disadvantage, and the sGrol Ma palace during this period engaged in rather extensive trading and tried to keep its living expenses and donations to religious projects at modest levels.

Payment of Officials

A final cost of government in Sa sKya was the payment of the officials of the several establishments. The principal method of payment was to turn over to an official a certain amount of land which he could use as he saw fit and on which he paid no revenue in kind. Grants of land went to three officials of the KHri CHen, the eight sKu Drag officials of the Religious Establishment, the nine members of the Work Corps, the thirteen higher Government officials, and the eight District Officers of Sa sKya proper. The amounts of these grants varied with the importance of the office; there is no way to determine them. It seems that they all sufficed to provide a tolerable standard of living for any official who had no other means of supporting himself. If that living standard averaged about 50 KHal of barley per year, the cost was about 2,870 rDo TSHad. The officials also received many gifts that must be considered an unavoidable cost to the people, but this cost cannot, unfortunately, be estimated.

Certain officials could increase their incomes by serving as "revenue collectors" (bsDus Pa). Ten or twelve men went out each year and each returned with about 10 to 12 rDo TSHad in currency and goods. (This estimate is based on the specific memory that in the late 1940's an official of the KHri CHen returned from a "collection" trip with 13 rDo TSHad in cash and another 3 or 4 rDo TSHad in meat, skins, and homespun cloth. This was considered by his fellow "collectors" to have been a very good haul.) The total is about 120 rDo TSHad a year, with about half coming from the people of Sa sKya proper. The

officials who went on these "collection" trips were the three
Secretaries, the KHri CHen's Butler, Valet, and Treasurer, the
two Keepers of the Keys, the four Liaison Officials, the Archivist, the members of the Work Corps, the two Doormen of the
KHri CHen, and the Candidates. Three Candidates went on
these trips each year; one-third of the others went out each year,
but each Doorman went out only once in six years.

On the basis of these partial and approximate figures, we offer
the following conclusions. Maintaining a governmental apparatus cost the people of Sa sKya proper about 17,100 rDo TSHad
per year in the late 1940's, or about 1 rDo TSHad per person.
The several governmental agencies during that period spent about
21,500 rDo TSHad (omitting all levied labor); about 53 per cent
of the total went directly for religious purposes, about 15 per
cent to pay governmental officials, about 23 per cent to maintain
the royal family, and the remaining 9 per cent for miscellaneous
purposes. The annual expenditure of about 11,465 rDo TSHad
for religious purposes brought the government about 8,865 rDo
TSHad from the religious collectors each year.

There is another way to check our conclusion that the total
expendable income of the establishments was about 20,530 rDo
TSHad. Our respondents estimated that the Government and
the KHri CHen were saving from 16 to 20 per cent of their
incomes during the period from 1935 until 1945. In 1945 a pillar
in the southwest corner of the Great God House of the South
Monastery collapsed, bringing down the two stories above it but
leaving the outside walls of the monastery intact (Chapter 11,
sections I and XI). The structure had to be rebuilt, idols and
books had to be repaired and replaced, and it was decided to
repaint the whole hall. The cost of repairs was estimated to be
about equal to the financial reserves of the Government and
KHri CHen, which some wanted to use to pay for the restoration. Instead a loan was sought from outside, and the government
at Lhasa advanced an interest-free loan of 10,000 rDo TSHad

and donated the labor of 270 workers for 45 months, which represented the labor levy on about 540 families in 16 Dzong of the Lhasa government, the men working about nine months per year for five years. To this was added the labor of about 30 Sa sKya men working for 45 months; voluntary donations from the Sa sKya officialdom totaling about 1,500 rDo TSHad; voluntary contributions from the subjects of Sa sKya totaling about 1,120 rDo TSHad (about 4,000 KHal of barley); about 1,000 rDo TSHad worth of material contributed by the KHri CHen; and one-third of the special religious collection of NGag dBang Kun dGaa PHrin Las (Appendix E, section V), worth about 5,865 rDo TSHad. All the workers were fed but given no wages. The total cost of the restoration was 19,485 rDo TSHad.

The total cost of repairs was about half again as large as the estimated annual expendable income of the Government and the KHri CHen, which means that to accumulate the 19,485 rDo TSHad in ten years, they would have saved about 15 per cent of this income each year. Thus there is additional evidence supporting the reasonableness of our estimates of governmental income.

Appendix E

Monastic Affairs

I. Support of the Capital Monks

Our respondents estimated that the five hundred monks of the North and South Monasteries were supported at the level of 60 KHal of barley per year per monk, a yearly expense of 8,400 rDo TSHad. (This standard of living includes housing, the cost of which should be subtracted from this amount. We could not, however, estimate this cost.) The Steward provided about half this amount from the revenue of the subjects of the Religious Establishment and from the special 1 per cent levy on animals (Chapter 9, section I). One Steward told our respondents that in three years 10,000 sheep and goats had been slaughtered for consumption by the monks, and this checks with the probable total number of these animals in Sa sKya.

The six-year collectors, upon their return, gave feasts for the monks out of their own pockets, and this added about 220 rDo TSHad a year to the income of the monasteries. Although this was a small amount, the method by which we calculated it can be given here as an example of the way we arrived at many of our estimates of income and expenses. Each collector used his own judgment regarding the extent and lavishness of his entertainment, but probably three-quarters gave a moderate half-day feast for the monks of both the North and South Monasteries. For five hundred monks, one-half-day's worth of mutton cost about 375 Srang (50 Srang equal one rDo TSHad): each monk, for a single meal during the half day, had to be given about three-quarters of a pound of mutton that cost 1.5 Srang per

pound. Tea, butter, salt, and barley cost about 800 Srang, calculated in the same way. The collector was also expected to give a
small amount of cash to each monk, say 1 Srang, for a total of
500 Srang; and to give about fifteen officials greeting scarves that
cost about 25 Srang apiece, for a total of 375 Srang. Material for
religious observance cost about 150 Srang: 1.5 KHal of butter
for the lamps, 1.5 KHal of barley for offerings, and 50 Srang
worth of incense. The total is about 2,200 Srang, or 44 rDo
TSHad.

The accompanying table provides a list of the regular annual
feasts given to some or all of the five hundred monks by the
several establishments. The total cost of these feasts was 2,066
rDo TSHad, minus the Religious Establishment's own contribution of 450 rDo TSHad, or about 1,600 rDo TSHad per year.
(On these feast days, the poor laity of the capital, and some from
outlying districts who specialized in this type of thing, gathered
round the Monasteries and received gifts from the monks
[Chapter 10, section VII]. The cost to the subjects of maintaining the monasteries was thus lowered by the amount of these
gifts, an amount impossible to estimate.)

The Steward of the Religious Establishment clothed the
young monks until they reached the age of sixteen. There were
probably about seventy young monks, who each needed about
two and one-half complete outfits of clothing from the age of six
until the age of sixteen. Each complete outfit cost about 12 rDo
TSHad, and hence the Steward's annual expenditure for this
item was about 210 rDo TSHad. After sixteen, the monks
bought their own clothing with what they received in cash.
When an active monk died, his clothing was sold within his
monastery for about half price.

The above items of income total about 6,000 rDo TSHad. Of
the remaining 2,400 rDo TSHad, at least 900 no doubt came
from the Government (see Appendix D, section IV); and, if the
Government spent 85 per cent of its income (rather than 80 per
cent as we have assumed); another 400 rDo TSHad would have

Regular Annual Feasts for Monks

Time of year	Length of feast in days	Number of monks feasted	Sponsoring establishment	Occasion	Cost in rDo TSHad
1st moon	5	500	Government and Religious Establishment	Religious service	225
2nd moon	5	500	PHun TSHogs palace	Religious service	300
3rd moon	5	500	sGrol Ma palace	Religious service	300
4th moon	4	500	Government	Making magic pellets	105
5th moon	1	500	Government	Restoring mountain shrines	30
6th moon	1	100	Government	For the 16 Gling	4
7th moon	30	200	Government and Religious Establishment	Religious service	370
9th moon	9	500	Government and Religious Establishment	Honoring sect's founder	180
10th moon	30	100	Government and Religious Establishment	Religious service	90
Irregularly throughout year	36, total	200	Government and Religious Establishment	Death anniversaries of aKHon ancestors	432

been available. The remainder of the monks' support came from donations by private individuals and families. When a very wealthy nobleman died in the middle 1930's, his family gave the monks a feast that cost 100 rDo TSHad. More humble folk might have given a sheep, worth 0.4 rDo TSHad. Occasionally the monks profited from an anniversary of the birth of a living member of the aKHon family. On a male's thirty-seventh birthday, his palace gave a large feast worth 600 rDo TSHad; on the thirteenth, twenty-fifth, forty-ninth, and sixty-first birthdays, a 100 rDo TSHad feast was provided. Smaller amounts were provided for the anniversaries of living females of the family.

The monasteries of PHru Ma and Byas aGyur, with a total of twenty-three monks, were also fully supported by the Religious Establishment. The monastery of sPyi lHas, with fifteen monks, received special distributions from the Steward but not daily rations, and so did the nunneries of Sa bZang and Rin CHen sGang, with 110 nuns. The forty monks of the monastery at CHu aDus received 25 per cent of the Religious Establishment revenue from the area. For locations, see Map 3. The Religious Establishment also maintained the shrines in the capital and some of the small dwellings of the North Monastery monks, and it paid annual subsidies to the royal family.

On governmental income and expenditures, see also Appendix D, section IV.

II. Personnel of the North and South Monasteries

The following is a list of the officials of the North and South Monasteries (see also Appendix C, section II). We did not investigate the monasteries' internal operation.

The South Monastery (CHos sDe lHo):

Religious Officials

The abbot (mKHan CHen or KHri Ba), who was selected by the KHri CHen from two or three men suggested by the high officials of the monastery and was in charge of all discipline and religious practices

The chant master (dBu mDZad CHen Mo), who supervised and instructed eight assistants

Heads of the sixteen Gling (Gling dPon): a Gling, or hostel, was a separate living area in the rear of the monastery into which the monks were divided, originally according to their place of origin—there was, for example, a SHab Gling and a Ga Ra Gling. Each Gling had a schoolroom (Grwa SHag) and its own set of regulations (bCaa Yig)

Eight assistant chant leaders (bsKul CHung Pa)

Eight conch-blowers (Dung mKHan), who called assemblies, signified changes in ritual, and so forth

Twenty "doctors of theology" (bKaa Rab aByams Pa)

Officials for Managing the
Monastery (sPyi Sa CHen Mo)

The business manager (sPyi CHen dPon Slob)

The work manager (Las THog Pa)

The keeper of the Great God House (dKon gNYer CHen Mo)

Two thousand-offerings officials, or "butter-lamp officials" (sTong mCHod aGo Ba)

Two secretaries (Drung Yig)

108 keepers of ikonery (dKon gNYer)

Personal secretaries of the abbot and of any retired abbots (Drung CHen)

The religious law official (CHos KHrims Pa), who gained his position not by appointment but by communing with the supernatural

The assistant law official (CHos gZHon Pa)

The doorkeeper (sGo dPon)

Non-official Personnel

As many as forty debaters (bSHad Grwa), who were taught to debate according to the precepts of the religious sect

About forty monks (bKaa bCu Ba) who specialized in learning, memorizing, and debating sutras

About twenty monks (bSHad Pa) who studied the more obvious historical records

About twenty young monks, from seven to ten years old (bsDus Grwa), who were organized to debate among themselves

The North Monastery (CHos sDe Byang):

This monastery was divided into two "colleges," the "KHri CHen's College" (Bla Ma Ben TSHang Pa) and the "College of Secret Mantra Great Peace" (gSang sNGags bDe CHen Gling). The former ranked higher than the latter; its lowest official took precedence over the highest official of the other college.

Officials of the KHri CHen's College

The abbot (brGya TSHo dPon Slob)

The chant master (dBu mDZad CHen Mo)

Three assistant chant masters (dBu mDZad)

Two offerings officials (the mCHod dPon CHen Mo and the Grwa TSHang mCHod dPon, who was in charge of the candidates)

Two assistant chant masters (bsKul CHung Pa)

The beadle (dGe bsKos), who enforced discipline and maintained order and was considered important enough to have his appointment confirmed by the KHri CHen

Eight candidates (Bla Ma TSHang Pa)

Eight candidates of a lower rank without title, who entered regular candidacy according to seniority

Officials of the College of Secret Mantra Great Peace

Two head teachers (the dGe aPHel dPon Slob and the dGaa lDan dPon Slob)

The chant master (dBu mDZad CHen Mo)

The religious law official (CHos KHrims Pa), who maintained order and discipline

The head teachers and the chant master usually were appointed to their positions from candidacy in the KHri CHen's College. The law official was lower in rank than the candidates.

III. The Smaller Monasteries and the Nunneries of Sa sKya Proper

The following information was gathered in the course of pursuing other topics. We did not examine these monasteries and nunneries in detail. See Map 3 for their locations.

CHos aKHor lHun Po

CHos aKHor lHun Po, which housed about two hundred monks, was founded in the fourteenth or fifteenth century by gZHung brGya Ba dNGos Grub dPal aBar. When the aKHon family split at the end of the eighteenth century (Chapter 1, section X), the two younger brothers who were monks sided with Yab CHen Kun dGaa Rin CHen, who founded the PHun TSHogs palace. Later the older of these two monks, dNGos Grub dPal aBar, was discovered to be a reincarnation of the founder of CHos aKHor lHun Po, and hence became the monastery's first—and, as it developed, last—emanation body. The monastery thus came to have a special relationship to the PHun TSHogs palace.

The abbot was selected by the head of the PHun TSHogs palace from a list of candidates submitted by the monastery. The abbot's term was limited to three years; but if after a year the monks were dissatisfied with him, the palace could be requested to replace him. When an abbot was selected, the palace notified the ZHabs Pad who called the selectee to the capital for a ceremony of congratulations.

The monastery had a business manager (sPyi Ba) and three assistant managers; two chant leaders, one ranking above the other; a beadle; and eight keepers of images, one for each of seven temples and one for the main image house. In this monastery the business manager outranked the chant leaders, a most

unusual arrangement, emphasizing the monastery's worldly orientation.

gDong dGaa CHos sDe

gDong dGaa CHos sDe contained about fifty monks. Its abbot
(dPon Slob, see section IV below) was appointed by the capital
and he outranked all other abbots outside the North and South
Monasteries. The reason for his high status and special title was
connected with the marriage to KHri CHen Kun dGaa Rin
CHen (1517–1584) of two daughters of the local political
leader, who subordinated his political power in return for special
deference as a religious leader. Its last abbot had been promoted
from assistant chant leader of the North Monastery.

The monastery also had a chant leader (who also outranked
other chant leaders outside the capital); a beadle; a business
manager and two assistant managers; and a keeper of images. In
the smaller monasteries, the officials usually operated as a com-
mittee. The importance of the business manager depended upon
the personality of the abbot and upon the monastery's need to
use business ventures to help support itself. Perhaps 70 per cent
of the monks of gDong dGaa CHos sDe were from the immediate
vicinity.

The monastery had enough private land to provide subsistence
for its monks; and since it had a good religious reputation, it was
probably also well supported by the local people. The monks
lent some money, but were not known for their business ability.
They had some sharecroppers on their land. The capital helped
these smaller monasteries in emergencies. On one occasion the
buildings of gDong dGaa CHos sDe were badly damaged, and on
its request the Government sent materials (wood, paint, glass,
etc.) and the Religious Establishment food and labor.

Monks in Sa sKya proper were allowed to engage in trade and
other business activities, save for the highest order, which was
forbidden to engage in mundane affairs. Monks performed all
the tasks of skilled artisans within their monasteries, but were

allowed to do only printing and idol-making for outsiders, and they were supposed to receive no payment for their idols. Monks who were not good at their studies became menials within their monasteries. Lower-order monks could not plow, but they could sow and reap as a service and not for pay. They rarely worked in the fields. The monks of the North and South Monasteries, of course, spent a minimum of time in such pursuits.

THub bsTan dGe aPHel

THub bsTan dGe aPHel contained about fifty monks (see Chapter 1, section V). The abbot (mKHan Po) was selected by the capital. There were also a chant leader, a business manager, and an image-keeper.

The monastery had enough private land to support itself and a good religious reputation that brought it additional income. Its monks engaged in a limited number of business ventures. It had a reputation as a comfortable place to live.

Monastery at CHu aDus

The monastery at CHu aDus, whose name is not recalled, contained about forty monks. This monastery had two unique features: its abbot (mKHan Po) was chosen by the monks themselves; and it received about one-quarter of the revenue in kind from Religious Establishment lands in the CHu aDus District. Its other officials were a chant leader, a business manager, a beadle, and four keepers of imagery. There were only about twenty Religious Establishment families in the district, so the monastery received the revenue of about five families, but it had land of its own. It had only a middling religious reputation and did only a moderate amount of business. It was, however, described as a well-ordered monastery.

KHa Ba lHas

Nothing was known about the monastery of KHa Ba lHas except that it contained about forty monks.

NYi SHar

NYi SHar, which contained about 24 monks, was composed of a group of three small units, each with about eight monks. The abbot (Bla Ma TSHab) in charge of all three was appointed by the capital. He was assisted by a chant leader, a business manager, and a keeper of images. The monastery had some land and conducted some business, but apparently the combined returns were not enough to support the monks. It was said to have had only a fair religious reputation, which meant that the local population did not donate as liberally as elsewhere in Sa sKya. Periodically the monastery requested permission from the capital to solicit in order to maintain itself.

bDe Can

bDe Can, housing about fifteen monks, was a monastery for retired monks. Nothing was known about it, except that it also contained about five retired nuns.

Byas aGur

Byas aGur, containing about fifteen monks, was headed by a chant master, who was usually a retired official from the North or South Monastery, assisted by a beadle. This monastery was for monks who failed their examinations in the capital monasteries. The monks were supported by the Steward of the Religious Establishment, and they performed religious services for the local population and pilgrims. The monastery had no land of its own.

sKyi lHas

sKyi lHas, also called KHau Brag rDZong, housed about fifteen monks. It was a monastery for retired monks, headed by a dPon Slob. The Steward of the Religious Establishment did not provide daily rations for these monks, but only shares of the special distributions. The monks apparently lived on donations from pilgrims who visited the birthplace of dKon mCHog rGyal Po, the founder of the Sa sKya sect, which was in the neighborhood.

sGra aDrai

sGra aDrai, with about eight monks, was a monastery for monks from the area who had retired from the North and South Monasteries. They appointed their own abbot, who was assisted by a keeper of images, and they lived solely by performing religious services for and receiving donations from the local population.

Brag Po CHe

Brag Po CHe, having about eight monks, was a monastery for retired monks. Nothing more was known.

PHru Ma

PHru Ma housed about eight retired monks fully supported by the Steward of the Religious Establishment.

Bya gSHong

Bya gSHong contained about seven monks. The monastery had an abbot (mKHan Po), a chant leader, and an image keeper. At one time this was a very large monastery, and buildings remained that were large enough to accommodate a thousand monks. It was founded at the time of the founding of the sect. The monastery had some land which apparently supported the monks.

aJigs sKyob

aJigs sKyob contained about four retired monks, with no officials, apparently supported by monastery land.

Sa bZang

Sa bZang was a nunnery containing about sixty nuns. It had no abbot, but a chant leader, beadle, business manager, offerings official, and two or three image-keepers. The abbot of the North

Monastery presided over the summer and winter convocations. The nunnery had been a monastery, but had declined in numbers and so was made a nunnery. Most of its nuns were levied. The nunnery probably had some land of its own.

Rin CHen sGang

Rin CHen sGang, with about fifty nuns, had the same organization, type of personnel, and manner of support as Sa bZang.

KHa Gung dGon Pa, rTSe Drung, and La SHar dGon Pa

The nunneries of KHa Gung dGon Pa and rTSe Drung each having about fifty nuns, and La SHar dGon Pa, with about thirty nuns, were all located in Ko CHag and were organized under a single monk, whose title was Bla Ma rTSe Drung and who was appointed by the capital. Each nunnery had its own chant leader, business manager, beadle, offerings official, and several keepers of images. The nunneries had land of their own, but the nuns still went out to work about half of the time. These contacts with the outside made the keeping of vows particularly difficult for the nuns of Sa sKya.

dGon Pa rGyas

dGon Pa rGyas had about twenty nuns. The nunnery had no abbot, but a chant leader, business manager, beadle, offerings official, and three image-keepers. The dGe aPHel dPon Slob (Appendix E, section II) of the North Monastery came here for important convocations. The nunnery had a good religious reputation and enough private land to support some sharecroppers.

lHau

lHau, which had about eight nuns, had the same organization as dGon Pa rGyas, but only one image-keeper.

IV. Monastic Officials Sent Out from Sa sKya Proper

The monastic officials sent out from Sa sKya proper had three titles, but a man's title was not very descriptive of his function.

The most common title was Bla Ma TSHab, or "substitute lama," which suggested a focus of faith and belief, a man representing the emanations of the Sa sKya sect. Most of the officials who brought wealth back to Sa sKya proper had this title. The second most frequent title was mKHan Po, or "abbot," which connoted administration and instruction. Most of the officials who served as abbots on indefinite tenure had this title. The least frequent was dPon Slob, or "official-teacher," which suggested a certain amount of worldliness and a connection with political affairs. Some monastery officials within Sa sKya proper also had these titles.

We were able to identify forty-four officials and their destinations (Map 1):

Two Bla Ma TSHab were sent for six years to the monastery sDeu CHos rJe, with about 500 monks, the headquarters of the Sa sKya sect in northeast Tibet (Amdo). The two had only one collection quota to meet.

One Bla Ma TSHab was sent for six years to the monastery Zur sBug, with about 50 monks, near Dar rTSe mDo, or Kangting.

One Bla Ma TSHab was sent for six years to the monastery lHa aBri dGe aPHel Gling, with about 100 monks, the largest of about twenty-five monasteries northwest of Kangting.

One Bla Ma TSHab was sent for six years to the monastery rMa Ya Ta, with about 1,250 monks, in the vicinity of Kweiteh.

One Bla Ma TSHab was sent for six years to the monastery Glang Nag, with about 100 monks, the largest of five monasteries near Kantse.

One Bla Ma TSHab was sent for six years to the monastery Gling TSHang, with about 400 monks, the largest of a number of monasteries west of Derge.

One Bla Ma TSHab was sent for six years to the monastery Rag CHu, with about 100 monks, east of aDam THog near Droma Lhakang.

One Bla Ma TSHab was sent for six years to the monastery Rin CHen Gling, with about 100 monks, north of aDam THog.

One Bla Ma TSHab was sent for six years to the monastery NYi SHar, with about 130 monks, between aDam THog and Mar KHams rGya KHag.

One Bla Ma TSHab was sent for six years to a monastery whose name was not recalled, with about 130 monks, in the area of AH bSod mDo CHang, marked without a name on Map 1 to the northeast of Mar KHams rGya KHag.

One Bla Ma TSHab was sent for six years to the monastery PHrin bsDu sKal bZang, with about 500 monks, to the north of Jyekundo.

One Bla Ma TSHab was sent for six years to the area of Mor aGol rGyas, near the monastery PHrin bsDu sKal bZang to collect from about 3,000 nomad families.

One Bla Ma TSHab was sent for six years to the monastery ZHau mDo, with about 200 monks, near Jyekundo.

One Bla Ma TSHab was sent for six years to the monastery Bon aGrub Gling, with about 1,050 monks, near Jyekundo.

One Bla Ma TSHab was sent for six years to the monastery gTSang mDaa, with about 200 monks, the largest of seven monasteries about 150 miles west of aDam THog.

Three Bla Ma TSHab were sent for six years to Derge, where there were many monasteries with a total of about 2,000 monks. The PHur Pa (dagger) Bla Ma went to the monastery Yi Na Bla Brang, with about 300 monks. The sMan Pa (medicine) Bla Ma went to a district of Derge. The gYang Ra (adobe fence) Bla Ma went to the monastery Rab bsTan, with about 150 monks.

One Bla Ma TSHab was sent for six years to the monastery bDe Cen Grwa TSHang bsTan aPHel Gling, with about 300 monks, south of Mar KHams rGya KHag in the district of rGya KHag. His principal function was collection.

A dPon Slob was also sent for six years to the monastery bDe Cen Grwa TSHang bsTan aPHel Gling. His principal functions were administrative.

Two Bla Ma TSHab were sent for six years to the monastery aDam THog, with about 400 monks. These two were the only six-year collectors sent to a Sa sKya territory.

One Bla Ma TSHab was sent for six years to a monastery called Rong mDo CHang. Its size and location, somewhere in Khams, were not remembered.

One Bla Ma TSHab was sent for six months to the monastery PHi Wang, with about 25 monks, in westernmost Tibet in the area of Gu Ge. Each six-month collector was provided with a document (Slong Yig) that authorized his collecting, and he was usually accompanied by a steward who did some trading.

One Bla Ma TSHab was sent for six months to the area of sPu Hreng in western Tibet.

One Bla Ma TSHab was sent for six months to the area of Byang THang, north of Sa sKya proper.

One Bla Ma TSHab was sent for six months to the area of Gro gSHod in western Tibet.

One Bla Ma TSHab was sent for six months to the area of mNGaa Ris in western Tibet.

One Bla Ma TSHab was sent for six months to the area of Nag CHu, north of Lhasa.

One bsKor dPon Slob was sent for nine months to travel throughout Tibet, except in the east, northeast, and far west, and he usually had a two- to five-year appointment. When residing in the North Monastery three months of each year, he formally outranked everyone including the abbot. He had no power and brought back little wealth—but did rather well for himself. Apparently this post had its ancestry in some personal representative sent out by a former KHri CHen.

One mKHan Po was sent for an indefinite period to the monastery dBang lDan bDe Can, with about 300 monks, near Gyangtse.

One mKHan Po was sent for an indefinite period to the monastery rTa Mo Gling, with about 70 monks, located in the Sa sKya area of Mus.

One mKHan Po was sent for an indefinite period to the monastery dGaa rTSe aPHel CHos Grags, with about 30 monks, south of Sa sKya proper on Lake Tingkye.

One mKHan Po was sent for an indefinite period to the

monastery bZang lDan, with about 50 monks, near Ngangtse Lake, north of Mus.

One Bla Ma TSHab was sent for an indefinite period to the monastery of Yul CHen, with about 25 monks, in the Sa sKya area of Yul CHen.

One mKHan Po was sent for an indefinite period to the monastery rNan rGyal lHa rTSe, with about 15 monks, near Mustang in Nepal.

One Bla Ma TSHab was sent for an indefinite period to the monastery sPu Hreng rTag lHa, with about 35 monks, in the area of sPu Hreng in western Tibet. Although this official was appointed for an indefinite period and although his duties were principally administrative, he was supposed to return to Sa sKya proper upon his resignation with a specified amount of wealth accumulated from religious donations. If an incumbent had remained for many years without giving any sign of intending to return, the government inquired about his plans. This was the only exception to the principle that only six-year and six-month officials had to meet a collection quota. It was admittedly a confused arrangement.

One mKHan Po was sent for an indefinite period to the monastery THar Gling CHos sDe, with about 50 monks, south of Lhasa in the area of Yamdrok.

Two Bla Ma TSHab were sent for indefinite periods to monasteries near Punakha, Bhutan. One went to the monastery PHang Ya, and the other to a monastery whose name was not recalled. There were fewer than 20 monks in both monasteries.

Three officials were sent for indefinite periods to the monastery of bSam Yas, with over 500 monks, south of Lhasa. The officials were the Grwa TSHang mKHan Po, a Slob dPon, and the lCog mKHan TSHang sDe Pa, who was the interpreter of the oracle of bSam Yas.

In addition we identified a number of Sa sKya monasteries that appointed their own highest officials, with no control from Sa sKya proper. They were the monastery of THab bsDan rNam rGyal, with about 200 monks, in the area of rTa Nag

(Thubden), just north of Sa sKya proper; two large and several small monasteries in rTSe gDong; the monastery of Pe Har near the palace of the King of Derge; and five monasteries in CHab mDo. (Only monasteries with officials sent out from the capital are located on Map 1.)

V. Wealth Returned by Religious Collectors

Each collector had a precise quota of specific goods that he had to present to a specific number of people upon his return to Sa sKya proper. These amounts had probably not been changed for many years, and they varied only according to the number of members of the royal aKHon family. The six-year collectors went out on a staggered schedule, and probably about an equal number returned each year. Before leaving the North Monastery, a new appointee consulted, if possible, with his predecessor. When one of the six-year collectors arrived at rTSe gDong or thereabouts on his homeward journey, he sent word to the ZHabs Pad and had an audience with him upon his arrival at the capital—another indication of the government's involvement in the monastic empire. He then announced his arrival to the KHri CHen and went to the Chief Secretary for an official copy of his collection schedule, which he took, with the material owed them, to the people listed below. They indicated their receipt of the money and goods due them, and the collector returned the signed schedule to the Chief Secretary. The document then went into the Government archives. The short-term collectors followed the same procedure, without the preliminary formalities.

Most of the quotas and schedules for the six-year collectors were remembered in some detail. The monetary values are given in terms of prices in Sa sKya in 1947 of medium-quality materials and animals, which were usually the kind donated to religion by the laity. The quality of goods given by the collector to the people on his list was standard; he could not, for example, give all his best satin to the KHri CHen. The collectors returned with the animals and material from eastern Tibet and presented them to the officials and royalty. They did not bring money, for prices in Sa sKya were 150 to 200 per cent of those in the east. The values are given in the Tibetan unit, the rDo TSHad. One rDo TSHad was worth 50 Srang, the unit we use in dealing with daily living in Sa sKya (see Appendix D, sections II and III). For international comparison, 1 rDo TSHad was worth 3⅓ Mexican silver dollars or 2.4 Chinese taels (the Chinese ounce of silver).

The following are the schedules of the six-year collectors. The amounts due the first six recipients were remembered very clearly; the rest were estimated.

To the KHri CHen, the collector owed 100 rDo TSHad in currency, one roll of satin (2.5 ft. by 30 ft.) valued at 6 rDo TSHad, 200 pounds of tea worth 30 rDo TSHad, one first-quality riding mule worth 100 rDo TSHad, and one twelve-foot greeting scarf worth 5 rDo TSHad.

To each remaining male member of the aKHon family, he owed 66 rDo TSHad in currency, ⅔ roll of satin worth 4 rDo TSHad, 120 pounds of tea worth 18 rDo TSHad, and one small scarf worth 2 rDo TSHad.

To each daughter of the two palaces, and to the rGyal Yum (the son-bearing wife of the KHri CHen), he owed 50 rDo TSHad in currency, ½ roll of satin worth 3 rDo TSHad, 80 pounds of tea worth 12 rDo TSHad, and one small scarf worth 2 rDo TSHad.

To the bDags Mo (wives of aKHon males other than a rGyal Yum), he owed 33 rDo TSHad in currency, ⅓ roll of satin worth 2 rDo TSHad, 40 pounds of tea worth 6 rDo TSHad, and one small scarf worth 2 rDo TSHad.

To the Government, signed for by Keepers of the Keys, he owed 90 rDo TSHad in currency, one roll of satin worth 6 rDo TSHad, 200 pounds of tea worth 30 rDo TSHad, and about 4 pack animals, either mules or horses, total averaging about 100 rDo TSHad.

To the ZHabs Pad, for his personal use, the collector owed 10 rDo TSHad in currency, 20 pounds of tea worth 3 rDo TSHad, and one small scarf worth 2 rDo TSHad.

To the Steward, for the Religious Establishment, he owed 45 rDo TSHad in currency, 80 pounds of tea worth 12 rDo TSHad, and one small scarf worth 2 rDo TSHad.

To the Steward, for his personal use, he owed 7 rDo TSHad in currency, 25 pounds of tea worth 2 rDo TSHad, and one small scarf worth 2 rDo TSHad.

To the treasury of the KHri CHen, signed for by his Treasurer, he owed about the same as to the Steward for the Religious Establishment—hence 59 rDo TSHad in goods and currency.

To the Treasurer of the KHri CHen, for his personal use, he owed 12 pounds of tea worth 1 rDo TSHad and one small scarf worth 2 rDo TSHad.

To the Chief Secretary, for his personal use, he owed 5 rDo TSHad in currency, 10 pounds of tea worth 1.5 rDo TSHad, and one smaller scarf worth 1 rDo TSHad.

To each of the abbots of the North and South Monasteries, for their personal use, he owed 5 rDo TSHad in currency, 10 pounds of tea worth 1.5 rDo TSHad, and one smaller scarf worth 1 rDo TSHad.

To each Keeper of the Keys, for his personal use, he owed 3 pounds of tea worth 0.5 rDo TSHad and one smaller scarf worth 1 rDo TSHad.

Upon receipt of their dues, these people gave the collectors some gift, ranging from a suit of clothing and a slab of butter from the KHri CHen to a very small scarf from the lowest officials.

In 1947, including four male members of the aKHon family in addition to the KHri CHen, eight daughters, one rGyal Yum, and one bDags Mo, the total value of each six-year collector's quota was about 1,645 rDo TSHad.

The quotas for the six-month collectors were not remembered. One of them told our respondents that he could meet his quota with 120 rDo TSHad worth of goods and currency. On their schedules were the KHri CHen, all members of the aKHon family, the Government, the Religious Establishment, the abbot of the South Monastery, the ZHabs Pad, and the Butler and Valet of the KHri CHen. Of the 120 rDo TSHad, probably about 95 went to the royal family, 4 to the Government, 17 to the Religious Establishment, and 4 to the various officials. Nothing was known about the schedules of the bsKon dPon Slob and the Bla Ma TSHab of sPu Hreng rTag lHa (see section IV above).

There were supposed to be 56 men sent out from Sa sKya proper. We identified all the short-term collectors (six six-month and one nine-month), twenty-four six-year collectors, and thirteen men on indefinite tenures—a total of forty-four. To bring the total to fifty-six, we assume six more six-year officials and six more on indefinite tenures. This means that about five six-year collectors returned with wealth to Sa sKya proper each year, for their terms were staggered. On this assumption, in 1947 the six-year collectors returned with 8,225 rDo TSHad in currency and kind to meet their quotas. The six six-month collectors brought in 720 rDo TSHad in 1947. Each collector, it was estimated, had a surplus for himself of about half his quota. Hence the total wealth brought in in 1947 had the value of 13,417 rDo TSHad.

The reasonableness of these figures is supported by the results of a special collection trip to nomad country north of Sa sKya proper made in 1947 by NGag dBang Kun dGaa PHrin Las in order to help pay for the restoration of the Great God House of the South Monastery (Chapter 11, section IX). In a period of three months, in territory already worked over by the regular six-months collectors, this emanation body at the age of thirteen returned to Sa sKya with the equivalent of 17,595 rDo TSHad. The following items made up his collection: 4,500 rDo TSHad in currency, 1,000 yaks and yak cows @ 7 rDo TSHad, 5,000 sheep @ 0.4 rDo TSHad, 30 small horses @ 15 rDo TSHad, 30 oxen with loads and saddles @ 15 rDo TSHad, 600 KHal of butter @ 0.8 rDo TSHad, 160 KHal of dry cheese @ 0.28 rDo TSHad, 160 rolls of tent cloth @ 16 rDo TSHad, 250 tanned lambskins @ 0.12 rDo TSHad, 20 tanned lynx skins @ 3 rDo TSHad, and 20 fox skins @ 1 rDo TSHad.

Glossary

Abbot: mKHan Po (expert); or dPon Slob (official teacher); or Bla Ma TSHab (lama substitute)—see Appendix E, section IV

Acting (as ZHabs Pad): TSHab (substitute)

Allegiance: Mi KHongs (man midst)

Archivist: Yig TSHang gNYer (letter den steward)

Body Servant (of the KHri CHen): sKu mDun gSol dPon (body vis-à-vis serve official)

Building Official: KHang dPon (building official)

Butler of the KHri CHen: gSol dPon CHen Mo (serve official great one)

Candidacy: dKyus Drung (length near)

Capital: gDan Sa (seat soil or place)

Chef of the KHri CHen: Ja dPon CHen Mo (tea official great one)

Chief artisans: dBu mDZod (head doer)

Chief Secretary: Drung Yig CHen Mo (near letter great one)

Collector, religious: aDul sDud (gift gather)

District Office: gZHis KHa (locality part)

District Officer: gZHis KHa (locality part)

Doorman (of KHri CHen and ZHabs Pad): aGag Pa (stop one)

Emanation body: sPrul sKu (emanation body)

Equerry: CHibs dPon CHen Mo (horse official great one)

Flogger or policeman: Drul lCag (putrid whip)

Fodder Official: rTSwa gNYer (grass steward)

Fuel Official: SHing dPon (wood official)

Government: gZHung (central)

Great Assembly Meeting: TSHogs aDu CHen Mo (assembly gathering great one)

Great God House, of South Monastery: lHa KHang CHen Mo (god house great one)

Group Official: TSHo dPon (group official)

Herders: Sa Ma aBrog (neither soil nor wilderness)

Headman: bZaa dPon (eat official); or sDe Pa Lags (community one honorable); or (among herders) SHed dPon (strength official)

Hospitality Officials: ZHol rGan Po (village senior one)

Jailers: bTSon Srung (prison guard)

Keeper of the Keys: lDe aCHang Pa (key keeper)

Law Official: KHrims dPon (law official)

Liaison Officer: mGron gNYer (entertainment steward)

Liaison Official for the KHri CHen: TSHogs mGron (assembly invite)

Military Official: dMag sPyi (soldier manager)

Nobility: brGyud Pai sKu Drag or Drag bTSan—see Chapter 8

North Monastery: CHos sDe Byang (religion community north)

Offerings Official of the KHri CHen: mCHod dPon CHen Mo (offerings official great one)

Old sect: rNYing Ma Pa (old suasion one)

Palace: PHo Brang (male abode)

Policeman or flogger: Drul lCag (putrid whip)

Religious Establishment: CHos gZHi (religion estate)

Retired (as abbot or ZHabs Pad):   Zur (retired)

Scarves of greeting: KHa bTags (mouth tie)

Secretary: Drung Yig (near letter)

Sedan Officer: PHebs Byams aGo Pa (going chair chief)

Sharecropper: Dud CHung (smoke small)

South Monastery: CHos sDe lHo (religion community south)

Steward for the Government: aDren dPon (dish official)

Steward of the Religious Establishment: gNYer dPon (steward official)

Subject: Mi Ser (man yellow)

Transport levy: U Lags (from the Turkish)

Transportation Official: rTa gTang Pa (horse send one)

Treasurer of the KHri CHen: rTSe PHyag mDZod (peak hand do)

Valet of the KHri CHen: gZims dPon CHen Mo (sleep official great one)

Work Corps: Las TSHan Pa (work class ones)

Index

Tibetan words transcribed according to the system described in the Preface are listed in this index by the first capital letter occurring in them.